Public Trust in Business

Public trust in business is one of the most important but least
understood issues for business leaders, public officials, employees,
NGOs, and other key stakeholders. This book provides much-needed
thinking on the topic. Drawing on the expertise of an international
array of experts from academic disciplines including business,
sociology, political science, and philosophy, it explores long-term
strategies for building and maintaining public trust in business. The
authors look to new ways of moving forward, by carefully blending
the latest academic research with conclusions for future research and
practice. They address core drivers of public trust, how to manage it
effectively, the consequences of low public trust, and how best to
address trust challenges and repair trust when it has been lost. This is
a must-read for business practitioners, policy makers, and students
taking courses in corporate social responsibility or business ethics.

JARED D. HARRIS is Associate Professor at the Darden School
of Business, University of Virginia. His research centers on the
interplay between ethics and strategy, with a particular focus on
the topics of corporate governance, business ethics, and interorganizational trust. He is a fellow with the Business Roundtable
Institute for Corporate Ethics and a senior fellow with Darden's
Olsson Center for Applied Ethics. Harris is also a research partner
of Open Ethics and Compliance Group (OCEG) and the Institute of
Management Accountants (IMA). He consults with several leading
financial services companies on the topics of strategic management,
ethics, and compliance.

BRIAN T. MORIARTY is Director of the Business Roundtable Institute
for Corporate Ethics, and Adjunct Professor at the Darden School
of Business, University of Virginia. He leads the Project on Public
Trust in Business, a joint initiative with the Arthur W. Page Society.
In 2013 and 2014 he was selected as one of the Top 100 Thought
Leaders in Trustworthy Business Behavior by Trust Across America.

ANDREW C. WICKS is the Ruffin Professor of Business Administration and Director of the doctoral program at the Darden School of Business, University of Virginia. He is Director of the Olsson Center for Applied Ethics and academic adviser for the Business Roundtable Institute for Corporate Ethics. His research interests include stakeholder responsibility, stakeholder theory, trust, health care ethics, total quality management, and ethics and entrepreneurship. He is actively working with Ethics-LX, an entrepreneurial venture, to create a series of web-based simulations that incorporate ethics into the functional areas of business.

Public Trust in Business

Edited by

JARED D. HARRIS

BRIAN T. MORIARTY

ANDREW C. WICKS

CAMBRIDGE
UNIVERSITY PRESS

CAMBRIDGE
UNIVERSITY PRESS

University Printing House, Cambridge CB2 8BS, United Kingdom

One Liberty Plaza, 20th Floor, New York, NY 10006, USA

477 Williamstown Road, Port Melbourne, VIC 3207, Australia

314-321, 3rd Floor, Plot 3, Splendor Forum, Jasola District Centre, New Delhi - 110025, India

79 Anson Road, #06-04/06, Singapore 079906

Cambridge University Press is part of the University of Cambridge.

It furthers the University's mission by disseminating knowledge in the pursuit of education, learning and research at the highest international levels of excellence.

www.cambridge.org
Information on this title: www.cambridge.org/9781107023871

© Cambridge University Press 2014

First published 2014

A catalogue record for this publication is available from the British Library

Library of Congress Cataloging in Publication data
Public trust in business / edited by Jared D. Harris, Brian T. Moriarty, Andrew C. Wicks.
    pages   cm
ISBN 978-1-107-02387-1 (Hardback) – ISBN 978-1-107-65020-6 (Paperback)
1. Trust.   2. Public relations.   3. Business ethics.   4. Business–Public opinion.   5. Corporate culture.   I. Harris, Jared D.   II. Moriarty, Brian T.   III. Wicks, Andrew C.
HF5387.P83 2014
659.201´9–dc23   2014007006

ISBN 978-1-107-02387-1 Hardback
ISBN 978-1-107-65020-6 Paperback

Contents

Figures

Tables

Notes on contributors

EDITORS

Jared D. Harris is Associate Professor of Business Administration at the University of Virginia's Darden Business School, a Fellow with the Business Roundtable Institute for Corporate Ethics, and a Senior Fellow with Darden's Olsson Center for Applied Ethics. He is the editor of *Kantian Business Ethics: Critical Perspectives* (with Denis G. Arnold). He has published numerous articles and chapters on corporate governance, business ethics, and interorganizational trust.

Brian T. Moriarty is Director at the Business Roundtable Institute for Corporate Ethics and Adjunct Professor of Management Communications at the University of Virginia's Darden Business School. His current scholarship on public trust in business focuses on the relationship of employee engagement to stakeholder trust and reputation.

Andrew C. Wicks is the Ruffin Professor of Business Administration, Director of the Olsson Center for Ethics, and Director of the Doctoral Program at the University of Virginia's Darden Business School. He is an academic adviser at the Business Roundtable Institute for Corporate Ethics. His prior books include *Stakeholder Theory: The State of the Art* (Cambridge University Press, with R. E. Freeman, J. Harrison, B. Parmar, and S. DeColle), *Managing for Stakeholders: Survival, Reputation and Success*, and *Business Ethics: A Managerial Approach*.

CONTRIBUTING AUTHORS

Paul Argenti is Professor of Corporate Communication and Faculty Director for the Leadership and Strategic Impact Program at the Tuck School of Business at Dartmouth. He is the author of *Digital Strategies for Powerful Corporate Communication* (with C. Barnes), *The Power of Corporate Communication* (with J. Forman), *The Fast Forward MBA Pocket Reference* (2nd edn), and *Corporate Communication* (6th edn).

Reinhard Bachmann is Professor of Strategy at the Surrey School of Business and Deputy Editor-in Chief of the *Journal of Trust Research*. He is the author of several books including *The Handbook of Trust Research* (with A. Zaheer), *Trust within and between Organizations* (with C. Lane), and *Landmarks Papers on Trust* (with A. Zaheer).

Robert Bies is Professor of Management and Founder of the Executive Master's in Leadership Program at the McDonough School of Business at Georgetown University. He is co-author of the book, *Getting Even: The Truth about Workplace Revenge – And How to Stop It*. Professor Bies's research focuses on leadership, the delivery of bad news, organizational justice, trust and distrust dynamics, and revenge and forgiveness in the workplace

Karen S. Cook is the Ray Lyman Wilbur Professor of Sociology and Director of the Institute for Research in the Social Sciences at Stanford University. She has edited a number of books in the Russell Sage Foundation Trust Series that she co-edits with M. Levi and R. Hardin, including *Trust and Distrust in Organizations: Emerging Perspectives* (with R. Kramer) and *e-Trust: Forming Relationships in the Online World* (with C. Snijders, V. Buskens, and C. Cheshire). She also co-authored *Whom Can We Trust?* (with M. Levi and R. Hardin).

Gjalt de Jong is Associate Professor of Strategy at the Faculty of Economics and Business, University of Groningen. His research interests and publications include the management of strategic alliances; business ethics in transition economies; the strategy, structure, and organization of multinational enterprises; and the causes and consequences of national rules. Prior to his current position, he was senior management consultant for PricewaterhouseCoopers and KPMG.

Edeltraud Hanappi-Egger is Professor for Gender and Diversity in Organizations and head of the Gender and Diversity Management Group at Vienna University of Economics. She is the author of the book *The Triple M of Organizations: Man, Management and Myth* and has published more than 200 articles on gender and technology, diversity management, and organization studies.

Roderick Kramer is the William R. Kimball Professor of Organizational Behavior at the Graduate School of Business at Stanford University. He has also been a visiting professor at the Kellogg Graduate School at Northwestern University, the Kennedy School of Government at Harvard University, the London Business School, and Oxford University. Kramer is the author or co-author of more than 150 scholarly articles and essays. Kramer is also the author or co-author of numerous books, including *Negotiation in Social Contexts; The Psychology of the Social Self; Trust in Organizations: Frontiers of Theory and Research; Power and Influence in Organizations; Trust and Distrust within Organizations;* and *Restoring Trust in Organizations and Leaders: Enduring Challenges and Emerging Answers.*

Deepak Malhotra is a Professor in the Negotiations, Organizations, and Markets Unit at the Harvard Business School. Malhotra has won numerous awards for his teaching, including the HBS Faculty Award

xii NOTES ON CONTRIBUTORS

by Harvard Business School's MBA Class of 2011, and the Charles
M. Williams Award from the Harvard Business School. His first book
*Negotiation Genius: How to Overcome Obstacles and Achieve
Brilliant Results at the Bargaining Table and Beyond* (with
M. Bazerman) was awarded the 2008 Outstanding Book Award by
the International Institute for Conflict Prevention and Resolution.
His second book, *I Moved Your Cheese*, is a Wall Street Journal
Best-Seller.

Kirsten Martin is Assistant Professor of Strategic Management and
Public Policy at the George Washington University School of Business
and serves on the US Census Bureau's National Advisory Committee
on Racial, Ethnic, and Other Populations. Her research interests
include business ethics, privacy, technology, stakeholder theory, on
which she has published many articles and chapters.

Bart Nooteboom is Emeritus Professor of Innovation Policy. He is
author of eleven books and over 300 articles on small business,
entrepreneurship, innovation and diffusion, innovation policy,
transaction cost theory, inter-firm relations, trust, networks, and
organizational learning. He is a member of the Royal Netherlands
Academy of Arts and Sciences. He was awarded the Kapp prize for his
work on organizational learning, the Gunnar Myrdal prize for his book
on trust and the Schumpeter prize for his book on a cognitive theory
of the firm. His most recent book, *Beyond Humanism* (2012) is a
philosophy book on humanism.

Bidhan L. (Bobby) Parmar is Assistant Professor of Business
Administration at the University of Virginia's Darden School of
Business. He is a Fellow at the Business Roundtable Institute for
Corporate Ethics and at the Olsson Center for Applied Ethics.
Parmar authored the book *Stakeholder Theory: The State of the
Art* (Cambridge University Press, with R. E. Freeman, A. Wicks,
J. Harrison, and S. DeColle). Parmar is a lead author of Ethics-LX,™

a series of ethically charged online-learning experiences tailored to every core course in a typical MBA program.

Michael Pirson is an assistant professor at the Fordham Schools Business and a research fellow at Harvard University. His most recent books include *Humanistic Ethics in the Age of Globality* (with C. Dierksmeier, E. Kimakowitz, and H. Spitzeck) and *Cases in Sustainability and Social Entrepreneurship* (with J. Hamschmidt). He is also a founding partner of the Humanistic Management Network, an organization that brings together scholars, practitioners, and policy makers around the common goal of creating a 'life-conducive' economic system. He co-edits the book series, Humanism in Business, published by Palgrave McMillan.

Laura Poppo is the Edmund P. Learned Professor in Business at the University of Kansas School of Business. Her research areas include outsourcing, alliances, vertical integration, contracting, trust, social networks, the multi-divisional corporation, and information technology. She has published numerous journal articles and book chapters in these areas.

Donald J. (DJ) Schepker is Assistant Professor of Management at the Darla Moore School of Business at the University of South Carolina. His research is in strategic management and focuses on corporate governance, executive dismissal, and decision making at the board of directors and firm level. His research has appeared in the *Journal of Management* and *Corporate Reputation Review*.

Oliver Schilke is a doctoral candidate in the Department of Sociology at the University of California at Los Angeles. Previously he was a research fellow at Stanford University's Institute for Research in the Social Sciences. Schilke's research interests include trust development between individuals and between organizations, institutionalization processes, collective identity, and organizational capabilities. His research has appeared in academic journals such as the *Journal of Management, Journal of Product Innovation Management, Entrepreneurship Theory and Practice*, and *Journal of Marketing Research*, among others.

Eric M. Uslaner is Professor of Government and Politics at the University of Maryland, College Park. He is Senior Research Fellow, at the Center for American Law and Political Science, Southwest University of Political Science and Law, Chongqing, China. He is the author of several books, including *The Moral Foundations of Trust* (Cambridge University Press) and *Corruption, Inequality, and the Rule of Law: The Bulging Pocket Makes the Easy Life* (Cambridge University Press), *Segregation and Mistrust* (Cambridge University Press) and approximately 120 articles.

Rosalinde Klein Woolthuis is Associate Professor of Economics and Business Administration at the VU University Amsterdam, and a consultant at TNO Strategy and Policy. Her research focuses on the diffusion of sustainable innovations and practices which transform existing business models and industries. Key concepts in her work are innovation, collaboration, trust, contracts, and dependence. She has published papers in journals such as *Organization Studies, Technovation*, and *Technological Forecasting & Social Change*. She is a consultant to national and international governmental bodies on how sustainable innovation can be promoted through measures such as stimulating entrepreneurship and modernizing rules and regulations.

Preface: discovering new territory in public trust in business

Despite the importance of public trust in business, very little scholarly work has been written on this topic. While the literature on organizational trust – both interpersonal and interorganizational – is vast and growing rapidly – particularly in the field of management – much less academic research has been conducted on public trust in business as an institution. Based on top executives identifying trust in business as their biggest concern,[1] we held several seminars with executives, journalists, and governance experts during 2007, in both Washington, DC and New York, to seek their input and increase our understanding of their practical perspective on the crisis of trust in business. Based on what we learned, and with the further erosion of public trust in business with the onset of the global financial crisis, we issued both a preliminary report on the topic,[2] and convened the 2009 Ruffin Summit on Public Trust at the University of Virginia's Darden School of Business, which involved twenty-five top thought leaders on trust across a variety of disciplines. This volume includes papers presented at the summit, and other invited papers, to gather what we believe to be the best current thinking on the problem.[3] The scholarship in this volume speaks in

---

[1] Business Roundtable Institute for Corporate Ethics, *Mapping the Terrain: Issues that Connect Business and* Ethics (May, 2004). Highlights of this survey are available online at www.corporate-ethics.org/pdf/mapping_terrain_business_ethics_2004.pdf.

[2] Roger Bolton, R. Edward Freeman, Jared Harris, Brian Moriarty, and Laura Nash, *The Dynamics of Public Trust in Business – Emerging Opportunities for Leaders* (Business Roundtable Institute for Corporate Ethics white paper, 2009). This report is available online at www.corporate-ethics.org/pdf/public_trust_in_business.pdf.

[3] The editors of this volume are listed in alphabetical order as all three contributed greatly to this book which has been a team effort.

detail to this critically important topic, and raises a variety of questions that beg for further attention.

Part I of this volume focuses on public trust in business as an institution. In Chapter 2, Eric M. Uslaner analyzes data from multiple surveys of the US population to determine the extent to which the global economic crisis caused a reduction of trust in government and in generalized trust. Using these same data sets, he explores whether the economic crisis played a key role in support of the Tea Party movements, and whether these movements in turn lowered levels of trust.

In Chapter 3, Deepak Malhotra argues that the economic crisis of 2008 and the subsequent bail-out of "too big to fail" firms revealed that the dynamics of stakeholder trust have dramatically shifted. Stakeholder dynamics have changed, this chapter argues, due to two significant changes: the compartmentalization of action within organizations and the complexity of action among organizational actors. The former impedes trustworthy behavior on the part of organizations and the latter inhibits the ability of stakeholders to judge the trustworthiness of organizations. Malhotra examines the implications that this new trust environment has for business leaders and researchers, offering a set of proposals for improving how we manage trust moving forward.

Robert Bies, in Chapter 4, argues that current analyses of public trust in business fails to recognize that trust and distrust are two distinct phenomena that coexist side by side in the current state of affairs. Analyzing survey data, Bies demonstrates that distrust is a resilient phenomenon, which indicates that it is a critical factor for leaders who have responsibility for managing stakeholder relationships.

In Chapter 5, Kirsten Martin, Michael Pirson, and Bidhan L. Parmar explore the factors that govern public trust in business. This chapter employs the results of a factorial vignette study conducted by the authors to clarify the impact that various determinants – e.g., size of the company, industry sector, integrity, value congruence, etc. – have on public trust.

Chapter 6, by Karen S. Cook and Oliver Schilke, examines the role that three different forms of trust – public trust, relational trust, and organizational trust – currently play in economic affairs. The authors apply literature on relational trust from the field of medicine to show how this form of trust could create further value for business and argue that the shift to institutional footings for maintaining trust are inevitable in an era marked by dramatic change.

Part II of this volume explores critical aspects of public trust with respect to business organizations. In Chapter 7, Jared D. Harris and Andrew C. Wicks develop a theoretical model for understanding the relationship between public trust in business and trust in particular firm–stakeholder interactions. This chapter makes stakeholder theory a central position, assessing how issues of goodwill and competence are of varying importance to different stakeholders and the impact this has on public trust in business and in particular companies.

In Chapter 8, Roderick Kramer examines the concept of presumptive trust and the advantages this form of trust could have for building organizations that are more trustworthy and more trusting. Taking an inside-out approach, Kramer argues that efforts to build trust with the public must begin by building more trustworthy organizations. Kramer's proposed barometer for assessing the effectiveness of these efforts is the level of presumptive trust, "a 'background expectation' that animates action within an organization without conscious calculation or premeditation on the part of organizational members."

Paul Argenti argues, in Chapter 9, that while public trust in business has never been more challenged, it has also never been of greater importance. Argenti's chapter explores opportunities for building trust by examining multiple case studies that suggest particular actions in the area of reputation management which leaders can employ to deliver improved levels of trust in their companies.

In Chapter 10, Reinhard Bachmann and Edeltraud Hanappi-Egger examine the relationship between interpersonal trust and institutionalized distrust within German and Austrian companies that operate under a two-tiered corporate governance system. This study shows how some level of distrust between the supervisory board and the executive board can limit the potential for negative impacts, such as corruption, which become more likely if there is too much trust between these two parties.

In Chapter 11, Rosalinde Klein Woolthuis, Bart Nooteboom, and Gjalt de Jong examine the role of third parties in trust repair via an empirical study of alliance managers in the high-tech sector. Such alliances are critical for innovation, and, thus, a crucial factor in remaining competitive. This study compares the impact of third-party involvement with other common inter-firm trust strategies, such as the use of contracts and legal haggling, to demonstrate which options are most likely to be effective for managers.

Chapter 12 by Laura Poppo and Donald J. (DJ) Schepker develops a conceptual framework for restoring public trust in the wake of organizational failures. The authors differentiate between organizational failures that are within the firm's control and those that are outside of the firm's control. Recognizing this difference and determining whether the violation is the result of incompetence or lack of integrity, this chapter claims, is critical for choosing an appropriate and effective response strategy.

Each of the chapters begins with an executive summary, composed by the editors, which highlights the particular situation, key questions, new knowledge and main lessons contained in each chapter. The book concludes with a final chapter by the editors which provides a brief overview of research areas of public trust in business that lie on the horizon. It is the editors' hope that this volume will serve as a catalyst for further research.

Acknowledgments

The authors thank the Business Roundtable Institute for Corporate Ethics (the Institute) and participants in the Project on Public Trust in Business, a joint initiative of the Institute and the Arthur W. Page Society. We are grateful to the CEOs of Business Roundtable for bringing this issue to the fore, and to Business Roundtable for their continuing support of the Institute's work.

In particular we would like to acknowledge those who contributed to the report, *The Dynamics of Public Trust in Business*. These include our terrific co-authors – Roger Bolton, R. Edward Freeman, Dean Krehmeyer, Laura Nash, and Michael Wing – as well as our exceptional trust panel participants – Paul Argenti, Harold Burson, Alice Eldridge, David Frishkorn, Francesco Guerrera, Chris Hill, Jon Iwata, Leah Johnson, Linda Kelleher, Jeff Mahoney, Thomas Nicholson, W. D. (Bill) Nielsen, Steve Rochlin, John W. (Jack) Rowe, M. D., Kurt Schacht, Johanna Schneider, Harold Tinkler, Frank Vogl, and Sandra Waddock.

We are also grateful for the contributions of Thomas Cervelloni, Jennifer Hicks, Karen Musselman, David Newkirk, Elizabeth Rothburd, and Lisa Stewart, who helped to organize the Ruffin Summit on Public Trust in Business, an event held at the University of Virginia's Darden School of Business in 2009, with the aim of catalyzing and shaping research in this emerging area of academic inquiry. We appreciate the sponsorship of Olsson Center for Applied Ethics of this event and its ongoing support throughout this process.

Joshua Metz was tremendously helpful in preparing the manuscript for this book and we appreciate his efforts.

As always, we thank our families and colleagues for their support of our work.

I Public trust in business: what's the problem and why does it matter?

Andrew C. Wicks, Brian T. Moriarty,
Jared D. Harris

EXECUTIVE SUMMARY

THE SITUATION

Survey data indicates that low public trust in business is an enduring phenomenon, but does not illuminate the underlying causes of this reality. While significant academic research has been done in the areas of interpersonal and interorganizational trust, little has been done in the area of public trust in business. This makes it difficult for business leaders to truly understand the problems posed by a lack of public trust and creates hurdles for their efforts to build and maintain public trust.

KEY QUESTIONS

What do business leaders know about building public trust in their companies? What don't they know and how might that be important for their particular business? What factors play a role in low levels of public trust in business? Why does trust matter to companies? What are the core dynamics of trust in business?

NEW KNOWLEDGE

Public trust in business is a highly complex phenomenon that is impacted by social and technological change. Low trust in business is not the result of a single factor, but rather emerges from the interaction of multiple causes. Some aspects of what shapes public trust in business seem fairly constant and stable over time (e.g., suspicion of large institutions) other dimensions seem more contextual and fluid (e.g., the rise of the internet, information sharing, and the decrease in direct human interaction as a part of business).

Trust matters deeply to business. Public trust impacts reputation, business performance, valuation, and the regulatory environment.

While public trust is complex, understanding the three core dynamics of trust can provide business leaders with a useful framework for managing stakeholder relationships.

KEY LESSONS

Understanding the relationships of the various drivers of trust is critical for business leaders seeking to build and maintain trust. Building and maintaining healthy levels of public trust in business is an undertaking that should be the joint venture of business leaders, scholars, government officials, and other stakeholders in the institution of business.

Business is a human institution – at its core it is about people working together to create value that no one of us could create on our own. In this context business has much to learn from research in social science and the humanities.

What happens inside organizations impacts the larger social environment (and vice versa).

INTRODUCTION

Distrust of the institution of business is not new; declining trust in business predates the current crisis,[1] and has long hovered between 10 percent and 20 percent.[2] Nevertheless the already dismally low levels of institutional trust have declined over the years it has been measured,[3] and the recent Occupy movement demonstrates its relevance as a building crisis for business; trust in business, though historically always low, has declined sharply. But what does this tell us, and why does this matter? The crisis of trust in business presents an opportunity to better understand the phenomenon of trust in business as an institution, where it comes from, and what can be done about it.

---

[1] Bolton *et al.*, 2009.   [2] Gallup, 2011.   [3] Van de Ven and Ring, 2006.

Low trust in business appears to be an enduring phenomenon. While measures of trust in business have experienced dips during times of economic crisis, they have not exhibited significant rebounds during economic boons. The high watermark for business in the already mentioned Gallup survey is 25 percent, achieved in 1990 and 2001. Measures of trust in other professions – such as nurses and firefighters who typically score above 80 percent in the same survey – suggest such gains are marginal.

While significant academic research has been completed in the areas of interpersonal and interorganizational trust, there is a dearth of research in the area of public trust in business. This knowledge gap makes it difficult for business leaders seeking to build and maintain public trust to do so effectively.

As Anne Mulcahy, former Chairperson of the Board and Chief Executive Officer of Xerox, wrote in 2009: "Current knowledge gaps in the dynamics of public trust … present serious challenges to leaders concerned with developing and implementing an effective long-term strategy for building mutuality and public trust."[4] Specifically, business leaders may find it difficult to answer questions about: how public trust in business impacts their company; what effects low levels of trust have upon regulators; which trust drivers are most effective with different stakeholder groups; which business outcomes derive from various types of trust; and how organizations should measure public trust. In a world where scandals and financial crises occur with some regularity, it becomes vital to have an understanding of the role of trust in markets – and the extent to which public trust is critical to the healthy function of markets.

In the face of scandals and crises, governments and stakeholders often call for more regulation to rebuild public trust. To what extent does this work, and allow us to rebuild trust in business? To what extent does such regulation reveal and enshrine a lack of trust and constrain the proper function of markets? We all have a stake in the

---

[4] Mulcahy, 2009.

answers to these questions – and we need a deeper understanding of public trust in business to answer them.

Currently, scholars have little insight to offer business leaders with respect to such questions, which is why there is such a need for the kind of new research found in this volume. The problem of public trust in business is a tangled knot that calls for joint efforts among scholars, business leaders, regulators, and other stakeholders affected by public trust in business. Together, we must build a robust understanding of public trust in business – how it works, how it can be altered, and what can be done to foster healthy levels of it.

THE NATURE OF THE PROBLEM – A KNOT OF KNOTS

It is important to recognize the extremely complex nature of the problem of public trust in business. Knowing that trust in business is low is akin to measuring an elevated body temperature. Without further knowledge of secondary symptoms and underlying causes, proper diagnosis and effective treatment eludes us. Our current efforts to (re)build public trust may resemble the efforts of doctors during the Middle Ages who used leaches and bleedings to "heal" sick patients – the best wisdom of the time, but practices that not only didn't help, but also often exacerbated the patient's condition.

We should begin with basics. As Russell Hardin has noted, trust is at minimum a three-part relationship that focuses on expectations of future behavior. For example, A trusts B to do C. But as Hardin has also indicated, these trust relationships exist within various social environments that influence the relationship – e.g., A trusts B to do C in context D.[5] This provides a common reference point for thinking about trust and how it functions in a social context.

While the basic structure of trust relationships in business have not altered that much over time, the contexts in which these relationships exist have experienced tremendous and continual change, particularly over the last three decades. Numerous sources

[5] Hardin, 2004.

note the rapid pace of globalization and its widespread effects on the structure of business and society. Combined with the spread of the internet and its increasingly ubiquitous role in our everyday life, the world has never been smaller or more interconnected. People can now talk and interact with people (and businesses) all over the world almost instantaneously and at virtually no cost.

While globalization has brought many benefits – easy access to more goods, services, and people at relatively low cost – it has also generated many unpopular effects. The growth of globalization has led to "outsourcing" (particularly unpopular in more developed economies which tend to see a decrease in jobs due to outsourcing), it has been associated with a growth in income inequality, and it has fostered outrage on the part of a variety stakeholder groups.

One of the more striking recent social movements is the "Occupy Wall Street" (Occupy) protest, which began in New York in September 2011 and quickly expanded into a global movement. Although the protest grew to encompass an expansive variety of issues and vague demands, it struck some common themes reflecting a deep dissatisfaction with modern capitalism: growing wealth inequality, corporate influence on democracy, business corruption, and lack of accountability – particularly in the financial services sector.[6] And even though the movement has been controversial – it has been lauded by some (e.g., *Time Magazine*'s person of the year: the protester)[7] and derided by others (e.g., Ovide, in his *Wall Street Journal* article from October 2011) – nearly three-quarters of American citizens see the Occupy movement as having a legitimate point.[8] For better or worse, this populist movement draws attention to an underlying crisis of trust in business as an institution.

Another notable trend that is met with anxiety by some members of the public is the increasing concentration of wealth within companies. In 1996, according to a report from the Institute for Policy Studies, for the first time in history, more than half of the

---

[6] Apps, 2011.   [7] Andersen, 2011.   [8] Becker, 2011.

world's 100 largest economies were companies, not nations.[9] The authors determined the relative magnitude of economies by comparing corporate sales figures with GDP.

On January 12, 2010, as the global economy was continuing to recover, the Haitian earthquake hit, resulting in thousands of deaths and mass destruction. Two weeks later, Goldman Sachs announced its bonus pool. Shortly thereafter, the headline "GDP of Haiti: $8.5 billion. Goldman Sachs bonus pool: $20 billion," went viral on the internet. A statement from the National Council of Churches remarking on the disparate concentration of wealth between this company and country noted that "The earthquake devastation in Haiti creates a painful context for news that Goldman Sachs has approved a bonus pool of $20 billion."[10] The implication is that some stakeholders view business as a game rigged in favor of the powerful. Views of business as being about making the rich richer, question basic fairness and undercut public trust in business.

The computing and communications revolutions offer additional challenges for building and maintaining public trust. Business interactions become less personal and driven more by indirect forms of interaction. More and more of our interaction in organizations (and within society) is done via email, text, tweet, and other social media. While there are distinct advantages to this development, there are also decided costs – particularly in terms of the richness and context of our interactions, which in turn, impacts the dynamics of trust. A decrease in the richness of contact leaves people with less information from which to understand core messages, interpret motivations, and appreciate the importance of the communication – all of which can invite distrust or at least erode the potential for building trust through communication. This is true for all organizations, which may explain why the US Postal Service is listed repeatedly by Americans as the most trusted federal agency in the Ponemon Institute's annual survey.[11] Most members of the public

---

[9] Anderson and Cavanagh, 2000.   [10] Jenks, 2010.   [11] Ponemon, 2010.

have regular, personal interactions with their mail carrier, which is not the case with employees of other agencies.

At the same time, the ability to reach a vast array of individuals and groups all over a country or the globe may open up new possibilities for building relationships and fostering trust. One of the things the Obama administration is noted for is their use of social media and the internet to contact potential voters and use these points of contact to build a connection with their audience – which, in turn, may have substantially impacted voter turnout and voter preferences.

Government regulators attempt to keep up with changes in practice which they deem related to negative social impacts. Most often the stimulus for new regulatory action arises in the form of a business scandal or series of scandals that has damaged public confidence in some area of business. For example, Sarbanes–Oxley legislation was written and passed on the heels of the Enron and WorldCom scandals. However, as Larry D. Thompson, the former Deputy Attorney General who led the Enron investigation famously said, "Regulations expand with each ensuing scandal to encompass every possible abuse ... except for the next one."[12] Regulation is expensive and reactive by its very nature, even as it may be essential to maintain healthy institutions. The key is discerning when regulation is needed and useful and when it becomes excessive and value destroying.

As the Sarbanes–Oxley legislation illustrates, a critical part of our framework for evaluating regulation may be not only the costs and benefits one can measure from the specifics of the policies – but the intangible impacts of such new laws on public trust. Sarbanes–Oxley may impose massive new costs and responsibilities onto companies – some of which make little sense or have unintended negative consequences – but was it a necessary step by the government to restore confidence in markets? Had we not passed Sarbanes–Oxley (or something like it) would public trust in business

---

[12] Thompson, 2003.

have eroded further and possibly led to even worse consequences for both business and society?

Keeping up with the pace of change is not only difficult for regulators, it is also a tremendous challenge for business leaders. Many business leaders may feel helpless in the face of new scandals and the threat of new regulations. When business leaders are not part of the companies or industries where scandals take place, they have no direct involvement in the events that erode trust. Yet business leaders are keenly aware that they are impacted by what happens around them and the corresponding loss in public trust.[13] Such changes may have a direct and substantial impact on your business and your ability to lead effectively. The question then becomes, what can I do as a business leader – both to protect and preserve trust in my business and to help rebuild public trust in business?

The problem of public trust in business appears to be a complex knot consisting of various knots and threads that reflect an environment of dynamic change. Business leaders and policy makers seeking to build public trust in business may be best served by approaches that are correspondingly multifaceted.

PUBLIC TRUST MATTERS TO BUSINESS

From the perspective of business leaders, declining trust in business constitutes a top concern.[14] Executives may worry that public displeasure may result in increased government regulation, a decline in customer confidence and corresponding sales, or even a "brain drain" of more top college graduates choosing a future outside the corporate world. No doubt executives desire social acceptability and admiration, and would be happier if business were regarded as more noble and appreciated, rather than as a kind of "dirty work."[15] Business leaders may wish to avoid negative press coverage, out of concern

---

[13] Bolton et al., 2009, 6.
[14] Business Roundtable Institute for Corporate Ethics, 2004.
[15] See Ashforth and Kreiner, 1999; Hughes, 1958.

that negative media accounts will encourage more regulation; a concern that appears to be well founded.[16]

A broader perspective suggests the importance of public trust in the institution of business, as well. Given the legal embracing of corporate "personhood" in the United States and the corresponding ability to directly donate to domestic political campaigns,[17] public trust in business is more closely related than ever to larger issues of trust in broad societal institutions.[18] Business has an increasingly large influence on public policy, social welfare, and public goods – relationships that may be exaggerated in the developing world, where multinationals are often the most robust institutions.[19]

The importance of the issue therefore requires us to seek a better understanding of how perceptions of business as an institution are formed. For instance, despite widespread concern about the health of the global economy and high unemployment across the globe,[20] the crisis of trust in business appears to be particularly concerned with ethics, business integrity, and corporate responsibility, rather than with business efficiency or economic viability.[21] If true, this may suggest that business entities should be as concerned about their reputations for integrity and accountability as they are about their ability to add more employees to the payroll.

The fact is, reputation has never been of greater importance to companies. For example, John Gerzema and Edward Lebar Prahalad contend that the approximate percentage of company value attributable to intangibles had increased from just over 30 percent in the 1950s to approximately 62 percent by 2008.[22] According to Interbrand's 2011 survey, the total value of the top 100 global brands is roughly $1.25 trillion, with Coca-Cola alone valued at $71.8 billion. The majority of these valuations are tied to reputation and trust – things that do not show up on balance sheets.

---

[16] Cavazos and Rutherford, 2011.   [17] Toobin, 2012.
[18] Brossard, 1996; Fukuyama, 1995.   [19] Hargrave, 2009.
[20] *Economist*, 2012.   [21] Porter, 2012.   [22] Gerzema and Lebar, 2008.

Chief executives and directors responding to an Economist Intelligence Unit Survey listed "events that undermine public trust in your products or brand" as the single most significant threat to a company's global business operations.[23] Similarly, a 2011 report from Deloitte identifies reputational risk as a meta risk that is "an even greater hazard to organizational survival than a financial restatement or problematical findings in a compliance report."[24] The widespread availability to the general public of inexpensive communications channels that have a global reach not only gives brands a reality beyond firsthand experience, but also makes brands more vulnerable to public scrutiny of company actions. BP, for example, lost $74 billion (or 40 percent) of their market cap in the first six weeks after the Gulf of Mexico oil spill.[25]

While the balance of power between companies, interest groups, and the broader public continues to evolve, there are other key areas of concern for executives trying to manage risks associated with corporate reputation. As Charles Fombrum and Violina Rindova have indicated, "a firm's relative standing ... internally with employees" is also an important contributor to a company's reputation.[26] Research suggests that many companies are some ways from maximizing the engagement of their employees. For example, one survey of employees found that only 10 percent of workers believe their senior leaders treat employees as key assets.[27] While we know that employee assessments have an impact on the reputation of their particular firms, we do not know how – or even if – this impacts the broader issue of public trust in business. Focus on executive compensation as a key reason for public distrust in business, however, indicates a potential connection between workplace experience and public trust in business. As a 2009 Conference Board report states, "executive compensation has become a flashpoint for ... frustration and anger"

[23] Economist Intelligence Unit, 2005.   [24] Deloitte, 2011.
[25] Mufson and Vargas, 2010.   [26] Fombrun and Rindova, 1996.
[27] Towers Perrin, 2007–2008.

over the global economic crisis that "has led to a loss of public trust in corporations and other institutions."[28] The report lists total compensation that is fair to employees as part of it "guiding principles" and key recommendations.[29]

THE THREE CORE DYNAMICS OF PUBLIC TRUST

So how are business leaders to build and maintain public trust in this complex and dynamic environment? Current research and dialog with business leaders indicates that there are three core dynamics of public trust in business: mutuality, balance of power, and trust safeguards.[30]

Mutuality – a sense of shared values, purpose, or interests – is the most crucial and central dynamic. Mutuality connects directly with the core purpose of business as a form of social cooperation that creates value for people. Business leaders and the general public identify many of the same issues – e.g., health care, privacy, education, energy – as being the most crucial issues facing society.[31] While differences of perspective are sometimes emphasized in news accounts about pressing issues, the commonality of concern represents a significant opportunity for meaningful dialog or other activities that can create greater mutuality and trust.

Balances of power, the second core dynamic of public trust, are equilibriums which ensure that one party or group is not able to unfairly impose its will upon another. The founders of the United States, for example, purposefully embedded checks and balances between the three branches of the US federal government because they believed such measures were necessary to maintain liberty and halt tyranny. Because trust involves voluntary vulnerability, extreme imbalances of power can disrupt opportunities for building and maintaining trust. The communications revolution which has given millions of people an unprecedented ability to communicate about brands may be helpful for counterbalancing the rise of corporate

---

[28] Conference Board, 2009, 6.   [29] Ibid., 11.
[30] Bolton et al., 2009, 22–27.   [31] Ibid., 23–24.

power signified by the unprecedented concentration of wealth decried by groups like Occupy.

The final core dynamic is trust safeguards, or legal and compliance mechanisms meant to mandate fairness in the presence of intractable power imbalances and to require reparations when vulnerable parties have suffered abusive behavior. Most trust safeguards exist in the form of regulation, such as consumer protection laws, but also include voluntary efforts on the part of an industry sector. For example, in 1986 after a series of overpricing scandals involving sales to the US federal government, defense contractors launched the Defense Industry Initiative, a voluntary effort to self-regulate by creating ethics and compliance measures to prevent further bad behavior.[32]

While mutuality is the most critical dynamic, business leaders and policy makers would be well served to consider the potential roles of all three core dynamics when assessing opportunities for building and trust with the public and other stakeholders. As we noted in our 2009 report, the three core dynamics of public trust are not mutually exclusive and "operate most effectively when they work together like gears in a machine."[33]

CONCLUSION

This book represents a concerted effort to highlight the timeliness and importance of research on public trust in business – and to take some key first steps in better understanding this phenomenon. It is not a complete description of the problem or an exhaustive study of the topic. Indeed, one of the things we hope emerges from this volume is the push for more discussion and focused research so that the collaboration between scholars and business leaders (as well as other related stakeholders) can take hold and deliver the results we need. We can all appreciate that public trust is low and that there are many existing forces that risk driving it lower; we all appreciate the stakes involved

---

[32] *Ibid.*, 27.   [33] *Ibid.*, 22.

and the impact of low public trust in business. What we need is to foster a set of conversations and focused inquiry that allows us to better understand how public trust in business works and how we can rebuild it. If we want healthy institutions, particularly healthy markets that consistently deliver outstanding value to a wide array of stakeholders, then we need to understand the dynamics of public trust. A look around at the state of the world and the pressure being put on business leaders highlights the practical importance of this topic – but we can also point to our present and future generations and note that doing a better job on this front is vital to their ability to thrive. The time has come. We hope this volume moves us forward and sparks the kinds of conversations and research that we need.

REFERENCES

Andersen, K. (2011), 'The protester.' *Time*, December 26, 53–89.

Anderson, S. and Cavanagh, J. (2000), *The Rise of Corporate Global Power: Institute for Policy Studies*, white paper.

Appiah, K. (2008), *Experiments in Ethics*. Cambridge, MA: Harvard University Press.

Apps, P. (2011), 'Wall Street action part of global Arab Spring?' Reuters, October 11, retrieved November 24, 2011.

Ashforth, B. E. and Kreiner, G. E. (1999), 'How can you do it: dirty work and the challenge of constructing a positive identity.' *Academy of Management Review*, 24, 413–434.

Becker, B. (2011), 'The Hill Poll: fears about income inequality grow,' *The Hill*, October 31.

Bolton, R., Freeman, R. E., Harris, J. D., Moriarty, B., and Nash, L. (2009), *The Dynamics of Public Trust in Business: Emerging Opportunities for Leaders*. Charlottesville, VA: Business Roundtable Institute for Corporate Ethics, white paper.

Brossard, M. A. (1996), 'Americans losing trust in each other and in institutions.' *Washington Post*, 28–29 January, A1.

Business Roundtable Institute for Corporate Ethics (2004), *Mapping the Terrain: Issues that Connect Business and Ethics*, white paper.

Cavazos D. E. and Rutherford, M. (2011), 'Examining how media coverage impacts the regulatory notice and comment process.' *American Review of Public Administration*, 41(6), 625–638.

Conference Board (2009), *The Conference Board Task Force on Executive Compensation*, 6, www.conferenceboard.org/pdf_free/ExecCompensation2009.pdf (accessed July 8, 2013).

Deloitte (2011), *A Risk Intelligent View of Reputation*. White paper: Risk Intelligence Series, no. 22.

The Economist (2012), 'The never-ending crisis.' July 24.

Economist Intelligence Unit (2005), *Reputation: Risk of Risks*, white paper.

Fombrun, C. J. and Rindova, V. (1996), *Who's Tops and Who Decides? The Social Construction of Corporate Reputations*. New York University, Stern School of Business, working paper.

Fukuyama, F. (1995) *Trust: The Social Virtues and the Creation of Prosperity*. New York: Free Press.

Gallup (2011), 'Honesty/ethics in the professions,' November 28–December 1.

Gerzema, J. and Lebar, E. (2008), *The Brand Bubble: The Looming Crisis in Brand Value and How to Avoid It*. San Francisco, CA: Jossey-Bass.

Hardin, R. (2004), *Trust and Trustworthiness*. New York: Russell Sage Foundation, 9.

Hargrave, T. (2009), 'Moral imagination, collective action, and the achievement of moral outcomes.' *Business Ethics Quarterly*, 19(1), 87–104.

Harris, J. D. and Edward Freeman, R. (2008), 'The impossibility of the separation thesis.' *Business Ethics Quarterly*, 18(4), 541–548.

Hughes, E. C. (1958), *Men and Their Work*. Glencoe, IL: Free Press.

Jenks, P. (2010), Editor's note to 'For Haiti, A Modest Proposal,' George Hunsinger and Michael Kinnamon. National Council of Churches website, www.ncccusa.org/news/100203hunsingerkinnamon.html (accessed July 8, 2013).

Mufson, S. and Vargas, T. (2010), 'BP loses 15 percent of market value as US launches criminal probe of spill.' *Washington Post*, June 2.

Mulcahy, A. M. (2009), *Introductory Letter to the Dynamics of Public Trust in Business: Emerging Opportunities for Leaders*. Business Roundtable Institute for Corporate Ethics, white paper.

Ovide, S. (2011), 'Billionaire tells Occupy Wall Street to get off his lawn.' *Wall Street Journal*, October 11.

Parker, S. L. and Parker, G. R. (1993), 'Why do we trust our congressman?' *Journal of Politics*, 55 (2), 442–453.

Ponemon Institute News Release (2010), 'US Postal Service tops Ponemon Institute List of Most Trusted Federal Agencies,' 30 June, www.ponemon.org/news-2/32 (accessed July 8, 2013).

Porter, E. (2012), 'The spreading scourge of corporate corruption.' *New York Times*, July 10.

Searle, J. R. (1964), 'How to derive "ought" from "is."' *Philosophical Review*, 73(1), 43–58.

Thompson, L. D. (2003), *Senior Fellow*. Brookings Institute, Federalist Society Address 2, November 14.

Toobin, J. 2012. 'Money unlimited.' *New Yorker*, May 21.

Towers Perrin (2007–2008), *Closing the Engagement Gap: A Road Map for Driving Superior Business Performance*, white paper.

Van de Ven, A. H. and Ring, P. S. (2006), 'Relying on trust in cooperative inter-organizational relationships.' In R. Bachmann and A. Zaheer (eds.), *Handbook of Trust Research*, Cheltenham, UK: Edward Elgar, 144.

Wicks, A. C., Berman, S., and Jones, T. (1999), 'The structure of optimal trust: Moral and strategic implications.' *Academy of Management Review*, 24(1), 99–116.

PART I　Trusting the institution of business

2 The economic crisis of 2008, trust in government, and generalized trust

Eric M. Uslaner

EXECUTIVE SUMMARY

THE SITUATION

The global economic crisis of 2008 damaged trust in the institutions of business and government among the American public. The Tea Party in particular stands out as a political movement that responded by viewing both big business and big government as being at fault.

KEY QUESTIONS

Was the economic crisis responsible for reducing trust either in government or in other people more generally? What factors shape different forms of trust? How does survey data contribute to our understanding of political movements (such as the Tea Party movement) with respect to trust in institutions?

NEW KNOWLEDGE

When survey researchers ask whether "most people can be trusted," respondents interpret this question as referring to strangers, *not to people we know.* They do not tend to see the question as reflecting their life experiences, but rather as reflecting a general worldview. However, trust in people we know and people we don't know are *not* the same thing, nor can we readily move from the former to the latter.

I am grateful to the Graduate School of the University of Maryland, College Park for a Research and Scholarship Award (RASA) that assisted me greatly in preparing this chapter.

Generalized trust, the belief that "most people can be trusted," does not vary much over time. It is a moral value learned early in life from your parents or other influential figures, and remains relatively stable over time, in contrast to trust in particular institutions, like the government. For example, people who are the angriest about the state of the economy are 16 percent more likely to distrust government but have only a 1 percent greater probability of distrusting other people.

A sense of shared beliefs or membership in a group, makes a huge difference. The principal "real world" factor shaping trust (and optimism) is the level of economic inequality in a society. The more inequality, the less likely people will see a common fate – or view people from different economic (and often ethnic/racial backgrounds) as part of their "moral community." The economic crisis exacerbated inequality.

Polarization among the public has been growing sharply in recent years, reaching record levels. The economic crisis, which galvanized Tea Party groups, merely pushed these divisions to new plateaus. When people do not see others as part of their moral community, they will not believe that "most people can be trusted." Movements such as the Tea Party are best characterized as a result of skepticism about the role of government and about finding common cause with people of different backgrounds.

Our polarized political system has taken a toll on how we view our political leaders. Trust has become an uncommon commodity in politics.

Education is the strongest predictor of generalized trust: people with postgraduate training are 36 percent more likely to trust others than are respondents with only a grade school education. Education, however, has no significant effect on trust in government.

KEY LESSONS

Trust is a complex idea. Institutional trust (in specific institutions, like the government) and generalized trust (in other people more generally) have different foundations – one based upon experience, the other independent of individual experience. There is thus little reason to expect the same theoretical model to account for both trust in government and trust in people.

Political variables such as support for the Tea Party have powerful effects on trust in government, but not on (generalized) trust in people. Trust in government largely reflects satisfaction with the direction of the country – how well the economy is performing, not how well people are doing personally.

INTRODUCTION

The financial crisis of 2008 shook the social and political foundations of the country. The worst economic downturn since the Great Depression of the 1930s was not just a temporary downturn. Unemployment, which had been as low as 4.5 percent for much of 2006 and 2007, rose steeply in 2008 and 2009 before peaking at almost 10 percent in December, 2010 – and remaining at 9 percent or more through May, 2011.[1] The downturn became critical in September when the federal government placed the two largest mortgage holders, Fannie Mae (Federal National Mortgage Association) and Freddie Mac (Federal Home Loan Mortgage Corporation), into conservatorship as many mortgage holders defaulted on their loans and housing values dropped sharply. Investment Manager Bernard Madoff bilked more than $65 billion dollars from people who entrusted their money to him.[2]

President Barack Obama's first order of business after taking office in 2009 was a $787 billion stimulus program and a relief program for the hard-hit automobile industry. As the unemployment rate began to climb and the value of retirement accounts plummeted with falling stock prices, companies that were on the brink of failure were rescued by government programs – and then rewarded their top executives with generous bonuses: the insurance company AIG received a government rescue package of $173 billion and awarded its top employees with bonuses of $165million.[3]

---

[1] Data from www.google.com/publicdata/explore?ds=z1ebjpgk2654c1_&met_y=unemployment_rate&tdim=true&dl=en&hl=en&q=trends+in+unemployment, accessed July 7, 2011.

[2] Shear and Kane, 2009, A1; Barry, 2009.   [3] *Economist*, 2009, 77.

The economic traumas quickly turned into a crisis of public confidence. People felt betrayed by businesses that they saw as playing fast and loose with financial instruments that few seemed to understand. The economic collapse was widely called a crisis of trust for an outraged public.[4] The Pew Center for the People and the Press argued that the crisis led to "a perfect storm of conditions associated with distrust of government – a dismal economy, an unhappy public, bitter partisan-based backlash, and epic discontent with Congress and elected leaders."[5]

When government was called upon to rescue the automobile industry and the banks, many Americans felt that the system was "stacked" against them. Bankers and automobile makers were rescued, but there was little relief for the average person as the unemployment rate doubled from 5 percent in May, 2008 to 10 percent in October, 2009.[6] Americans have long been skeptical of anything big – big government, big business, big labor,[7] and the 2008 crisis led people to lose faith in both business and government. I shall present some evidence that attitudes toward business and government were strongly related, though a more extensive analysis challenges this argument at least in part. On the other hand, there is far weaker evidence that the crisis of 2008 led to less social cohesion, or trust in other people.

The *cri de cœur* against bigness was the Tea Party movement – actually "movements," since the Tea Party is a catch-all term for various anti-government groups including the Tea Party Nation, the Tea Party Patriots, the Tea Party Express, the Boston Tea Party, Freedom Works, and others.[8] The impetus for the movement came in a "rant" by reporter Rick Santelli on the cable network CNBC on February 19, 2009. Santelli called for a new Tea Party in the mold of the 1773 Boston Tea Party where colonists protested a tax on tea

---

[4] Barry, 2009; *Economist*, 2009, 77.
[5] Pew Center for the People and the Press, 2010, 1
[6] The unemployment data can be found at http://data.bls.gov/timeseries/ LNS14000000, accessed May 23, 2012.
[7] Lipset and Schneider, 1983.   [8] Karpowitz *et al.*, 2011

imposed by King George III of the United Kingdom without their consent. Santelli argued that the "government is promoting bad behavior" by providing generous grants to corporations and their leaders when ordinary people were losing their houses because they couldn't pay their mortgages.[9]

The Tea Party linked big business and big government, but what seemed to be a protest against both political leaders and corporations ultimately turned into a movement aimed primarily at Washington – in particular, the dominant party (the Democrats) and its policy agenda. There was a residue of complaints against big business, but waning confidence in business was becoming "de-linked" from the loss of faith in government.

Tea Party organizations sprung up, virtually spontaneously, across the country following Santelli's rant. By the 2010 election, Tea Party organizations had endorsed 149 Republican challengers and open-seat candidates. More than half of them (77) were elected in November and once the 112th Congress convened in 2011, members of the new Tea Party Caucus in the House of Representatives were more likely than other Republicans to vote against the "continuing resolution" that keeps the government running in the absence of a budget accord.[10]

The Tea Party movement is an expression of distrust in government – a protest against big government generally.[11] The Tea Party set out to undo much of the work of the Democratic Congress in the first two years of the Obama administration: the health care legislation, the "cap-and-trade" environmental proposal, TARP, and the economic stimulus – though only in more conservative districts for the latter.[12]

The Tea Party is also a protest movement against "politics as usual," and especially of making deals to get things done.

---

[9] Bedard, 2010; the video of Santelli's comment is available at http://video.cnbc.com/gallery/?video=1039849853, accessed July 7, 2011.

[10] Bailey et al., 2011, 6, 20–22.   [11] Pew Center for the People and the Press, 2010, 1.

[12] Brady et al., 2011; Masket and Greene, 2011.

Compromise became a dirty word in the Tea Party movement,[13] which was named, after all, for the event that gave rise to the American Revolution. The ideological and partisan polarization underlying the "no compromise" position is indicative of a much wider distrust of those who may be different from yourself – a distrust of people in general.[14]

What is striking is how the Tea Party arose as a reaction to the economic crisis – to the government "bail-outs" of the banks and the automobile industry (the Troubled Asset Relief Program, or TARP). But the government rescue programs were bipartisan – TARP was a program of the Bush administration. The protest movement shifted away from criticism of big business (even though this is where it started) toward fighting big government and the policy agenda of the Obama administration – and even to cultural issues underlying partisan polarization (see below). Resentment of Wall Street did not fade; it just took a back seat to larger political causes.

I do not suggest that the Tea Party movements are the cause of mistrust of government or of other people. Rather, the Tea Party is better characterized as a result of skepticism about the role of government and about finding common ground with people of different backgrounds. Polarization among the public has been growing sharply in recent years, reaching record levels: the economic crisis, which led to the formation of Tea Party groups, merely pushed these divisions to new plateaus.[15] When people do not see others as part of their moral community, they will not believe that "most people can be trusted."[16]

THE DATA

Was the economic crisis responsible for reducing trust either in government or in other people more generally? I examine these questions

[13] Lightman and Douglas, 2010; See also www.portagecountyteaparty.com/news/other-tea-party-news/when-compromise-is-going-soft.html, accessed July 7, 2011.
[14] Uslaner, 2000.   [15] Jacobson, 2011.   [16] Uslaner, 2002, 1.

in two surveys of the American public. The first is the Chicago Booth/ Kellogg School Financial Trust Index Survey (FTIS), a quarterly look at Americans' trust in the nation's financial system, measuring public opinion over three-month periods to track changes in attitude. It was sponsored by the University of Chicago Booth School of Business and the Kellogg School of Management at Northwestern University over seven waves from December, 2008 through June, 2010.[17] I obtained access to variables on levels of trust in different institutions and other people as well as anger over the state of the economy. I use this survey to present some time trends in trust and to test basic models of trust in people and in government.

The second data set will allow me to test a more comprehensive model. It is the Pew Trust in government survey in April 2010.[18] I use this data set to develop probit models for trust in government and generalized trust. In these models, I examine the impact of support of the Tea Party movement as the key factor affecting trust. Tea Party support should *not* by itself shape either form of trust. Instead, it is a proxy for anxiety over the state of the economy, fear of government, and disapproval of both financial institutions and a key policy of the Obama administration (health care). These variables, together with measures of ideology, optimism, a sense of cultural alienation, and some demographics will be used as instruments for Tea Party support.

Since the models from the FTIS data include few variables and more than 6,600 cases, it is not surprising that attitudes toward financial institutions and anger over the state of the economy shape both trust in government and generalized trust. However, the impacts are considerably stronger for trust in government – and this result also holds for the Pew data. The lessons from this more comprehensive

---

[17] On the FTIS, see Guiso (2010). The Chicago Booth/Kellogg School Financial Trust Index dataset is produced and distributed with primary funding from the University of Chicago Booth School of Business and the Kellogg School of Management at Northwestern University (www.financialtrustindex.org). I am grateful to Paola Sapienza and Luigi Zingales for providing the data.

[18] Pew Center for the People and the Press, 2010.

data set are similar to what I have reported elsewhere: political variables such as support for the Tea Party have powerful effects on trust in government, but not on (generalized) trust in people.[19]

The two measures of attitudes toward the financial industry in the Pew survey – on Wall Street and banks – have either modest or insignificant effects as instruments for Tea Party support. In a truncated model of Tea Party support, both are significant, but still lag far behind opposition to Obama's health care legislation. The rise of the Tea Party was more a protest against big government, with the financial crisis playing a subsidiary role.

Before discussing the data analysis, I consider the factors that we should expect to shape trust in government and generalized trust. I turn to that discussion now.

WHAT SHAPES TRUST?

We tend to think of trust as a single syndrome. Lane sees trust in government as part of the same general outlook as trust in people.[20] It is also common to argue that trust of all sorts "spreads" from specific experiences to more general expectations.[21] And people tend to see most institutions in the same light – support for government goes hand in hand with confidence in institutions in the private sector.[22]

This suggests that we need either a single measure of trust or a single model that would explain both trust in government and trust in other people. Trust, however, is not a single idea. People have more confidence in some institutions than in others: the military, the scientific community, medicine, the Supreme Court, and education (in that order) traditionally gain the public's confidence far more than does the executive branch, Congress, television, and the press more generally. The differences are substantial: The public had more than five times as much confidence in the military than in

<hr/>

[19] Uslaner, 2002, ch. 5.   [20] Lane, 1959, 165–166.
[21] Putnam, 2000, 288; Hardin, 2002.   [22] Lipset and Schneider, 1983.

the press in 2008.[23] Trust in institutions – even different branches of government – elicit varying levels of support from the public.

Beyond institutional trust, faith in our fellow men and women is also distinctive in two ways. First, trust in people we know and people we don't know are *not* the same thing, nor can we readily move from the former to the latter. We can't base trust in strangers upon experience because we don't have experience with them – and it may not be so reasonable to extrapolate from our interactions with people we know (largely our friends and family) to people who may be quite different from ourselves.

When survey researchers ask whether "most people can be trusted," respondents interpret this question as referring to strangers, *not to people we know.* They don't see the question as reflecting their life experiences, but rather a general worldview.[24] So, second, this suggests an alternative, if complementary, notion of trust. Generalized trust is *not* faith in specific persons, but the belief that you *ought to treat people as if they were trustworthy.* It is all about acting on faith, hope, and an optimistic worldview.

This suggests, third, that institutional trust and generalized trust (in other people) have different foundations – one based upon experience, the other not. There is thus little reason to expect the same model to account for both trust in government and trust in people.

Trust in government largely reflects satisfaction with the direction of the country, how well the economy is performing, and approval of leaders.[25] What matters are national economic conditions, not how well you are doing personally: most people don't believe that government is responsible for their own economic situation.[26] When economic conditions are bad – as reflected in the overall state of the nation – people are less likely to have confidence in the government. I present a graph from the Pew Center in Figure 2.1 that shows the tight connection between trust in government and satisfaction with

---

[23] Uslaner, 2011, 115.   [24] Uslaner, 2002, 68–74.
[25] Citrin, 1974; Hetherington, 1998.   [26] Kinder and Kiewiet, 1979.

Trust in Government
and Views of National Conditions

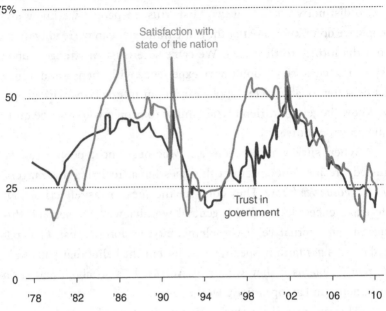

FIGURE 2.1 Trends in trust in government: Pew Center for the People
and the Press
Source: http://people-press.org/2010/04/18/distrust-discontent-anger-
and-partisan-rancor

the direction of the country. It is not surprising that the historic
lows (at least since the trust in government question was first asked
in 1960) occurred in 1994 and in October, 2008 – both periods of
economic turmoil *and* public reaction against major expansions of
the government role by Democratic administrations.[27] Figure 2.1
shows the wide swings in trust in government over time.

Generalized trust, the belief that "most people can be trusted,"
does *not* vary much over time. It is a moral value learned early in life

[27] See the interactive chart at http://people-press.org/2010/04/18/public-trust-in-
government-1958-2010. When one moves the mouse over the circles on the bottom,
pop-ups "explain" the levels of trust at each time period (accessed July 7, 2011).

from your parents and remains stable over time, in contrast to trust in government.[28] Generalized trust is *not* based upon experiences in adult life.[29] Instead, trusting people shake off negative experiences as exceptions to a more general rule. Generalized trust is based upon the psychological foundations of optimism and control – life is good, it will get better, and you can help make it better. Distrusters see the world as a dark and dangerous place where forces beyond their control shape their destiny. The optimism underlying generalized trust is a long-term faith in the future. Generalized trust is *not* based upon today's financial conditions, but on expectations for the more distant future – notably whether life will be better for the next generation. Trust in government *does* reflect satisfaction with current conditions.

The principal "real world" factor shaping trust (and optimism) is the level of economic inequality in a society: the more inequality, the less likely people will see a common fate – or view people from different economic (and often ethnic/racial backgrounds) as part of their "moral community."

Trust in government and generalized trust have different consequences. Confidence in political institutions makes it easier to enact programs such as health care, which expand the responsibilities of the government. If you don't trust the government, you won't want to expand its scope.[30] Generalized trust doesn't lead to the enactment of any specific programs, but it does promote *getting something done*. Low levels of trust lead to more stalemates in Congress.[31] When you see others as part of your moral community, you are more likely to accept compromising with them.

Trust in government and trust in other people are largely independent of each other, at least at the individual level.[32] The simple correlations between the two measures are: 110 for the FTIS and .079 for the Pew survey. And the reason seems clear: while confidence in government has seesawed over time, trust in other

---

[28] Uslaner, 2002, 60–65.   [29] This discussion is based upon *ibid.*, chs. 2, 4, and 6.
[30] Hetherington, 2004.   [31] Uslaner, 2002, 212–215.   [32] *Ibid.*, 151–153.

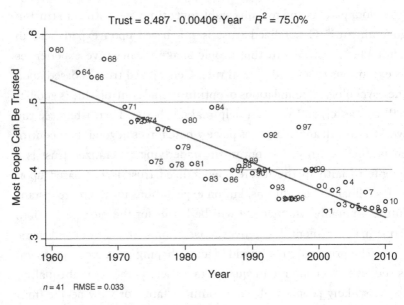

FIGURE 2.2 Generalized trust over time

people has declined sharply (see Figure 2.2) – moving in tandem with economic inequality.[33]

The financial crisis might affect both types of trust, but for different reasons. On trust in government, many Americans clearly saw the crisis as the result of poor regulation – and were also highly critical of the government's decision to bail out the banks, investment firms, and the automobile industry – especially as the unemployment and foreclosure rates soared. As *The Economist*'s columnist Lexington wrote, "The biggest cause of anger is [President Barack] Obama's willingness to bail out everyone with a tin cup, from bankrupt bankers to incompetent car makers to their over-their-ears mort-gage-holders. People who have borrowed prudently and lived within their means are livid that they are being asked to bail out neighbors who splurged on McMansions and giant televisions."[34] The govern-ment had become too distant from ordinary people – enacting

[33] *Ibid.*, 186–188, 230–237.   [34] Lexington, 2009, 42.

programs that were not popular (health care), growing to a size that many found out of control, and not competent in getting the economy back on track. The founding of the Tea Party groups and their success in the 2010 elections are testimony to the low level of trust in government – that has barely rebounded since its low in 2008.

On generalized trust, the key factors that might lead to a decline in generalized trust were: (1) perceptions of growing inequality and the belief that the rich were getting special treatment from the government and ordinary people were being left to fend for themselves as the economy tumbled; (2) the belief that we have lost control over our destiny to forces we cannot control – and for many in 2010 this was the federal government; and (3) a rise in pessimism – the system is fundamentally broken and not easily reparable.

There was plenty of reason to believe that some people are treated better than others in the financial crisis, notably the huge payments that chief executives reaped while ordinary citizens suffered. The economic crisis exacerbated inequality. While inequality, as measured by the Gini index, actually fell slightly from 2007 to 2008 and then ticked up slightly thereafter,[35] wealth at the very top increased substantially over time, especially compared to the income of the average American. While average wage income rose 26 percent from 1970 to 2005, the salaries of executives rose by 430 percent.[36] When the auto executives flew to Washington in 2009 in private jets to ask for bail-outs for their companies, there was a strong public reaction.[37]

The current situation is hardly unique: economic crises and rising inequality go together. Moss argues: "There are remarkable correlations between bank failures (and financial crises), financial regulation/deregulation, and income inequality across U.S. history."[38] The direction of causality is unclear: Moss seems to presume that inequality might have led to crises by giving too much power to the

[35] Data are from www.census.gov/hhes/www/income/data/historical/inequality/index.html, Table H4. Accessed May 23, 2011.
[36] Whoriskey, 2011.   [37] Lexington, 2009, 42.   [38] Moss, 2010.

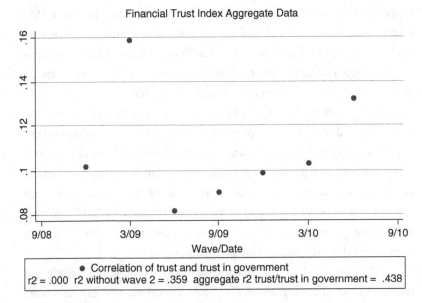

FIGURE 2.3 Correlation of trust and trust in government

entrepreneurs on Wall Street, especially since peaks in inequality seem to have occurred *before* the crises.[39] What is critical, from my perspective, is not *when* inequality rose (and it didn't seem to grow by much), but whether people saw unequal treatment in the wake of the crisis.

Second, the rise of the Tea Party was predicated on the idea that government had become too powerful and had usurped the power of local authorities: 85 percent of Tea Party supporters agreed with this statement, while 55 percent who did not support the Tea Party in the Pew survey disagree. Finally, many people came to believe that the political system was fundamentally broken – that it could not be repaired. Such a sentiment reflects longer-term pessimism, which is anathema to generalized trust.

Did the economic crisis lead to declines in trust? There is evidence that it had at least a short-term effect in Figure 2.3. Here

---

[39] Story, 2010; Moss, 2010.

I present the simple correlations of trust in government and trust in people from the FTIS data aggregated by wave of the sample. In the aggregate, over a short time period, trust in government and trust in people are highly correlated ($r^2 =.438$) but there is no trend for the size of the individual level correlations over time ($r^2 =.000$).

One data point is an outlier – for wave 2 (conducted in March 2009). The individual-level correlation between trust in government and generalized trust is at a maximum (.16) for this wave – considerably above all other correlations other than the last survey in June 2010. Trust in people increased very modestly, but trust in government rose considerably from the first wave. The rise in trust in government may seem puzzling since this wave was conducted right after Rick Santelli made his "Tea Party" comment and citizens were organizing Tea Party groups across the country. February, 2009 was also a time when there were new government initiatives on financial recovery: the announcement by Treasury Secretary Timothy Geithner of the Financial Stability Plan as well as the President's announcement of programs of mortgage relief and the Trouble Assets Relief Fund,[40] which was not yet so widely unpopular. Government was taking action – so even as the Tea Party movement was just beginning to get organized, the administration seemed to be taking action to resolve the economic crisis.

Since generalized trust is a stable value, it is not surprising that it shows little variation across the seven waves. There is no time trend and the variations are within sampling error. Trust in government is more variable. To make more sense of the data I dichotomized the measures. The low point for trust in government, with just 14 percent expressing confidence, occurs in the first wave (December, 2008), a time when there was no single major event, but nevertheless a barrage of bad news from at home and abroad on the effects of crisis. Trust

---

[40] See the financial turmoil timeline from the New York Federal Reserve Bank at www.newyorkfed.org/research/global_economy/Crisis_Timeline.pdf, accessed July 8, 2011.

rose steadily over 2009, to 19 percent in March, 23 percent in June, and 25 percent in September before falling to 17 percent in March, 2010. The rise in confidence shows that no news – the dominant pattern throughout 2009 – may be good news. The absence of any more traumatic announcements led faith in government to rise again (see note 8). The increases in trust in government in 2009 correspond to small upticks in both consumer sentiment and in satisfaction with the direction of the country. Overall, however, trust in government, from both the FTIS and Pew data, was very low and had fallen sharply not only from the high after the September 11, 2001 terrorist attacks but also from public disenchantment over the war in Iraq and even the government's handling of Hurricane Katrina in 2005 (see the source in note 5).

WHAT THE DATA SHOW

I turn first to the FTIS data. Both trust questions are five point scales so I estimate the models for each by ordered probit (see Table 2.1).[41] I present the coefficients, their standard errors, z ratios, and effects. Effects are the changes in probabilities in the independent variables, holding other predictors at their original values and evaluating the independent variables at their minimum and maximum values – the

---

[41] The trust questions are five-point scales: "On a scale from 1 to 5, where 1 means 'I do not trust them at all' and 5 means 'I trust them completely,' can you please tell me how much do you trust (the government) (other people in general)." The standard trust questions are "How much of the time do you trust the government in Washington to do what is right?" and "Generally speaking, do you believe that most people can be trusted or can't you be too careful in dealing with people?" Pew uses these questions. The trust in government question is a four-point scale ranging from "just about always" to "never" (volunteered). The generalized trust question is a dichotomy. I also dichotomized the trust in government question for two reasons. First, I estimate identical models for the two types of trust, so I needed to collapse the trust in government question. Second, only 2.9 percent of the respondents answered "just about always," so collapsing the data makes sense. The standard dichotomy on generalized trust is a preferable measure, especially with an odd number of cases, where responses tend to "clump" in the middle (neutral) category (Uslaner, in press (a), Uslaner, in press (b)).

Table 2.1 *Ordered probits for trust in government and generalized trust: Financial Trust Index Survey*

Variable	Coefficient	Std Error	z Ratio	Effect†
Trust in government				
Trust banks	.067****	.012	5.43	−.082
Trust Federal Reserve	.421****	.012	34.77	−.517
Angry over state of the economy	−.138****	.010	−13.32	.163
Generalized trust				
Trust banks	.125****	.012	10.44	−.055
Trust Federal Reserve	.057****	.011	5.09	−.025
Angry over state of the economy	−.027***	.010	−2.64	.011

Notes:
* p <.10
** p <.05
*** p <.01
**** p <.0001
−2*Log Likelihood ratio = 17744.90 for trust in government, 17711.76 for generalized trust
Cutpoints not reported
† Change in probability for not trust at all

"effects" of each predictor.[42] For the ordered probits, the effects are the changes in probability of not trusting government (people) at all.

The models using the FTIS data include just three predictors: trust banks, trust the Federal Reserve Bank, and anger over the state of the economy. The huge sample sizes mean that all three variables are significant, at least at p <.001 for both trust measures. But the effects for each measure are far greater for trust in government than for trust in other people. People who have trust in banks are 8 percent less likely to

[42] Rosenstone and Hansen, 1992. For dichotomies, I estimate these probabilities using the margins command in Stata, followed by the lincom command for the instrumental variables probit models for the Pew data. Details are available on request.

have no confidence in government and 5.5 percent less likely to have little faith in other people. People who are the angriest about the state of the economy are 16 percent more likely to distrust government have only a 1 percent greater probability of mistrusting other people. Since many of the efforts to stimulate the economy involved the Federal Reserve Bank (and Ben Bernanke, the Chairman of its Board of Governors), it is not surprising that the biggest effects for trust in government are for confidence in the Fed. People with complete confidence in the Federal Reserve Board are 52 percent less likely to express strong distrust of government, compared to those with the least faith in the Fed. The effect is far more modest for trust in people, just 2.5 percent.

The financial crisis had much stronger effects on trust in government than on trust in people according to the analysis based upon FTIS data. This seems reasonable, especially since the available variables do not tap either inequality or long-term pessimism.

The Pew Trust in government survey provides a broader opportunity to examine the impact of the financial crisis on trust. The estimation strategy I have chosen is instrumental variable probit. I use probit because the two trust questions are dichotomies/dichotomized (see note 9). I want to examine the effects of both Tea Party support and the economic crisis, but it is not realistic to assume that they are independent of each other. So the models for trust include the measure of agreement with the Tea Party. But I treat support for the movement as depending upon attitudes toward the economic crisis, as well as on perceptions of whether the government is a threat, if it interferes with local initiatives, whether the system is broken, ideology and positions on health care, satisfaction with the direction of the country, whether government helps the average person, and whether the entertainment industry has a positive effect on the country.

TRUST, THE TEA PARTY, AND THE ECONOMIC CRISIS:
THE PEW SURVEY

I turn now to an examination of the roots of trust in government and generalized trust in the Pew Trust in government survey. The Pew survey has a more comprehensive set of questions – though it is clearly more designed to examine trust in government than generalized trust. It also permits me to consider whether the economic crisis played a key role in support for the Tea Party – and whether in turn this led to lower levels of support for either form of trust.

While trust in government and generalized trust have different roots, I estimate identical models for them. In part, I do this because the survey is thin on determinants of generalized trust.[43] Identical models also allow us to see how some factors influence one type of trust and not another.[44]

The models I estimate are instrumental variable probits. I use probits because the trust measures are dichotomies (see note 9). One of the key predictors is support for the Tea Party.[45] As I have argued above, the influence of the economic crisis on either form of trust is not likely to be direct, but rather through its effect on Tea Party support. So I estimate a model for Tea Party support as part of the trust estimations – and then use the predicted values for Tea Party support in the trust equations.[46] I consider the estimations for the two forms of trust and Tea Party support and then I also examine a simpler model for Tea Party support alone.

The trust models include, in addition to attitudes on the Tea Party, satisfaction with the direction of the country, whether the government threatens your rights and freedoms, whether the federal government interferes with the role of state and local government, whether the political system is broken or can be repaired with new people, ideology, whether one owns a gun, age, education, and race. Satisfaction with the direction of the country is a widely used measure of government performance (and the Pew survey does not have a question on satisfaction with the economy). The two questions on government – is it a threat and is the federal government infringing

[43] See Uslaner, 2002, ch. 4.   [44] *Ibid.*, 154–158.
[45] The middle category is "no opinion." I considered dropping such responses (treating them as missing data), but this would have reduced the sample size dramatically.
[46] I use the ivprobit command in Stata for these estimations.

on the role of the states and localities – should tap different dimensions of trust. Government as a threat may shape both types of trust. If we see government as a threat, we would be less likely to trust it. Perceiving threats may just as likely reflect a worldview that our life is not within our control – and that we should not be so ready to put our faith in *anyone* outside our immediate circle of family and friends.[47] The Pew survey has no question that directly taps economic inequality. The closest is whether government helps the average person rather than special interests. A similar question – whether officials don't care for the average person – was (other than age) the strongest predictor of generalized trust in one model I estimated.[48] It is thus a reasonable measure of perceptions of inequality.

Anderson *et al.* argue that identifiers of the in-party will be more trusting of government than out-party supporters.[49] Rather than party identification, I include ideology in the trust equations because all predictors in the trust equations are also employed as instruments for Tea Party support. Since almost all Tea Party candidates were Republicans, party identification would likely swamp all other effects in that equation.[50] The strong overlap between ideology and party identification rules out including both of them.[51] One of the cultural issues shaping distrust in government is gun control. Gun owners are, according to one study, less likely to trust government.[52] Some Tea Party candidates – notably Sharron Angle, the Republican nominee for the United States Senate from Nevada in 2010, argued that people needed to assert their "Second Amendment rights" to protect themselves from government abrogation of their rights. Finally, generalized trust is lower among the young, the least educated, and African-Americans.[53]

The instrumental variables for Tea Party support include all of the predictors for trust[54] as well as four other determinants of Tea

---

[47] Banfield, 1958, 110.   [48] Uslaner, 2002, 98–100.   [49] Anderson *et al.*, 2005.
[50] Bailey *et al.*, 2011.   [51] Jacobson, 2011.
[52] Jiobu and Curry, 2002.   [53] Uslaner, 2002, ch. 4.
[54] This is standard in instrumental variable estimation in Stata. The equations for Tea Party support including such variables are called the "reduced form."

Party support: two measures of attitudes toward the financial crisis – whether banks have a positive effect on the country and whether Wall Street gets more attention than it deserves – as well as government interference with state and local authorities and attitudes toward the Obama administration's Affordable Health Care Act. The rationale for the economic measures is straightforward: it was the economic crisis that spurred Rick Santelli to call for a new American Tea Party. Arguing that the federal government has usurped the powers of state and local authorities is a likely source of mistrust of government – and of support for the Tea Party movement.[55] For many, the health care bill was a federal intrusion into areas of state responsibility – and fourteen state attorneys general filed suit to declare the act unconstitutional.[56]

I present the results of the instrumental variable probits in Tables 2.2 and 2.3. Table 2.2 has the estimates for trust in government and the associated instruments for Tea Party support. Table 2.3 has similar estimates for generalized trust and the instruments. The estimates for the instruments are, of course, similar for both estimations. However, trust in government and generalized trust have – as in other analyses – different foundations. The effects tell the story clearly. The Tea Party instrument is by far the most important factor shaping trust in government. It is the only variable significant at p <.01 or better. More critically, the strongest Tea Party supporters are 76.3 percent less likely to trust government than are those most skeptical of the movement. The Tea Party instrument is not significant in the generalized trust equation and the effect is a mere .026: Strong supporters are 2.6 percent less trusting of other people than are opponents, a minuscule effect.

The second largest effect for trust in government is for age, though this result is less compelling since it may be ephemeral: young people, most notably 18-year-olds, are 13 percent more likely to put faith in government than are older people (aged 75). This may reflect the greater enthusiasm of young people for President Obama and the

[55] Berkowitz, 2010.   [56] Williams, 2010.

Table 2.2 *Instrumental variable probit: trust in government*

Variable	Coefficient	Std error	z Ratio	Effect
Tea Party Agreement (instrument)	−.777****	.203	−3.83	−.763
Satisfaction with direction of country	.422**	.211	2.00	.103
Government threatens your rights and freedoms	−.076	.185	−.41	−.035
Government doesn't do enough to help average American	−.100	.121	−.82	−.046
Political system is broken	−.174	.159	−1.10	−.040
Ideology	−.112	.121	−.92	−.100
Own gun	.002	.170	.01	.000
Age	−.010**	.005	−2.12	−.134
Education	−.053	.053	−1.00	−.073
African-American	.445**	.243	1.83	.138
Constant	2.071	1.404	1.47	

Notes:
* p <.10
** p <.05
*** p <.01
**** p <.0001
N= 489 Wald χ^2 = 72.32

Democratic Party rather than any other rationale for confidence in the system per se.[57] Indeed, consistent with much other research, older people are substantially *more* likely to say that "most people can be trusted."[58] The effect in Table 2.3, .194, is the third largest in the model. African-Americans are also more trusting of government (by 11 percent); hardly surprising since Barack Obama is the first black President of the United States. But they are also 14 percent less trusting of other people, again consistent with previous research and hardly surprising.[59]

[57] Keeter *et al.*, 2008.   [58] Brehm and Rahn, 1997; Uslaner, 2002, 98–107.
[59] Uslaner, 2002, 98–107.

Table 2.2 (continued) *Estimates for Tea Party Agreement Instrument*

Variable	Coefficient	Std error	z Ratio
Tea Party Agreement			
Satisfaction with direction of country	−.100	.110	−.91
Government threatens your rights and freedoms	−.250****	.058	−4.32
Government doesn't do enough to help average American	.052	.059	.88
Political system is broken	−.011	.088	−.13
Government interferes too much in state and local matters	−.317****	.052	−6.13
Entertainment industry has positive effect on country	−.115	.111	−1.04
Banks have positive effect on country	.109	.141	.77
Wall Street gets more attention from government than it deserves	.089*	.055	1.63
Favor health care legislation	−.704****	.124	−5.68
Age	−.002	.003	−.71
Education	−.064**	.031	−2.09
African-American	.014	.177	.08
Constant	5.498****	.314	17.53

Notes:
  * p <.10
  ** p <.05
  *** p <.01
  **** p <.0001

Satisfaction with the direction of the country leads to a 10 percent boost in the likelihood of trusting government. Counterintuitively, those who are most satisfied are 9 percent *less* likely to trust other people. However, this effect is far from statistically significant: the standard error is six and a half times as great as the probit coefficient. The only other factor with a measurable effect is ideology: strong conservatives are 10 percent less likely to trust government than are very liberal respondents.

Table 2.3 *Instrumental variable probit: generalized trust*

Variable	Coefficient	Std error	z Ratio	Effect
Tea Party Agreement (instrument)	−.019	.149	−.13	−.026
Satisfaction with direction of country	−.027	.173	−.16	−.090
Government threatens your rights and freedoms	−.246**	.104	−2.37	−.162
Government doesn't do enough to help average American	−.349****	.097	−3.61	−.244
Political system is broken	−.332***	.134	−2.48	−.111
Ideology	.012	.090	.14	.016
Own gun	−.037	.146	−.25	−.012
Age†	.010***	.004	2.36	.194
Education	.179****	.046	3.89	.357
African-American	−.428**	.232	−1.85	−.138
Constant	−2.376**	.910	−2.61	

Notes:
   * p <.10
   ** p <.05
   *** p <.01
   **** p <.0001
N= 489 Wald χ^2 = 72.32
† Effects for age calculated at 18 and 75

WHAT SHAPES GENERALIZED TRUST?

The factors shaping generalized trust are very different from those for trust in government. Education is, as elsewhere,[60] the strongest predictor of trust: people with postgraduate training are 36 percent more likely to trust others than are respondents with only a grade school education. Education has no significant effect on trust in government.

Perhaps a bit ironically, three perceptions of government matter for generalized trust, but not for confidence in government. Most

[60] Brehm and Rahn, 1997; Uslaner, 2002, 98–107.

Table 2.3 (continued) *Estimates for Tea Party Agreement Instrument*

Variable	Coefficient	Std error	z Ratio
Tea Party Agreement			
Satisfaction with direction of country	−.130	.110	−1.18
Government threatens your rights and freedoms	−.251****	.058	−4.31
Government doesn't do enough to help average American	.048	.059	.81
Political system is broken	.001	.086	.01
Government interferes too much in state and local matters	−.303****	.052	−5.84
Entertainment industry has positive effect on country	−.026	.094	−.28
Banks have positive effect on country	.171	.057	1.45
Wall Street gets more attention from government than it deserves	.084*	.057	1.48
Favor health care legislation	−.743****	.116	−6.38
Age	−.001	.003	−.52
Education	−.056**	.031	−1.80
African-American	.044	.180	.25
Constant	5.399****	.315	17.14

Notes:
   * p <.10
   ** p <.05
   *** p <.01
   **** p <.0001

notable is the powerful effect of whether the government helps the average person. Believing that the failure of government to act on behalf of the "common man (and woman)" is a major problem and leads to a .24 drop in the probability of trusting others. The idea that government is a threat to you makes you 16 percent less likely to put faith in others. If you say that the system of government is broken, you will be 11 percent less likely to be a generalized truster. None of these measures leads to a significant drop in trust in government.

The factors shaping trust in government and generalized trust are thus very different: political attitudes – notably Tea Party support and ideology as well as short-term satisfaction with the direction of the country – affect confidence in government, but not generalized trust. Views about who gets what, whether you face threats from forces you cannot control, and whether you can fix problems shape generalized trust, but not confidence in the state. Older people have more trust in other people, but less in government, while the opposite is true for African-Americans. Owning a gun is the only factor that shapes neither form of trust.

WHAT SHAPES TEA PARTY SUPPORT?

What underlies Tea Party support? I first examine the first stage estimates in the instrumental variable probits. This estimation technique does not permit an estimation of probit effects, so I have to rely upon the significance of the variables. In the trust in government model, people who believe that Wall Street receives too much attention from Washington are significantly more likely to support the Tea Party. The effect is weaker in the generalized trust first stage estimation, but here the belief that banks are having a *positive* effect on the country seems to increase support for the movement (though the wrongly signed coefficient is not significant). The economic crisis did seem to boost support for the Tea Party – but the effect seems modest compared to more explicitly political variables: Worrying about governmental interference in state and local affairs, seeing government as a threat to your rights, conservatism, and especially opposition to the administration's health care legislation drove support for the Tea Party. Only education, of all the other variables, had a significant effect on backing the movement (more highly educated people are less supportive).

The initial call for a new Tea Party from Rick Santelli was based upon conservative populist rhetoric that demonized the unequal treatment of the rich on Wall Street and in the banking community at the expense of the average person. Yet, the perception that the government did not help the common men and women was not a significant predictor of Tea Party support. Neither was satisfaction with the state of the country or even the belief that the system is broken. The rhetoric also emphasized a cultural gap between liberals and conservatives. Yet, a classic demon of the right – the entertainment industry – did not affect support for the Tea Party. Neither did gun ownership.

Finally, I estimated a "bare bones" standalone model of Tea Party support. To obtain effects that are easier to understand, I collapsed the measure of approval into a dichotomy.[61] The model includes only one cultural factor (the entertainment industry), two economic indicators (Wall Street and bankers), the government interference measure, support for the health care law, and education.

Economics matters – but only for Wall Street. Believing that Wall Street gets too much attention leads to a 15 percent greater likelihood of backing the Tea Party. Beliefs that banks have a positive effect on the country continue to lead to more support for the movement. This is not a statistical aberration due to the confounding influence of other variables (e.g., highly collinear predictors). The two economic indicators are barely related (r =.019). And the zero-order correlation between perceptions of bankers and Tea Party support is positive, if small (r =.065). There is also modest support for a cultural effect: seeing a positive effect for the entertainment industry drives Tea Party support down by 15 percent. But the effect of health care is twice as large and belief in government interference increases backing by 46 percent.

REPRISE

The economic crisis clearly had political effects: the very high unemployment rate was in the minds of voters in 2010. The state of the economy was the most important issue in the election and voters

---

[61] I coded support and strong support as 1; opposition, strong opposition, and no opinion are coded as 0.

Table 2.4 *Probit for Tea Party Agreement (dichotomized)*

Variable	Coefficient	Std error	z Ratio	Effect
Entertainment industry has positive effect on country	−.546****	.144	−3.80	−.146
Banks have positive effect on country	.335	.153	2.19	.089
Wall Street gets more attention from government than it deserves	.288****	.080	3.57	.153
Government interferes in state/local area	.553****	.081	6.82	.458
Favor health care legislation	−1.057****	.140	−7.55	−.314
Education	−.052*	.038	−1.38	−.082
Constant	1.129****	.253	4.46	

Notes:
  * p <.10
  ** p <.05
  *** p <.01
  **** p <.0001
McKelvey–Zavoina R^2 =.546 percent predicted correctly: 76.7 (Model)
60 (Null)
−2*Log likelihood ratio = 554.05

who held the economy to be central were more supportive of Republicans. Two-thirds of voters who were very worried about the economy said that they voted Republican – and this was half of the electorate. The election was also about health care and the power of the federal government. Only a third of voters blamed Wall Street for the country's economic woes and 57 percent of them voted Republican.[62]

Why didn't the economic crisis have bigger effects on trust? For generalized trust, the answer may be twofold. First, generalized trust

---

[62] See www.cnn.com/ELECTION/2010/results/polls/#val=USH00p3 and www.cnn.com/ELECTION/2010/results/polls/#val=USH00p2, accessed July 12, 2011.

is learned early in life and is largely resistant to adult experience. Second, trust in people is not based upon short-term economic trends and it may be too early (or we may not have the right questions) to determine whether the long recession has led to pessimism for the long term. In 2010 slightly more people thought that life for the next generation would be worse than now (39 percent) than who thought it would be better (32 percent, see note 15). Americans may be less optimistic than in the past, but the economic crisis has not led to a collapse in confidence.

The economic crisis had a greater impact on trust in government, but even here the impacts were limited. The Tea Party movement may have been started as a protest against Wall Street, but the movement quickly transformed itself into a more general movement against big government and Obama's health care bill in particular. Votes for the President's economic stimulus and for TARP did come back to hurt Democratic members of Congress, but health care seemed more important.[63] The Tea Party emerged as the ideological forefront of the Republican Party, not as a protest movement against bigness per se. Moreover, the public has long been skeptical of big business. In 1973, the first time the General Social Survey asked the question, just 31 percent of respondents said that they had confidence in business. This figure bounced up and down until 2001, when it began a steady decline. It reached a low of 13 percent in 2010, but was only 16 percent in 2008 (before the crisis hit).

There is some evidence that the crisis did lead to less trust in government. In recent years, Americans have not expressed much confidence in their leaders even when times have been better. Our polarized political system has taken a toll on how we view our political leaders. Trust has become an uncommon commodity. You can't destroy what isn't there. Once the protest movement that stemmed from the crisis became so highly partisan, Tea Party supporters could not bring themselves to believe that the system was fundamentally

---

[63] Brady *et al.*, 2011; Jacobson, 2011, 48–49.

broken. If this were so, they would have no rationale for their campaigns. For once, it wasn't (in the words of Bill Clinton's political strategist James Carville in 1992) "the economy, stupid."

REFERENCES

Anderson, C. J., Blais, A., Bowler, S., Donovan, T., and Listhaug, O. (2005), *Losers' Consent: Elections and Democratic Legitimacy*. New York: Oxford University Press.

Bailey, M. A., Mummolo, J., and Noel, H. (2011), 'The Tea Party and congressional representation: tracking the influence of activists, groups, and elites,' unpublished paper, Georgetown University Department of Government, accessed July 8, 2011. www9.georgetown.edu/faculty/baileyma/Papers.htm,.

Banfield, Edward. 1958. *The Moral Bases of a Backward Society*. Glencoe, IL: Free Press.

Barry, Dan. 2009. "Broken trust shakes web from farmer to cow," *New York Times* (March 23), A9, A13.

Bedard, Paul. 2010. 'Washington whispers: Rick Santelli gets credit for Tea Party movement,' *US News and World Report* (January 25), www.usnews.com/news/blogs/washington-whispers/2010/01/25/rick-santelli-gets-credit-for-tea-party-movement (accessed July 7, 2011).

Berkowitz, Peter. 2010. "Why liberals don't get the Tea Party movement," *Wall Street Journal* (October 16), http://online.wsj.com/article/SB10001424052748704631504575531913602803980.html (accessed July 11, 2011).

Brady, D. W., Morris, P. F., and Wilkins, A. S. (2011), "The 2010 elections: why did political science forecasts go awry?," *PS: Political Science and Politics*, 44, 247–250.

Citrin, J. (1974). "Comment: the political relevance of trust in government," *American Political Science Review*, 68, 973–988.

Economist (2009). "Coming down to earth" (March 28), 28–30.

Guiso, L. (2010), 'A trust-driven financial crisis, implications for the future of financial markets.' EUI Working Paper ECO 2010/07, European University Institute, http://ideas.repec.org/p/eie/wpaper/1006.html (accessed July 8, 2011).

Hardin, R. (2002), *Trust and Trustworthiness*. New York: Russell Sage Foundation.

Hetherington, M. J. (1998), 'The political relevance of political trust.' *American Political Science Review*, 92, 791–808.

Hetherington, M. J. (2004), *Why Trust Matters: Declining Political Trust and the Demise of American Liberalism*. Princeton, NJ: Princeton University Press.

Jacobson, G. C. (2011), 'The Republican resurgence in 2010.' *Political Science Quarterly*, 126:27–52.

Jiobu, R. M. and Curry, T. J. (2002), 'Lack of confidence in the federal government and the ownership of firearms.' *Social Science Quarterly*, 82, 77–88.

Karpowitz, C. F., Quin Monson, J., Patterson, K. D., and Pope, J. C. (2011), 'Tea time in America? The impact of the Tea Party movement on the 2010 midterm elections.' *PS: Political Science and Politics*, 44, 303–309.

Keeter, S., Horowitz, J., and Tyson, A. (2008), *Young Voters in the 2008 Election*. Pew Research Center Publications, http://pewresearch.org/pubs/1031/young-voters-in-the-2008-election (accessed July 12, 2011).

Kinder, D. R. and Roderick Kiewiet, D. (1979), 'Economic discontent and political behavior: the role of personal grievances and collective economic judgments in congressional voting.' *American Journal of Political Science*, 23 (August), 495–527.

Lane, R. E. (1959), *Political Life*. New York: Free Press.

Lexington (2009), 'Anger Management.' *Economist* (March 7): 42.

Lightman, D. and Douglas, W. (2010), 'Republican plan: no compromise with the Democrats,' www.mcclatchydc.com/2010/11/04/103223/gop-agenda-make-the-democrats.html (accessed July 7, 2011).

Lipset, S. M. and Schneider, W. (1983), *The Confidence Gap: Business, Labor, and Government in the Public Mind*. New York: Free Press.

Masket, S. E. and Greene, S. (2011), 'When one vote matters: the electoral impact of roll call votes in the 2010 congressional elections.' Presented at the Annual Meeting of the Midwest Political Science Association, Chicago, April.

Moss, D. (2010), 'Comments on bank failure/regulation/inequality chart,' www.tobinproject.org/conference_economic/papers/BankFailures_Chartwith Comments_Moss.pdf (accessed July 10, 2011).

Pew Center for the People and the Press (2010), *The People and Their Government: Distrust, Discontent, Anger, and Partisan Rancor*. Washington, April 18, http://people-press.org/2010/04/18/distrust-discontent-anger-and-partisan-rancor (accessed July 7, 2011).

Putnam, R. (2000), *Bowling Alone*. New York: Simon & Schuster.

Rosenstone, S. J. and Hansen, J. M. (1992), *Mobilization, Participation, and Democracy in America*. New York: Macmillan.

Shear, M. D. and Kane, P. (2009), 'Anger over firm depletes Obama's political capital,' *Washington Post* (March 17), A1, A5.

Story, L. (2010), "Income Inequality and Financial Crises," *New York Times* (August 21), 2011 www.nytimes.com/2010/08/22/weekinreview/22story.html? pagewanted=print (accessed July 10).

Uslaner, E. M. (2000), 'Is the Senate more civil than the House?' In Burdett Loomis (ed.), *Esteemed Colleagues: Civility and Deliberation in the Senate* Washington, DC: Brookings Institution.

Uslaner, E. M. (2002), *The Moral Foundations of Trust.* New York: Cambridge University Press.

Uslaner, E. M. (2011), 'Trust and the economic crisis of 2008.' *Corporate Reputation Review*, 13, 110–123.

Uslaner, E. M. In press (a) 'The generalized trust questions in the 2006 Anes Pilot Study.' In John Aldrich and Kathleen McGraw (eds.), *Improving Public Opinion Surveys: Interdisciplinary Innovation and the American National Election Studies.* Princeton, NJ: Princeton University Press.

Uslaner, E. M. In press (b) "Measuring interpersonal trust: in defense of the standard question." In Fergus Lyon, Guido Möllering, Mark Sanders, and Tally Hatzakis (eds.), *Handbook of Research Methods on Trust.* London: Edward Elgar.

Whoriskey, P. (2011), "Income gap widens as executives prosper," *Washington Post* (June 19), A1, A16–A17.

Williams, P. (2010), "State attorneys general sue over health bill," www.msnbc.msn.com/id/36001783/ns/politics-health_care_reform/t/state-attorneys-general-sue-over-health-bill (accessed July 11, 2011).

3 Too big to trust? Managing stakeholder trust in business in the post-bail-out economy

Deepak Malhotra

EXECUTIVE SUMMARY

THE SITUATION

This chapter considers the aftermath of the financial crisis of 2008, and specifically the subsequent "bail-out" of the large financial institutions by the American government, from the perspective of trust in the post-bail-out economy. The author considers the impacts of both the compartmentalization of action within companies, and the increased complexity of interaction within business, on stakeholder trust in organizations.

KEY QUESTIONS

To what extent does compartmentalization of action within companies inhibit trustworthy behavior on the part of organizations? To what extent does the complexity of interactions in business inhibit the ability of stakeholders to make accurate judgments of organizational trustworthiness? What is distrust in business and how is the *nature* of distrust evolving? Is stakeholder trust today more difficult to build and sustain than in response to previous crises?

NEW KNOWLEDGE

Some of the operating assumptions made in most models of stakeholder trust may no longer hold. For example:

- Relevant organizational actors, and associated behaviors, are no longer easily identified by the stakeholder.

- The relevant trust dimension implicated in an organization's behavior is no longer easy to identify.
- Who an organizational decision will impact is no longer well understood.
- The link between organizational action and organizational impact is no longer straightforward.

Here is a more disconcerting thought: *what if stakeholder trust was not misplaced?* What if, for the most part, the bailed-out companies *did* earn the trust of their various stakeholders through actions that were demanded by their respective stakeholders? A consideration of this question leads to two sets of insights: the bigger the business and the more complex the economy in which it operates: (a) the more distant the organizational actors are likely to be from the stakeholders that their actions impact; and (b) the less aware they are likely to be of the sheer number and types of stakeholders they impact.

The bigger the business and the greater the degree of interaction with different elements of the broader economy, the more difficult it is: (a) to predict the effects of any one organizational actor; and (b) for firms to internalize the externalities their behaviors create.

INTRODUCTION

In early February, an article entitled "Distrust of Corporate Management" appeared in the *New York Times*. The opening paragraph read as follows:

> One of the most formidable obstacles to a revival of financial
> and business confidence is the almost universal distrust of the
> management of great companies and of a certain class of financial
> institutions. The distrust is the more serious because it is
> reasonable. A senseless panic will wear itself out. Sweeping
> accusations based on exceptional wrong seldom do much mischief.
> But when, as in this case, the doubts that prevail are the result of
> an experience too recent to be explained away, and too widely

> injurious to be attributed to accidental causes, their frank
> recognition is the first step toward improvement.

Predictably, the article went on to discuss problems of insufficient transparency, the complex task of assessing true firm worth in an environment where stock prices are behaving erratically and seemingly at the whim of short-term investors, the loss of faith in the character of managers and executives, and the drying up of much-needed liquidity in the market. The article appeared on February 2. The year was 1877.

It was a different crisis, with a different cast of characters. The article bemoaned the behavior of railroad executives and the conspicuous profits of the coal industry. Similar articles would be written 132 years later that bemoaned the behavior of auto executives and the conspicuous profits of the oil industry. The *NYT* article extended its attack to include financial institutions. The financial institutions to be derogated in similar articles 132 years later would be larger, more complex, and more varied in strategy and structure. The cast of characters differs today, but the story seems strangely similar. But it is not entirely.

As I discuss in detail below, the 2007–2009 financial crisis – and in particular, the corporate behaviors and government actions involving firms that were considered "too big to fail" (TBTF) – have brought to light a fundamental problem with the co-evolution of big business and the complex global economy. In addition to enormity of scale – which is the definitional hallmark of firms that are TBTF – business activity within organizations and industries is now increasingly compartmentalized into silos of atomistic activity that interact in complex ways to produce stakeholder outcomes. The core argument of this chapter is that this compartmentalization of action and complexity of interaction has two crucial effects regarding stakeholder trust. First, it increases the social distance between organizational actors and stakeholders, making it easy for organizational actors to ignore the externalities and broader consequences of their activities. Second, it complicates the stakeholder's task of evaluating organizational trustworthiness. The first consequence inhibits trustworthy behavior on the part of organizations. The second consequence inhibits accurate judgments of organizational trustworthiness on the part of stakeholders. Each of these is problematic, but their coincidence can produce especially dangerous outcomes – for example, a reduction in organizational trustworthiness with no accompanying reduction (and possibly an increase) in stakeholder trust.

The chapter is organized as follows. I begin by providing some evidence for the decline in trust following the recent financial crisis. I then define stakeholder trust and elaborate some of the assumptions underlying traditional models of stakeholder trust. Next, I illustrate why the problem of managing stakeholder trust is not only different, but also more difficult following TBTF, and explain why the assumptions that underlie traditional models of stakeholder trust may be inappropriate in the post-TBTF economy. I then propose a re-characterization of the nature of organizational action that may be more suited to studying stakeholder trust in the current context, and elaborate on two specific trust problems that have emerged in this context – the problem of sustaining organizational trustworthiness and the problem of accurately judging trustworthiness. I conclude with a set of implications for research on organizational trust, trust development, and trust repair, and for restoring and managing trust in business in the current context.

TBTF AND DISTRUST IN BUSINESS

The recent financial crisis has led to a number of commentaries regarding the need to reconsider regulatory reform and enforcement, the problems associated with asymmetric monetary policy, and the kinds of incentive problems that can surface within firms and in regulatory frameworks.[1] Perhaps the most viscerally charged

---

[1] Acharya and Sundaram, 2009; Cooley and Philippon, 2009; Richardson and White, 2009; Saunders *et al.*, 2009; Rajan, 2010.

commentary and debates, however, have surrounded the realization that firms can destroy incredible amounts of value, elicit the wrath not only of the masses but also of the market, and still emerge intact (due to government-led bail-outs) – despite the harsh judgment that market forces were prepared to unleash on them. Accordingly, at some point in the middle of 2008, a somewhat irksome phrase crept into the American lexicon: "too big to fail."

Too big to fail refers to businesses that are perceived (or argued) to be so large and/or interconnected with myriad components of the economy that allowing them to fail would cause widespread economic damage – well beyond what would be suffered by the firm's own shareholders and employees.[2] The idea of TBTF has been around for decades – as have been the government bail-outs that TBTF demands (e.g., Chrysler in the 1980s). What changed in 2008 was not only the unprecedented extent to which TBTF became a global concern for policy makers, but also the extent to which it became a topic of debate among the public at large. The TBTF argument, while seemingly odious to politicians and the public alike, was nonetheless effective: not every firm that could claim TBTF standing was offered a government bail-out (e.g., Lehman Brothers), but many were – including many of the largest players in the financial industry, as well as the entire US auto industry.[3] Much has been written since on the appropriate use of bail-outs and on the need to carefully balance systemic risk and moral hazard.[4] The purpose of this chapter is different: to consider the aftermath of TBTF from the perspective of trust.

Admittedly, trust is not easily measured or benchmarked, and it is notoriously difficult to rigorously support any claims regarding the erosion of trust. Nonetheless, if one *were* to seek out a canary in the coalmine – a gauge by which to measure how bad things had

---

[2] Stern and Feldman, 2004.
[3] Johnson and Kwak, 2010. For a complete list of who received bail-out funds, and how much has been paid back, see: http://projects.propublica.org/bailout/list.
[4] See, e.g., Acharya and Richardson, 2009.

gotten following TBTF – it might look something like the following. In February 2009, a CNN/Opinion Research Corp. survey asked Americans who they trusted to make the right decisions with regard to fixing the economy.[5] Fifty-three percent had confidence in Congressional Republicans, 66 percent had confidence in Congressional Democrats, and 75 percent had confidence in President Obama. In contrast to the level of trust in politicians, only 28 percent had confidence in bankers and executives of financial firms.

A more rigorous analysis of the decline in trust in business is offered by the annual Edelman Trust Barometer,[6] a yearly international survey of trust among the "informed public."[7] According to their results, "with only 38 percent of informed publics in the United States trusting business today, levels are the lowest they have been in the Barometer's tracking history – even lower than in the wake of Enron and the dot-com bust." Figure 3.1, based on data from the 2009 Edelman Trust Barometer report (and including trust data dating back to 2001), provides a graphic display of the severity of the trust problem in the US following TBTF.

In all likelihood, this precipitous drop in trust was multiply determined, with the effects of TBTF, news of Wall Street bonuses, the stock market crash, and other such events each contributing to the trust crisis. Additional evidence suggests that the key players in TBTF – i.e., big businesses, business executives, and bankers – may have been pivotal in undermining trust. Gallup Poll data from 1998 to 2009 documents the level of public confidence in "Big Business" and "Small Businesses" across the years.[8] While confidence in Small

[5] Steinhauser, 2009.   [6] Edelman, 2009a.
[7] According to the Edelman Trust Barometer website (www.edelman.com/trust/2009/), "a 30-minute telephone survey was conducted among 4,475 people in 20 countries ... between November 5 and December 14, 2008 ... The informed publics interviewed in the 2009 survey: are college-educated; report a household income in the top quartile of their country (per age group); report significant media consumption and engagement in business news and public policy."
[8] See www.gallup.com/poll/1597/Confidence-Institutions.aspx. Data on confidence in Small Businesses was not collected by Gallup from 1999–2006.

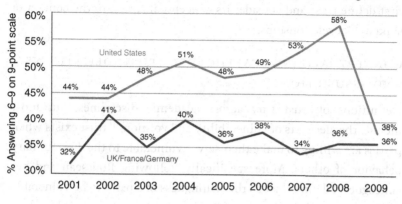

FIGURE 3.1 Trust in business (2001–2009)
Source: Edelman Trust Barometer (2009)

Business is consistently higher than trust in Big Business, the gap widens considerably in early 2009 – i.e., post-TBTF. Notably, confidence in both Small and Big Business had increased in the year leading up to TBTF; the following year, confidence in Small Business increased while trust in Big Business dropped. Gallup Poll data also shows that between late 2007 to late 2008 – i.e., before and after TBTF – trust in business executives declined and trust in bankers plummeted. This was not due to a more general trust decline: trust in lawyers, advertising professionals, and car salespeople was increasing during this time period. Notably, of the twelve professions for which Gallup collected data in 2007 and 2008, only three showed *any* amount of decline in trust.[9]

While such data focuses on the *degree* of distrust, and suggests that the recent decline in stakeholder trust is noteworthy in its severity, it does not address the possibility of the changing *nature* of distrust – and to the ways in which stakeholder trust today may be more difficult to build and sustain than in previous crises. Before we

---

[9] See www.gallup.com/poll/1654/Honesty-Ethics-Professions.aspx.

turn to a discussion of the changing nature of trust problems, let us first define trust and consider its conceptualization in the context of stakeholder relationships.

CONCEPTUALIZING STAKEHOLDER TRUST: DEFINITIONS AND ASSUMPTIONS

Definitions of trust vary across academic disciplines, but most include the elements of vulnerability and volition;[10] trust exists when parties are willing to make themselves vulnerable to the discretionary behavior of others. More specifically, following Rousseau and her colleagues, I define trust as the willingness of a party to be vulnerable to the actions of another party (individual or organization) based on positive expectations regarding the other party's motivation and/or behavior.[11] The focus of this chapter is on stakeholder trust in business,[12] which implicates the individual-to-organizational level of analysis.[13] Accordingly, I define stakeholder trust in business as *the willingness on the part of individual stakeholders (e.g., customers, employees, investors, community members, etc.) to accept vulnerability to the actions of the organization.*[14] Importantly, in conceptualizing stakeholder trust in business, I presume that stakeholder expectations regarding a firm's likely behavior will stem, at least in part, from expectations regarding the likely behavior of relevant organizational actors.[15]

Trust, defined as the psychological willingness to accept vulnerability, can be meaningfully distinguished from the underlying *dimensions* of trustworthiness (e.g., integrity and competence). Attributions of the other party's trustworthiness along these

---

[10] Rousseau *et al.*, 1998.   [11] Ferrell, 2004; Mayer *et al.*, 1995.
[12] Freeman, 1984.   [13] See Zaheer *et al.*, 1998.   [14] See Freeman, 1984.
[15] See, e.g., Currall and Judge 1995; Inkpen and Currall 1998. While the survey data discussed earlier looks at trust in business among the population at large, in the absence of data on specific stakeholder groups (e.g., investors, customers, etc.), I use the available data as a proxy for stakeholder trust. In so doing, I am assuming, at least for the purposes of motivating discussion, that trust in business likely declined across most or all stakeholders in the wake of the financial crisis.

dimensions motivate a willingness to accept vulnerability among trusters.[16] In their seminal paper on organizational trust, Mayer *et al.* identify three primary dimensions of trustworthiness: *ability, benevolence,* and *integrity*.[17] Here I will occasionally make use of a more concise framework that differentiates simply between competence-based trust (comprising attributions of managerial and technical competence) and character-based trust (comprising attributions of integrity and benevolence).[18] This shorthand also maps onto characterizations of the crisis by media commentators, policy makers, and the lay public: they typically refer to "greed" and "incompetence" as the core problems underlying trust in business, implicating, respectively, the character and competence dimensions of trustworthiness.

Notably, while trust attributions are not always easy for a firm's stakeholders to make with great accuracy, most models of stakeholder trust consider the attribution process to be relatively "simple." This presumed simplicity stems from a set of assumptions that are (at least implicitly) made in most models of stakeholder trust.[19] These assumptions are as follows:

1. *The relevant organizational actors and behaviors are easily identified by the stakeholder.* For example, the investor knows to look to the behavior of executives when evaluating managerial competence, suppliers know to look at the expertise of engineers when evaluating technical competence, and employees know to look to the behavior of their managers when evaluating benevolence.

2. *The trust dimension implicated in an organization's behavior is easily identified.* For example, defects in the product are likely to implicate insufficient technical competence, a decision not to recall products with known defects is likely to implicate a lack of

---

[16] Kim *et al.* 2006; Weber *et al.* 2005. [17] Mayer *et al.* 1995.
[18] See: Nooteboom, 1996; Das and Teng, 1998.
[19] See, e.g., Sheppard and Sherman, 1998; Zaheer *et al.*, 1998

integrity, and mistreatment of subordinates is likely to implicate the benevolence dimension of trust.

3. *Who an organizational decision will impact is relatively well understood.* It is largely known, for example, who a layoff, a decision to forego a recall, or a decision to meet the bare minimum environmental standards will impact.

4. *The link between organizational action and organizational impact is relatively straightforward.* For example, the effect of retaining employees even during an economic downturn will save jobs and sacrifice potential profit; competing on price will increase sales but may diminish profits industry wide; introducing a new, patented technology will increase market share, but may spur competition.

These assumptions are seemingly ubiquitous in research on stakeholder trust in organizations.[20] In some cases, the assumptions are even quite explicit. Jones, for example, describes the nature of stakeholder trust in business as follows:

> First, assume that the behavior of corporations with respect to moral issues ("corporate morality"), like individual morality, is detectable ... Some of the firm's policies and decisions will be readily apparent to the stakeholders affected by them. For example, if a firm decides to lay off 10 percent of its salaried workforce in order to boost profits, the decision and its implications will be well known to salaried employees. If a company establishes a strict policy of "no returns" on merchandise, the policy will soon become known to dealers and certain customers. These decisions are "visible" to the affected stakeholders, and the company's reputation among its employees and customers, respectively, will be affected accordingly. Further, decisions and policies of this type are likely to influence the judgments of stakeholders other than

[20] See, e.g., Simons, 2002; Becerra and Gupta, 2003; Dyer and Chu, 2003; Huff and Kelley, 2003; Hodson, 2004; Schoorman *et al.*, 2007; Castaldo *et al.*, 2009; Pirson and Malhotra, 2010.

those immediately affected. That is, the effect of these decisions and policies on the firm's reputation is likely to transcend the relationship between the firm and the immediately affected stakeholder group. For example, if the firm reneges on its pension obligations to company retirees, it will probably have difficulty maintaining the trust of its current (or potential) employees ... If a single firm made all three of the decisions used as examples above, its reputation would reflect, in some measure, opportunistic policies toward employees, customers, and pensioners. Thus, the firm's reputation, and that of its top managers, will be partly a direct function of its policies and decisions.[21]

Together, the four basic assumptions underlying research on stakeholder trust suggest that trust-relevant organizational action is enacted in ways that makes it easy for stakeholders to evaluate the trustworthiness of the firm, and for firms to manage stakeholder trust by taking appropriate, targeted actions. While there have always been contexts in which these assumptions were somewhat flawed, none of the assumptions have traditionally been considered too daring. However, all of these assumptions are suspect in the post-TBTF economy.

THE NATURE OF DISTRUST FOLLOWING TBTF: AN ILLUSTRATION

To illustrate the emerging problems of evaluating and managing stakeholder trust, consider the position of a stakeholder who wishes to evaluate the character and competence of *Companies A, B, C,* or *D.* Their (simplified) story goes as follows:

> *Company A* is a large mortgage lender. It employs hundreds of brokers tasked with originating loans in a regulatory environment where proof of income and independent appraisals of home value are not deemed necessary for the issuance of "Alt-A" loans. The mortgage broker, like thousands of others like him throughout

[21] Jones, 1995, 418.

the economy, evaluates the buyer's application on stated values, and goes out of his way to help the customer purchase his dream home. The high-interest mortgage is approved and quickly resold in the secondary market, and then packaged along with many other such mortgages to create mortgage-backed securities.

Company B is an investment bank, and purchases such mortgage-backed securities, combines them, and creates tranches of the asset to be sold off as bonds. Another recombination of assets ensues, and is followed by yet another effort to create different tranches of bonds.

A group of traders at *Company C*, a large broker-dealer, buys these bonds; their colleagues down the hall purchase other investment vehicles that, in fact, are similarly structured collateralized debt obligations (CDOs). Because of the pace of business and the presumed stability of a market for CDOs, no one in Company C knows exactly what percentage of the assets underlying the securities are subprime or other high-risk mortgages. In any case, all of the bonds are highly rated by the appropriate rating agencies. Still, as a means of diversifying risk, Company C trades actively with its peer firms and even purchases insurance against the possibility that its bond issuers end up defaulting.

To do so, Company C invests in credit default swaps (CDSs) issued by the large and well-reputed insurance firm, *Company D*. Meanwhile, traders in Company D's small Innovative Products division are happily issuing hundreds of billions in CDSs – without having to post any collateral for such contracts – to any firm that is willing to trade away its exposure to defaults, especially in AAA-rated tranches of debt.

Companies A, B, C, and D are all doing extremely well – they are well trusted by their various stakeholders. Each has profits that are much higher than peer firms, each is considered extremely well managed, and two of them (Companies C and D) are considered technical innovators in the field of finance; all around, investors are jubilant. Employees at all of these companies are treated well and paid handsomely (especially in Companies B and D). Customers are also happy: homeowners are ecstatic with the level of concern showed by mortgage brokers at Company A; the banks, hedge funds, and other companies purchasing mortgage-backed securities from Company B are extremely happy with the returns these are generating; Company C's customers – e.g., those who have their savings invested in money-market accounts – are thankful not only for the great customer service, but also for the high, above-market yields being offered; and seemingly everyone on Wall Street is happy with Company D for helping them wash away their exposure to risk. Public perception of Companies A, B, C, and D could not be better: Company A is a large and growing employer in many big cities; Company B sets the standard for professionalism among investment banks and has underwritten some of the biggest deals of the last fifty years; Company C has recently completed an extremely successful marketing campaign in which it highlighted its focus on the needs of the individual customer and on the well-being of society; Company D is a household name with an impeccable reputation for meeting its insurance obligations.

Then trouble begins. As the housing market begins to unravel, many of the mortgages that Company A is holding are deemed to be worth very little. Company A begins to post losses as a large percentage of homebuyers are unable to meet their payment obligations. The stock price of Company A plummets further when it is unable to sell any of the mortgages it now holds. Very quickly, financing for Company A dries up entirely. Company B finds that its bonds are worth very little, but it is unclear exactly how little. When Company B is forced to mark down the value of some of these assets, its stock price starts to plummet. Because Company B depends in large part on short-term financing, its ability to rollover its debt and continue operations is severely curtailed. Company C is holding the largest percentage of the toxic assets.

At least some of the firms Company C trades with are holding similar assets – but no one knows who exactly is at risk of going under, so trading between these firms freezes up. As a swath of CDS counterparties reach out to Company D for collection, Company D finds that it is unable to meet this demand. Its credit rating is downgraded and a key clause of the CDS contracts kicks in – Company D is now forced to put up collateral. Of course, Company D is too highly leveraged at this point and, worse, also relies upon short-term financing to fund its operations. With the credit freeze now spreading, Company D does not have the money to put up the collateral. Company D starts selling off parts of its business, but at fire-sale prices that do not raise enough capital. Company D goes to the government for a bail-out. The government has to step in, lest a large part of the economy which has purchased insurance through Company D for asset-backed securities of almost every kind suddenly finds itself completely exposed in an unraveling market. Meanwhile, Company C and its peers are shocked to see that their CDSs provide no real insurance, and that their myriad of complex contracts makes it unclear which peer firm owes which other firm how much. It almost does not matter, as no one is ready to make any payments until the smoke clears. To make matters worse, banks have also stopped lending to Companies A, B, C, and D, partly because they have their own toxic assets and partly because they have no idea which company is going to survive the growing crisis. Six months later, the CDOs are still perceived as worthless, Company D has been bailed out, Company C is being transformed into a bank holding company so that its customers' investments can be eligible for government insurance, Company B is lobbying for government loans, and Company A has gone bankrupt. No one trusts anybody.

Every one of these companies was highly trusted all the way until cataclysmic events unfolded. So what went wrong? *Was the problem caused by misplaced stakeholder trust?* And, if so, which errors of trust attribution prevailed? Were investors overestimating the competence of key decision makers of firms that were consistently growing revenues and posting huge profits in highly competitive markets? Should employees have mistrusted the benevolence of employers who treated them well and rewarded their hard work with high levels of compensation? Should customers have distrusted the integrity of those that were giving them better returns than competitors? Should the public have questioned the values of organizations that were breaking no laws, paying taxes, employing tens of thousands of Americans, giving to charity, and serving the needs of many millions of depositors, investors, homeowners, and corporations – all the while attempting to meet their fiduciary duties to investors?

Here is a more disconcerting thought: *What if stakeholder trust was not misplaced?* What if, for the most part, each of these four companies *did* earn the trust of their various stakeholders through actions that were demanded by their respective stakeholders? Consider the actions of Company C, whose investment in CDOs may be heralded as evidence of untrustworthy behavior: Company C only invested in AAA-rated securities, it relied upon a network of trading partners to diversify risk, and it even sought to insure against the risk of default among bond issuers by purchasing CDSs – all the while treating its employees, customers, and investors extremely well. Or, consider the actions of Company A, whose approval of high-risk loans may be presented as evidence of untrustworthy corporate actions: Company A encouraged brokers to put the needs of customers first; it followed the law and trusted customers when asking them to self-report their ability to pay; it even charged appropriately high interest rates to reflect the high-risk nature of the loan – all the while being entirely transparent regarding the risk characteristics of these loans to those that purchased and repackaged them. Did these companies really deserve to be mistrusted *ex ante?* If so, on what basis should stakeholders have mistrusted them?

In short, it *may* be possible to construct a defense of the trustworthiness of Companies A, B, C, and D that is not entirely specious.[22] And yet, we must face the reality that stakeholder trust in companies such as these has clearly declined following the corporate and governmental actions surrounding TBTF. If we are to reconcile these two factors, perhaps the best question to ask is this: *how should we revise our models of stakeholder trust to reflect the new face of stakeholder vulnerability to organizational actors?* We should begin with the assumptions.

FLAWED ASSUMPTIONS

Having considered the case of Companies A, B, C, and D, let us revisit the assumptions underlying traditional models of stakeholder trust. The shortcomings of each now appear glaring.

Flawed assumption 1: relevant organizational actors and behaviors are easily identified by the stakeholder

In fact, it is very difficult to know which organizational actor's motivations or behavior will affect a particular stakeholder's interests. For example, *whose* competence should Company C's investors be expected to judge? Should they evaluate the competence of traders who purchased the CDOs recommended by rating agencies? Or should they judge the competence of rating agencies themselves? Should they judge the competence of those that purchased the CDSs based on a presumption that Company D had not over-committed itself in the issuance of this type of contract? Or should they be expected to judge the competence of that small group of financial innovators in Company D that might have taken on too much exposure by issuing these CDSs? Or should investors evaluate the competence of those, higher up in Company C, who are still unable to say exactly how much exposure the firm has to the housing market because they have no way to know exactly how many more

---

[22] This is not to say that unethical, malevolent, or incompetent behavior was entirely absent in the tale of Companies A, B, C and D. Rather, the important point here is that *even if* everyone in Companies A–D was ethical, well intentioned, and competent, it may not have averted the financial – and trust – crisis.

homeowners will default – nor which of their trading partners is holding toxic debt?

Flawed assumption 2: the trust dimension implicated in an organization's behavior is easily identified

Why did Company C invest so heavily in CDOs, a decision that ultimately forced it to seek government assistance? Does this reflect technical incompetence, as evidenced by the fact that traders did not fully understand the risks they were taking on? Or does this reflect a lack of integrity and greed because the pursuit of high-risk assets was motivated by a desire to offer higher returns to money-market customers? Or, was this a failure of management, which failed to reconcile conflicts between competitive positioning and risk? Similarly, why did Company A approve so many subprime and Alt-A mortgages? Does this represent greed or incompetence? Or might it have been an issue of malevolence, as evidenced by a lack of concern among some brokers for customers they knew could never afford the high-interest mortgages their adjustable rates would soon be creating.

Flawed assumption 3: who an organizational decision will impact is relatively well understood

If there is one concept above all that stakeholders have been forced to grapple with in the post-TBTF economy, it is "externalities." Organizational actions can have unintended and even unanticipated consequences for various parties that are not involved in the exchange. When Company C invests in high-risk CDOs to boost its money-market yields, it inspires competitors to do the same. As demand builds, it encourages Company A to originate more high-risk mortgages, Company B to package more high-risk CDOs, and Company D to issue additional CDSs aimed at insuring this growing market. Ironically, the actions of Company A begin to fuel the housing bubble at the exact same time as the actions of Company D are making it difficult for it to meet its CDS obligations in the event that the housing market is experiencing a bubble. The rest is history.

*Flawed assumption 4: the link between organizational action
and organizational impact is straightforward*

When Company A decided to vigorously pursue the issuance of Alt-A
mortgages, it was probably motivated by the direct impact this would
have on shareholder value. It is extremely unlikely that any organizational actor realized that its actions would contribute to a potentially
global financial crisis. In fact, the actions of Company A alone were
far from sufficient causes of the subprime mortgage crisis – it
required the existence of hundreds of other entities pushing high-
risk mortgages at the same time, a lax regulatory environment, eager
buyers of mortgage-backed securities, and eager insurers for those
holding these securities. Likewise, when traders at Company
B decided that bundling and selling tranches of mortgage-backed
securities would be a good way to make money and meet demand
among customers for highly rated bonds, they probably did not antici-
pate that months later, business activity between Company C and its
peers would come to a halt because the assets were considered toxic
and no one knew – or had to reveal – how exposed they were. And
who caused Company D to fail? Was it the actions of those in the
Innovative Products division who created too many CDSs? Or was it
the actions of Company A and its peers who flooded the market with
too many high-risk mortgages, which not only facilitated the housing
market collapse, but simultaneously led to a freezing of the credit
markets upon which Company D relied for short-term financing to
cover its CDSs?

If we are to do justice to the increasingly complex task of
gauging trust post-TBTF, we will have to shed flawed assumptions
regarding the nature of organizational action. Moreover, if we are to
recommend a way forward, whereby researchers can more accurately
conceptualize – and stakeholders can more accurately gauge – the
trustworthiness of business, we will have to replace these assumptions with a re-characterization of organizational action in the context
of stakeholder trust.

RE-CHARACTERIZING ORGANIZATIONAL BEHAVIOR: SCALE AND SILOS

When politicians, regulators, and economists talk about the problems associated with firms that are deemed too big to fail, they are almost exclusively referring to the problem of *scale*.[23] The problem of scale can manifest in two distinct but related ways. First, when scale increases, so can the number of economic entities that directly rely upon the existence of the firm. For example, as General Motors grew in size, so did the number of dealers, suppliers, and employees that relied upon its continued success. Second, when scale increases, so might the level of systemic risk imposed upon the economy. For example, in the financial industry (think AIG and its clients), as financial instruments became increasingly complex, securitization proliferated, and as leverage reached new heights, the assumption that a failure of firm X would be uncorrelated with a failure of firm Y became increasingly tenuous.[24] Either effect of scale can trigger the political and economic motivation to bail out a firm that is TBTF; when both aspects co-occur, the argument for government intervention becomes especially strong.

Problems of scale fuel debates regarding whether to bail out a particular TBTF firm, and more complex analyses among politicians, regulators, and economists regarding which regulatory reforms (if any) are likely to prevent future financial crises. In addition to scale, however, TBTF exposes a structural aspect of big business that has received far less attention, but which has significant implications for the current *trust crisis*. This is the problem of silos.

Literally, the term "silo" refers to a storage unit, e.g., an underground bunker used for storing and shielding missiles. In the current context, I use the term silos to refer to the increasingly *compartmentalized* and *shielded* nature of activity in organizations, and the increasingly *complex* nature of interorganizational activity and impact. It is useful to elaborate on each of these aspects of silo structure:

---

[23] Bernanke, 2009; Lo, 2009.   [24] Rajan, 2010.

Compartmentalized: The tasks for which organizational actors are employed and evaluated are becoming increasingly narrow *relative to the scope of their overall impact.*

Shielded: Organizational actors are increasingly shielded from both the intended and the unintended ultimate consequences of their actions.

Complex: The number and types of interactions between the firm and its environment have grown tremendously. Organizational actors interact *and co-act* with counterparties in a wide variety of other organizations in myriad components of the economy. As a result, the prospect of "emergent phenomenon" that is not simply an aggregate of volitional individual acts increases.[25]

Charles Perrow touched on some of these issues in what may be considered examinations of earlier generations of siloed organizations. Although his emphasis was on the impact of hierarchy and bureaucracy *within* organizations, his analyses are more generally applicable to complexity in *interorganizational* systems. In describing "the unexpected interactions that can occur in reasonably complex systems," Perrow observed:

> While most accidents in risky systems stemmed from a major failure that could have been prevented, a substantial minority resulted from the unexpected interaction of two or more small failures ... The resulting accidents were "system accidents," arising from the ability of the system to permit the unexpected interactions of failures. They were, in a sense, "normal accidents" because it is normal (though rare) for such interactions to occur.[26]

In the current context, characterizing the nature of activity within and between organizations as compartmentalized, shielded, and

---

[25] Holland, 1995; Stacey, 1995.   [26] Perrow, 1986, 147.

complex yields a set of propositions regarding trust-relevant organizational action:

> **Proposition 1**: The bigger the business and the more complex the economy in which it operates, the smaller will be the ratio, for organizational actors, of job description to stakeholder impact.
>
> **Proposition 2**: The bigger the business and the more complex the economy in which it operates: (a) the more distant the organizational actors are likely to be from the stakeholders that their actions impact; and (b) the less aware they are likely to be of the sheer number and types of stakeholders they impact.
>
> **Proposition 3**: The bigger the business and the greater the degree of interaction with different elements of the broader economy, the more difficult it is: (a) to predict the effects of any one organizational actor; and (b) for firms to internalize the externalities their behaviors create.

Arguably, none of the characteristics of silo structure described above is inherently perverse. Compartmentalization is seemingly a natural consequence of the division of labor and the pursuit of efficiency. Likewise, it would be natural for organizational actors in large organizations to be shielded from the ultimate impact of their actions, and for economic phenomena to diverge from what an aggregation of *individual* interests and decisions might predict. As we have seen, however, these aspects of silo structure, albeit natural, also have consequences for the prospects of building or restoring stakeholder trust. As I elaborate in the following section, they also have implications for the study of stakeholder trust.

IMPLICATIONS FOR RESEARCH ON STAKEHOLDER TRUST

The siloed nature of organizational action not only makes it difficult to evaluate organizational trustworthiness, it also puts into question the nature of organizational trust itself. From the firm's perspective, silos – and in particular, the emergent nature of organizational impact – make it difficult for organizations to behave in a trustworthy manner and/or to signal trustworthiness. This complicates the agenda of researchers interested in trust development from the perspective of managerial or organizational action.[27]

Here I consider some of the specific conceptual challenges – and research opportunities – that emerge in the context of silos. What follows is not meant to be an exhaustive delineation. Rather, it is an attempt to draw attention to some of the problems that need further study.

Revising our conceptualization of competence-based trust

As the recent financial crisis has shown, the competence demanded of organizational actors is often narrowly defined, even though these actors make decisions that rely on a large number of (often hidden) assumptions regarding myriad interactive components of their organization, and of the economy.[28] Related to this, the competence of organizational actors is often narrowly evaluated by stakeholders, even though their decisions have significant externalities (i.e., spillovers) elsewhere in the organization and in the economy.[29] The gap between *evaluated* competence and *requisite* competence is wide and, in all likelihood, growing. How the gap can be bridged is a question that requires additional research. How might firms reconcile the difference between "job description" and "job impact" of organizational actors? If this requires the internalization of externalities, how might that be accomplished? How might performance measures be improved to align requisite and demanded competence? How might stakeholders improve their evaluation of organizations and organizational actors? Might this require a much broader approach to transparency, one that reveals not only an organization's direct

---

[27] See, e.g., Whitener *et al.*, 1998; Simons, 2002; Ferrin and Dirks, 2003; Hodson, 2004; Scott and Walsham, 2005; Gillespie and Dietz, 2009.
[28] Perrow, 1986.   [29] See Ethiraj and Levinthal, 2009.

impact, but also how the firm impacts stakeholders when co-acting with other organizations?

Revising our conceptualization of character-based trust

As suggested by our discussion of decision making by organizational actors in Companies A–D, the compartmentalized and shielded nature of organizational activity promotes abstract analysis and does not lend itself to promoting a "moral" frame for decision-making.[30] This exposes what has come to be understood as the inherent distinction between what may be considered to be the "trait" ethicality of an individual (something that we do not expect to vary across contexts), and the ethicality of that individual's behavior *in situ* (as influenced by the decision frame, or situation). As Bazerman and colleagues have argued in their work on "bounded ethicality," many (and perhaps most) of the unethical behaviors that occur in organizations may result from ordinary and predictable psychological processes, such as the narrowing of decision makers' focus on short-term economic consequences, rather than on social or long-term consequences.[31] This raises fundamental questions regarding how ethicality is to be assessed, and how ethical behavior may best be promoted. For example, it may be more effective for organizations to create the types of organizational structures that promote ethical considerations than to screen for ethical individuals at the time of recruitment. More fundamentally, what types of organizational structures are more/less likely to promote ethical considerations and trustworthy behavior? A second set of issues surrounds the need to understand the impact of social distance on trustworthy behavior. In the early 1960s, psychologist Stanley Milgram conducted a number of now classic experiments on obedience to authority, in which individual subjects (called "teachers") were asked by the experimenter to administer electric

---

[30] Brewer and Kramer, 1986; Pinkley, 1990; Tenbrunsel and Messick, 1999.
[31] Murnighan *et al.*, 2001; Bazerman and Banaji, 2004; Chugh *et al.*, 2005; Bazerman and Greene, 2009.

shocks of increasing voltage to a "learner" in the other room.[32] These studies not only revealed the appalling degree to which individuals might be induced to inflict pain on others, but also that the willingness to inflict pain (under orders) increased as a function of the distance between the "teacher" and the "learner." In contrast, when the distance diminished, and the teacher could see and touch the learner, behavior became much more humane. Relatedly, silos increase the social distance between organizational actors and stakeholders, thereby reducing concern for individuals impacted by organizational actions.[33] How can large organizations overcome this tendency while reducing social distance? If it is possible to do so, how costly would such changes be and are they worth it on balance?

The need to understand trust attribution processes in complex environments

It is difficult for stakeholders to evaluate character or competence on the basis of actions that do not have a clean causal link to outcomes. This is the case when actions are not *pivotal* in producing a consequence, as when the decisions of multiple actors combine to produce an adverse effect. How do stakeholders make trust judgments when organizational action is situated in, and operates through, a complex environment in which the decisions of multiple disparate entities combine to create impact? Moreover, how might we improve the accuracy of such judgments? There is also a need to understand trust attributions in contexts involving rare events. Starbuck identifies many reasons (including cognitive limitations, biases, and the paucity of data) why it is difficult to learn, generally, from rare events, all of which seem relevant to learning about trustworthiness in particular.[34] It is easy for stakeholders to evaluate character or competence on the basis of decisions that produce outcomes with regularity (e.g., turnover, revenues, market share, employee satisfaction) but difficult to evaluate competence based on decisions that produce catastrophic

[32] Milgram, 1974. [33] Charness and Gneezy, 2008. [34] Starbuck, 2009.

events with low probability (e.g., over-leveraging, or exposing the firm to systemic risk). How should stakeholders evaluate trustworthiness in light of this problem? From the firm perspective, how might trustworthiness judgments be made robust to negative, low-probability events?

The need to work toward a systems-level theory of organizational trust

The preceding discussion raises another basic and important question: is it even reasonable for stakeholders to judge the trustworthiness of an organization that operates in sufficiently complex environments? If the behavior of organizational actors must combine, often in non-linear ways, with the behavior of myriad other entities in the economy before stakeholder impact can be assessed, how useful or appropriate is it to make trust judgments at the level of the organization? Might it be more appropriate to evaluate trustworthiness at the level of an industry, institution, or system? For example, it is worth studying the conditions under which trust judgments regarding one's doctor or hospital become overshadowed by trust judgments regarding the "health care system." A second issue emerges within organizations. Because expertise is often focused on narrow domains, whereas managerial problems are almost boundless in scope, it is difficult to know where competence *should* lie – i.e., which individual or group should be responsible for the collection and analysis of information that pertains to externalities, emergent phenomenon, and systemic risks. Should it be those who have strong-but-narrow technical expertise, or those with lesser technical ability but a better view of the system?

It is worth noting that some of these problems are, in fact, "new." Consider, for example, the most recent crisis of trust prior to 2008: the Enron crisis. There is some evidence to suggest that trust in "Big Business" declined more severely after Enron than it has during the current financial crisis.[35] Yet, despite the gravity of the trust

---

[35] See www.gallup.com/poll/1597/Confidence-Institutions.aspx.

problem then, and the sizable list of companies implicated in corporate scandals at the time (e.g., Enron, Arthur Andersen, Tyco, WorldCom), the *nature* of the trust problem was much simpler then. The problem was largely perceived to be a lack of integrity, the people to blame were either top executives or those with a conflict of interest (e.g., auditors), and the solution was regulation aimed at greater transparency and a reduction in conflicts of interest. In comparison, the current crisis is a quagmire: was it incompetence or greed or neither? Who is to blame, or was it an emergent problem? Is there a solution?

The way forward in the current crisis, almost inevitably, will involve both regulatory reform as well as initiatives by firms that are motivated to win back valuable stakeholder trust. With an appreciation for the complexities discussed here, let us consider how this might happen.

IMPLICATIONS FOR MANAGEMENT OF STAKEHOLDER TRUST

The story of Companies A, B, C, and D is about thousands or millions of individual actors, all working in silos, making decisions that are devoid of an understanding of impact, and lacking in appreciation for the ethical dimension of their decisions. How might such behaviors be curtailed? Also, how might stakeholders judge whether such behaviors have been curtailed? And, finally, how might firms that are interested in building stakeholder trust signal that they deserve to be trusted?

As a means of organizing the discussion, consider the following proposals for managing stakeholder trust. These extend from the conceptual analysis contained in this chapter, rather than any elaborate empirical research on trust in complex systems (which is largely lacking). Moving ahead with any of the proposals would require much more rigorous analysis of costs and (potentially unintended) consequences than can be addressed in this chapter.[36] In their current

---

[36] See Greenwood, 2007.

form these proposals are simply designed to motivate discussion and to inspire consideration of innovative ways in which firms and their stakeholders can collaborate on the important task of restoring trust in business. Notably, the presumption is not that firms would be motivated to pursue such actions simply because they wish to restore "trust in business" generally; rather, it is presumed that there are firms that will realize that they stand to gain by increasing their stakeholders' trust in them.

1. *Stakeholder impact analysis:* An important initiative for businesses motivated to win back trust may take the form of educating all organizational actors on the breadth of impact that their actions (individually and in aggregate) have on stakeholders. This might take the form of a "Stakeholder Impact Report" (SIR) that all organizational actors must take part in creating. The SIR would consider not just the direct effects of actions on all stakeholder groups, but also the effects that the organization and its employees have when acting in concert with other economic entities. The report would document not only the potential impact on stakeholders, but also assess the conditions that would increase or decrease the likelihood of such impact.

2. *Managing stakeholder impact:* To the extent possible, and pursuant to the development of the SIR, appropriate teams or divisions would be delegated the task of – and provided *incentives* for – mitigating risks that are exposed by the SIRs. For example, a group of Company C traders who have created an SIR might discover that the same unlikely events which increase the likelihood of a bond issuer defaulting on their CDOs would also increase the likelihood that Company D would be unable to insure the CDOs! At this point, they might: (a) do an internal study of the extent to which high-risk mortgages were underlying their CDOs; (b) approach Company D to learn more about its exposure and ability to post collateral in the event of a credit crunch and a rating downgrade; (c) decide whether to diversify risk further by

purchasing CDSs from a Company D competitor that does not rely so heavily on short-term financing; and (d) decide whether decreasing exposure to CDOs altogether is a good idea.

3. *Appointment of a chief risk officer (CRO):* Lo suggests that there is a strong need for an executive-level position to evaluate and mitigate the firm's contribution to and exposure to systemic risk. Lo describes the would-be CRO as someone who "reports directly to the board of directors and whose compensation is tied to the stability of the company and not to last year's profits."[37] CROs should also be responsible for overseeing the myriad SIRs of the firm, as well as for a firm-level evaluation of "risks to stakeholders" that goes beyond the fiduciary responsibility of assessing risks to investors.

4. *Report out to a stakeholder panel:* In addition to reporting to the board of directors, the CRO would ideally provide an annual report – in writing and in person – to a panel of stakeholders representing (among others) customers, employees, members of the local community, regulators, and competitors.[38] The objective of the report would be to provide stakeholders a realistic analysis of the ways in which the organization and its activities impact the interests of various stakeholders, to discuss industry and economic trends of potential consequence, and to create a dialogue aimed at better understanding and targeting stakeholders' vulnerabilities.

5. *Interorganizational panel on stakeholder impact:* For many of the problems that can surface in the post-TBTF environment, no single organization is pivotal. Such problems need coordinated action from firms that are currently co-acting blindly. Stakeholder impact may also be most accurately evaluated and targeted via inter-firm coordination. As an example: Company C did not create the high levels of demand for subprime mortgage-backed securities by

---

[37] Lo, 2009.

[38] Competitors are included in this list because, as the example of Companies A–D reveals, competitive pressures are what often drive decision making that, when aggregated across firms, leads to mutually destructive outcomes.

acting alone; competitors were pursuing these same assets. In
fact, even if Company C had seen the writing on the walls, it would
have had a hard time leaving this market lest it yield many
millions in profit to its competitors. And even then, the financial
crisis may have eventually crippled Company C. The most
effective way for Company C to help *prevent* the crisis would
have been to act in concert with its competitors. While talk of
coordination inevitably raises antitrust concerns, there are many
avenues for competitors to legally pursue joint action aimed at
forestalling crises. As an example, Company C and its competitors
could agree to greater transparency regarding who holds which
types of assets, and a coalition of Companies such as C and D could
work together to create an exchange for high-stakes CDSs that
would replace the current system of structuring idiosyncratic
over-the-counter contracts.

6. *Governmental report on stakeholder impact:* In an environment
where it is notoriously difficult to force firms to internalize the
externalities they impose on the economy and on non-investor
stakeholders, there is clearly a place for regulatory action. Others
have discussed in some detail the need for a regulatory board that
evaluates systemic risks in the economy. For example, Lo suggests
the creation of a "Capital Markets Safety Board" that would be
modeled after the National Transportation Safety Board and would
be responsible for investigating financial crises, for "managing data
related to systemic risk, and creating high-level risk analytics such
as a network map of the financial system, estimates of illiquidity
exposure, leverage, and asset flows," and for serving as a central
command of sorts for coordination and communication during an
economic crisis.[39] A similar agency, board, or commission – more
likely modeled after the Government Accountability Office or the
Congressional Budget Office – could serve the purpose of reporting
on stakeholder vulnerabilities to the actions of individual firms

---

[39] Lo, 2009.

as well as groups of economic entities. A "Stakeholder Impact and Vulnerability Board" (SIVB) would be expected to issue reports on the business, economic, and political activities of large and/or heavily interconnected firms, with an emphasis on the effects of individual and aggregate actions, and complex interactions, on various stakeholders. The reports would be made public so that consumers, employees, local communities, etc. could make informed decisions regarding whether to trust and interact with firms that impose large negative externalities on others, and/or how to manage the risks that are unavoidable.

CONCLUDING REMARKS

The global financial crisis of 2007–2009 has led to a variety of realizations among academicians, business executives, policy makers, and alleged media "watchdogs." These realizations pertain to the need for regulatory reform and enforcement; the high degree of interconnectedness, complexity, and vulnerability of the global economy; the problems associated with asymmetric monetary policy; the dangers associated with flawed financial modeling; and the kinds of incentive problems that can surface within firms and within regulatory frameworks. These and other problems have led many die-hard *laissez-fairians* to decry the failings of unregulated capitalism and the need for a better understanding of how atomistic individual and firm decisions aggregate into global economic trends. Most notable in this regard has been Alan Greenspan's admission that "those of us who have looked to the self-interest of lending institutions to protect shareholders' equity are in a state of shocked disbelief." As it turns out, also in shocked disbelief are millions of stakeholders who never realized that the safeguarding of their interests depended upon organizational actors whom they could not observe or evaluate, and at whose discretion they had never knowingly accepted vulnerability. This is the new face of distrust.

The corporate behaviors and governmental actions surrounding TBTF did not cause the crisis of trust, but they revealed what may be wrong with old assumptions regarding the basis of stakeholder trust. Firms that, *ex ante*, showed no signs that they deserved to be mistrusted by *any* stakeholders were suddenly declared to be completely untrustworthy, lacking in character as well as competence. The current examination of the aggregation of organizational behaviors into stakeholder impact – as in the analysis of Companies A–D – reveals some of the flaws with traditional approaches to understanding stakeholder trust. Exposing these flaws and re-characterizing the nature of organizational behavior as it pertains to trust judgments can help lay the groundwork for more exciting and promising research on stakeholder trust, and for the possibility of developing more effective tools for the management of stakeholder trust in the post-bail-out economy.

REFERENCES

Acharya, V. V. and Sundaram, R. K. (2009), 'Governance, incentives, and fair value accounting overview.' In V. V. Acharya and M. Richardson (eds.), *Restoring Financial Stability: How to Repair a Failed System*. Hoboken, NJ: Wiley.

Bazerman, M. H. and Banaji, M. R. (2004), 'The social psychology of ordinary unethical behavior.' *Social Justice Research*, 17(2), 111–115

Bazerman, M. H. and Greene, J. D. (2009), 'In favor of clear thinking: incorporating moral rules into a wise cost–benefit analysis.' *Perspectives on Psychological Science*, 5, 209.

Becerra, M. and Gupta, A. K. (2003), 'Perceived trustworthiness within the organization: the moderating impact of communication frequency on trustor and trustee effects.' *Organization Science*, 14(1) 32–44.

Bercovitz, J., Jap, S. D., and Nickerson, J. A. (2006), 'The antecedents and performance implications of cooperative exchange norms.' *Organization Science*, 17(6), 724–740.

Bernanke, B. S. (2009), 'Financial reform to address systemic risk.' Address to the Council on Foreign Relations, Washington DC, March 20.

Brewer M. B. and Kramer, R. M. (1986), 'Choice behavior in social dilemmas: effects of social identity, group size, and decision framing.' *Journal of Personality and Social Psychology*, 50, 543–549.

Castaldo, S., Perrini, F., Misani, N., and Tencati, A. (2009), 'The missing link between corporate and social responsibility and consumer trust: the case of fair trade products.' *Journal of Business Ethics*, 84(1), 1–15.

Charness, G. and Gneezy, U. (2008), 'What's in a name: anonymity and social distance in dictator and ultimatum games.' *Journal of Economic Behavior and Organization*, 68(1), 29–35.

Chugh, D., Banaji, M., and Bazerman, M. (2005), 'Bounded ethicality as a psychological barrier to recognizing conflicts of interest.' In D. Moore, D. Cain, G. Loewenstein, and M. Bazerman (eds.), *Conflicts of Interest: Challenges and Solutions in Business, Law, Medicine, and Public Policy*. New York: Cambridge University Press.

Cooley, T. F. and Philippon, T. (2009), 'The role of the Federal Reserve.' In V. V. Acharya and M. Richardson (eds.), *Restoring Financial Stability: How to Repair a Failed System*. Hoboken, NJ: Wiley.

Currall, S. C. and Judge, T. A. (1995), 'Measuring trust between organizational boundary role persons.' *Organizational Behavior and Human Decision Processes*, 64(2), 151–170.

Das, T. K. and Teng, B. S. (1998), 'Between trust and control: developing confidence in partner cooperation in alliances.' *Academy of Management Review*, 23, 491–512.

Dyer, J. H. and Chu, W. J. (2003), 'The role of trustworthiness in reducing transaction costs and improving performance: empirical evidence from the United States, Japan, and Korea.' *Organization Science*, 14(1), 57–68.

Edelman and Associates (2009a), Edelman Trust Barometer (available at: www.edelman.com/trust/2009).

Edelman and Associates (2009b), Special Midyear Trust Survey (available at: www.edelman.com/trust/midyear).

Ethiraj, S. K. and Levinthal, D. 2009. 'Hoping for A to Z while rewarding only A: complex organizations and multiple goals.' *Organization Science*, 20 (1), 4–21.

Ferrell, O. C. (2004), 'Business ethics and customer stakeholders.' *Academy of Management Executive*, 18(2), 126–129.

Ferrin, D. L. and Dirks, K. T. (2003), 'The use of rewards to increase and decrease trust: Mediating processes and differential effects.' *Organization Science*, 14(1), 18–31.

Freeman, R. E. (1984), *Strategic Management: A Stakeholder Approach*. Boston, MA: Pitman.

Friedman, M. (1970), 'The social responsibility of business is to increase its profits.' *New York Times*, September 13.

Gillespie, N. and Dietz, G. (2009), 'Trust repair after an organization-level failure.' *Academy of Management Review*, 34(1), 127–145.

Greenwood, M. (2007), 'Stakeholder engagement: beyond the myth of corporate responsibility.' *Journal of Business Ethics*, 74(4), 315–327.

Hodson, R. (2004), 'Organizational trustworthiness: findings from the population of organizational ethnographies.' *Organization Science*, 15(4), 432–445.

Holland, J. H. (1995), *Hidden Order*. Reading, MA: Perseus Books.

Huff, L. and Kelley, L. (2003), 'Levels of organizational trust in individualist versus collectivist societies: a seven-nation study.' *Organization Science* 14(1) 81–90.

Inkpen, A. and Currall, S. C. (1998), 'The nature, antecedents, and consequences of joint venture trust.' *Journal of International Management*, 1, 1–20.

Johnson, S. and Kwak, J. (2010), *13 Bankers: The Wall Street Takeover and the Next Financial Meltdown*. New York: Pantheon Books.

Jones, T. M. (1995), 'Instrumental stakeholder theory: a synthesis of ethics and economics.' *Academy of Management Review*, 20(2), 404–437.

Kim, P., Dirks, K. T., Cooper, C. D., and Ferrin, D. L. (2006), 'When more blame is better than less: the implications of internal vs. external attributions for the repair of trust after a competence- vs. integrity-based trust violation.' *Organizational Behavior and Human Decision Processes*, 99, 49–65.

Lewicki, R. J. and Bunker, B. B. (1996), 'Developing and maintaining trust in work relationships.' In R. M. Kramer and T. R. Tyler (eds.), *Trust in Organizations: Frontiers of Theory and Research*. Thousand Oaks, CA: Sage, 114–139.

Lo, A. W. (2009), 'Regulatory reform in the wake of the financial crisis of 2007–2008.' *Journal of Financial Economic Policy*, 1(1), 4–43.

Mayer, R. C., Davis, J. H., and Schoorman, F. D. (1995), 'An integrative model of organizational trust.' *Academy of Management Review*, 20(3), 709–734.

Milgram, S. (1974), *Obedience to Authority: An Experimental View*. New York: Harper & Row.

Murnighan, J. K., Cantelon, D. A., and Elyashiv, T. (2001), 'Bounded personal ethics and the tap dance of real estate agency.' In J. A. Wagner III, J. M. Bartunek, and K. D. Elsbach (eds.), *Advances in Qualitative Organizational Research*, 3: 1–40. New York: Elsevier/JAI.

Noteboom, B. (1996), 'Trust, opportunism, and governance: a process and control model.' *Organizational Studies*, 17(6), 985–1010.

Perrow, C. (1986), *Complex organizations: A critical essay* (3rd Edition). Newbery Award Records, Inc.: New York, NY.

Pinkley R. L. (1990), 'Dimensions of conflict frame: disputant interpretations of conflict.' *Journal of Applied Psychology*, 75(2), 117–126.

Pirson, M. and Malhorta, D. K. (2010), 'Antecedents of stakeholder trust: what matters to whom.' Fordham University School of Business Research Paper No. 2010–016.

Rajan, R. (2010), *Fault Lines: How Hidden Fractures Still Threaten the World Economy*. Princeton, NJ: Princeton University Press.

Richardson, M. and White, L. J. (2009), 'Rating agencies: is regulation the answer?' In V. V. Acharya and M. Richardson (eds.), *Restoring Financial Stability: How to Repair a Failed System.* Hoboken, NJ: Wiley.

Rousseau, D. M., Sitkin, S. B., Burt, R. S., and Camerer, C. (1998), 'Not so different after all: a cross-discipline view of trust.' *Academy of Management Review,* 23(3), 393–405.

Saunders, A., Smith, R. C., and Walter, I. (2009), 'Enhanced regulation at large, complex financial institutions.' In V. V. Acharya and M. Richardson (eds.), *Restoring Financial Stability: How to Repair a Failed System.* Hoboken, NJ: Wiley.

Schoorman, F. D., Mayer, R. C., and Davis, J. H. (2007), 'An integrative model of organizational trust: past, present, and future.' *Academy of Management Review,* 32(2), 344–354.

Scott, S. V. and Walsham, G. (2005), 'Reconceptualizing and managing reputation risk in the knowledge economy: toward reputable action.' *Organization Science,* 16(3), 308–322.

Sheppard, B. H. and Sherman, D. A. (1998), 'The grammars of trust: a model and general implications.' *Academy of Management Review,* 23(3), 422–437.

Simons, T. (2002), 'Behavioral integrity: the perceived alignment between managers' words and deeds as a research focus.' *Organization Science,* 13(1), 18–35.

Stacey, R. D. (1995), 'The science of complexity: an alternative perspective for strategic change processes.' *Strategic Management Journal,* 16(6), 477–495.

Starbuck, W. H. (2009), 'Cognitive reactions to rare events: perceptions, uncertainty, and learning.' *Organization Science,* 20(5), 925–937.

Steinhauser, P. (2009), 'Poll: politicians trusted more than business leaders on economy.' Retrieved from CNN.com, February 24, 2009.

Stern, G. H. and Feldman, R. J. (2004), *Too Big to Fail: The Hazards of Bank Bailouts.* Harrisonburg, VA: R. R. Donnelley

Tenbrunsel, A. E. and Messick, D. M. (1999), 'Sanctioning systems, decision frames, and cooperation.' *Administrative Science Quarterly,* 44(4), 684–707.

Tomlinson, E. C. and Mayer, R. C. (2009), 'The role of causal attribution dimensions in trust repair.' *Academy of Management Review,* 34(1), 85–104.

Watts, D. (2009), 'Too big to fail? How about too big to exist?' *Harvard Business Review,* 87(6), 16.

Weber, J. M., Murnighan, J. K., and Malhotra, D. (2005), 'Normal acts of irrational trust: motivated attributions and the trust development process.' *Research in Organizational Behavior,* 26, 75–101.

Whitener, E. M., Brodt, S. E., Korsgaard, M. A., and Werner, J. M. (1998), 'Managers as initiators of trust: an exchange relationship framework for understanding managerial trustworthy behavior.' *Academy of Management Review*, 23(3), 513–531.

Williams, M. 2001. 'In whom we trust: group membership as an affective context for trust development.' *Academy of Management Journal*, 28(3), 377–396.

Wilson, J. 2007. 'Shielding money clashes with elders' free will.' *New York Times*, December 24.

Zaheer, A., McEvily, B., and Perrone, V. (1998), 'Does trust matter? Exploring the effects of interorganizational and interpersonal trust on performance.' *Organization Science*, 9(2), 141–159.

4   At the crossroads of trust and distrust: skepticism and ambivalence toward business

Robert Bies

EXECUTIVE SUMMARY

THE SITUATION

Current analyses of public trust in business do not capture the new relationships and realities facing business in the twenty-first century.

KEY QUESTIONS

What do high levels of distrust in business really mean? Is there a "new normal" with respect to trust and distrust in business? Should business leaders and policy makers be concerned about levels of trust in business? Are business accountability strategies and analytic tools effective for building public trust in business?

NEW KNOWLEDGE

Trust and distrust are not ends of the same continuum; rather, trust and distrust are two distinct phenomena, and both can exist simultaneously with respect to the public's attitudes toward business. The simultaneous coexistence of trust and distrust creates the condition of *ambivalence* toward business. Trust tends to be a fairly stable phenomenon, but distrust also appears to be a resilient phenomenon, defining a new business landscape in which it does not fade away but is always present, if not always salient.

Accordingly, there is a mismatch between corporate views of accountability and those held by the public. While some compliance-focused accountability strategies employed by organizations are important management tools, they fall short of the public's central concerns about how individuals are treated by businesses. The public wants responsiveness in the form of engagement and fair treatment from business, not just accountability strategies grounded in analytic tools and the reporting of statistics.

KEY LESSONS

Both trust and distrust are relatively stable and resilient, and, as such, our theoretical frameworks and practical recommendations with respect to trust must reflect this new social reality.

Studies suggest that business must address public anger, not just public distrust. Public anger about the economic crisis of 2008 is grounded in a moral judgment that something *wrong* has occurred and that it must be addressed.

The failure to establish a human connection signals to people that a company does not respect them or care about them. Legalistic remedies fail to address value congruence and human engagement which are critical for building public trust. In an environment where trust is scarce, trust emerges as a new organizational imperative that deserves the attention of leaders in the public and private sectors.

INTRODUCTION

As we enter the second decade of the twenty-first century, the introductory sentences from *A Tale of Two Cities* by Charles Dickens come to mind: "It was the best of times, it was the worst of times, it was the age of wisdom, it was the age of foolishness, it was the epoch of belief, it was the epoch of incredulity, it was the season of Light, it was the season of Darkness, it was the spring of hope, it was the winter of despair."[1] Those words are as relevant today as they were when they were written over 150 years ago.

We began the new millennium filled with great possibilities only to be met with 9/11. The first decade began with great prosperity driven by globalization only to end with global recession and growing

---

[1] Dickens, 1859/1997.

distrust of business and its leaders. The decade that began with optimism and hope had given way to pessimism and despair. And this shift
in mindset and mood parallels the erosion of trust and the emergence
of distrust of business that we are witnessing around the world today.

In this chapter, I will argue that current analyses of public trust
in business do not capture the new relationships and realities facing
business in the twenty-first century. More specifically, trust and
distrust are not ends of the same continuum; rather, trust and distrust
are two distinct phenomena, and both can exist simultaneously with
respect to the public's attitudes toward business.[2] The simultaneous
coexistence of trust and distrust creates the condition of *ambivalence*
toward business. I will review data from surveys of public trust in
business that support this line of reasoning.

I will further argue that this ambivalence is a rational response
on the part of the public in its dealings with business. As part of this
argument, I will emphasize the importance and functionality of distrust
in the public's attitudes toward business, a view that is gaining increasing support from scholars.[3] While distrust creates challenges to organizations and its leaders in restoring trust,[4] the focus on simultaneous
trust and distrust identifies new directions for theory and research on
public trust in business. Drawing on complementary conceptual frameworks advanced by Lewicki *et al.*[5] and Sitkin and Roth,[6] I will also
suggest new approaches to be taken by business to rebuild the public's
trust in business while managing the public's distrust of business.

The next section begins a discussion of the public's distrust of
business. As current events demonstrate, and a look back at history
underscores, the public's distrust of business has always been present,
while not always figural it has always been in the background.
As such, researchers and leaders must embrace the reality that trust
and distrust are both resilient phenomena, and our conceptual
frameworks and recommendations must reflect this new social reality.

[2] Lewicki *et al.*, 1998.   [3] See, e.g., Hardin, 2004; Sievers, 2003.
[4] Kramer and Pittinsky, 2012.   [5] Lewicki *et al.*, 1998.   [6] Sitkin and Roth, 1993.

THE PUBLIC'S DISTRUST OF BUSINESS

Current events and a historical perspective

> Those who cannot remember the past are condemned to repeat it.
>
> *George Santayana*

Current events and history provide consistent evidence of the public's distrust of business. The current event is the Occupy Wall Street movement. But this social movement is not a new phenomenon; for, across the decades there have been cries of outrage and distrust of business, often resulting in actions taken against business to correct their mistakes. A review of history suggests there has been a recurring cycle of public trust and distrust of business, and this "track record" of bad actions by business is persuasive evidence for skepticism toward business to be a rational response on the part of the public.

The Occupy Wall Street movement: "mad as hell" at "greed is good"

The movement known as Occupy Wall Street (Occupy) began on September 17, 2011 in Liberty Square in Manhattan's Financial District. Organizing around the theme that "We Are the 99 percent that will no longer tolerate the greed and corruption of the 1 percent," it has spread to over 100 cities in the United States. And this movement has become a global phenomenon, with actions in over 1,000 cities beyond the United States. It is a movement that cuts across race, gender, and political persuasion. While people debate the political impact and influence of the Occupy movement, there is little doubt that this movement has become the human face, its vocal and visible expression, of the distrust and anger that people have about business.

The Occupy movement recalls the most memorable scene in one of the greatest morality tales ever shown on the silver screen, *Wall Street*. That scene was the (in)famous "greed is good" speech given by Gordon Gekko to the shareholders of Teldar Paper:

> Greed is right. Greed works. Greed clarifies, cuts through, and captures the essence of the evolutionary spirit. Greed, in all of its forms – greed for life, for money, for love, knowledge – has marked the upward surge of mankind. And greed – you mark my words – will not only save Teldar Paper, but that other malfunctioning corporation called the USA.

That speech could be viewed as the marching orders not just for Wall Street in the first decade of the twenty-first century, but also for so many other corporations here in the United States and around the world. And it is that "greed is good" philosophy that the Occupy movement is protesting.

This obsession with greed led some leaders down a road toward reckless choices, particularly in, but not limited to, the banking and financial sectors. Even as the year 2012 reaches its midpoint, there are still daily, if not hourly, reports of bad economic and financial news. The internet and online blogs report the news of failures and scandals drawn right out the Gordon Gekko playbook. These failed plays, implemented by leaders across all industry sectors and around the world, have created a harsh reality where the public is rightfully worried about their way of life and their children's futures. And even as we work our way out of these difficult times, business and its leaders are reckoning with the anger and distrust of the public at large.

And it is the anger that business must address, not just the distrust. For people are angry, *really* angry. Actually, people have been angry for some time, but the recent headlines have stoked this anger, not just here in the United States but also abroad. "Obscene" was the headline in the British newspaper, the *Daily Express*. The headline referred to the actions of Sir Fred Goodwin, former CEO of Royal Bank of Scotland (RBS). RBS lost $34.2 billion in 2008, and as Goodwin was being forced out, he negotiated a pension in the amount of $980,000 per year – for life! And to make matters worse, most of the pension is to be paid by British taxpayers. Hence, the *Daily Express* headline.

A decade before the movie *Wall Street*, the film *Network* gave rise to another memorable speech of the silver screen. At the end of his newscast, Howard Beale, who was fed up with the hypocrisy and greed of his time, uttered these words, which could be the rallying cry of those expressing anger at today's world: "I'm as mad as hell, and I'm not going to take this anymore!"

This is not just any anger – this is *righteous anger*.[7] Righteous anger is not just a swirling cauldron of emotions; righteous anger is grounded in a moral judgment that something *wrong* has occurred and it must be corrected and changed.[8] And that righteous anger is one of the key motivators of the Occupy movement.

This erosion of trust while distrust rises is not a new social phenomenon facing business. Indeed, it is a familiar refrain, a recurring theme, in the history of the United States and around the world.[9] To provide a historical context to understand the public trust in business in today's world, it is illustrative to review key events in the cycle of trust to distrust – and then back to trust – in business over the past 100 years. As is evident from this walk down memory lane, history may not repeat itself, but it surely does appear to rhyme.

TRUST IN BUSINESS

A historical perspective

As human beings, trust is our default position, particularly with respect to business.[10] Yet, across the past century, our trust in business has been severely tested, if not shattered, due to the scandals, financial crises, and abuses by business. But through decisive leadership by some industry titans and corporate leaders, and governmental intervention through regulation and the creation of safeguards to rebuild the confidence in business, one finds trust in business to be a resilient, if not robust, phenomenon. A few examples from the last 100 years will illustrate this phenomenon.[11]

---

[7] Bies and Tripp, 1996.   [8] Tripp and Bies, 2009.
[9] Kramer, 2009.   [10] *Ibid.*   [11] *Ibid.*

Let us begin this walk through history in 1907. The collapse of Knickerbocker Trust caused by stock market schemes created a financial panic. In an act of decisive leadership, J. P. Morgan "persuades" leading bankers to bail out weaker institutions, to restore stability and trust. This Panic of 1907 also motivated the United States Congress to create the Federal Reserve System, a strong central bank to help avert monetary shortages (a role it plays even today in the United States and globally due to the financial crises of 2008 and beyond).

While the United States stock market boomed in the Roaring Twenties, it crashed in October, 1929, leading to the Great Depression. To rebuild trust in business, the United States government created such regulatory bodies as the Federal Deposit Insurance Corporation (FDIC) and Securities and Exchange Commission (SEC), as watchdogs and safeguards for the American public. Rachel Carson's book, *Silent Spring* (1962), and Ralph Nader's book, *Unsafe at Any Speed* (1965), heightened awareness that business interests often clashed with those of citizens, helping to motivate and mobilize the United States Congress to pass environmental and safety legislation.

There have been several breakthroughs and innovations in trust building led by business. For example, in 1983, Jack Stack, CEO of Springfield Remanufacturing Corporation, began the *open-book management* movement by sharing all financial information with employees and teaching them the skills to understand and interpret the information. And, in 1997, eBay instituted its feedback stars system allowing for buyers to assess the (un)trustworthiness of sellers, a system that became a huge success for eBay.

However, for all of the attempts by business to build trust, events always seem to occur that take attention away from such initiatives. In 1984, one such event occurred on a global scale that reverberated for many years to follow. That event involved the Union Carbide chemical gas spill in Bhopal, India. The scale of this event and the tragic consequences associated with it created greater skepticism and distrust about how multinational corporations operate in developing countries.

But with the dawn of the new millennium, we witnessed events that contributed to a growing distrust of, and anger toward, business. Beginning with the dot.com bubble burst in 2000, and compounded by the collapse of Enron and WorldCom in 2001, financial ruin and fraud contributed to distrust in business, a phenomenon that permeates society today. This distrust reached a pinnacle in 2008 with the collapse of the real-estate bubble and reckless, if not illegal, financial machinations, plunging the United States into a severe recession that expanded globally. In 2009, the distrust created in 2008 widened and deepened with government bail-outs of corporations, some of which used the bail-out money to pay millions of dollars to their executives (e.g., AIG).

This recurring cycle of trust to distrust to trust in business provides an historical context to the current state of affairs facing business. It may provide some reassurance to business in that trust appears to be a resilient phenomenon.[12] But it also provides a reference point to highlight differences in how today's state of affairs facing business may be different than in the past. For it appears that distrust is also a resilient phenomenon, defining a new business landscape in which it does not fade away but is always present, if not salient. Indeed, one could argue that skepticism, if not distrust, toward business may be a rational response on the part of the public. The next section reviews empirical evidence gathered from surveys of the public that support this line of reasoning.

SURVEYS OF PUBLIC TRUST IN BUSINESS

A review of empirical evidence

In this section, I draw on the four most recent Edelman Trust Barometer surveys (2009, 2010, 2011, and 2012), which yield new insights into what is influencing and shaping people's trust in – and distrust of – business. In addition, I review a study by Public Agenda

---

[12] *Ibid.*

and the Kettering Foundation from 2011 that examined how the public views initiatives by business to rebuild trust through different accountability strategies. The study reveals the unintended and negative views of these corporate strategies in the eyes of the public.

The Edelman Trust Barometer: a global survey of the public

The Edelman Trust Barometer is an annual trust and credibility survey that samples thousands of informed publics in two age groups (25–34 and 35–64). According to Edelman, informed publics meet the following criteria: "college-educated; household income in the top quartile for their age in their country; read or watch business/news media at least several times a week; follow public policy issues in the news at least several times a week."[13] The Edelman Trust Barometer is a global survey that examines public trust in business and the factors that shape the public's viewpoint.

Beginning with the 2009 Edelman Trust Barometer, which is based on survey data gathered in the last quarter of 2008, just as the severe recession is taking hold in the United States. Not surprisingly, 62 percent of the global survey said they trust business less than they did a year prior, and 77 percent of the United States sample of informed publics said they trusted business less than they did a year prior. In the United States, when asked how much they trust business to do what is right, there was a 20-point drop in people's trust from 2008 to 2009, dropping from 58 percent to 38 percent. This trust level was lower than the post-Enron level.

Trust in nearly every industry sector dropped, although there were differences between sectors. The Technology and Biotech/Life Sciences sectors were the two most trusted sectors while insurance, media companies, and banks were the lowest trusted sectors. Globally, the credibility of all information sources declined strongly in most markets among 35- to 64-year-old respondents, with the biggest erosion in TV and radio channels.

[13] Edelman, 2010.

As public trust in business fell, calls for action rose from the public. This lack of trust was associated with calls for more government regulation and control. Among the global sample of 25- to 64-year-old informed publics, there was a 3 to 1 margin in favor of government intervening to regulate and exercise greater control over business.

And the survey evidence suggested that trust may impact the public's assessment of overall corporate reputations. In the global sample, the survey results identified the five most important factors shaping evaluations of overall corporate reputation in order of importance were: "offering high quality products or services; a company treats its employees well; communicates frequently and honestly about the state of its business; a company I trust; and gives value for money."

In 2010, the Edelman Trust Barometer found a modest global rise in trust in business, even in the United States (60 percent to 71 percent). But that trust is fragile, as nearly 70 percent of informed publics expect business and financial companies to revert to "business as usual" after the recession. And in the United States and Europe, it was the banking industry that showed the biggest drop in trust, where less than 30 percent of the informed publics in those countries believed that business would do the right thing.

As was found in the 2009 survey, trust and transparency emerged as key factors influencing assessments of corporate reputation, even more important than financial performance. In the 2010 survey, the five most important factors shaping overall evaluations of corporate reputation in order of importance were: "transparent and honest practices; a company I trust; high quality products or services; a company treats its employees well; communicates frequently; and treats its employees well." In essence, trust emerges as a new line of business.

In 2011, the Edelman Trust Barometer found that trust increased in all institutions globally (54 percent to 56 percent), but in the United States there was a decline in the trust that business would do the right thing (54 percent to 46 percent). Again, globally, trust varied by sector: technology was the most trust sector while the bottom three sectors were insurance, banks, and financial services.

The 2011 Trust Barometer identified four key factors that mattered in evaluations of corporate reputations. In order of importance, these factors were "high quality products or services, transparent and honest business practices, a company I can trust, and treats employees well." Across three years of surveys, it was the same factors that influenced people's evaluations of overall corporate reputation. This suggests a new reality facing business and its leaders.

The 2011 survey also suggests that trust protects reputations. For example, when a company is trusted, 51 percent of the respondents will believe positive information about the company after hearing that news one to two times while only 25 percent will believe negative information about the company after hearing that news one to two times. However, when a company is distrusted, 57 percent of the respondents will believe negative information about the company after hearing that news one to two times while only 15 percent will believe positive information about the company after hearing that news one to two times.

In 2012, the Edelman Trust Barometer found that, in the majority of countries surveyed, trust in business held steady. As in the previous Edelman Trust Barometer surveys, trust in the technology industry was the highest while the banking and financial services industries remain the least trusted.

Taken together, Edelman's surveys of public trust in business revealed the same factors influencing the public's evaluations of overall corporate reputation. Further, trust factors emerged as key elements in those evaluations. That trust matters is not shocking news, but how it matters – and what new trust factors are emerging – suggests a new landscape for analyzing the public's trust in business.

As to what the new landscape looks like, Edelman argues that survey results suggest that there has been a transformation of trust frameworks.[14] The old trust framework was based on four factors: control information, focus solely on profit, protect the brand, and

---

[14] Edelman, 2011.

stand alone. The new trust framework is based on three factors: transparency (how), engagement (where), profit with purpose (what). The 2012 Edelman Trust Barometer survey results provide additional support for the new trust framework.

ASSESSING THE "ACCOUNTABILITY MOVEMENT"

The Public Agenda and Kettering Foundation study

Public Agenda and the Kettering Foundation conducted a study that examined how institutions demonstrate they are responsive and effective, as part of an "accountability movement" that has as one of its missions the building of public trust in business.[15] After looking at the findings from this study, which will be discussed below, Matthews posed this provocative and important question: "If this movement is demonstrating true accountability, why, then ... do institutions suffer from a huge loss of public confidence?"[16] Answers to that question are found in this chapter.

This study employed a qualitative research approach. One part of this study involved focus group discussions with members of the public. The other part of this study employed a key informant strategy, which involved individual interviews with experts and leaders who have studied accountability issues in different sectors.

Several key findings emerge from this study that inform and provide new insights for an analysis of public trust in business. First, from the focus group discussions with members of the public, a core accountability issue was a belief that too many Americans were exhibiting more selfish behavior rather than fulfilling their responsibilities to society or a greater good. For the public, accountability meant acting more honorably, focusing on personal responsibility for actions as a key criterion.

A lack of perceived fairness also emerged as a key concern for the public. For example, there was the perception that more than just a few people had circumvented the rules as a path to their prosperity

---

[15] Public Agenda and Kettering Foundation, 2011.   [16] Matthews, 2011, 3.

while most people were held accountable to those same rules and literally paid the price. This concern about fairness echoes the refrain of those in the Occupy movement.

Fairness emerged in another way for the public. From the focus group discussions, people made clear that they wanted to be able to reach someone who would actually listen to them and treat their ideas and questions respectfully. Establishing this "human connection" with a company was meaningful to the public, and an important dimension of accountability. The failure to establish this human connection signaled to people that a company did not respect them or did not care about them, which is a core aspect of interpersonal fairness.[17] Moreover, research on procedural justice underscores the importance of participation and voice in creating respect, which is at the foundation of trust in authorities and institutions.[18]

But the corporate vision of accountability was much different than the public's vision. Corporations implemented *accountability strategies* as a primary mechanism to build confidence and trust in business. Data collection, judging performance on quantitative measures, and assessing progress on benchmarks were the corporate response to accountability, a response which fell short of the public's most potent concerns.

What this research uncovered was that, while business and the public both agree that rebuilding public confidence is an important objective, they approach the issue from very different starting points. While the accountability strategies employed by business are important management tools, they fall short of the public's central concerns about how they are treated by business. This pattern of data creates what I call *the trust paradox*.[19]

The accountability movement has created a legalistic mindset in its leaders and managers.[20] Increasingly, managerial actions are becoming dominated by a concern for what is legally defensible

---

[17] Bies and Moag, 1986.   [18] Tyler and Lind, 1992.
[19] See Sitkin and Bies, 1993.   [20] See Jos and Tompkins, 2004.

at the expense of broader social considerations such as trust and fairness.[21] In the context of public trust in business, the trust paradox is revealed when corporations rely on accountability strategies to build trust they are actually *creating* distrust in business. For the accountability strategies actually do not respond to the trust concerns of the public, and, in fact, undermine it. For the public wants responsiveness in the form of engagement and fair treatment from business, not just accountability strategies grounded in analytic tools and the reporting of statistics, however meaningful they may be.

As Brian Cook describes this phenomenon:

> An increasingly vicious circle has emerged in which anxiety about control and accountability ... has led to more extensive, more complex controls, which in turn have increased the bureaucratic distance between administrators and the public they are expected to serve. This distance then raises new worries about control and accountability and brings about the introduction of another layer of controls.[22]

At a fundamental level, this research suggests that leaders and the public have different definitions of accountability, creating a gap between what business *thinks* that the public wants in terms of accountability and what the public actually *wants* from business in terms of accountability. The report refers to this difference in conceptual terms as the Corporate Model versus the Public Model. Table 4.1 highlights some of the key differences relevant to public trust in business.

The 2011 Public Agenda and the Kettering Foundation study drew two important conclusions that are relevant to public trust in business. First, business must "acknowledge and accept the legitimacy of the public's alternative framework."[23] Second, business must "depend less on data and standard communications strategies and more on dialogue."[24]

---

[21] Sitkin and Bies, 1994.   [22] Public Agenda and Kettering Foundation, 2011, 5.
[23] *Ibid.*, 13.   [24] *Ibid.*, 14.

Table 4.1 *The Corporate Model versus the Public Model*

The Corporate Model	The Public Model
Accountability as measurement	Accountability as responsibility
A reliance on technical solutions	A focus on moral problems
Quantitative measures	Qualitative measures
A focus on performance	A yearning for people to be responsible
Risks and rewards understood statistically	Risks and rewards understood personally
Interest of the institution	Interest of the public
A confidence in the benefits of transparency and disclosure	Confusion and lack of trust

Taken together, the Edelman Trust Barometer surveys and the Public Agenda and Kettering Foundation study reveal a new social geography facing business – a world in which distrust is also a resilient phenomenon while coexisting with trust. Further, while attempts to build trust and confidence through accountability strategies, corporations are contributing to skepticism and distrust about their actions to build trust, paradoxically. Coupled with the public's sense of injustice created the perception of selfish and uncaring behavior by corporations, new conceptual frameworks to analyze the challenges facing business and its leaders – and to suggest new approaches to be taken by business and its leaders to defuse the anger and rebuild the public trust in business – are needed. It is those analytic frameworks that I turn my attention to in the next section.

TRUST AND DISTRUST

A new reality and new relationships for business

The issue of trust is at the center of all interpersonal and organizational relationships. Understanding why people trust, and how that trust shapes social relations, has been the focus of researchers from a variety of disciplines, including psychology,[25] sociology,[26] political science,[27] and economics.[28] Trust is important as it facilitates cooperation[29] and it enhances the stability of social institutions and markets.[30]

While previous theory and research has brought great insight and understanding into trust dynamics, Lewicki *et al.* argue that the guiding analytical frameworks are rooted in core theoretical assumptions that are incomplete, or even no longer valid.[31] More specifically, the governing paradigm on trust is guided by assumptions of balance and consistency, and the relationships are, for the most part, viewed as dominantly "uniplex" in nature. Let me first outline the core arguments of Lewicki *et al.* and then apply it to the context of public trust in business.

Simultaneous trust and distrust: the Lewicki, McAllister, and Bies model

According to Lewicki *et al.*:

Relationships are multifaceted and multiplex. In other words, we relate to each other in multiple ways. We have different encounters in different contexts with different intentions that lead to different outcomes. These encounters accumulate and interact to create a rich texture of experience. The concept of *link multiplexity* within network relations provides an essential mechanism for depicting the richness for interpersonal relationships ... There has been a tendency among social network scholars to assume that multiplex relations are simply (and unidimensionally) trusting and fair in nature.[32]

Lewicki *et al.* challenge this view and argue that trust and distrust can and do exist within multiplex relations. Their view is grounded in an appreciation of "the potential breadth of the *bandwidth* and *richness*

[25] Deutsch, 1962; Worchel, 1979.   [26] Gambetta, 1988.   [27] Barber, 1983.
[28] Axelrod, 1984.   [29] Barnard, 1938.   [30] Williamson, 1975; Zucker, 1986.
[31] Lewicki *et al.*, 1998.   [32] *Ibid.*, 442.

of ongoing relationships ... We see relationships composed of *facets*: basic components of experience that an individual has with another." These facets aggregate into *bands*, which are groupings of facets across personal qualities that come to define our experience with a single individual in a single context. The broader the experience across multiple contexts, the broader the bandwidth. In addition to breadth, we recognize the potential for richness in the texturing of relationships. That is, although some relationships may be understood provisionally in general terms, mature relationships tend to be characterized by greater specification and detail across the bandwidth. For example, as a relationship matures, an emphasis shifts from "How much do I trust?" to "In what areas and in what ways do I trust?"[33]

They challenge:

> The traditional assumption of models of interpersonal behavior that are strongly grounded in notions of balance and consistency. Not all of one party's experiences with another are consistent. Although parties may pursue consistency and the resolution of inconsistent views, the more common state is not one of balance but, rather, of imbalance, inconsistency, and "uncertainty." Balance is a transitional state we pass through as we process information; the continually arriving wealth of new information, the salience and prominence of that information continually push as toward *inconsistency* and *incongruence*. Balance and consistency depictions may be more accurately represented as single-frame snapshots of a dynamic time-series process.[34]

In their analysis, Lewicki *et al.* define trust as "confident positive expectations regarding another's conduct" and distrust as "confident negative expectations regarding another's conduct."[35] Another's conduct refers to the words, actions, decisions of another. Confident positive expectations reflect a propensity to attribute virtuous intentions to another and the willingness to act on the basis of another's

---

[33] *Ibid.*, 442–443.   [34] *Ibid.*, 443.   [35] *Ibid.*, 439.

conduct. Confident negative expectations reflect a propensity to attribute sinister intentions to another and the desire to protect one's self from another's conduct.

They argue that trust and distrust are distinct and separate dimensions, with low and high levels, creating a 2 × 2 table with four cells: low trust/low distrust (cell 1); high trust/low distrust (cell 2); low trust/high distrust (cell 3); and high trust/high distrust (cell 4). Of most interest and relevance to the analysis of public trust in business are cells 2, 3, and 4.

Cell 2 (high trust/low distrust) is characterized by hope, faith, and assurance, where opportunities are pursued and new initiatives are undertaken. Cell 3 (low trust/high distrust) is characterized by fear, skepticism, and vigilance, where harmful motives are assumed and interdependence is managed as a defensive strategy. Cell 4 (high trust/high distrust) is characterized by hope and fear, faith and skepticism, where the operating philosophy is "trust but verify" and activities are carefully monitored.

Finally, Lewicki *et al.* highlight the condition or state of *ambivalence* as central to understanding trust and distrust dynamics. Ambivalence is the human and social response to trust and distrust existing simultaneously.

> Individuals experience ambivalence when positive and negative attitudes toward a single target exist ... Of course, in organizational settings where complexity, uncertainty, and role conflict are commonplace, and where ongoing interpersonal relationships mature over time and are multiplex in nature, the potential for ambivalence – simultaneous trust and distrust – too is considerable.[36]

Moreover, this ambivalence may serve a functional role in social relations. Building on Luhmann,[37] Lewicki *et al.* argue that social structures that are the most stable are the ones with healthy doses

---

[36] *Ibid.*, 448–449. [37] Luhmann, 1979.

of both trust and distrust, "a productive tension of confidences exists."[38] For if one trusts too much, they are a candidate for betrayal and harm. However, if one does not trust enough, nothing gets done. In other words, the key is to manage distrust and suspicions while at the same time building trust and relationships.

The Lewicki *et al.* model provides a framework for making sense of the surveys of public trust in business. In reviewing the findings from the three Edelman Trust Barometer surveys, there was evidence consistent with the public's ambivalence toward business. Some industry sectors were still found to be trusted (e.g., technology) while other sectors were distrusted (e.g., banking). And in those distrusted sectors, the surveys found the public expressed greater desires for more government intervention and regulation, revealing the public distrust of business. The question then arise as to how business can initiate trust building efforts while implementing distrust management efforts at the same time. Sitkin and Roth provide additional insight that complements and supports the Lewicki *et al.* framework.[39]

VALUE CONGRUENCE AND RELIABILITY

The Sitkin and Roth model

Sitkin and Roth clarify the distinction between trust and distrust. They argue that "trust is violated to the extent that expectations about context-specific task reliability are not met ... Distrust is engendered when an individual or group is perceived as not sharing key cultural values."[40] As did Lewicki *et al.*, Sitkin and Roth conceptualize trust and distrust as two separate dimensions, each based on different expectations. The keen insight from Sitkin and Roth is that there must be different remedies for different types of violations.

Sitkin and Roth argue that organizations often adopt legalistic "remedies" when trust is lacking. Such remedies would include

[38] Lewicki et al., 1998, 450.   [39] Sitkin and Roth, 1993.   [40] Ibid., 371.

formal rules and contracts. But the research on the effectiveness of these legalistic remedies finds that they fail to restore trust relations.[41] Furthermore, Sitkin and Roth argue, these legalistic remedies can lead to "an 'inflationary spiral' of increasingly formalized relations," creating further distrust.[42]

Sitkin and Roth provide a framework for making sense of the 2011 Public Agenda and Kettering Foundation study. For example, the accountability strategies employed by business to build trust actually undermine trust, as Sitkin and Roth would predict. The accountability strategies employed by business further formalize the relations and increase the psychological distance between the public and business. Such strategies may address reliability issues, but what the public also wants is value congruence from business to build trust. And that expectation for value congruence is expressed in demands for human engagement with – and being treated fairly by – business. In other words, business must undertake initiatives to build trust while continuing to employ accountability strategies to manage distrust. And there are ways to improve the communication of accountability strategies to make them more engaging.

NEW DIRECTIONS FOR UNDERSTANDING THE PUBLIC'S TRUST AND DISTRUST OF BUSINESS

Managing the tensions between responsibility and accountability

The 2011 Public Agenda and Kettering Foundation study provided evidence suggesting that the public wants business to act more responsibly, and by that meaning that business acts more honorably, engages the public directly, and treats the public fairly.[43] In the Sitkin and Roth model, this would be value congruence. But the accountability strategies are also important for business as it provides data to the public as to how corporations have performed. In the Sitkin and

---

[41] *Ibid.*   [42] *Ibid.*, 367.   [43] See Feldheim and Wang, 2004.

Roth model, this would be reliability. Managing both responsibility and accountability will create tensions for leaders to manage, and also will contribute to the ambivalence the public has toward business, as suggested by Lewicki *et al.*[44]

To build trust and manage the distrust of business, Bies argues that leaders must act responsibly and with honor while being held accountable for their actions.[45] He identifies five principles as the foundation for leadership action, three which deal with responsibility and two that deal with accountability. The three responsibility principles are: (1) tell the truth; (2) listen, listen, and listen; and (3) treat people fairly. The two accountability principles are: (4) share information on a regular basis; and (5) over-communicate and practice C3. The first of those three principles are fundamental to building trust and the last two principles are fundamental to managing distrust.

Principle 1: Tell the truth: With all due respect to Jack Nicholson in the movie, *A Few Good Men*, people *can* handle the truth. What they find difficult is handling the lies. So leaders must start telling the truth. If a leader's actions played a role in creating a bad situation, then they must explain their actions. What the public is looking for first in the offering of truth is a sincere and honest explanation. The explanation must acknowledge responsibility, and, not just privately, but also publicly.

The offering of truth may be one reason why doctors who give apologies for medical errors are sued for malpractice less often than doctors who refuse to give apologies (often out of fear that the apology will be perceived as an admission of guilt that may be used against them in court).[46] As Richard C. Boothman, Chief Risk Officer for the University of Michigan, explained to the US Senate:

> Despite widespread convictions that patients see lawyers because they are looking for a financial windfall, studies done to understand why some patients hire lawyers all yield the same results: patients

---

[44] Lewicki *et al.*, 1998.   [45] Bies, 2010.   [46] Tripp and Bies, 2009.

are actually seeking accountability, answers, and assurances that the same complication will not befall anyone else.[47]

This is why many states have considered bills for "I'm sorry" laws that would give doctors legal immunity for admitting mistakes. The intent is to help improve communication between doctors and their patients and avoid conflict escalation.

Society at large is no different in terms of its expectations from business. People want an explanation for controversial management decisions and for leaders' behaviors, particularly when those decisions or behaviors result in bad news. In the face of bad news, secrecy seems to be the default response of many leaders. Too often leaders say it is "on a need to know basis and *you* don't need to know." To rebuild trust, tell the truth and take responsibility for your actions. Don't shift the blame or pass the buck. This is a matter of honor.

Principle 2: Listen, listen, and listen: Leaders are signal-senders. One of the most important signals that leaders can send to convey that they care is this: *listen!* Listening is the most important leadership skill. Why? Because when leaders listen, the public will tell them *lots* of stuff. And when leaders listen, and we mean *really* listen, the public will feel valued and important. Indeed, the 2012 Edelman Trust Barometer survey results found that listening to customer needs and feedback was the most important attribute to respondents in building future trust in business.

Listening is absolutely critical for (re)building trust. And as leaders listen, they should do the following: listen for the *content* (what are people concerned about?); listen for the *emotions* (what are people afraid of?); but also listen to *act* (are people suggesting solutions or new ideas to act on, to help the organization?).

There are great examples of how business is merging twenty-first-century technology – building their Twitter strategies – with old-fashioned listening – and how it works.[48] Smart companies are

---

[47] Boothman, 2006, 7.   [48] Holmes, 2011.

viewing Twitter as more than just a new way to communicate; in addition, it can be a conversation that engages the public and be a channel to dealing with threats to trust or engage in trust building.

Holmes provides three case studies of how companies use Twitter as part of trust building and reputation protection.[49] First, Southwest Airlines has ten people involved in their Twitter account. These people are responsive to customer questions about everything from delayed flights to lost baggage. As soon as a complaint is tweeted to @SouthwestAir, there is an immediate response to the person complaining. At Southwest Airlines, the communications department works with the customer relations department to teach and train employees how to use Twitter. There is always someone monitoring the account from 5 a.m. to 11 p.m., which is the Southwest Airlines flight schedule, and the team is always on call in the case of bad weather or service disruptions.

Second, Whole Foods has one employee, its global online community manager, handling shoppers' questions, spending about a third of his day monitoring the Twitter account. The online community asks questions and makes complaints seven days a week, so the Twitter account is monitored seven days a week. Best Buy takes a hands-on, more-is-more approach to Twitter. Over 3,000 employees have signed up to answer tweets sent to Best Buy's help desk. This allows Best Buy to connect a tweet to the right person with the expertise to respond. Often, senior leaders at Best Buy will respond to the tweets, providing their personal email addresses as a means of engaging the customer.

Principle 3: Treat people fairly: If we conceptualize rebuilding trust as an exercise in service recovery, then research from the field of marketing suggests many new and different insights into rebuilding the public's trust in business.[50] In their review of the literature, Michel et al identify two consistent findings with respect to customer recovery. First, perceived fairness is critical in shaping customer

---

[49] *Ibid.*   [50] Michel *et al.*, 2009.

satisfaction with the recovery effort. Second, business can recover customers after one failure, but not after multiple failures.[51]

Let us begin with the fairness dimension. Justice research has identified three core dimensions – distributive, procedural, and interactional – and all three dimensions have been found to be associated with customer satisfaction with the recovery efforts of business.

Distributive justice focuses on the perceived fairness of the outcome.[52] In a customer context, did the person get the expected benefits of the product or service given relative to the price paid? Falling short of the public's expectations creates a sense of unfairness. To recover from this failure, businesses may expect a variety of remedies ranging from an apology to some form of compensation.[53]

Procedural justice refers to the fairness of the decision-making process.[54] In other words, what are the procedures used by a company in the attempted resolution of the service failure. To recover from this failure, businesses should provide opportunities for customers to present their complaint to a real person. In addition, the speed of recovery by a business and any recourse to appeal the recovery outcome will be key procedural justice factors for the public.

Interactional justice refers to the interpersonal treatment received by the customer.[55] To recover from the failure, businesses should provide an explanation for the failure and the expected timeline for recovery to occur. Businesses should show concern and empathy, and be very attentive to the customer. And this requires a human touch.

"Do not fail twice" is another keen insight from the research on service recovery.[56] Customers may forgive once, but not twice. The second failure may lead to the customer engaging in revenge to get even with the company.[57] As Parasuraman et al. demonstrate, customers have a "zone of tolerance" about what they expect to receive

---

[51] Ibid.   [52] Adams, 1965.   [53] Bowen and Johnston, 1999.
[54] Thibaut and Walker, 1975; Leventhal, 1980.   [55] Bies and Moag, 1986.
[56] Michel et al., 2009.   [57] Tripp and Bies, 2009.

and what they actually receive.[58] The zone of tolerance is wider when the public assesses a company's product or service delivery, but is much narrower when they evaluate the efforts at service recovery.

Principle 4: Share information on a regular basis: An important way that leaders can manage distrust and trust is to share information with the public – early and often. Keep the public informed as to how things are going, whether it is good news or bad news. Sharing information is one of the sure ways to (re)build trust.

But often leaders want to withhold information out of the need for control or power. Leaders operate under the mistaken belief that, by sharing the information, it will only make matters worse. But, by withholding information, it will only make matters worse for you in terms of (re)building trust. Why? The reason: in the absence of information, people will create rumors, which contributes to everyday paranoia.[59] What are the situational conditions that encourage rumors? Two conditions: lack of information and the existence of an important issue. What are the situational conditions that encourage everyday paranoia? Two conditions: lack of information and the existence of status uncertainty. What do rumors and paranoia have in common? Both are fuelled by a lack of information. While rumors and paranoia are created by the landscape of bad news, leaders can lessen their negative impact on the public by sharing information on a regular basis.

Principle 5: Over-communicate and practice C³: At the core of the accountability movement is reporting the results of corporate performance against standards and benchmarks. These results must be communicated through a variety of media channels to make sure that the public has access to this information. But, as the Public Agenda and Kettering Foundation found, this strategy may actually increase distrust from the public.[60]

To address this limitation of accountability strategies, leaders need to practice C3, or *crystal clear communication*.[61] That means

<hr>

[58] Parasuraman *et al.*1991.   [59] Bies *et al.*, 1997; Tripp and Bies, 2009.
[60] Public Agenda and Kettering Foundation, 2011.   [61] Bies, 2010.

speak and report the results in simpler, more understandable terms. The example of Jack Stack, CEO of Springfield Remanufacturing Corporation, who began the *open-book management* movement, could be instructive for business. By sharing financial information and corporate performance with the public and, most importantly, teaching them the skills to understand and interpret the information, would be a welcome outreach education to the public from business.

As a rule of thumb, communicate more than feels normal. By the way, because over-communication will involve all the senior leadership team, make sure everyone stays on message! This is the challenge – and where leader's trust in his or her team is so vital.[62] Unauthorized comments and "leaks" to the press seem to be a persistent, thorny problem for organizations – even those highly motivated to tell the truth!

AT THE CROSSROADS OF TRUST AND DISTRUST

Virtue and vigilance

Leaders must lead in good times *and* in bad. In fact, a leader's ability is most tested in times of distress when public anger and distrust seem most immediate. It is a call to action for leaders to imagine new and more effective ways to build public trust in business. Indeed, it is that call to leadership that is found in the words of David Starr Jordan, first president of Stanford University: "Wisdom is knowing what to do next. Skill is knowing how to do it. Virtue is doing it."

Sounds too simple? It's not, but it is basic. This is why when the cynics and critics say that this is a warmed-over recommendation from the past, we reply: "Go back to basics; we know what works." In fact, what got us in this mess were leaders ignoring those tried-and-true basics. While the prescriptions for (re)building trust may seem like common sense, it is prudent to remember the words of Voltaire: "Common sense is not so common."

---

[62] Kramer, 2002.

But as history suggests, trusting the virtue of business and its leaders is probably not a prudent response, requiring the need for more skepticism and vigilance.[63] That vigilance must be institutionalized in business practices. Janis suggests a variety of institutional practices to promote vigilant problem solving to avoid errors in judgment and bad action.[64]

The skepticism and vigilance must also be external to the corporation. Consumer watchdogs, political groups, and the media must play a key role in vigilance.[65] Corporations might reach out to external groups to create innovative mechanisms to assess trustworthy behavior. Some variation of eBay's feedback stars system would be a possible innovation.

To bring this chapter to a conclusion, I would like to offer the best advice for the public when it comes to the issues of trust and distrust of business. That advice is found in a famous Russian proverb: *Doveryai, no Proveryai*. Translation: "Trust, but verify." This proverb became famous in 1987 when President Reagan quoted it as a "guiding maxim" in his negotiation of the Intermediate-Range Nuclear Forces Treaty (INF) with Secretary Gorbachev of the Soviet Union.[66] And, because of the actions of business in the recent and distant past, it should be the guiding maxim for the public in its present and future dealings with business in the twenty-first century.

REFERENCES

Axelrod, R. (1984), *The Evolution of Cooperation*. New York: Basic Books.
Barber, R. (1983), *The Logic and Limits of Trust*. New Brunswick, NJ: Rutgers University Press.
Barnard, C. I. (1938), *The Functions of the Executive*. Cambridge, MA: Harvard University Press.
Bies, R. J. (2010, April), 'Leading change in the era of bad news: Dealing with anger, distrust, and revenge in the workplace.' Paper presented at the ProSci Global Conference, Las Vegas, NV.

[63] Kramer, 2009.   [64] Janis, 1989.   [65] Kramer, 2009.   [66] Shultz, 1993.

Bies, R. J. and Moag, J. S. (1986), 'Interactional justice: communication criteria of fairness.' In R. J. Lewicki, B. H. Sheppard, and M. H. Bazerman (eds.), *Research on Negotiation in Organizations*. Greenwich, CT: JAI Press, 43–55.

Bies, R. J. and Tripp, T. M. (1996), 'Beyond distrust: getting even and the need for revenge.' In R. Kramer, and T. R. Tyler (eds.), *Trust in Organizations: Frontiers of Theory and Research*. Thousand Oaks, CA: Sage Publications, 246–260.

Bies, R. J., Tripp, T. M., and Kramer, R. M. (1997), 'At the breaking point: cognitive and social dynamics of revenge in organizations.' In R. A. Giacalone and J. Greenberg (eds.), *Anti-social Behavior in Organizations*. Thousand Oaks, CA: Sage, 18–36.

Boothman, R. C. (2006), 'Medical justice: making the system work better for patients and doctors.' Testimony before the United States Senate, Committee on Health, Education, Labor and Pensions, June 22.

Bowen, D. E. and Johnston, R. (1999), 'Internal service recovery: developing a new construct.' *International Journal of Service Industry Management*, 10, 118–132.

Carson, R. (1962), *Silent Spring*. New York: Houghton Mifflin.

Deutsch, M. (1962), 'Cooperation and trust: some theoretical notes.' *Nebraska Symposium on Motivation* (pp. 275–320). Lincoln, NE: Nebraska University Press.

Dickens, C. (1859/1997), *A Tale of Two Cities*. New York: Signet Classics.

Edelman Trust Barometer (2009), www.edelman.com/trust/2009.

Edelman Trust Barometer (2010), www.edelman.com/trust/2010.

Edelman Trust Barometer (2011), www.edelman.com/trust/2011.

Edelman Trust Barometer (2012), http://trust.edelman.com.

Feldheim, M.A., & Wang, X. (2004), 'Ethics and public trust: results from national survey.' *Public Integrity*, 6, 63–75.

Gambetta, D. (1988), *Trust: Making and Breaking Cooperative Relations*. New York: Blackwell.

Hardin, R. (2004), 'Distrust: manifestations and management.' In R. Hardin (ed.), *Distrust*. New York: Russell Sage Foundation, vol. VIII, 3–33.

Holmes, E. (2011, December 9), 'Tweeting without fear: how three companies have built their twitter strategies.' *Wall Street Journal*, B1.

Janis, I. L. (1989), *Crucial Decisions: Leadership in Policymaking and Crisis Management*. New York: Free Press.

Jos, P. H. and Tompkins, M. E. (2004), 'The accountability paradox in an age of reinvention: the perennial problem of preserving character and judgment.' *Administration & Society*, 36, 255–281

Kramer, R. M. (2002), 'When paranoia makes sense.' *Harvard Business Review*, 80(7), 62–69.

Kramer, R. M. (2009), 'Rethinking trust.' *Harvard Business Review*, 87(6), 69–77.

Kramer, R. M. and Pittinsky, T. L. (eds.) (2012), *Restoring Trust in Organizations and Leaders: Enduring Challenges and Emerging Answers*. New York: Oxford University Press.

Leventhal, G. S. (1980). 'What should be done with equity theory? New approaches to the study of fairness in social relationship.' In K. Gergen, M. Greenberg, and R. Willis (eds.), *Social Exchange: Advances in Theory and Research*. New York: Plenum Press, 27–55.

Lewicki, R. J., McAllister, D. J., and Bies, R. J. (1998), 'Trust and distrust: new relationships and realities.' *Academy of Management Review*, 23(3), 438–458.

Luhmann, N. (1979), *Trust and Power*. Chichester, UK: Wiley.

Matthews, D. (2011), 'Accountability and democracy.' In Public Agenda and Kettering Foundation, *Don't Count Us Out* (3–5) (at: www.publicagenda.org/dont-count-us-out).

Michel, S., Bowen, D., and Johnston, R. (2009), 'Why service recovery fails: tensions among customer, employee, and process perspectives.' *Journal of Service Management*, 20, 253–273.

Nader, R. (1965), *Unsafe at Any Speed: The Designed-in Dangers of the American Automobile*. New York: Grossman.

Parasuraman, A., Berry, L. L., and Zeithaml, V. A. (1991), 'Understanding customer expectations of service.' *Sloan Management Review*, 32(3), 39–48.

Public Agenda and Kettering Foundation (2011), *Don't Count Us Out: How an Overreliance on Accountability Could Undermine the Public's Confidence in Schools, Business, Government, and More* (at www.publicagenda.org/dont-count-us-out).

Santayana, G. (1905), *Life of Reason*. New York: C. Scribner's Sons.

Shultz, G. (1993), *Triumph and turmoil: My years as Secretary of State*. New York: Scribner.

Sievers, B. (2003), 'Against all reason: Trusting in trust.' *Organizational & Social Dynamics*, 3, 19–39.

Sitkin, S. B. and Bies, R. J. (1993), 'The legalistic organization: Definitions, dimensions and dilemmas.' *Organization Science*, 4, 343–349.

Sitkin, S. B. and Bies, R. J. (eds.) (1994), *The Legalistic Organization*. Newbury Park, CA: Sage.

Sitkin, S. B. and Roth, N. L. (1993), 'Explaining the limited effectiveness of legalistic "remedies" for trust/distrust.' *Organization Science*, 26, 367–392.

Thibaut, J. W. and Walker, L. (1975), *Procedural Justice: A Psychological Analysis*. Hillsdale, NJ: Erlbaum.

Tripp, T. M. and Bies, R. J. (2009), *Getting even: The Truth about Workplace Revenge – And How to Stop It.* San Francisco, CA: Jossey-Bass.

Tyler, T. R. and Lind, E. A. (1992), 'A relational model of authority in groups.' In M. Zanna (ed.), *Advances in Experimental Social Psychology.* New York: Academic Press, vol. XXV, 115–192.

Williamson, O.E. (1975). *Markets and hierarchies: Analysis and antitrust implications.* New York: Free Press.

Worchel, P. (1979). 'Trust and distrust.' In W. G. Austin and S. Worchel (eds.), *The Social Psychology of Intergroup Relations.* Belmont, CA: Wadsworth, 174–187.

Zucker, L.G. (1986). 'Production of trust: institutional sources of economic structure, 1840–1920.' In B. M. Staw and L. L. Cummings (eds.), *Research in Organizational Behavior.* Greenwich, CT: JAI Press, vol. VIII, 53–111.

5   Public trust in business and its determinants

Michael Pirson, Kirsten Martin,
Bidhan L. Parmar

EXECUTIVE SUMMARY

THE SITUATION

As the importance of public trust in business becomes ever more obvious to both practitioners and scholars, the levels of generalized trust in business have reached alarmingly low levels.

KEY QUESTIONS

Is an emerging trust gap – where the need for trust outpaces the actualization of trust in business – likely to impair successful business development? What are the determinants of public trust in the institution of business? Do stakeholder-role-specific perspectives impact public trust in business? If so, how do they do so?

NEW KNOWLEDGE

Men tend to be more trusting of business than are women. Age plays a role in people's trust in business, with those 23 years old or younger being much *more* likely to trust business.

 While it is commonly supposed that the public has greater trust in smaller companies, this study finds that changing the size of the firm from small, regional, national, or global does not substantially "move the dial" for trust. The authors' research, however, does find that public trust in business will be affected by a firm's industry.

KEY LESSONS

Public trust in the institution of business matters to all companies, since it colors stakeholder trust in particular businesses.

Age and gender play a role in stakeholder trust. Business leaders should be cognizant of these differences when assessing the status of their relationships with various stakeholders.

INTRODUCTION

Trust has been called the lubricant of society,[1] and public trust legitimizes large institutions such as business. Without trust many institutions, including business and government, would not be productive.[2] Trust in the business context has been widely recognized as a key enabler of organizational success,[3] a facilitator of efficient business transactions,[4] a prerequisite for customer satisfaction,[5] and an enhancer of employee motivation and commitment.[6] More generally, trust promotes cooperative behavior within organizations[7] and between organizational stakeholder groups,[8] as it fosters commitment,[9] motivation,[10] creativity, innovation, and knowledge transfer.[11] As such, by strengthening relationships between the firm and its various stakeholders, including the public, trust can serve as a source of competitive advantage for the organization.[12]

Public trust in business, or the degree to which external stakeholders such as the public trust business in general is largely understudied.[13] As the relevance of public trust in business becomes ever more obvious to practitioners and scholars, the levels of trust in business have reached alarmingly low levels.[14] On the one hand, political, economic, societal and technical developments lead to more need

---

[1] Luhmann, 1979.   [2] Fukuyama, 1995.   [3] Davis et al., 2000.

[4] Noteboom, 1996; Williamson, 1988, 1993.

[5] Doney and Cannon, 1997; Ganesan, 1994; Morgan and Hunt, 1994.

[6] Ganesan, 1994; Lewis, 1999; Osterloh and Frey, 2000; Sprenger, 2002.

[7] Dirks and Ferrin, 2001; Gulati and Westphal, 1999; Williams, 2001.

[8] Gulati, 1995; Jensen, 2003; Uzzi, 1997.

[9] Ganesan, 1994; Mayer and Gavin, 2005.   [10] Dirks, 1999.

[11] See, e.g., Clegg et al., 2002; Holste and Fields, 2005; McAllister, 1995; Nahapiet and Ghoshal, 1998; Osterloh and Frey, 2000; Politis, 2003; Tsai and Ghoshal, 1998.

[12] Barney and Hansen, 1994; Jensen, 2003; Nahapiet and Ghoshal, 1998.

[13] Poppo and Schepker, 2010.   [14] See, e.g., Edelman, 2011; Forum, 2005.

for public trust in business,[15] on the other hand, organizations, especially corporations, are arguably further eroding public trust.[16] Hence, an
emerging trust gap, where the need for trust outpaces the actualization
of trust in business, is likely to impair successful business development.
Therefore business executives and scholars have become interested in
how organizations can reestablish and maintain public trust in order to
remain legitimate and thereby secure their long-term survival. Before
scholars and practitioners can answer this important question, we must
better understand the concept of public trust and understand the determinants of said public trust. To conceptualize public trust more clearly,
this chapter suggests four domains of existing trust research that
scholars of public trust in business can draw from. Then we propose
several hypotheses which aim to predict the determinants of public trust
and test these hypotheses using a factorial vignette methodology. These
results provide scholars with more direction as this is, to our knowledge,
the first empirical study of public trust determinants. Furthermore
the study will enable those companies interested in increasing public
trust to better understand respective determinants of public trust.

This design mitigates several concerns in trust research. First,
trust research is fraught with respondent bias where respondents
inflate their concern for certain antecedents which may not reflect
their true attitude. The factorial vignette survey methodology is
specifically designed within sociology to avoid respondent bias by
indirectly measuring the determinants and their relative importance
of respondents informing normative judgments. Second, respondents
may not agree with a theoretical definition of trust while still
retaining ideas of trust. Trust is a complicated phenomenon requiring
sophisticated techniques to examine individual responses to trust
violations within specific contexts. In particular public trust involves
a distant vulnerability or the intention to trust in a yet-to-be-realized
relationship. Therefore the components of public trust draw on
multiple theories of trust. Public trust is, therefore, more complicated
and less well defined. This study focuses on the differences in trust

[15] Pirson, 2007.   [16] See, e.g., Edelman, 2011.

judgments across hypothetical firms and not whether or not the respondents agree with a theoretical definition of trust.

THE NOTION OF PUBLIC TRUST IN BUSINESS

Blois states that trust suffers in large part from being "superficially obvious";[17] it is so often used in everyday discourse that everyone knows what it means and how it should be used contextually.[18] Similarly, the notion of *public* trust only receives more scrutiny when it has been violated e.g., by unethical corporate conduct.[19] *Trust* and *public trust* are complex phenomena that can take various forms. Currently there is little consensus on the theoretical concept of public trust, therefore we argue that there are four theoretical streams of trust research that public trust can be viewed from. Public trust requires elements from each of these four streams of research and cannot be reduced to any one of them.

Generalized trust

A first perspective can be developed through the notion of generalized trust. Simmel was the first to distinguish between personalized and generalized trust, in 1908. Rotter *et al.* stated that "a generalized expectancy of trust" toward businesses determines the behavior of market actors and influences the success of the enterprises.[20] Coleman claimed that the functioning of economic institutions such as business assumed a foundation of generalized and almost unreflected trust on behalf of the public.[21] Parsons suggests that once the public starts reflecting this form of generalized trust in business, trust is already reduced and mechanisms such as money or credit will work less effectively (e.g., see causes of the financial crisis).[22] Parsons's view closely resembles what Luhmann later referred to as "system trust"[23] and Giddens calls "trust in expert systems."[24] Public trust accordingly is based on collective attributes based upon relationships between people in a social system.[25]

---

[17] Blois, 1999.   [18] Barber, 1983.   [19] Swift, 2001.
[20] Rotter *et al.*, 1972, 40. See also Fukuyama, 1995.   [21] Coleman, 1984.
[22] Parsons, 1961.   [23] Luhmann, 1979.   [24] Giddens, 1996.
[25] Lewis and Weigert, 1985.

Zucker explicitly states that these collective attributes encompass social expectations shared by everyone involved in an economic or any other exchange.[26] Rather than viewing public trust within a specific context of business, public trust in this theoretical conception represents a general, non-reflective attitude of the public toward business, which can be captured in general attitude measures toward the institution of business.

Institutional trust

A second and related theoretical perspective is presented by the notion of institutional trust. Institutional trust concerns trust in the guiding principles, routines, and controlling mechanisms of an institution such as business,[27] including external regulations. In contrast to the prevailing conceptions of trust, institutional trust represents a form of impersonal trust[28] and, similar to generalized trust, is less reflective. Following McKnight and Chervany,[29] institutional trust is defined as the subjective belief with which organizational members collectively assess favorable conditions in place for successful transactions.[30] Public trust in business according to this perspective refers to the trust by the public in the norms and procedures of business, for example executive compensation. Giddens argues that in modern times personal trust has been increasingly replaced by institutional trust.[31] Cook et al. (2005, 196) similarly argue that "Societies are essentially moving away from trust relationships toward externally regulated behavior."[32] Cook and Schilke further suggest that the public may increasingly be unable to judge trustworthiness of certain institutions because of lack of knowledge. As such, low levels of public trust result from insufficient knowledge and may not be harmful at all if external regulation can act as substitute.[33] Understanding public trust within this perspective highlights the importance of the context. In contrast to generalized trust institutional trust is more

---

[26] Zucker, 1986.   [27] Sztompka, 1999.   [28] Rousseau et al., 1998.
[29] McKnight and Chervany, 2002.   [30] Saparito et al., 2004.
[31] Giddens, 1996.   [32] Cook et al., 2005, 196.   [33] Cook and Schilke, 2010.

context specific, and as such the importance of the regulatory environment of the industry or the size of the business becomes relevant.

Reputation-based trust

A third theoretical perspective informing the study of public trust is reputation-based trust. Since members of the public are increasingly unlikely to form first-hand knowledge of all businesses, they will need to rely on third party accounts. As Rousseau *et al.* (1998) posit, third-party relations impact trust, "where existing social structures shape a person's reputation based upon a third party's ability to tell stories that corroborate one's trustworthiness (or lack of it)."[34] In addition, trust judgments will be fed by what Freeman labels "background narratives." These background narratives will likely be influenced by stories forming the historical trustworthiness of parties, the social context (e.g., networks) that makes reputational effects possible, and the social norms that shape beliefs regarding the intentions of others.[35] Thus, public trust can be influenced by micro-level arrangements – in particular, how individuals representing a business relate to members of the public.[36] This perspective highlights how, for example, the role of CEOs and their portrayal in the media can influence perceptions of public trust through reputation.

Stakeholder trust

A fourth theoretical perspective informing the discussion of public trust is the perspective of stakeholder trust.[37] Stakeholder trust in organizations entails willingness on the part of individuals (e.g., customers, employees, or members of the public) to accept vulnerability to the actions of an organization. Based on this perspective the public, as stakeholder, and each member of the public individually forms a trust judgment based on attributions of business in general. This process is considered to be reflective, rational,

[34] Rousseau *et al.*, 1998. See also Burt and Knez 1996.   [35] Whitener *et al.*, 1998.
[36] Fichman and Goodman, 1996.   [37] See, e.g., Pirson and Malhotra, 2011.

informed, and organization specific. The attributions made by stake-holders toward a specific business are informed by trustworthiness dimensions of ability, benevolence, integrity,[38] transparency, and value congruence.[39]

Public trust

Based on these four streams of existing trust research, we argue that public trust encompasses elements of generalized, institutional, reputation-based, and stakeholder trust. Members of the public will express trust in business largely along the lines of generalized and institutional trust – as a largely unreflective attitude toward business and its norms. However, we argue that the public's attitude – the willingness to become vulnerable to business – is informed by experiences with business in their respective roles as stakeholders of a subset of businesses as well as third party, reputational information about a larger subset of businesses.

In our further inquiry we therefore define public trust as *the willingness of the public as a stakeholder to become vulnerable to the actions of business as a general institution*. That trust in turn, is based on generalized non-reflective attitudes that relate to the norms, rules, and regulations within business, which can be informed by third-party accounts (including background narratives) and more direct attributions along the trustworthiness dimensions of relevant actors.

DETERMINANTS OF PUBLIC TRUST

Having outlined the concept of public trust and the different concep-tions that feed into it, our goal in this research is to understand determinants of public trust to provide the basis for a more informed discussion on how business could manage public trust. As Noteboom (1996) and others criticize, the notion of public trust as a mere unre-flective attitude becomes almost meaningless to examine as it is unclear what determines certain survey outcomes.[40] In this chapter,

---

[38] Mayer *et al.*, 1995.   [39] Pirson and Malhotra, 2011.   [40] Noteboom, 1996.

we explore the determinants of public trust by embedding the generalized notion of public trust in business. We argue that public trust as defined above will be influenced by a wide variety of factors. In the following we wish to highlight our theoretical reasoning to test a critical subset of these factors. In the relationship between the public and business, the public can be referred to as the truster – the actor that entertains a willingness to become vulnerable to another party. Business can be understood as the trustee – the actor that influences the truster's willingness to become vulnerable by the perception of his/her trustworthiness.

Truster-related determinants of public trust

In this section we describe the determinants of public trust which are related to the truster – or individual member of the public who chooses to become vulnerable to business. We posit that a member of the public will decide the level of willingness to be vulnerable to business in general using all the information accessible at a given point in time.[41] While public trust in business refers to a generalized institution, with whom no actor can have a full interaction trust related information will be less complete than in individual trust relationships. However, we argue that the amount of interactions experienced by a specific member of the public will increase the knowledge on which to base a trust judgment.[42] As such we suggest that any member of the public will be influenced in their trust decision by their experience with the business world (e.g., working in a business). Furthermore we argue that the amount of knowledge about business will grow with age of a person as with increased age the probability for interactions with business will raise.

Hypothesis1a: Public trust in business will be affected by a
    member of the public's level of experience with business.
Hypothesis1b: Public trust in business will be affected by a
    member of the public's age.

[41] See, e.g., Hardin, 2002.   [42] See, e.g., Lewicki and Bunker, 1996.

A variety of studies have suggested that trusting behavior is often influenced by general trust dispositions,[43] including attitudes and expectations. Gilligan argues that gender shapes such dispositions and attitudes.[44] She further suggests that gender influences moral judgments and finds that women in their judgment rely more on contextual information, whereas men tend to judge more instrumentally. Based on such arguments it could be construed that men trust instrumental profit-maximizing business organizations much more than women that take into account the consequences of such instrumental behavior. Empirical evidence for the role of gender in trusting decisions is mixed, however.[45] Glaeser et al. (2000) report that female undergraduates are less likely than others to trust in the context of trust games.[46] Buchan et al. (2008) find in a large-scale experiment that female students are less likely to trust than male students.[47] In contrast, Eckel and Wilson are among the few who report a higher trust rate for American women than for men.[48] Whereas empirical results of gender differences in mainly interpersonal trust contexts yield mixed evidence, it is possible that in terms of generalized expectations related to business gender differences are more pronounced.

Hypothesis1c: Public trust in business will be affected by gender.

Gender, age, and experience with business will influence a general attitude toward business in the sense of generalized trust. Furthermore, public trust judgments are likely to be influenced by generalized attitudes and expectations based on personal value sets. Schwartz proposes a set of 7–10 meta values that are universal in content and useful for explaining systematic relations between value priorities and a variety of attitudes and behaviors.[49] Schwartz's theory adopts a definition of human values as desirable goals, varying in importance, that serve as guiding principles in people's lives.[50] The crucial content

---

[43] See, e.g., Rotter, 1971.   [44] Gilligan, 1982.   [45] Bohnet and Zeckhauser, 2004.
[46] Glaeser et al., 2000.   [47] Buchan et al., 2008.   [48] Eckel and Wilson, 2003.
[49] Schwartz, 1994.   [50] Rokeach, 1973.

aspect that distinguishes among values is the type of motivational goal they express. With regard to public trust, members of the public, who find their values represented by a business organization, would theoretically behave differently in their trusting behavior than those members of the public that do not find their values represented. Pirson and Malhotra (2011) indeed find that stakeholders that perceive high value congruence with a business organization report significantly higher trust values than those with low perceived value congruence.[51] Businesses that are viewed as "good" usually benefit in terms of financial performance as well.[52]

> *Hypothesis1d: Public trust in business will be affected by a member of the public's general attitude toward business.*

Trustee-related determinants of public trust

Public trust, as the willingness of members of the public to become vulnerable to business, also depends on attributes of business as the trustee. While the attributes of the truster influence generalized trust in business, the attributes of the trustee will be shaped along the conceptualizations of institutional trust, reputation-based trust and stakeholder trust. We suggest that the size of the business, the industry a business operates in, the objective function of said business as well as the trustworthiness dimensions of the business including ability, benevolence, integrity, transparency, value congruence are critical influences of public trust.

Size of the firm. Institutional norms differ according to organizational size. In larger entities norms of behavior are more likely to be rule-based or command-and-control oriented, whereas in smaller organizations behavior can be based on interpersonal trust. As Luhmann (1979) suggests, the size of an organization determines the amount of risk and contingencies regarding organizational behavior.[53] The larger an organization, the higher the number of actors involved

---

[51] Pirson and Malhotra, 2011.
[52] Collins and Porras, 2002; Fombrun and van Riel, 2003.   [53] Luhmann, 1979.

which results in higher levels of information asymmetry. As Cook et al. state, increased anonymity in larger organizations will cause large businesses to be less trusted.[54] According to public trust surveys, small firms are indeed consistently more trusted than big national firms, whereas the multinational firms receive the lowest levels of public trust.[55] Cook et al. suggest, however, that that lack of trust of larger organizations could be compensated by regulatory safeguards, such as instated for the banking industry. Despite the regulatory substitute, we suggest that public trust can be influenced by the size of a business, with smaller businesses deemed less threatening and therefore more trustworthy.

Hypothesis 2a: Public trust in business will be affected by the size of a specific business.

Industry: Institutional norms are determined in part by the context a business is operating in.[56] The industry a business operates in influences the rules and norms of behavior, especially when external regulations are in place. Banking or consulting businesses operate differently from mining businesses or businesses in the defense industry. The way business is conducted in the oil industry differs from the emerging energy sector that is less established. As various reputation based surveys indicate, public trust in business seems to be influenced by the industry in which a business operates.[57] The technology industry usually commands much higher levels of public trust than for example the oil industry. In that sense the "contextuality" of trust in business is critical in influencing public trust.[58]

Hypothesis 2b: Public trust in business will be affected by the industry a specific business is in.

Objective function: Institutional norms are influenced by the objective an organization pursues. Trustworthiness, in turn, is judged

---

[54] Cook et al., 2005. [55] Forum, 2006. [56] See, e.g., Dacin, 1997.
[57] Edelman, 2011; Fombrun and van Riel, 2003. [58] Edelman, 2011.

in part by perceived intention of the trustee. Mayer et al. suggest that the level of perceived benevolence determines the willingness to become vulnerable across levels (individual, organization, etc.).[59] On the organizational level, the objective function presents a basis for attributions about intention and level of benevolence. Common objective functions in business range from profit maximization to job creation, stakeholder value creation, or societal well-being. Edelman finds that a large majority of the public globally rejects the notion of profit maximization as the fundamental objective function of business.[60] He also suggests that to increase trust companies should pursue a purpose beyond profit maximization. Porter and Kramer (2011) similarly propose that business focus on the creation of shared value to maintain its legitimacy.[61]

> *Hypothesis 2c: Public trust in business will be affected by the objective function of the particular business.*

Trustworthiness dimensions: As members of the public have increasingly less direct information about all businesses, third-party accounts become increasingly relevant. Such third party accounts culminate in the reputation of business, which is judged along several dimensions. Fombrun and colleagues suggest to measure reputation along perceptions of trust, admiration, high esteem, and good feeling and evaluates companies with regard to their citizenship, governance, workplace, leadership, financial performance, and innovation.[62] Focusing on trust, we build on the notion of reputation yet extend it with insights coming from stakeholder trust research.[63] Such research suggests several direct trustworthiness dimensions including ability, benevolence, and integrity as put forth by Mayer et al. as well as the notion of transparency and value congruence (or identification).[64]

Stakeholder trust is based in large part on the perceived *ability* of the organization to provide goods and services that benefit the

---

[59] Mayer et al., 1995.   [60] Edelman, 2011.   [61] Porter and Kramer, 2011.
[62] Fombrun, 1996; Fombrun and van Riel, 2003.
[63] Pirson and Malhotra, 2011.   [64] Mayer et al., 1995

stakeholder.[65] In addition, stakeholder trust is also based on the perceived *motivation* as captured by integrity and benevolence.[66] Integrity refers to an organization's general tendency (or propensity) to act fairly and ethically, benevolence refers to the organization's concern for their stakeholders' well-being.[67] Transparency is also likely to be of relevance to public stakeholders.[68] According to Hardin and McKnight *et al.*, when there is little previous interaction and information asymmetry is high, all trust-relevant information is sought and scrutinized.[69] This should accentuate the importance of transparency. For example, corporate communication initiatives and newly developed reporting standards (e.g., the Global Reporting Initiative) are aimed at building trust with stakeholders (e.g., investors) who might otherwise not have access to information regarding organizational behaviors and motives. Transparency may also be a more important element of trust in shallow relationships due to recent corporate scandals.[70] Finally, in line with Rousseau *et al.* and Pirson and Malhotra[71] we argue that the relationship between the public and business in general will be based in part on perceptions of value congruence,[72] and more generally, the ability to identify with business as an institution.[73]

> *Hypothesis 2d: Public trust in business will be affected by the ascribed trustworthiness of a business along the dimensions of ability, benevolence, integrity, transparency, and value congruence.*

METHOD

The goal of this research is to identify the determinants of public trust. This research aims to deconstruct what individuals mean when

---

[65] McAllister, 1995; Mayer *et al.*, 1995.   [66] *Ibid.*
[67] See also Whitener *et al.*, 1998.   [68] Sheppard and Sherman, 1998.
[69] Hardin, 2002; McKnight *et al.*, 1998.
[70] Dervitsiotis, 2003; DiPiazza, 2002; Turnbull, 2002.
[71] Rousseau *et al.*, 1998 and Pirson and Malhotra, 2011.
[72] Lewicki and Bunker, 1996.
[73] Enz, 1988; Lewicki and Bunker, 1996; Yaniv and Farkas, 2005.

they assert that they do or do not trust 'business' by varying firm-related trust factors and capturing truster-related measures based on the trust literature outlined above and in Table 5.1.

Toward this end, the factorial vignette survey methodology, developed to investigate human judgments,[74] was employed. In a factorial vignette survey, a set of vignettes is generated for each respondent, where the vignette factors or independent variables are controlled by the researcher and randomly selected, and respondents are asked to evaluate these hypothetical situations. Factorial survey methodology allows for the simultaneous experimental manipulation of a large number of factors through the use of a contextualized vignette.[75] The factorial vignette approach allows the researcher to examine: (1) the elements of information used to form judgments; (2) the weight of each of these factors; and (3) how different subgroups of the respondents agree on (1) and (2).[76] These factors and their associated coefficients are the *equations-inside-the-head* of respondents as to judgments of trust.[77]

The vignettes were constructed by varying several factors along dimensions or levels. A deck of vignettes for each respondent was randomly created with replacement as the respondent was taking the survey from a vignette universe. For each rated vignette, the associated rating, factor levels, and vignette script were preserved as well as the vignette sequence number. The vignette format is also provided in the Appendix below with a sample vignette and the vignette template.

This is a proof-of-concept examination – a theoretical examination[78] – therefore the findings will support or not support the hypothesized relationships between trust factors and trust judgments. Such research seeks the generalizability of ideas rather than

[74] Rossi and Nock, 1982; Jasso, 2006; Wallander, 2009.
[75] Ganong and Coleman, 2006. In comparison, in experiments, factors are designed orthogonally to each other but manipulated one at a time; however, in a traditional survey, many factors are examined but are not necessarily orthogonal to each other (Appelbaum *et al.*, 2006).
[76] Nock and Gutterbock, 2010.   [77] Jasso, 2006.   [78] Lynch, 1982.

Table 5.1 *Public trust in business, or the degree to which external stakeholder such as the public (Poppo and Schepker, 2010) trusts business in general*

Trust literature	Summary	Contributions to public trust in business construct	Implication to study of public trust	Implications to this study
Generalized	• Referred to as "system trust" (Luhmann) and "trust in expert systems" (Giddens) • Non-reflective • As distinct from personalized trust (Giddens)	Public trust accordingly is based on collective attributes based upon relationships between people in a social system (Lewis and Weigert, 1985)	Public trust in this theoretical conception represents a general, non-reflective attitude of the public toward business, which can be captured in general attitude measures toward the institution of business	• General trust in business rating as possible factor of trust in a firm • Non-specified firm (no name) in vignettes • General trust in a firm as the 1st rating task
Institutional	• Impersonal, less reflective • Concerns trust in the guiding principles, routines, and controlling	Public trust in business refers to the trust by the public in the norms and procedures of business, e.g., executive compensation, codes of	Institutional trust is more context-specific, and as such the importance of industry or size of the business becomes relevant	• Inclusion of objective or mission statements • Industry, size as contextual factors

		conduct, performance assessment, etc.	
		• The subjective belief with which organizational members collectively assess favorable conditions in place for successful transactions (Saparito et al., 2004)	
Reputational	• In case of no personal interaction third-party accounts become relevant for trust formation	Public trust can be influenced by micro-level arrangements – in particular, how individuals representing a business behave toward members of the public (Fichman and Goodman, 1996)	Public trust in business is influenced by "background narratives" (Freeman) Public trust is influenced by general reputations of certain firms Reputations of firm representatives, such as the CEO can influence	• third-party reporting in vignette • Industry, size as contextual factors • Inclusion of objective or mission statements • Profitability as common metric offered in third-party accounts
	• Where existing social structures shape an organization's reputation based upon a third-party's ability to tell stories			

mechanisms of an institution (Sztompka, 1999)

Table 5.1 (*cont.*)

Trust literature	Summary	Contributions to public trust in business construct	Implication to study of public trust	Implications to this study
	that corroborate trustworthiness or lack of it (Burt and Knez, 1996)		perceptions of public trust through reputation	
Stakeholder	• Entails willingness on the part of individuals (e.g., customers, employees, or members of the public) to accept vulnerability to the actions of an organization (Pirson and Malhotra, 2011)	The public, as a stakeholder, and each member of the public individually forms a trust judgment based on attributions of business in general.	Public trust is organization-specific The attributions made by stakeholders toward a specific business are informed by trustworthiness dimensions of ability, benevolence, integrity, (Mayer *et al.*, 1995) transparency, and value congruence (Pirson and Malhotra, 2011)	• Stakeholder-focused trust rating task • Firm-level vignettes • Ability, benevolence, integrity, transparency, and value congruence as factors in vignette

the generalizability of data patterns within a specific population.[79] In other words, the findings from this experimental study will identify truster measures and trustee factors important to understanding public trust in business.[80]

VIGNETTE FACTORS

Generalizability for theoretical research, as compared to effects application research, investigates relationships among ideas or constructs, and the researcher "seeks to understand those constructs that have influence on a variety of behaviors in a variety of situations."[81] As such, naturally occurring stimuli and responses are often ill-suited to testing hypotheses of interest to theoretical researchers leading such researchers into the laboratory "where manipulations and measures can be concocted that have relatively simple mappings onto the constructs of concern."[82] Here, we representatively sampled factors in order to test the hypotheses based on the trust scholarship explored above and outlined in Table 5.1.

The number and levels of factors combine to create the universe of possible vignettes[83] and should be guided by theory, reasoning, and wisdom.[84] Here, the use of computer programming to design and create the vignettes and web-based tools to administer the survey alleviated many of the logistical limitations on the number of factors and levels to include. Based on the hypotheses developed, the study must include (1) different technologies or 'locations' for the vignettes and (2) privacy factors that may vary in importance across locations. The Appendix contains the vignette factors as well as a sample vignette.

TRUSTEE-RELATED FACTORS

The vignettes were constructed from two sets of factors. The first set focused on facets of the firm – the *size, industry, mission statement,*

---

[79] *Ibid.*   [80] Levitt and List, 2007.   [81] Lynch, 1982.   [82] *Ibid.*, 233.
[83] Nock and Gutterbock, 2010.   [84] Jasso, 2006; Wallander, 2009.

profitability, and *stated values* – that may impact public trust in a firm. Specifically, firm size included small, regional, national, and global firms. For industry, firms were assigned industries of financial services, oil and gas, pharmaceuticals, and solar based on recent focus on these industries in the press. The objective function or mission statement of the firm focused on creating value, generating employment, bettering society, or increasing firm profitability based on the reputational trust literature. In addition, profitability was included as a generally communicated firm metric and added realism to the reported attributes of the firm in the vignettes based on reputational trust literature.

The second set of factors focused on known factors for stakeholder trust, where *ability, benevolence, integrity*, and *value congruence* are the main drivers of trust within a direct firm–stakeholder relationship. The vignettes also included *transparency* as a possible factor of trust, as transparency has been widely suggested as a solution to building trust in the public but has not been empirically examined as a factor of public trust. A grade was assigned, from F to A+, of the firm's ability, benevolence, integrity, and transparency in the vignettes in order to analyze how much a grade change in these trustee-related factors would move the dial on trust for the respondents. Value congruence was measured by: (1) assigning two values from the list in the Appendix to the firm in the vignette; (2) capturing the respondents' ranking of values in business at the end of the survey; and (3) creating a dummy variable indicating if the vignette included values that matched the respondents' stated preferred values for business. The vignette factors and dimensions are provided in a table in the Appendix are linked to the trust literature in Table 5.1.

TRUSTER-RELATED MEASURES

Respondent-level data was captured at the beginning of the survey to support the testing of hypotheses 1a–1c. In addition to age, gender, and years of business experience, the respondent was told "Tell us how much you agree with the statements below. On the sliding scale below, with a rating to the left being 'strongly disagree' to the right being 'strongly agree.'" The rating task stated "I trust this business." Additionally, at the end of the vignettes, the respondents selected five values they look for in business from a list. The list was generated by sampling from the ten categories of values from Schwartz' taxonomy of universal values, using only those values that would be most applicable and realistic to organizations.[85] See the Appendix for a complete list. Each firm in the vignette was randomly assigned two (2) values with the other randomly assigned factors; the respondent and the firm could have 0, 1, or 2 values in common. We measured the number of common values as our value congruence measure with two values matching being a strong agreement.

RATING TASK

For each vignette, respondents were given two rating tasks and asked "Tell us how much you agree with the statements below: on a scale of (1–5), 1 being 'strongly disagree' to 5 being 'strongly agree.'" The first rating task stated "I trust this company" and captured the respondent's general trust in the described firm based on generalized trust theory. The second rating task varied *between* respondents – each respondent was assigned one of the following second rating tasks:

- I would work with this company
- I would invest in this company
- I would work for this company
- I would buy products and services from this company

The second rating task captured the stakeholder-role-specific trust as suggested in the stakeholder trust literature. This second rating task was assigned randomly for each individual and kept constant throughout all forty vignettes for that respondent.

[85] Schwartz, 1994.

SAMPLE

The respondents were contacted via email through distribution lists provided by the Business Roundtable Institute for Corporate Ethics in addition to postings on the Institute's website and emails to students at two universities in the Mid-Atlantic. Out of 436 respondents who answered *any* vignettes, 332 (76.15 percent) answered all 40 vignettes and 49 (11.24 percent) stopped within the first three vignettes. These 332 respondents answered 11,800 vignettes out of 13,929 total vignettes answered. The sample was 44.6 percent male and 76.8 percent over 23 years old (non-undergraduates) with an average of 12.26 years of business of experience.

RESULTS

Hypotheses 1a–c

Hypotheses 1a–1c predict that *public trust in business will be affected by a member of the public's level of experience with business, age, and gender.* To test the first set of hypotheses, a regression analysis of the first rating task on the trustee (firm) factors and truster control measures was conducted. The results are in Table 5.2 with Model A representing the regression of the first rating task for all respondents (Trust DV; $N = 11,800$). The findings support the prediction in Hypothesis 1a that public trust in business will be affected by a member of the public's level of experience with business. The results in Table 5.2 illustrate that the more experience in business, the less trust an individual will have in a firm ($\beta = -0.211$, $p = 0.00$), thus supporting Hypothesis 1a that public trust in business will be affected by a member of the public's level of experience with business even controlling for age.

The findings support the prediction in *Hypothesis 1b* that *public trust in business will be affected by a member of the public's age.* A dummy variable was created to signify if the respondent's age was over 23 (AgeOver23) roughly approximating undergraduate and non-undergraduate status. The results in Table 5.2 show that age is negatively related to trust in a firm with those over 23 years old rating a firm 2.201 points lower (p =.0.03) than respondents under 23 years old even when controlling for years of experience.

The findings support the prediction in *Hypothesis 1c* that *public trust in business will be affected by a member of the public's gender*. The results in Table 5.2 illustrate that males rate firms more trustworthy (β = 3.912, p = 0.00) than females, thus supporting Hypothesis 1c that public trust in business will be affected by a member of the public's gender. In sum, the results suggest public trust in business is affected by a member of the public's experience, age, and gender. Specifically, experience and age are negatively correlated with public trust in a firm and males rate firms more trustworthy than females.

Hypothesis 1d

Hypothesis 1d predicts *Public trust in business will be affected by a member of the public's general attitude toward business*. To test Hypothesis 1d, the full regression analysis in Table 5.2 contains the impact of a respondent's general trust in the institution of business on their more specific trust in a firm (Trust in Business). The findings support the prediction in Hypothesis 1d. Specifically, a respondent's trust-in-business rating explains 16.3 percent of their trust rating in a particular firm. For every additional point a respondent trusted the institution of business, their trust in a particular firm increased 0.163 points (p = 0.00), thus supporting Hypothesis 1d that public trust in business will be affected by a member of the public's general attitude toward business.

Hypotheses 2a–c

Hypotheses 2a–2c predict public trust in business will be affected by the firm's size, industry, and objective function. To test the second set of hypotheses, a dummy variable for each dimension of the trustee factors – size, industry, and objective function was created to isolate the impact of each level on the trust in a firm. The findings *do not*

Table 5.2 Full regression of all factors and control measures

		All respondents		Male		Female		Age over 23		Age under 23	
		Model A		Model B		Model C		Model D		Model E	
		β	p > |t|	β	p > |t|	β	p > |t|	β	p > |t|	β	p > |t|
Control variables	Male	3.912	0.00	(omitted)	0.00	(omitted)	0.00	3.244	0.00	5.071	0.00
	AgeOver23	−2.201	0.03	−4.730	0.00	0.218	0.87	(omitted)	0.00	(omitted)	0.00
	BusExpYrs	−0.211	0.00	−0.121	0.01	−0.342	0.00	−0.205	0.00	−1.267	0.00
	TrustinBus	0.163	0.00	0.183	0.00	0.143	0.00	0.183	0.00	0.102	0.00
Trust factors	Ability	2.380	0.00	2.263	0.00	2.486	0.00	2.539	0.00	1.842	0.00
	Benevolence	3.091	0.00	2.958	0.00	3.213	0.00	3.094	0.00	3.177	0.00
	Integrity	5.997	0.00	5.970	0.00	6.000	0.00	5.959	0.00	6.097	0.00
	Profitability	1.681	0.00	1.458	0.00	1.856	0.00	1.707	0.00	1.588	0.00
	Transparency	3.204	0.00	2.882	0.00	3.457	0.00	3.378	0.00	2.642	0.00
Industry	Pharma	−3.559	0.00	−4.091	0.01	−3.088	0.03	−3.703	0.00	−3.184	0.13
	OilGas	−4.665	0.00	−3.874	0.02	−5.227	0.00	−5.830	0.00	−0.893	0.66
	FinancialS~s (Solar)	−2.338	0.03	−2.126	0.19	−2.579	0.08	−3.106	0.02	−0.025	0.99

Size	SmallCo	0.886	0.40	1.214	0.45	0.469	0.74	−0.059	0.96	3.710	0.07
	RegionalCo	0.224	0.84	−1.088	0.50	1.293	0.37	0.797	0.53	−1.614	0.43
	NationalCo (Global)	0.357	0.74	0.575	0.72	−0.085	0.95	0.348	0.78	0.107	0.96
Mission	ValueFcn	0.569	0.59	1.698	0.29	−0.394	0.78	−0.477	0.70	3.467	0.09
	WorkFcn	1.999	0.06	0.023	0.99	**3.566**	**0.01**	1.544	0.22	3.581	0.08
	SocietyFcn (ProfitFcn)	1.553	0.15	−0.165	0.92	**3.018**	**0.04**	0.804	0.52	**4.356**	**0.04**
	Cons.	−100.476		−90.589		−104.937		−103.526		−95.397	
	R2	0.2995		0.2926		0.3063		0.2983		0.3098	
	N =	11800		5200		6600		8920		2880	

Notes: Bold signifies p<0.05.
Factor labels and definitions in the Appendix.

support the prediction in *Hypothesis 2a* that *public trust in business will be affected by the size of a specific business*. The results in Table 5.2 show that changing the size of the firm in the vignette from small, regional, national, or global does not move the dial for trust, therefore not supporting Hypothesis 2a that public trust in business will be affected by the firm's size.

The findings support the prediction in *Hypothesis 2b* that *public trust in business will be affected by a firm's industry*. The results in Table 5.2 illustrate that changing the industry of the firm in the vignette from solar does move the dial on trust for respondents. Specifically, the pharmaceutical, oil and gas, and financial services industries are less trusted in comparison to the solar industry, thus supporting Hypothesis 2b that public trust in business will be affected by the *industry* of a particular firm.

The findings are mixed in regards to the prediction in *Hypothesis 2c* that *public trust in business will be affected by the mission statements of the particular businesses*. The results in Table 5.2 illustrate a mission statement focused on employment is slightly more trusted than one focused on profitability. All other mission statements were statistically identical to a mission statement focused on profitability.

Hypothesis 2d

Hypothesis 2d predicts *public trust in business will be affected by the ascribed trustworthiness of a business along the dimensions of ability, benevolence, integrity, transparency, and value congruence.* To test Hypothesis 2d, the full regression of the first rating task on the trustee factors and truster measures in Table 5.2 is used to test the importance of ability, benevolence, integrity, and transparency. The findings support the prediction in Hypothesis 2d. The results in Table 5.2 illustrate that ability, benevolence, integrity, transparency, and profitability are all statistically significant in a respondent's judgment of trust. For example, for each increase in grade in integrity, the respondent rated the firm 5.996 points higher in trust ($p = 0.00$).

In comparison, for each letter grade increase for profitability, the respondents rated a firm 1.681 points higher in trust (p = 0.00).

In addition, value congruence was tested by examining a subset of the vignettes associated with those respondents who ranked their top business values at the end of the factorial vignette survey. A vignette-level variable was created signifying if both values assigned to the firm in the vignette matched those ranked by the respondent. This variable is listed as "Value Agree" in Table 5.3. Where a firm had strong value congruence with the respondent, in other words where the values of the firm and respondent matched, respondents rated the firm as more trustworthy (β = 4.446, p = 0.00). In summary, the findings support Hypothesis 2d that public trust in business will be affected by the ascribed trustworthiness of a business along the dimensions of ability, benevolence, integrity, transparency, and value congruence.

DISCUSSION

In this chapter we first defined public trust as a distinct type of trust which draws on existing research of generalized, institutional, reputation-based, and stakeholder-based forms of trust. We contribute to theory by distinguishing public trust from these other types of trust, and highlight how existing trust research streams can inform the study of public trust. We then proceeded to empirically test the determinants of public trust. Moving beyond general attitude-based measures of trust-in-business used by public relation firms, we provide one of the first empirical studies of the determinants of public trust in business. Employing a more comprehensive view of public trust, we examined two classes of variables in detail: attributes of the truster – in our case members of the public, and attributes of the trustee – in our case generalized business institutions. By deploying a factorial vignette methodology we found considerable empirical support for our hypotheses. However, we also discovered several unexpected findings. For example, we hypothesized that the level of trust in a business would be affected by its size, with larger more

Table 5.3 Regression for value congruence

Regression for value congruence

	All respondents		Male		Female		Over 23		Under 23	
	β	p > |t|	β	p > |t|	β	p > |t|	β	p > |t|	β	p > |t|
Control variables										
Male	3.455	0.00	(omitted)		(omitted)		2.712	0.06	2.720	0.20
AgeOver23	-2.248	0.15	-1.710	0.45	-1.556	0.49	(omitted)		(omitted)	
BusExpYrs	-0.216	0.00	-0.170	0.01	-0.308	0.00	-0.227	0.00	-0.995	0.03
TrustinBus	0.191	0.00	0.148	0.00	0.219	0.00	0.269	0.00	-0.014	0.60
Value Agree	4.446	0.02	4.357	0.12	4.314	0.09	5.670	0.01	0.979	0.79
Trust factors										
Ability	2.581	0.00	2.751	0.00	2.428	0.00	2.709	0.00	2.185	0.00
Benevolence	3.136	0.00	3.498	0.00	2.814	0.00	3.188	0.00	3.175	0.00
Integrity	6.104	0.00	6.383	0.00	5.872	0.00	5.793	0.00	6.815	0.00
Profitability	3.269	0.00	3.115	0.00	3.375	0.00	3.156	0.00	3.398	0.00
Transparency	1.705	0.00	1.678	0.00	1.774	0.00	1.725	0.00	1.546	0.00
Industry Pharma	-2.990	0.07	-3.701	0.13	-2.224	0.33	-3.203	0.11	-2.633	0.38
OilGas	-4.526	0.01	-3.077	0.21	-5.950	0.01	-6.356	0.00	-0.635	0.83
Financial Svc	-2.711	0.11	-0.980	0.69	-4.263	0.07	-4.332	0.03	1.154	0.69
Size SmallCo	1.417	0.39	0.347	0.89	2.521	0.26	-0.408	0.84	5.210	0.08
RegionalCo	0.527	0.75	-1.813	0.45	2.942	0.20	1.298	0.52	-0.809	0.78
NationalCo	0.958	0.56	-1.112	0.65	2.954	0.19	-0.315	0.87	3.078	0.30
Mission ValueFcn	0.795	0.63	2.548	0.30	-1.174	0.60	-1.232	0.54	6.162	0.03
WorkFcn	2.504	0.13	0.718	0.77	4.123	0.07	1.434	0.47	6.173	0.04
SocietyFcn	-0.860	0.60	-1.580	0.52	-0.426	0.85	-2.607	0.18	5.122	0.09
Cons.	-105.66	0.00	-104.91	0.00	-103.00	0.00	-104.90	0.00	-106.39	0.00

bureaucratic firms having less public trust. Our data, in contrast to other general attitude-based surveys, did not support this claim. Additionally, empirical support for industry and objective function were mixed. Experience, age, and gender were all significant predictors of the level of trust in business. It might be interesting to explore why the younger generation trusts business generally more than the older generations, despite the claim that millennials are less materialistic and more purpose oriented. Overall, we find that truster-related determinants are much more predictive of public trust in business than trustee-related determinants. That in turn, leaves practitioners and policy makers less leeway for managing public trust. The fact that the people trust business less the more they have been exposed to it is reflective of larger generational phenomena sociologists have long noted.[86] However, some levers that are at the disposal of the trustee related to stakeholder trust attributes do have significant influence on public trust. This opens the perspective of managing public trust similarly to stakeholder trust.

These results represent a first attempt at empirically evaluating the determinants of public trust. However, much work remains to be done. While we establish a first set of determinants, this set is not comprehensive and alternative determinants need to be explored. Furthermore, this study sets up several interesting questions to explore regarding public trust in business. First, we find that truster-related attributes are driving trust in business more systematically than trustee-related attributes. This suggests that we can possibly identify better how members of the public generate their "individual equations in the head" for determining public trust in business. Subsequent studies could explore how these equations are formed, and under what conditions they change. This study focused on broad characteristics of the business and of the public. It could be interesting to see how more specific institutional arrangements, such as executive compensation patterns, corporate governance structures or

---

[86] See, e.g., Paxton, 1996; Putnam, 2000.

corporate social responsibility activities affect individuals' assessment of trust in business. Finally, this work sets up a subsequent body of research on repairing public trust in business by examining stakeholder-level trustworthiness dimensions. Further studies could examine strategies available to organizational actors, and how can they best be deployed to increase public trust in business.

CONCLUSION

The Occupy Wall Street movement highlights the public's low level of trust in business. Business practitioners feel the effects of such reduced trust, e.g., some bankers report that they are afraid to talk about where they are working, posing as consultants. Policy makers are searching for ways to increase the level of public trust in business. Scholars have so far not adequately addressed this issue. While there is existing research that we can draw on, in this chapter we develop a notion of public trust that can support endeavors to increase public trust in business. By distinguishing public trust from previous concepts of trust in the literature and empirically testing its determinants, this study gets us one step closer to better understanding the drivers of public trust in business.

Appendix

ESPOUSED VALUES — USED FOR VALUE CONGRUENCE FACTOR

The theory adopts a definition of human values as desirable goals, varying in importance, that serve as guiding principles in people's lives.[87] The crucial content aspect that distinguishes among values is the type of motivational goal they express.

Ten motivationally distinct types of values have been derived from the universal requirements of human existence and verified in cross-cultural research.[88] These value types are organized on two basic, bipolar dimensions.

- Power: social status and prestige, control or dominance over people and resources (social power, authority, wealth).
- Achievement: personal success through demonstrating competence according to social standards (successful, capable, ambitious, influential).
- Hedonism: pleasure and sensuous gratification for oneself (pleasure, enjoying life).
- Stimulation: excitement, novelty, and challenge in life (daring, a varied life, an exciting life).
- Self-direction: independent thought and action-choosing, creating, exploring (creativity, freedom, independent, curious, choosing own goals, intelligent).
- Universalism: understanding, appreciation, tolerance and protection for the welfare of all people and for nature (broadminded, social justice, equality, a world at peace, a world of beauty, protecting the environment).
- Benevolence: preservation and enhancement of the welfare of people with whom one is in frequent personal contact (helpful, honest, forgiving, loyal, responsible, true friendship).
- Tradition: respect, commitment and acceptance of the customs and ideas that traditional culture or religion provide (humble, accepting my portion in life, devout, respect for tradition).

[87] See: Kluckhohn, 1951; Rokeach, 1973.
[88] Schwartz, 1994; Schwartz and Sagiv, 1995.

- Conformity: restraint of actions, inclinations, and impulses likely to upset or harm others and violate social expectations or norms (politeness, self-discipline, honoring parents and elders).
- Security: safety, harmony and stability of society, or relationships, and of self (family security, national security, moderate, protect public image)

VIGNETTE FACTORS

	Factors		Dimensions		Variable name
1	Size	0	small		SmallCo
		1	regional		ReginalCo
		2	national		NationalCo
		3	global		[NULL]
2	Industry	1	financial services		FinancialSvc
		2	oil and gas		OilGas
		3	pharmaceutical		Pharma
		4	solar		[NULL]
3	Objective	1	maximize *profits* for shareholders		[NULL]
	function	2	maximize *value* for all stakeholders		ValueFcn
		3	*being the best place to work for our employees*		WorkFcn
		4	create general *well-being to society*		SocietyFcn
4	Values		Two values from the list below were randomly assigned to the firm		StrongAgree
			leadership ambition creativity independence curiosity		
			wisdom social justice equality protecting the environment honesty		
			loyalty responsibility self-discipline spirituality		
5	Ability	1–11	continuous variable: Grade A+ through F		AbilityId
6	Benevolence	1–11	continuous variable: Grade A+ through F		BenevolenceId
7	Integrity	1–11	continuous variable: Grade A+ through F		IntegrityId
8	Transparency	1–11	continuous variable: Grade A+ through F		TransparencyId
9	Profitability	1–11	continuous variable: Grade A+ through F		ProfitabilityId

SAMPLE VIGNETTE

A regional company in the oil and gas industry has a stated goal to create value for investors, society, and the environment. Its core values, as stated in the mission statement, are leadership and ambition.

In addition, the oil and gas company received the following scores by an established business magazine.

Ability	Integrity	Benevolence	Transparency	Profitability
Technically and managerially competent	Honest with stakeholders	Cares for stakeholders	Communicates openly with stakeholders	Able to make money consistently
C+	B	D	A+	B

Tell us how much you agree with the statements below.

Question 1: *I trust this company*

Strongly disagree   Strongly agree

SLIDING SCALE

Question 2: *Given the opportunity, I would be willing to work with this company.*

Strongly disagree   Strongly agree

SLIDING SCALE

VIGNETTE TEMPLATE

A [SIZE] company in the [INDUSTRY] industry has stated goal to [FUNCTION]. Its core values, as stated in the mission statement, are [VALUE1] and [VALUE2].

In addition, the [INDUSTRY] company received the following scores by an established business magazine.

Ability	Integrity	Benevolence	Transparency	Profitability
Technically and managerially competent	Honest with stakeholders	Cares for stakeholders	Communicates openly with stakeholders	Able to make money consistently
[ABILITY]	[INTEGRITY]	[BENEVOL]	[TRANSP]	[PROFIT]

ADDITIONAL QUESTIONS

Introductory questions						
Age						
Gender	Male	Female				
Education Level	High school/ GED	2-yr college	4-yr university	Master's	Professional (JD, MD)	Ph.D.
Country of origin	DDLB					
Ethnicity	DDLB					
In what zip code do you reside?						

Experience with business:

How many years of experience do you have working in a business?

Check the industries you or a family member have experience in:

List from above

Tell us how much you agree with the statements below

*In general, I find the **institution** of business to be trustworthy.*

Strongly disagree   Strongly agree

SLIDING SCALE

*In general, I find **people** in business are trustworthy.*

Strongly disagree   Strongly agree

SLIDING SCALE

Asked at the end of the survey:

Please pick your top 5 values from the list ...	Leadership Wisdom Loyalty	Ambition Social justice Responsibility	Creativity Equality Self-discipline	Independence Protecting the environment Spirituality	Curiosity Honesty

REFERENCES

Barber, B. (1983), *The Logic and Limits of Trust*. New Brunswick, NJ: Rutgers University Press.

Barney, J. B. and Hansen, M. H. (1994), 'Trustworthiness as a source of competitive advantage.' *Strategic Management Journal*, 15, 175–190.

Blois, K. J. (1999), 'Trust in business to business relationships: an evaluation of its status.' *Journal of Management Studies*, 36(2), 197–215.

Bohnet, I., and Zeckhauser, R. (2004), 'Trust, risk and betrayal.' *Journal of Economic Behavior and Organization*, 55(4), 467–484.

Buchan, N., Croson, R., and Solnick, S. (2008), 'Trust and gender: an examination of behavior and beliefs in the Investment Game.' *Journal of Economic Behavior and Organization* 68, 466–476.

Clegg, C., Unsworth, K., Epitropaki, O., and Parker, G. (2002), 'Implicating trust in the innovation process.' *Journal of Occupational and Organizational Psychology*, 75(4), 409–423.

Coleman, J. S. (1984), 'Introducing social structure into economic analysis.' *American Economic Review*, 74, 84–88.

Collins, J. and Porras, J. (2002). *Built to Last*. New York: HarperCollins.

Cook, K. and Schilke, O. (2010), 'The role of public, relational and organizational trust in economic affairs.' *Corporate Reputation Review*, 13, 98–109.

Cook, K. S., Hardin, R., and Levi, M. (2005), *Cooperation without Trust?*. New York: Russell Sage Foundation.

Dacin, M. T. 1997. 'Isomorphism in context: the power and prescription of institutional norms.' *Academy of Management Journal*, 40(1), 46–81.

Davis, F. D., Schoorman, F. D., Mayer, R. C., and Tan, H. H. (2000), 'The trusted general manager and business unit performance: empirical evidence of a competitive advantage.' *Strategic Management Journal*, 21(5), 563–576.

Dervitsiotis, K. N. (2003), 'Beyond stakeholder satisfaction: aiming for a new frontier of sustainable stakeholder trust.' *Total Quality Management*, 14(5), 511–524.

DiPiazza, S. A. (2002), *Building Public Trust – The Future of Corporate Reporting*. New York: Wiley.

Dirks, K. T. (1999), 'The effects of interpersonal trust on work group performance.' *Journal of Applied Psychology*, 84, 445–455.

Dirks, K. T. and Ferrin, D. L. (2001), 'The role of interpersonal trust in organizational settings.' *Organization Science*, 12(4), 450–467.

Doney, P. M. and Cannon, J. P. (1997), 'An examination of the nature of trust in buyer–seller relationships.' *Journal of Marketing*, 61, 35–51.

Eckel, C. and Wilson, R. (2003), 'Conditional trust: sex, race, and facial expressions in an experimental trust game.' Virginia Tech University Department of Economics Working Paper Series.

Edelman, R. (2011), Trust Barometer 2011. In E. P. Relations (ed.), http://edelman.com/trust/2011.

Enz, C. (1988), 'The role of value congruity in intraorganizational power.' *Administrative Science Quarterly*, 33, 284–304.

Fichman, M. and Goodman, P. S. (1996), 'Customer supplier ties in interorganizational relations.' In B. M. S. L. L. Cummings (ed.), *Research in Organizational
Behavior*. Greenwich, CT: JAI Press, vol. XVIII, 286–329.

Fombrun, C. J. (1996), *Reputation: Realizing Value from the Corporate Image*.
Boston, MA: Harvard Business School Press.

Fombrun, C. J. and van Riel, C. (2003), *Fame and Fortune – How Successful
Companies Build Winning Reputations*. Upper Saddle River, NJ: Financial
Times-Prentice Hall.

Forum, W. E. (2005), Decline in Trust, 2006: www.weforum.org/site/homepublic.
nsf/Content/Trust+in+Governments,+Corporations+and+Global+Institutions+
Continues+to+Decline.

Forum, W. E. (2006), Decline in Trust, 2006: www2.weforum.org/site/homepublic.
nsf/Content/Full+Survey_+Trust+in+Governments,+Corporations+and+Global
+Institutions+Continues+to+Decline.html: World Economic Forum.

Fukuyama, F. (1995), *Trust: The Social Virtues and the Creation of Prosperity*.
New York: Simon & Schuster.

Ganesan, S. (1994), 'Determinants of long-term orientation in buyer–seller relationships.' *Journal of Marketing* (April), 1–19.

Giddens, A. (1984), *The Constitution of Society: Outline of the Theory of Struc-
turation*. Cambridge: Polity.

Gilligan, C. (1982), *In a Different Voice: Psychological Theory and Women's
Development*. Cambridge, MA: Harvard University Press.

Glaeser, E., Laibson, D., Scheinkman, J., and Soutter, C. (2000), 'Measuring trust.'
Quarterly Journal of Economics, 115(3), 811–846.

Gulati, R. (1995), 'Does familiarity breed trust? The implications of repeated ties
for contractual choice in alliances.' *Academy of Management Journal*, 38(1),
85–112.

Gulati, R. and Westphal, J. D. (1999), 'Cooperative or controlling? The effects of
CEO–board relations and the content of interlocks on the formation of joint
ventures.' *Administrative Science Quarterly*, 44, 473–506.

Hardin, R. (2002), *Trust and Trustworthiness*. New York: Russell Sage Foundation.

Holste, J. S. and Fields, D. (2005), 'The relationship of affect and cognition based
trust with sharing and use of tacit knowledge.' *Academy of Management Best
Conference Paper, MED*, B3–B7.

Jasso, G. (2006), 'Factorial survey methods for studying beliefs and judgments.'
Sociological Methods and Research, 34(3), 334–423.

Jensen, M. (2003), 'The role of network resources in market entry: commercial
banks' entry into investment banking, 1991–1997'. *Administrative Science
Quarterly*, 48, 466–497.

Kluckhohn, C. (1951), 'Values and value-orientations in the theory of action: an exploration in definition and classification.' In T. Parsons and E. Shils (eds.), *Toward a General Theory of Action*. Cambridge, MA: Harvard University Press, 388–433.

Levitt, S. D. and List, J. A. (2007), 'What do laboratory experiments measuring social preferences reveal about the real world?' *Journal of Economic Perspectives*, 21(2), 153–174.

Lewicki, R. J. and Bunker, B. B. (1996), 'Developing and maintaining trust in work relationships.' In R. M. Kramer, and T. R. Tyler (eds.), *Trust in Organizations: Frontiers of Theory and Research*. Thousand Oaks, CA: Sage, 114–139.

Lewis, D. J. and Weigert, A. (1985), 'Trust as a social reality.' *Social Forces*, 63(4), 967–985.

Lewis, J. D. (1999), *Trusted Partners – How Companies Build Mutual Trust and Win Together*. New York: Simon & Schuster.

Luhmann, N. (1979), *Trust: A Mechanism for the Reduction of Social Complexity*. New York: Wiley.

Lynch, J. (1982), 'The concept of external validity.' *Journal of Consumer Research*, 9(3), 240–244.

McAllister, D. J. (1995), 'Affect- and cognition-based trust as foundations for inter-personal cooperation in organizations.' *Academy of Management Journal*, 38(1), 24–59.

McKnight, D. H. and Chervany, N. L. (2002), 'What trust means in e-commerce customer relationships: an interdisciplinary conceptual typology.' *International Journal of Electronic Commerce*, 6(2), 35–53.

McKnight, D. H., Cummings, L. L., and Chervany, N. L. (1998), 'Initial trust formation in new organizational relationships.' *Academy of Management Review*, 23(3), 473–490.

Mayer, R. C., Davis, J. H., and Schoorman, F. D. (1995), 'An integrative model of organizational trust.' *Academy of Management Review*, 20, 709–734.

Mayer, R. C. and Gavin, M. B. (2005), 'Trust in management and performance: who minds the shop while the employees watch the boss?' *Academy of Management Journal*, 48(5), 874–888.

Morgan, R. M. and Hunt, S. D. (1994), 'The commitment–trust theory of relationship marketing.' *Journal of Marketing*, (58), 20–38.

Nahapiet, J. and Ghoshal, S. (1998), 'Social capital, intellectual capital, and the organizational advantage.' *Academy of Management Review*, 23(2), 242–266.

Nock, S. and Gutterbock, T. M. (2010), 'Survey experiments.' In J. Wright and P. Marsden (eds.), *Handbook of Survey Research*, 2nd edn. Bingley, UK: Emerald, 837–864.

Noteboom, B. (1996), 'Trust, opportunism and governance: a process and control model.' *Organizational Studies*, 17(6), 985–1010.

Osterloh, M. and Frey, B. S. (2000), 'Motivation, knowledge transfer, and organizational forms.' *Organization Science*, 11(5), 538–550.

Parsons, T. (1961), *Theories of Society: Foundations of Modern Sociological Theory*. New York: Free Press of Glencoe.

Paxton, P. (1999), 'Is social capital declining in the United States: a multiple indicator assessment.' *American Journal of Sociology*, 105(1): 88–127.

Pirson, M. (2007), *Facing the Trust Gap: How Organizations Can Measure and Manage Stakeholder Trust*. St. Gallen: University of St. Gallen.

Pirson, M. and Malhotra, D. (2011), 'Foundations of organizational trust: what matters to different stakeholders?' *Organization Science*, 22(4), 1087–1104.

Politis, J. D. (2003), 'The connection between trust and knowledge management: what are its implications for team performance.' *Journal of Knowledge Management*, 7(5), 55–66.

Poppo, L. and Schepker, D. J. (2010), 'Repairing public trust in organizations.' *Corporate Reputation Review*, 13, 124–141.

Porter, M., and Kramer, M. (2011), 'The big idea: creating shared value.' *Harvard Business Review*, January–February(1), 1–17.

Putnam, R. D. (2000), *Bowling Alone: The Collapse and Revival of American Community*. New York: Simon & Schuster.

Rokeach, M. (1973), *The Nature of Human Values*. New York: Free Press.

Rossi, P. and Nock, S. (eds.) (1982), *Measuring Social Judgments: The Factorial Survey Approach*. Beverly Hills, CA: Sage.

Rotter, J. B. (1971), 'Generalized expectancies for interpersonal trust.' *American Psychologist*, (26), 443–452.

Rotter, J. B., Chance, J. E., and Phares, E. J. (1972), *Applications of a Social Learning Theory of Personality*. New York: Holt, Rinehart & Winston.

Rousseau, D. M., Sitkin, S. B., Burt, R. S., and Camerer, C. (1998), 'Not so different after all: a cross-discipline view of trust.' *Academy of Management Review*, 23(3), 393–405.

Saparito, P. A., Chen, C., and Sapienza, H. J. (2004), 'The role of relational trust in bank–small firm relationships.' *Academy of Management Journal*, 47(3), 400–410.

Schwartz, S. H. (1994), 'Are there universal aspects in the content and structure of values?' *Journal of Social Issues*, 50: 19–45.

Schwartz, S. H. and Sagiv, L. (1995), 'Identifying culture-specifics in the content and structure of values.' *Journal of Cross-Cultural Psychology*, 26(1), 92–116.

Sheppard, B. H. and Sherman, D. A. (1998), 'The grammars of trust: a model and general implications.' *Academy of Management Review*, 23(3), 422–437.

Simmel, G. (1908), *Soziologie. Untersuchungen über die Formen der Vergesellschaftung*. Berlin: Duncker and Humblot Verlag.

Sprenger, R. K. (2002), *Vertrauen führt- worauf es im Unternehmen wirklich ankommt*. Frankfurt am Main: campus.

Swift, T. (2001), 'Trust, reputation and corporate accountability to stakeholders.' *Business Ethics: A European Review*, 10(1), 15–26.

Sztompka, P. (1999), *Trust: A Sociological Theory*. Cambridge, UK: Cambridge University Press.

Tsai, W. and Ghoshal, S. (1998), 'Social capital and value creation: the role of intrafirm networks.' *Academy of Management Journal*, 41(4), 464–477.

Turnbull, S. (2002), *A New Way to Govern – Organizations and Society after Enron*. London: New Economics Foundation.

Uzzi, B. (1997), 'Social structure and competition in interfirm networks: the paradox of embeddedness.' *Administrative Science Quarterly*, 42, 35–67.

Wallander, L. (2009), '25 years of factorial surveys in sociology: a review.' *Social Science Research*, 38, 505–520.

Whitener, E. M., Brodt, S. E., Korsgaard, M. A., and Werner, J. M. (1998), 'Managers as initiators of trust: an exchange relationship framework for understanding managerial trustworthy behavior.' *Academy of Management Review*, 23(3), 513–531.

Williams, M. (2001), 'In whom we trust: group membership as an affective context for trust development.' *Academy of Management Journal*, 28(3), 377–396.

Williamson, O. E. (1988), 'Corporate finance and corporate governance.' *Journal of Finance*, 43(3), 567–591.

Williamson, O. E. (1993), 'Calculativeness, trust, and economic organization.' *Journal of Law and Economics*, 36(1), 453–486.

Yaniv, E., and Farkas, F. 2005. 'The impact of person–organization fit on the corporate brand perception of employees and customers.' *Journal of Change Management*, 5(4), 447–461.

Zucker, L. G. (1986), 'Production of trust: institutional sources of economic structure.' In B. M. S. L. L. Cummings (ed.), *Research in Organizational Behavior*. Greenwich, CT: JAI Press, vol. VIII, 53–111.

6 The role of public, relational, and organizational trust in economic affairs

Karen S. Cook and Oliver Schilke

EXECUTIVE SUMMARY

THE SITUATION

Trust not only saves on transaction costs, it also increases the overall efficiency of a system. It enables the production of more goods (or more of what a group values, if we focus on so-called public goods) at less cost. But trust cannot be simply produced on demand and it cannot be bought or sold on the open market.

The lack of mutual trust represents a loss: beyond the specific economic loss at the transactional level, there is a contribution to the deterioration in the effective functioning of the political system and other collective undertakings.

KEY QUESTIONS

To what extent does a lack of public trust weaken the foundations of the institutions that provide for the smooth functioning of society? What impact do public trust, relational trust, and organizational trust have on the economy?

NEW KNOWLEDGE

When two partner firms are very familiar with one another, organizational culture is a critical factor in trustworthiness. Contractual safeguards become more significant when the reputation of the alliance firm is less favorable.

Societies are evolving away from trust relationships toward externally regulated behavior. This is in part due to changes in the ways in which people relate to one another. People have gradually become less reliant on the "thick" relations of trust and normative control typical of small communities, and have come to depend on larger networks of "thin" relations of trust and cooperation that typify relationships spread out over geographic space.

KEY LESSONS

Verifying the trustworthiness of others has become a more difficult undertaking. The increasing complexity of business operations makes oversight more difficult, if not impossible.

In such a world, public trust in institutions may continue to be fairly low, even though at the personal level (my own banker or doctor) or even at the organizational level (my local bank or group medical practice) there may be room for increased trust, given proper organizational incentives.

INTRODUCTION

One of the most significant economists of our time is Kenneth Arrow, who argued over three decades ago that trust has implications for the economy as well as the polity. In the current "economic crisis" his words seem prophetic. For Arrow, trust has not only economic value but also sheer pragmatic value. It simply makes life easier. Like Luhmann, Arrow viewed trust as an important lubricant of a social system: "It is extremely efficient; it saves a lot of trouble to have a fair degree of reliance on other people's word."[1] Note here that the term trust is meant to imply honesty and integrity – that one's word can be counted on.

Arrow argues that trust not only saves on transaction costs (the concept Oliver Williamson made famous), it also increases the efficiency of a system. It enables the production of more goods (or more of what a group values if we focus on public goods) at less cost. But it cannot be simply produced on demand and it cannot be bought and sold on the open market, to carry his economic analysis of trust

[1] Arrow, 1974, 23.

further. In his words, "it is not even necessarily very easy for it to be achieved."[2] In fact he was not at all sure how it could be produced in societies in which it does not exist. Reflecting a theme that is central to the subsequent work of Francis Fukuyama, almost two decades later, Arrow argued that one of the properties of those societies classified as less developed economically is the lack of mutual trust (or what Fukuyama and others later came to refer to as generalized trust).[3]

The lack of mutual trust makes collective undertakings difficult, if not impossible, since individuals cannot know when they engage in an action to benefit another that the action will be reciprocated. It is not only the problem of not knowing who to trust, it is also the problem of having others not know whether they can trust you. Arrow's discussion of trust and its economic implications is brief, but brings to the surface some of the fundamental problems with treating markets (and prices) as the main mechanism for coordinating the interests of individuals within a society or at least the limits of price as a governance mechanism. The lack of mutual trust, Arrow points out, represents a distinct loss economically as well as a loss in the smooth running of the political system which requires the success of collective undertakings.

The economic value of trust in Arrow's view thus has mainly to do with its role in the production of public goods. Individuals have to occasionally respond to the demands of society even when such demands conflict with their own individual interests. Certainly, trust has been viewed over the decades as central in the solution of what has come to be known as the prisoner's dilemma and by extension many social dilemmas. The two prisoners captured and placed in separate rooms by interrogators must trust each other enough not to turn state's evidence on their partner in crime. If they do, both end up with the worst possible outcomes, mutual conviction. If they maintain mutual trust and remain silent, in the classic version of the prisoner's dilemma, they go free, obtaining the best possible outcome. Without trust, each defects independently sending them both to jail

[2] *Ibid.*, 36.   [3] Fukuyama, 1995.

for the maximum amount of time. A long tradition of experimental work in social psychology and economics provides evidence of the frequent failure of mutual trust under such circumstances.[4] As Arrow notes: "the agreement to trust each other cannot be bought."[5]

The work on collective trust, generalized trust, and, more recently what is called "public trust," that followed Arrow's famous essay continues to investigate the role of trust in the provision of public goods and in public life more generally. Without generalized trust, many argue that the collective action problems of our day cannot be solved easily. Ostrom and Walker, in their review of the various solutions to collective action problems, provide evidence of this fact.[6] There are many ways in which collective action problems are solved in different contexts, only one of which relies on the assumption that generalized trust works to solve the incentive problems involved. Without public trust many of the institutions that provide the foundations for the smooth functioning of society are weakened if not made wholly ineffective at best. At worst, lack of transparency and perceived incompetence serve as the seedbed of corruption.

Arrow's brief treatment of trust foreshadowed much later discussions of the role of trust in the economy. Perhaps the most widely read in the 1990s was Francis Fukuyama's major treatise, *Trust: The Social Virtues and the Creation of Prosperity*, on the economic implications of trust. This book investigates the links between social variables such as trust or reliability and various economic outcomes. He goes so far as to argue that there are major cultural differences in economic success that are based on the levels of what he terms general social trust in the societies he considers including, Japan, the United States, China, France, South Korea, Germany, Great Britain, Italy, and Russia. He analyzes some of the factors that support such a claim.[7]

If, as Fukuyama argues, the ability of companies to move from large hierarchies to flexible networks of smaller firms depends on the degree of trust and social capital in the broader society, then

---

[4] Cook and Cooper, 2003.   [5] Arrow, 1974, 26.
[6] Ostrom and Walker, 2003.   [7] Fukuyama, 1995.

understanding how trust emerges and how it varies across cultures is important in the effort to analyze what makes for economic success in different settings. Others are concerned less with economic performance and more concerned with the social and political consequences of different levels of trust in various cultures (e.g., Japan, China, Germany, the emerging capitalist societies in the former Soviet Union, and the United States). In the United States, for example, it is sometimes argued that it is the breakdown in community and the trust it fosters that is associated with increased criminal activity, violence, and anomie all of which have consequences for economic enterprises in urban areas. Uslaner and Brown and others have studied the links between general social trust and various indicators of inequality, which has been increasing in the United States as well as in many other countries and has been argued to be at the core of decreasing generalized trust.[8]

Fukuyama reasons that it is social trust that generates the conditions under which specific forms of organization emerge that facilitate competitive economic enterprise.[9] Arrow argues that economic productivity is hampered by monitoring and sanctioning, when it is required for managing relations based on distrust.[10] Both arguments are transaction cost arguments. It is the lack of social trust that Fukuyama identifies as the reason that organizations adopt a more hierarchical form (including large networks of organizations created by contracting). The more flexible networks of smaller firms that engage in exchange require trust. In Fukuyama's words: "A 'virtual' firm can have abundant information coming through network wires about its suppliers and contractors. But if they are all crooks or frauds, dealing with them will remain a costly process involving complex contracts and time-consuming enforcement. Without trust, there will be strong incentive to bring these activities in-house and restore old hierarchies."[11] Traditional hierarchical forms of governance are thus

---

[8] Uslaner and Brown, 2005.   [9] Fukuyama, 1995.
[10] Arrow, 1974.   [11] Fukuyama, 1995, 25.

viewed as inimical to modern global economic activity resulting in lower economic performance.

It is precisely the ability to be flexible and to form networks of small companies that can be responsive to change that Fukuyama identifies as central to economic growth and prosperity. Cultures that fit this motif are poised for economic success in the global economy. Ironically, he argues that it is precisely those cultures with strong and large families that have lower social trust and national prosperity. Fukuyama refers to this claim as the "paradox of family values."[12]

Oliver Williamson views trust as having a much narrower role in the economy, treating trust as largely relevant only in the realm of personal relations and not at all in economic relations that he characterizes as laden with opportunism. His work is at odds with much that has been written on the role of trust in the economy. In some respects Williamson has a more "romantic" view of trust, wanting to limit the term to the situation in which calculativeness is suspended. For Williamson, the concept trust loses its meaning if it is not restricted to apply exclusively to personal relations. In his view personal and commercial relations are based on completely different logics involving completely distinct forms of underlying calculus.[13] Other social scientists such as Fukuyama make much broader claims concerning the role of trust in society.

Bradach and Eccles in their *Annual Review of Sociology* article, for example, view trust as one type of control system to be distinguished from price and authority, building upon Arrow's early treatment of governance mechanisms.[14] Reliability and flexibility are important aspects of business relations and Bradach and Eccles associate these characteristics with trust relations. It is especially under uncertainty that trust becomes an important determinant of transactions as exchange partners seek out those who are trustworthy and likely to be reliable in continued exchange.

---

[12] *Ibid.*   [13] Williamson, 1993.   [14] Bradach and Eccles, 1989.

In related experimental literature Yamagishi *et al.*, among others, demonstrate that uncertainty leads to commitment among exchange partners as they attempt to avoid opportunism and potential exploitation or defaults.[15] This same phenomenon is called "relational contracting" in an older literature.[16] The tendency to form committed relations and to "lock-in" has some associated opportunity costs since committed exchange partners may not explore new relations that might yield better terms. It is this "stickiness" to certain partnerships often created by trust and commitment that may have significant effects on economic outcomes, especially if there are fundamental changes in the economy such as may be created by new technologies and new or rapidly expanding markets for trade and production. There is also the tendency to stick with exchange partners under conditions of high economic uncertainty and risk, which may lead to missed opportunities when economic conditions change.

Sociologists and anthropologists who study the economy have come to conclusions similar to those of Arrow concerning the role of trust in economic endeavors. Trust, when it exists, can reduce various kinds of costs, including, but not limited to, transaction costs. Granovetter, for example, views economic relations as one class of social relations.[17] In this view economic transactions are frequently embedded in social structures that are formed by the social ties among actors. A network of social relations thus represents a kind of "market" in which goods are bought and sold or bartered. In addition, they set the terms of exchange sometimes altering the mode of exchange as well as the content of the negotiations. Trust discourages malfeasance and opportunism in part because when transactions are embedded in social relations reputations come into play. Individuals, he argues, have an incentive to be trustworthy to secure the possibility of future transactions. Continuing social relations characterized by trust have the property that they constrain opportunistic behavior because of the value of the association. Hardin's book *Trust and*

---

[15] Yamagishi *et al.*, 1998.   [16] See Macauley, 1963.   [17] Granovetter, 1985.

Trustworthiness portrays an encapsulated interest theory of trust, which is also based on this logic.[18]

RELATIONAL TRUST

Trust can be defined in relational terms as the belief that the trustee will take one's interests to heart. In the encapsulated interest view of trust articulated in Hardin's 2002 book, *Trust and Trustworthiness* and expanded in Cook *et al.*, A trusts B with respect to x when A believes that her interests are included in B's utility function, so that B values what A desires *because* B wants to maintain good relations with A.[19] Others define trust as the belief that the trustee will not take advantage of one's vulnerability. If I perceive someone as trustworthy, I am less likely to monitor her behavior or performance. In this way trust reduces the cost of monitoring. It may also reduce transaction costs.

In a study of physician–patient trust Cook *et al.* argue that trust is central to the smooth functioning of professional–client relations in the medical world, as well as in other contexts.[20] But the perception of the extent to which physicians in general fulfill their fiduciary role to patients at large has clearly declined over the past few decades.[21] As Imber notes in his lengthy treatment of trust in doctors, the physician in the early decades was not only a healer, but also a "man" of integrity. A good physician was a "good man" who was competent and, importantly, someone who was a person of character and obligation, as immortalized by Hippocrates in what has become the sacred oath that physicians in training take.

One key reason for examining the role of trust in physician–patient relations is to investigate the ways in which trust "saves" not only on transaction costs but, literally, in terms of reductions in the cost of the delivery of care (e.g., a decrease in the duplication of services). Physicians often cited trust in a patient as one factor in their

---

[18] Hardin, 2002; see also Cook *et al.*, 2005.   [19] Hardin, 2002; Cook *et al.*, 2005.
[20] Cook, *et al.*, 2004a.   [21] Imber, 2008.

decisions regarding treatment options. In addition, both patients and physicians talked about how trust made it possible for the physician to respond to patient concerns over the phone or by email when they had established a long-term relationship characterized by trust.

Separate from the decline in trust in the "profession" of doctoring, public trust in those who manage and deliver health care has also declined. What we found in our interviews with patients and physicians is that often patients trusted their own personal physicians (especially if they had a longer-term relationship with them) and they sometimes transferred this trust to the group practice level and to the organization in which the practitioners were embedded, but this also depended heavily on the general reputation of the organization. Both past experience and reputation mattered in their assessments of trustworthiness.

In contrast, just one relatively negative experience with a physician in the group led to continued wariness and lack of trust that generalized to the organizational context. While there is no simple way in which dyadic, relational trust transfers to larger units in which the dyad is embedded, it is one path by which trust can be rebuilt when distrust exists. Both physicians and patients talked at length about the ways in which trust could be established through specific behaviors and about the value of trust for treatment decisions as well as compliance (or adherence to medical regimens). Several patients also spoke eloquently about the ways in which specific physician actions had undermined their trust in all physicians. In such situations it was difficult for these patients to trust any physician. With distrust that has generalized, rebuilding trust at the relational level may be one of the only mechanisms for resolving the underlying trust breach.

It is interesting that individuals often seem to maintain belief in the honesty and trustworthiness of their own physicians even as their confidence in the profession of medicine at large and the leaders in the field has diminished. This is also typically true of evaluations of local politicians in contrast to politicians in general. Organizational mechanisms for ensuring trustworthiness have arisen in part due to this decline in confidence in the profession of medicine (and health care in general). Ironically, the imposition of such mechanisms often undermines trust at the interpersonal level. But, despite the rise of organizational mechanisms for ensuring trustworthiness, trust still has an important role to play in physician–patient relations in which one party is more vulnerable (or less powerful) than the other and monitoring cannot be fully effective. The role of trust, however, has diminished over time as the stakes for malpractice have risen and economic factors have driven a wedge between patients and their physicians increasing the perception that conflicts of interest exist that undermine trust.[22] This macro-level fact has had negative implications for public trust in the healthcare system (as current news accounts reveal in the most recent efforts to reform the system in the United States).

There is an important distinction between trust in individuals and trust in the organization in which they are embedded, which is based in part on the nature of the roles individuals play in the organization and the extent to which they fulfill their roles. This is as true of physicians and nurses in the medical context as it is in the business world. Cook *et al.* discuss the nature of professional associations and the role they play in maintaining the reputation of the profession.[23] The AMA (American Medical Association) is an example of a proactive professional association that has worked hard to protect the reputation of physicians and their authority over the conditions of practice. At the same time, increasing public lack of trust in various professionals – not just doctors but priests, pastors, lawyers and teachers as well – has resulted in increasing organizational controls and monitoring of compliance with professional ethics. When people have little confidence not only in politicians, doctors, and lawyers, but also in business executives who distort stock prices or engage in "creative," but illegal accounting practices, attention shifts to the

---

[22] Mechanic, 1998.   [23] Cook *et al.*, 2005.

failure of organizational incentive structures and the relevant regulations to restrain opportunism, sanction the untrustworthy, and remove those who are grossly incompetent.

ORGANIZATIONAL TRUST

Powell conceives trust as similar to human or moral capital operating distinctly differently than physical forms of capital.[24] The supply of trust, he argues, increases with use rather than decreasing in value. Trust is not depleted in the same way that physical capital is over time when it is used. Powell identifies a number of types of business networks in which trust plays a role in the organization of economic activity.[25] For example, in research and development networks such as those in Silicon Valley, trust is formed and maintained through professional memberships in relevant associations, a high degree of information flow across the network and by frequent shifting of employees across organizational boundaries. In another example Powell explores the role of trust in business groups such as the Japanese keiretsu and the Korean chaebol. In these business groups trust emerges out of a mixture of common membership in the group, perceived obligation, and vigilance. Long-term repeat interactions are key to the establishment of trust relations in this context as well as in most circumstances in which trust relations emerge. Repeat interactions provide the opportunity for learning, monitoring, dyadic sanctioning, and increasing mutual dependence, which reinforces the basis for trust.

In a study of the garment industry, Brian Uzzi (1997) also identifies the nature of the social relations that link economic actors in ways that determine economic performance.[26] Two types of relationships seem to have been common among firms in the manufacturing business, those characterized as close relations, and those characterized as arm's-length relations. Those connected by "close" relationships were more likely to be trusting and cooperative, even

---

[24] Powell, 1996.   [25] *Ibid.*   [26] Uzzi, 1997.

though the same individuals could be self-interested and businesslike in their arm's-length relations. In the close relationships the individuals would more often engage in joint problem solving, transfer finer grained information to one another, and generally be more trusting. In contrast, the arm's-length relationships were more typically economic relations characterized by lack of reciprocity, less continuity, and a focus on narrowly economic matters. Trust developed in relations between manufacturers when extra effort was initially offered voluntarily and then reciprocated, in much the same way that Blau, in his influential 1964 book, *Exchange and Power in Social Life*, suggests that trust emerges in social exchange relations. Uzzi notes that this extra effort might involve giving an exchange partner preferred treatment, offering overtime, or placing an order before it was needed to help a partner during a slow time. Trust relations involved less monitoring.

In other industries, sociologists have found that trust relations can sometimes impede economic success. For example, Mizruchi and Stearns examined the role of trust in the closure of bank deals.[27] Under uncertainty, they discovered investment bankers turned to customers they had close ties to, involving trust relations. By engaging in deals with their close friends they were less successful in actually completing deals, thus this practice entailed an economic cost to the banking industry. It may have been that the bankers were unwilling to exercise the same degree of authority over their friends in bringing their deals to close. The latitude one extends a friend in this context thus had a negative impact on the profitability of the banks involved.

Trust between partners in an alliance reduces the need for hierarchical controls.[28] Higher levels of trust among partners to an alliance results in fewer concerns over opportunism or exploitation because the firms have greater confidence in the predictability and reliability of one another. Alliances between firms that view each

---

[27] Mizruchi and Stearns, 2001.　　[28] Gulati and Singh, 1998.

other as trustworthy lower coordination costs, improving efficiency in part because the firms are more likely to be willing to learn each other's rules and standard operating procedures. Without such trust, hierarchical controls and systems of monitoring and sanctioning are more often put into place to implement the alliance and to ensure success, though frequently increasing the overall cost of the enterprise.

Schilke and Cook specify one relatively simple model concerning the role of trust in strategic alliances formed between firms primarily for research and development in Germany.[29] They focus on the determinants of trustworthiness. In a recent study data were collected from firms that had been engaged in strategic alliances in various industries including chemicals, electronics, machinery, motor vehicles, and information technology. The core firms were asked to identify some of their key partners and data were then collected from the partner firms to provide dyadic data. Unfortunately, some of the firms in the sample were unwilling to provide the names and identifiers of their partner firms citing confidentiality (as well as strategic) reasons for maintaining the anonymity of their partners in ongoing ventures. The eventual sample of firms included dyadic data from 210 managers. Key informants in the R&D units of each firm provided relevant information on these alliances. The final dyadic sample included data on 167 dyads (after attrition at each stage of the study). Below we identify some of the relevant factors that entered into the trustworthiness assessments of these firms.

The two primary elements we examined in terms of assessments of the trustworthiness of alliance partners were organizational culture and level of contractual safeguards. We defined trustworthiness as an attribute of an exchange partner. Conceptually it refers to the extent to which that partner is viewed as unlikely to exploit any vulnerabilities the other partner has. The typical dimensions of trustworthiness identified in the organizational trust literature include ability (or competence), benevolence, and integrity.[30] All three

---

[29] Schilke and Cook, 2009.   [30] Mayer et al., 1995.

dimensions tend to be a part of trustworthiness judgments. We used scales previously developed for organizations. Ability refers to the competencies of the trustee that enable it to perform relevant tasks effectively. Benevolence refers to the extent to which the truster wants the trustee to do well. In personal relationships it refers to generosity and the willingness to help the trustee. Integrity is the extent to which one can rely on the word or promise entailed in the trust relationship. It involves the perception on the part of the truster that the trustee adheres to a set of principles that are known and that imply integrity. All of these dimensions are attributes of the trustee, while trust is typically a characteristic of a relationship between two entities.

In our study we used measures of ability that were adapted from Johnson *et al.* and measures of benevolence based on those used by Ganesan *et al.*[31] The integrity measures were developed based on the work of Dyer and Chu (2003).[32] The key independent variables, organizational culture, and contractual safeguards were also measured using items previously developed (or adapted) for the organizational level.

Contractual safeguards are stipulations included in the partnership agreement that impose penalties on a party for non-fulfillment of obligations or expected performance or for failure to cooperate as specified in the agreement.[33] Organizational culture has many dimensions but we used Barney's definition, which specifies culture as the complex set of beliefs, values, assumptions, and symbols that define the way a firm conducts its business.[34] Cameron and Freeman conceptualized and operationalized four key types of organizational culture (hierarchy, market, clan, and adhocracy).[35] Given that clan culture has been argued to be more closely linked to trust,[36] we measured the extent to which the firms in our sample could be

---

[31] Johnson *et al.*, 1996; Ganesan, 1994; Scheer, *et al.* 2003.
[32] Dyer and Chu, 2003. All scales were seven-point Likert scales ranging from 1 (strongly disagree) to 7 (strongly agree).
[33] Parkhe, 1993.   [34] Barney, 1986.   [35] Cameron and Freeman, 1991.
[36] McEvily *et al.*, 2003, 92.

characterized as having a clan culture, defined as emphasizing participation, cohesiveness, and teamwork.

Control variables included industry type, firm size, and firm
age, all factors that may impact the degree to which trustworthiness
matters. Moderating variables included familiarity – the extent to
which the exchange partners had had experience with each other,
and reputation – the extent to which the public knew about the firm
and their perception of its products and prospects in comparison with
competing firms in the industry. Based on previous research we
reasoned that familiarity and reputation would moderate the effect
of organizational culture and the presence of contractual safeguards
on assessments of trustworthiness. Both clan culture and contractual
safeguards are antecedents of trustworthiness, but their relative
importance in the establishment of the trustworthiness of the firm
varies by characteristics of the firm.[37] In particular, our research
indicates that when familiarity is high between two partner firms,
organizational culture is more important as the origin of trustworthiness. In addition, we find that contractual safeguards are more significant understandably when the reputation of the alliance firm is less
favorable. Such safeguards may be viewed as increasingly essential in
settings which are more economically volatile. Alliance partners will
require it and the public will want such assurance as a precursor to
investment decisions (sometimes made with very little information
when public trust and confidence in business was much higher).

Under some circumstances, research indicates that trust
and trustworthiness can improve the workings of organizations and
markets. In these instances, however, trust and trustworthiness tend
to be *complements* to structured incentives and to monitoring and
enforcement mechanisms.[38] The backdrop of third-party enforcement
can give individuals confidence to treat each other as if they are
trustworthy – at least in those domains where violations of trust will

[37] See Schilke and Cook, 2009 for more details of the study and the findings.
[38] See also Arrow, 1974, 24.

be punished or in which little is at stake. This may enable individuals to learn more about each other, to begin to take risks with each other, and in time to become trustworthy to each other. Examples of third-party enforcers abound: legal institutions that enforce contracts, managers who supervise employee relationships with clients, professional associations that investigate unethical behavior of their members, and hospital boards that inhibit malpractice. They not only boost the probability of reliable behaviors but also create the conditions for cooperation and trust. In an era of decreasing public trust in the world of business such mechanisms may be critical for the reestablishment of confidence and trust in economic institutions in general.

In the world of informal economies, Portes and Sensenbrenner analyze the role of trust in economic outcomes for immigrants to empirically demonstrate the impact of the embeddedness of economic activities in social relations.[39] In particular, trust plays a big role in the informal economy in which immigrants are able to barter and trade services outside of the formal economy with individuals they deem trustworthy in their personal networks. (Such informal economic transaction systems are rapidly growing as a result of the current economic crisis. Trade and barter of personal items and services now occurs over the internet and is spreading globally – e.g., Freecycle.org.) Immigrants also use their social networks as a kind of social capital when they enter a new country to provide access to critical resources such as educational and training opportunities, entry jobs, and the provision of food and shelter until they can become established on their own terms. These social networks provide the social capital the immigrants need to get established in a new land. Some of these network ties represent trust relations – others do not; thus, it is important to distinguish between trust and social capital. There are also downsides to the use of social networks for immigrants. Closed networks may result which lock the employees into low wage jobs with little time to develop the human capital

[39] Portes and Sensenbrenner, 1993.

that would be needed to move up and out of the protective environment of their enclave.

In an interesting historical study of the US economy between 1840 and 1920, Lynne Zucker identified three basic modes of trust production in society.[40] First, there is process-based trust that is tied to a history of past or expected exchange (e.g., gift exchange). Reputations work to support trust-based exchange because past exchange behavior provides accurate information that can easily be disseminated in a network of communal relations. Process-based trust has high information requirements and works best in small societies or organizations. The second type of trust she identifies is characteristic-based trust in which trust is tied to a particular person, depending on characteristics such as family background or ethnicity. The third type of trust is institutional-based trust, which ties trustworthiness to formal societal structures that function to support cooperation. Such structures include third-party intermediaries and professional associations or other forms of certification that remove risk. Government regulation and legislation also provide the institutional background for cooperation, lowering the risk of default or opportunism. High rates of immigration, internal migration, and the instability of business enterprises from the mid 1800s to the early 1900s, Zucker argues, disrupted process-based trust relations.

The move to institutional bases for securing trustworthiness was historically inevitable. Studies by Greif et al. and other economic historians of the emergence of various institutional devices for securing cooperation in long-distance trade in much earlier periods support this claim.[41] Such devices seem to be the focus of political and public attention in the current period of economic crisis and the reemergence of instability in businesses – including large banking and investment institutions formerly viewed as highly stable, and thus worthy of long-term investment. Restoring confidence in these institutions will require a lot of work by politicians as well as those in the business

---

[40] Zucker, 1986.   [41] Greif et al., 1995.

world. It is not at all clear that past mechanisms for ensuring trust-worthiness will garner the public trust after such cataclysmic losses and the attendant unemployment that has affected all sectors of the economy.

A number of economists and sociologists seem to agree that trust does play a role in the economy, but precisely how and in what ways is still under investigation. In Susan Shapiro's 1984 book, *Wayward Capitalists*, trust is viewed as the foundation of capital-ism. Building on the work of Macaulay and others,[42] she argues that financial transactions could not easily occur without trust because most contracts are incomplete. This theme is reflected in much of the work on contracts and is the reason for many alliances and cooperative agreements that build trust between the relevant parties. In significant ways, trust can be said to provide the social foundations for economic relations of exchange and production. Monitoring is often ineffective. Sanctioning can be costly. Transac-tion costs can be high. To the extent that actors are trustworthy with respect to their commitments such costs can be reduced within organizations and in the economy more broadly. But without the institutional backing of contract law and other forms of legal protec-tion, few societies rely strictly on the vagaries of personal relations. This seems only to happen when institutional backing is weak or non-existent and when interpersonal relations are the primary locus of exchange (often in developing countries suffering under political instability and corruption). In economies under transition from one major form of economic organization to another, as in the transitions that have occurred in post-communist societies, reliance on personal networks and trust relations can serve an important step in the evolution to systems of trade that require interactions with strangers in the context of market economies. This transition, however, can be highly problematic and can be fraught with risk, as in the case of Russia.[43]

---

[42] Shapiro, 1984; Macaulay, 1963.   [43] Radaev, 2004; Cook *et al.*, 2004b.

Restoring public trust in economic enterprises and in other arenas in society in which trust has declined (e.g., the world of professions including doctors, lawyers, priests, and politicians) will not be easy. We have tried to articulate in a few domains how personal relations of trust, organizational level trust, and general social trust are linked. But there is more work to be done on this topic, theoretically, methodologically, and empirically. Cook *et al.* argue that "Societies are essentially evolving away from trust relationships toward externally regulated behavior."[44] This is in part due to the change in the ways in which we relate to one another. We have evolved over long periods of time away from thick relations of trust and normative control in small communities to larger networks of thin relations of trust and cooperation with many people spread out in geographic space. This has altered the fundamental ways in which business is accomplished and has implications for the potential for trust relations, assessments of trustworthiness, and modes of cooperation. It also has implications for the capacity of the public to know enough to "trust" any institution in the traditional sense. The best we might accomplish is to regain confidence that these institutions are being given proper oversight and that there is legal recourse for those who are the victims of exploitation. A major difficulty is that the scale of business operations has become so complex and interrelated in many sectors that providing such oversight is increasingly complicated, if not impossible. In such a world, public trust in institutions may continue to be fairly low, even though at the personal level (my banker or doctor) or even at the organizational level (my local bank or group medical practice) there may be room for increased trust, given proper organizational incentives. Further research on these complex issues in an increasingly interdependent and global world of economic activity is needed.

[44] Cook *et al.*, 2005, 196.

REFERENCES

Arrow, K. J. (1974), *The Limits of Organization*. New York: W.W. Norton.

Barney, J. B. (1986), 'Organizational culture: can it be a source of sustained competitive advantage?' *Academy of Management Review*, 11(3), 656–665.

Barney, J. B. and Hansen, M. H. (1994), 'Trustworthiness as a source of competitive advantage.' *Strategic Management Journal*, 15(8), 175–190.

Blau, P. M. (1964), *Exchange and Power in Social Life*. New York: Wiley.

Bradach, J. L. and Eccles, R. G. (1989), 'Price, authority, and trust: from ideal types to plural forms.' *Annual Review of Sociology*, 15, 97–118.

Cameron, K. S. and Freeman, S. J. (1991), 'Cultural congruence, strength, and type: relationships to effectiveness.' In R. Woodman, and W. A. Passmore (eds.), *Research in Organizational Change and Development*. Greenwich, CT: JAI Press, vol. V, 23–58.

Cook, K. S. (ed.). 2001. *Trust in society*. New York: Russell Sage.

Cook, K. S. and Cooper, R. M. (2003), 'Experimental studies of cooperation, trust and social exchange.' In E. Ostrom and J. Walker (eds.), *Trust and Reciprocity: Interdisciplinary Lessons for Experimental Research*. New York: Russell Sage Foundation, 209–244.

Cook, K. S., Kramer, R., Thom, D., Bailey, S., Stepanikova, I., and Cooper, R. (2004a), 'Physician–patient trust relations in an era of managed care.' In R. Kramer and K. S. Cook (eds.), *Trust and Distrust in Organizations*. New York: Russell Sage Foundation.

Cook, K. S., Rice, E. R. W., and Gerbasi, A. (2004b), 'The emergence of trust networks under uncertainty: the case of transitional economies – insights from social psychological research.' In S. Rose-Ackerman, B. Rothstein, and J. Kornai (eds.), *Problems of Post Socialist Transition: Creating Social Trust*. New York: Palgrave Macmillan.

Cook, K. S., Hardin, R., and Levi, M. (2005), *Cooperation without Trust?* New York: Russell Sage Foundation.

Dyer, J. and Chu, W. (2003), 'The role of trustworthiness in reducing transaction costs and improving performance: empirical evidence from the United States, Japan, and Korea.' *Organization Science* (special issue: 'Trust in an organizational context'), 13(1), 57–68.

Fukuyama, F. (1995), *Trust: The Social Virtues and the Creation of Prosperity*. New York: Free Press.

Gambetta, D. and Hamill, H. (2006), *Streetwise: How Taxi Drivers Establish Customers' Trustworthiness*. New York: Russell Sage Foundation.

Gamesan, S. (1994), 'Determinants of long-term orientation in buyer–seller relationships.' *Journal of marketing*, 58(2), 1–19.

Granovetter, M. (1985), 'Economic institutions as social constructions: a framework for analysis.' *American Journal of Sociology*, 91, 481–510.

Greif, A., Milgrom, P., and Weingast, B. R. (1995), 'Coordination, commitment, and enforcement: the case of the merchant guild.' In J. Knight and H. Sened (eds.), *Explaining Social Institutions*. Ann Arbor, MI: University of Michigan Press, 27–56.

Gulati, R. and Singh, H. (1998), 'The architecture of cooperation: managing coordination costs and appropriation concerns in strategic alliances.' *Administrative Science Quarterly*, 43, 781–814.

Hardin, R. (1996), 'Trustworthiness.' *Ethics*, 107, 26–42.

Hardin, R. (2002), *Trust and Trustworthiness*. New York: Russell Sage Foundation.

Imber, J. (2008), *Trusting Doctors*. New York: Palgrave Macmillan.

Johnson, J. L., Cullen, J. B., Sakano, T., and Takenouchi, H. (1996), 'Setting the stage for trust and strategic integration in Japanese–US cooperative alliances.' *Journal of International Business Studies*, 27(5), 981–1004.

Leonidou, L. C., Palihawadana, D., and Theodosiou, M. (2006), 'An integrated model of the behavioural dimensions of industrial buyer–seller relationships.' *European Journal of Marketing*, 40(1/2), 145–174.

Macaulay, S. (1963), 'Non-contractual relations in business: a preliminary study.' *American Sociological Review*, 28, 55–67.

McEvily, B., Perrone, V., and Zaheer, A. (2003), 'Trust as an organizing principle.' *Organization Science*, 14, 91–103.

Malhotra, D. and Murnighan, K. (2002), 'The effects of contracts on interpersonal trust.' *Administrative Science Quarterly*, 47(3), 534–559.

Mayer, R. C., Davis, J. H., and Schoorman, F. D. (1995), 'An integrative model of organizational trust.' *Academy of Management Review*, 20(3), 709–734.

Mechanic, David. 1998. 'The functions and limitations of trust in the provision of medical care.' *Journal of Health Politics, Policy, and Law*. 23 (4): 661–86.

Mizruchi, M. S. and Brewster, L. (2001), 'Getting deals done: the use of social networks in bank decision-making.' *American Sociological Review*, 66, 647–671.

Ostrom, E. and Walker, J. (2003), *Trust and Reciprocity: Interdisciplinary Lessons for Experimental Research*. New York: Russell Sage Foundation.

Parkhe, A. (1993), 'Strategic alliance structuring: a game theoretic and transaction cost examination of interfirm cooperation.' *Academy of Management Journal*, 36(4), 794–829.

Portes, A. and Sensenbrenner, J. (1993), 'Embeddedness and immigration: notes on the social determinants of economic action.' *American Journal of Sociology*, 98, 1320–1350.

Powell, W. W. (1996), 'Trust-based forms of governance.' In R. Kramer and T. R. Tyler (eds.), *Trust in Organizations: Frontiers of Theory and Research*. Thousand Oaks, CA: Sage, 51–67

Radaev, V. (2004), 'How trust is established in economic relationships: when institutions and individuals are not trustworthy.' In S. Rose-Ackerman, B. Rothstein, and J. Kornai (eds.), *Problems of Post Socialist Transition: Creating Social Trust*. New York: Palgrave Macmillan.

Saxton, T. (1997), 'The effects of partner and relationship characteristics on alliance outcomes.' *Academy of Management Journal*, 40(2), 443–461.

Scheer, L. K., Kumar, N., and Steenkamp, J. B. E. M. (2003), 'Reactions to perceived inequity in US and Dutch interorganizational relationships.' *Academy of Management Journal*, 46(3), 303–316.

Schilke, O. and Cook, K. S. (2009), 'How do firms determine the trustworthiness of an alliance partner? The moderating effects of familiarity and reputation.' Unpublished paper.

Shapiro, S. (1984), *Wayward Capitalists*. New Haven, CT: Yale University Press.

Uslaner, E. M. and Brown. M. (2005), 'Inequality, trust, and civic engagement.' *American Politics Research*, 31, 868–894.

Uzzi, B. (1997), 'Social structure and competition in interfirm networks: the paradox of embeddedness.' *Administrative Science Quarterly*, 42, 35–67.

Williamson, O. E. (1985), *The Economic Institutions of Capitalism: Firms, Markets, Relational Contracting*. New York: Free Press

Williamson, O. E. (1993), 'Calculativeness, trust, and economic organization." *The Journal of Law & Economics*, 36(1–2), 453.

Yamagishi, T., Cook, K. S., and Watabe, M. (1998), 'Uncertainty, trust, and commitment formation in the United States and Japan.' *American Journal of Sociology*, 104, 165–194.

Zaheer, A. Lofstrom, S., and George, V. P. (2002), 'Interpersonal and interorganizational trust in alliances.' *Cooperative Strategies and Alliances*. London: Elsevier, 347–377.

Zaheer, A. and Harris, J. (2005), 'Interorganizational trust.' In O. Shenkar, J. J. Reurer(eds.), *Handbook of Strategic Alliances*. Thousand Oaks, CA: Sage, 169–197.

Zaheer, A., McEvily, B., and Perrone, V. (1998), 'Does trust matter? Exploring the effects of interorganizational and interpersonal trust on performance.' *Organization Science*, 9, 141–159.

Zucker, L. G. (1986), 'Production of trust: institutional sources of economic structure, 1840–1920.' In B. M. Staw and L. L. Cummings (eds.), *Research in Organizational Behavior*. Greenwich, CT: JAI Press, 53–112.

PART II   Public trust and business organizations

7 Public trust and trust in particular firm–stakeholder interactions: a theoretical model and implications for management

Jared D. Harris and Andrew C. Wicks

EXECUTIVE SUMMARY

THE SITUATION

Leaders need a better understanding of "public trust," what factors influence it, and what that means for organizational action.

We understand a great deal about organizational trust, but research generally assumes that all parties view trust in organizations the same way. *Stakeholder* trust – or, an analysis of differential stakeholder approaches to trust – has been relatively unexplored, with a few notable exceptions.

KEY QUESTIONS

What role can stakeholder theory play in understanding public trust in the institution of business?

How do different stakeholders conceptualize organizational trust, and what impact do these differences have? What does a better understanding of stakeholder trust tell us about public trust in business?

NEW KNOWLEDGE

Trust has at least two key components – trust that is based upon an assessment of integrity or goodwill and trust that is based on an assessment of competence. Competence-based trust may be a higher priority in certain stakeholder relationships, whereas in others goodwill-based trust may be more important. Recognizing and understanding which aspect of trust has priority in particular stakeholder relationships, and understanding how those stakeholders balance these two aspects of trust in their decisions, would be highly useful to business leaders.

KEY LESSONS

At the individual level, trust in the institution of business and trust in a particular business are distinct concepts.

Stakeholder roles (e.g., customer, employee, investor) differ *qualitatively* and engender different areas of emphasis when it comes to organizational trust; this has an important bearing on trust in business as an institution.

INTRODUCTION

We live in unprecedented times. The worst financial crisis in the past seventy-five years has raised vexing questions about the limits of markets, and particularly about the pathway to a prosperous future for the global economy. It has also brought to the forefront fundamental questions about public attitudes toward business. Although public trust in business is important to managers even in financially prosperous times – before the onset of the financial crisis, polls of executives showed public trust in business to be an important concern that impacts a range of other issues of vital importance – the current crisis highlights the salience of this issue.[1] This presents a paradox: on one hand, the trust of the public in business enterprise seems to be at an all-time low,[2] yet many see trust and public confidence as critical to rebuilding markets and re-strengthening the economy. Under such circumstances, how then does "public" trust get created? Although there is a wealth of management research on organizational trust, there is scant research exploring the concept of public trust in this literature.

[1] Brice, 2004.   [2] Garcia, 2009.

Given the currency of the subject and its direct relevance to managers, we believe it is critical to theoretically and empirically explore the topic of public trust in business in an effort to better understand it.

Organizational trust and its role in intra- and interorganizational relations is now a focal topic in business management and the wider literature on organizations. Yet, as we strive to better understand public trust and the role of trust in organizations, we suggest that there is a need to attend to the complexity of the phenomenon and how one's particular stakeholder position may influence one's perceptions of trust (or its absence). We need a better understanding of public trust, what factors influence it, and what that means for organizational action. We suggest that stakeholder theory can play a key role in understanding public trust in business.

Therefore, to provide a more fine-grained perspective on public trust, we will draw on insights from both the stakeholder literature and the trust literature, and propose a model for how such trust is formulated. We first lay out what we mean by "public trust," and then articulate several arguments that model public trust as a function of differential stakeholder perceptions and their preferences for different aspects of organizational trust. We crystallize these arguments into formal research propositions for empirical testing, and conclude with a discussion of implications and future research directions.

WHAT IS PUBLIC TRUST?

Typically, discussions about public trust in business reference aggregated data on attitudes toward business leaders and/or "business," generally speaking. The data often comes from public interest polls; such polls seek to capture widespread public opinion, and the polls often capture public attitudes about a variety of professional groups, such as national politicians, physicians, and military personnel, in addition to business executives. As such, poll questions typically ask respondents about their attitude toward "business" or "business leaders" in the most abstract sense, and these responses are aggregated to constitute "public trust in business."

For our purposes, a more precise conceptualization of public trust is both useful and necessary, in order to better understand where it comes from and what it entails. We suggest that at the individual level, trust in the *institution* of business and trust in a *particular* business are two different things. And as such, these concepts are not always synchronized. Much like in politics, where citizens' opinions of their own congressperson may not match their opinions of members of Congress generally,[3] the trust individuals have in business (i.e., institutional trust) is different than the trust individuals have in a *particular* business (i.e., organizational trust). Nevertheless these constructs are not completely orthogonal; indeed we aim to extend our understanding by building theory about the connection between the two.

The context of business is a special case for both managers and management researchers, who are interested in better understanding how public trust connects to the operations of a given company. As such, researchers need to better understand the organizational dynamics that determine both trust in particular firms and trust in business. The present chapter explores this relationship as one key ingredient in shedding light on the public trust.

Therefore, we conceptualize public trust as one's trust in business generally, and build a model for how such trust is constituted. As laid out in the next several sections, we argue such trust arises from particular stakeholder relations and correspondingly important aspects of trust valued by those stakeholders. We begin by discussing different aspects of organizational trust, and their importance to different stakeholders of the firm.

ASPECTS OF TRUST: GOODWILL AND COMPETENCE

Organizational trust is a multidimensional construct. Some have suggested that trust is largely a calculative consideration of another's competence,[4] whereas others have connected trust to forbearance

---

[3] See, e.g., Parker and Parker, 1993.   [4] Williamson, 1993.

from opportunism, and therefore to conceptions of goodwill and morality.[5] Although organizational research has increasingly conceptualized trust as embodying a focus on *both* competence and goodwill,[6] scholars have begun to empirically demonstrate that the goodwill and competence dimensions of trust, though related, have differential effects on organizational behavior,[7] reinforcing the idea that different types of trust matter for different reasons, and in different contexts. Indeed, Pirson and Malhotra's 2007 study of stakeholder trust pulls these two aspects of trust apart even further, identifying *six* different facets of trust: benevolence, integrity, managerial competence, technical competence, transparency, and value congruence. For our purposes, we focus on the two more generalized aspects of trust: goodwill and competence. However, we embrace and build on Pirson and Malhotra's critical shift in the literature: highlighting the significance of stakeholders as a way of better understanding the value of trust and the role it plays in making the firm a going concern.[8]

A STAKEHOLDER VIEW OF ORGANIZATIONAL TRUST

While it has been well established that trust is an important component of organizational action,[9] and that trust can improve intra- and interorganizational performance,[10] parties making up these organizational relationships are typically viewed as relatively homogeneous – that is, we understand a great deal about trust, but research generally assumes that all parties view organizational trust the same way. Hence the systematic examination of *stakeholder* trust – that is, an analysis of differential stakeholder approaches to trust – has been relatively unexplored, with a few notable exceptions.[11] How do different stakeholders conceptualize organizational trust, and what

---

[5] Baier, 1986.

[6] See, e.g., Bromiley and Cummings, 1995; Bromiley and Harris, 2006; Zaheer *et al.*, 1998.

[7] Jap and Anderson, 2003; Lui and Ngo, 2004; Saparito *et al.*, 2004.

[8] Pirson and Malhotra, 2007. [9] McEvily *et al.*, 2003.

[10] Dirks, 1999; Zaheer *et al.*, 1998. [11] See, e.g., Pirson and Malhotra, 2008.

impact do these differences have? And in turn, what does a better understanding of stakeholder trust tell us about public trust in business?

As a starting point, we consider the research of Pirson and Malhotra, who have opened the door to fuller consideration of differential stakeholder approaches to trust.[12] They argue for (and find evidence that) several psychological constructs – locus, a measure of whether a stakeholder is "internal" or "external" to the organization, and intensity, the frequency of interaction with the focal organization – are the dominant predictors of stakeholder trust. That is, as stakeholders vary with respect to these constructs, they will value different aspects of trust. Given their predictive framework, they suggest that certain stakeholders fit certain "archetypes" (e.g., customers have an external locus and high intensity, whereas employees have an internal locus and high intensity). Their work highlights the dual insights that trust has multiple dimensions, and stakeholders can vary in how they approach organizational trust – both concepts we explore further here.

In this chapter, we build upon these insights by exploring differential views of stakeholders regarding multiple facets of trust, but we do so by pursuing a different insight than Pirson and Malhotra: we argue that the stakeholder roles themselves (e.g., customer, employee, investor) differ *qualitatively*. In other words, we do not assume that all stakeholders are relatively homogeneous across different roles, varying primarily on the dimensions of locus and intensity. Rather, we argue that the stakeholder roles themselves engender different areas of emphasis when it comes to organizational trust.

The literature on interorganizational trust has placed a great deal of focus on supply chains as a context for exploring interorganizational trust.[13] Following Freeman's 1984 identification of five key

---

[12] Pirson and Malhotra, 2007; 2008.
[13] See, e.g., Dyer and Chu, 2000, 2003; Heide and John, 1990.

stakeholders, and in an effort to build our theoretical understanding of these stakeholders and their roles, we focus here on the four other key stakeholders – customers, employees, shareholders, and community – and their views of trust, in order to broaden our understanding of differential stakeholder views of trust. Let us discuss each of these stakeholders in turn.

Shareholders. When investors acquire an equity stake in a firm, the typical way of conceptualizing this is as an arm's-length, financially oriented transaction. As neoclassical theory suggests, people invest because they want a strong financial return. And, while the Socially Responsible Investing (SRI) movement has grown substantially in recent years, it continues to include a small minority of investors and investment dollars. The growth of SRI highlights that investors may well have multiple factors in mind when they invest, some of which explicitly include "social" or environmental issues, but there is little to suggest that these factors take priority over considerations of return. Even though many investors care about the social performance of the equity-granting firm,[14] the firm–shareholder relationship is potentially the most impersonal of the firm–stakeholder relationships, and therefore tends to be the most sterile. The liquidity of equity markets accentuates this feature; all the most referred-to metrics center on financial returns, and transaction costs are minimal. Furthermore, the intermediary dominated financial sector has created layer upon layer of investment practices that can serve to further remove investors from the equities they hold; for instance, how many investors know exactly what stocks are contained in their retirement portfolios, which are typically managed by professional mutual fund managers?

Thus it is no surprise that shareholders are significantly influenced by instrumental logic[15] and that managers operate under this frame of reference.[16] Therefore, we argue that the aspect of trust most important to shareholders is competence-based trust.

---

[14] Aguilera et al., 2007; Glac, 2009.   [15] Berman et al., 1999.   [16] Freeman, 1984.

Stated formally

Proposition 1a: To stockholders, competence-based trust will be more important than goodwill-based trust.

Proposition 1b: Stockholders will view competence-based trust as more important than goodwill-based trust and they will be relatively "imbalanced" in their indicated priorities.

Customers. As with other stakeholders, customers are likely to have a range of factors that matter to them which incorporate considerations of goodwill and competence. Customers, other things being equal, appear to want to buy from firms that have integrity, keep their promises, and will go the extra mile to look out for customers even when it may not pay to do so. At the same time, customers want high-quality products at an affordable price and they want to have confidence that the firm will continue to produce great products and service going forward. There are a number of reasons to believe the latter kinds of concerns, focused on competence, will tend to have primacy for customers.

First, studies done on the environment reveal that customers are willing to make only small increases in the price they pay and have even less tolerance for sacrificing product quality to get "greener" products.[17] Second, anecdotal evidence indicates that customers care more about products that meet their wants than they do about companies doing good things. Expediency is a primary concern of customers. Consider the fast food industry; even though substantial evidence exists suggesting fast food is unhealthy, potentially fosters obesity, and may even contribute to global environmental problems, fast food businesses remain incredibly popular and highly profitable because customers value expediency and competence. Third, the literature on brands suggests the power of perceived desirability for consumers in their buying behavior.[18] The perception of

[17] Auger and Devinney, 2007; Siegel, 2009.
[18] See, e.g., Aaker, 1997; Fournier, 1998.

quality and desirability are powerful draws that influence customer choices and would appear to be more salient and powerful than goodwill. Hence,

> Proposition 2a: To customers, competence-based trust will be more important than goodwill-based trust.
>
> Proposition 2b: Though customers will view competence-based trust as more important than goodwill-based trust, both will be important and relatively "balanced" in their indicated priorities.

Employees. At the core of any employer–employee relationship is a contract to work for financial compensation. Yet there is substantial evidence that what employees desire most is meaningfulness in their work.[19] Work becomes meaningful by achieving consonance between one's work and one's identity.[20] This suggests that many affective and subjective preferences are particularly salient in employees' evaluations of current or potential workplaces. This also appears to be true in the way that employees choose to interact with their coworkers *within* an organization. For example, in a study of three different organizations, employees' self-selection of coworkers to engage with in various work tasks is shown to be driven by affect and not the competence of the other party.[21] Similarly, we argue that employees generally have a heightened desire to possess goodwill-based trust in the organizations they work for, and that such considerations weigh heavier in the trust they have in their organization than competence-based considerations. In other words, the emphasis on goodwill, affect, and morality in employees' interpersonal relationships influences their desire for organizational identification.[22]

The central role of goodwill in the way employees identify with their organizations has support in several research streams; for instance, not only do individuals emphasize pro-social aspects of their

---

[19] Nord *et al.*, 1990; Pratt and Ashforth, 2003; Spreitzer, 1995.   [20] Kahn, 1990.
[21] Casciaro and Lobo, 2008.   [22] Sluss and Ashforth, 2008.

employment when they discuss and shape their work environment,[23] employees of organizations engaged in "dirty work" – firms that suffer from societal distrust or other social stigma – go to great lengths to resolve cognitive dissonance about their employment.[24] Entrepreneurs often leave the stability and "competence" of more established organizations to pursue socially responsible causes, even in the face of self-imposed economic costs and risks.[25] All of this work suggests that in the heightened interpersonal environment of the workplace, the aspect of organizational trust most important to employees is goodwill-based trust.

> *Proposition 3a: To employees, goodwill-based trust is more important than competence-based trust.*
>
> *Proposition 3b: Though employees will view goodwill-based trust as more important than competence-based trust, both will be important and relatively "balanced" in their indicated priorities.*

Community. Like other stakeholders, individuals operating from the community perspective will care about an array of factors. They want businesses to do well, create jobs, provide tax revenues, minimize any environmental or social "externalities" associated with their operations, and contribute to the overall well-being of the community. Communities will value competence in part because they want to see business continue to do things that will keep them profitable over a long period of time and avoid making mistakes that could have significant negative impacts on the community. However, they also care a great deal about the posture of companies toward the community in such things as charitable giving, community outreach, and leadership. As we consider the central issue of this chapter, public trust, it brings front and center the idea that it is absence of perceived goodwill by business that is in the forefront of people's minds as they think about the activities of business in their communities. Indeed, the language

---

[23] Grant, 2007; Sonenshein, 2006.   [24] Ashforth *et al.*, 2007.   [25] Baron, 2007.

of corporate citizenship and the corporate social responsibility movement appear to both focus primary attention on the issues linked to goodwill – that business should have a responsible and beneficent attitude toward the community. While all stakeholders have risks associated with the "imperfect" and "incomplete" contracts with the firm, communities are perhaps especially at risk and heavily reliant on the goodwill of companies. This is particularly true in terms of various externalities that a firm may (or may not) "dump" on a community. While concern with competence-related phenomena like jobs, profitability, and tax revenues are clearly important, they are likely to be less significant for these stakeholders than for others (e.g., employees, shareholders).

In their role as a member of the community, we believe that this concern with the posture or attitude of the business – in terms of their goodwill or not – will be particularly salient and important when we think about trust for this stakeholder group.

Proposition 4a: Community-oriented stakeholders value goodwill-based trust more than competence-based trust.

Proposition 4b: Community-oriented stakeholders value goodwill-based trust more than competence-based trust and they will be relatively "imbalanced" in their indicated priorities.

STAKEHOLDER TRUST

In this section we focus on the relationships between particular stakeholder roles and the overall levels of trust in *particular* businesses – hereafter referred to as stakeholder trust. We have previously argued that certain stakeholders will favor certain aspects of trust. We are now interested in better understanding which aspect of trust (competence or goodwill) and which levels of trust found with particular stakeholders are most likely to translate into the overall levels of trust that a stakeholder has in a given business.

We suggest that stakeholder roles – e.g., whether one is an employee or a customer – will factor prominently in explaining the

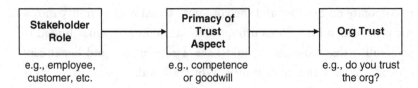

FIGURE 7.1 Stakeholder role and organizational trust

overall trust of that stakeholder in the referent business. As we have just argued, certain stakeholders tend to value one type of trust more than another. That being the case, we would expect to see that focal dimension of trust (e.g., competence or goodwill) playing a significant role in shaping the overall trust that stakeholder has toward a given company (see Figure 7.1). Hence

> *Proposition 5: The level of trust found in the type of trust determined to be most important to a given stakeholder (whether competence or goodwill) will be directly related to (and the best predictor of) overall trust in a particular business.*

While this basic relationship is important and anchors our stakeholder-driven perspective on trust, it is also critical to think about the role played by trust levels in the type of trust seen as less valued. For instance, the above proposition would suggest that for shareholders, given their emphasis on competence, we would expect that revealed levels of competence-based trust would be the best predictor of overall levels of trust in the firm. However, this leaves open the question of what role goodwill-based trust plays in their assessment.

We believe that the less preferred type of trust will have an impact on overall trust levels. However, we also think that salience, as revealed from a given stakeholder's perspective, will shape the degree of the impact: that is, for stakeholders that have a strongly skewed preference for one type of trust (either competence or good-will), the trust levels for the less-preferred type of trust will have little or no effect on overall trust levels. So, for instance, if shareholders truly do strongly prioritize competence-based trust over goodwill trust, we would argue that overall trust levels would closely mirror the level of revealed competence-based trust regardless of what answers were found for goodwill trust – even if goodwill-based trust were found to be very high or very low.

> Proposition 6: For stakeholders with a strong preference for one type of trust (either goodwill or competence), the less preferred type of trust will have little or no impact on the overall trust levels the stakeholder has in a given business.

In contrast, if a stakeholder clearly values both types of trust, then we would expect that the less preferred type of trust will make a significant difference in the overall trust assessment. Again, our argument is based on psychological salience linked to stakeholder perspective: if stakeholders value it and see it as important, then it should show up as a significant factor in their trust levels – even though their scores for individual trust types and overall trust are measured independently. Thus, for a stakeholder like an employee, who we argue cares about both goodwill and competence; we expect to see goodwill do the most work in determining overall trust levels. However, we would also expect to see competence influencing the overall trust – that if it is particularly high, then it might move overall trust significantly above what would be predicted from looking at goodwill alone; that if it is particularly low, then it might move overall trust significantly below what would be predicted from looking at goodwill alone.

> Proposition 7: For stakeholders with a weak preference for one type of trust (either goodwill or competence), the less preferred type of trust will have a significant relationship to the overall trust levels the stakeholder has in a given business, even though they will be less significant than the preferred trust type.

PUBLIC TRUST IN BUSINESS

Thus far our focus has been on trust in the relationship between stakeholders and particular firms. Yet a critical aspect of trust in the context of business is trust in business as a whole. We now turn to the connection between a particular stakeholder's trust in specific organization and their trust in the institution of business, i.e., public trust.

Anecdotal evidence suggests there may be a significant gap between the levels of trust we have in a particular business and our trust in the institution of business, with the former being significantly higher than the latter. Part of this effect is likely due to factors noted in other literature. For instance, we know from experimental work that psychological distance is a powerful factor in our sense of attachment to others.[26] An organization with which we have an ongoing relationship, and in which we may have developed relationships with particular people who represent that organization, is likely to garner far more trust from us than "business." Similarly, we know from studies in political science that people often demonstrate significant levels of trust in their own particular political representative, while having little trust for politicians in general.[27] Part of the explanation for this gap lies in familiarity and particularity that creates an emotional bond, but part of it may lie in additional factors that mediate the relationship – our deeper attitudes toward institutions, our place within social structures, and our sense of whether the existing system is corrupt and inefficient. In addition, some scholars have noted the power of scripts and background narratives for shaping individual attitudes and behaviors. The Zimbardo study,[28] where students took on the role of either a "guard" or "prisoner" in a mock prison, is one powerful example of research demonstrating how powerful certain labels and contexts may be for determining how we act: in this case, facilitating elaborate and frightening behaviors that individuals exhibited while occupying these roles. More recent work (e.g., Liberman *et al.*, 2004) reinforces the power of labeling and the associated implications for behavior.

In this vein, Freeman has hinted at the power of a "background narrative" believed to pervade modernized society, which in turn, shapes individual attitudes about business.[29] It provides a filter that

---

[26] See, e.g., Milgram, 1963.   [27] See, e.g., Parker and Parker, 1993.
[28] Haney *et al.*, 1973.   [29] Freeman, 1994.

allows people to interpret stimuli and information regarding the behavior of companies and firms, particularly through media outlets and particularly with respect to companies with which we have limited familiarity. In this view, despite living in a society whose values largely undergird and enable modern capitalism, most people see business as an inherently amoral or immoral enterprise. In particular, the focus on profits and revenue generation that characterize business seem fundamentally at odds with a conception of morality built around concern for others and indifference to one's own interests. If our societal conception of business suggests that businesses are all fundamentally cold-hearted and machine-like, completely absent of any consideration of ethics and focused solely on their own benefit, then trust in business may necessarily be generally low.

> Proposition 8: *Stakeholder trust in particular businesses will, other things being equal, be higher than trust in the institution of business.*

What is the relationship between stakeholder trust and public trust? Although the preceding discussion suggests that the societal background narrative about business will be generally negative, our model of public trust – acknowledging that institutionalized narratives can vary – seeks to combine this influence with the relationships we have previously hypothesized regarding stakeholder trust in a particular business. We come now to the consideration of the relationship between trust in specific businesses and one's generalized trust in business as an institution, in an attempt to begin to shed light on our understanding of trust as we move from the specific to the general.

Consistent with the constructionist view,[30] we suggest that individuals have a process of aggregating their respective experiences with particularized businesses into some larger, generalized view of trust in business. That is, individual commercial experiences matter,

---

[30] See, e.g., Berger and Luckmann, 1967.

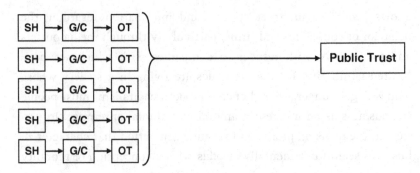

FIGURE 7.2 Additive model of generalized trust in business

and will have substantial impact on one's views of commerce generally. Viewed simply, one might suppose that this connection is simply additive (see Figure 7.2), and one's collection of trust in individual businesses aggregates into one's overall trust in business as in institution; for instance, the more one's specific experiences reflect or result in low trust, generalized trust will tend to also be low.

A more institutionalized view suggests an interaction between the background narrative about business, and one's more specific stakeholder experiences with trust (see Figure 7.3). As individuals aggregate their respective experiences of trust in particular businesses, not only might an overarching preference for a particular aspect of trust (e.g., competence or goodwill) emerge as a dominant influence on one's trust in the institution of business, but the influence of exogenous narratives about business – for good or ill – will *also* influence that generalized perception, both directly and indirectly.

In other words, as previously discussed, a negative narrative about business should have a dampening effect on one's public trust, even if trust in specific businesses is high. And although we have suggested that the effect for societal narratives about business will be overwhelmingly negative, we acknowledge that narratives can vary. For instance, background narratives could vary by geographic region or country, or they could vary depending on what kind of media one is exposed to, or based on the influence of NGOs or other third-party organizations.

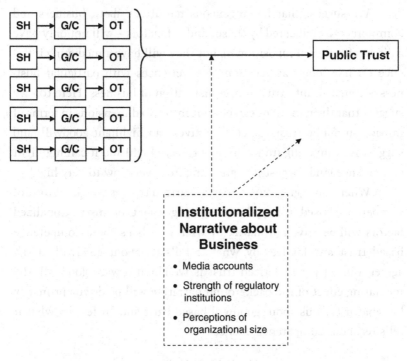

FIGURE 7.3 Institutionalized model of public trust

Institutionalized narratives about business may be culturally specific and shaped by how business is viewed within a particular context (e.g., stories about usury significantly shaped peoples' views of moneylending in many parts of Western Europe and continue to do so, just as stories about the Great Depression in the United States may still influence Americans' view of business). What might be some specific indicators of what one's narrative about business is? At the very least, one's contextualized narrative about business will be shaped by such factors as: (1) media accounts (specifically, how the media portray business); (2) one's confidence in the regulatory environment to curb either irresponsible opportunism or incompetence; and (3) the size of the institution the individual focuses on when they think of "business" (e.g., large or small).

We suggest that heterogeneous narratives about business and commerce – as indicated by these kinds of factors – will not only have a direct effect (see Proposition 8), but they will have a mediating influence on how one's aggregation of experiences with particular businesses translate into trust in the institution of business. Here too we suggest that the narratives can be split into two dimensions in terms of impact on public trust – such narratives can highlight goodwill (and suggest it is anything from very low to very high) and it can highlight competence (and suggest it is anything from very low to very high).

When the aggregation of particularized trust is weighted toward competence-based trust, the mediating effect of institutionalized factors will be driven primarily by what it tells us about competence based trust and far less by what it tells us about goodwill. If the aggregation of particularized trust is weighted toward goodwill, the mediating effect of the background narrative will be driven primarily by what it tells us about goodwill based trust and far less by what it tells us about competence. Hence

Proposition 9: *Public trust will be driven by individual aggregation of particularized trust in business and mediated by the contextual narrative about business, including media accounts, attitudes toward political institutions as an effective check on business, and perceptions about organizational size. Specifically:*

(a) *For individuals whose aggregation of particularized trust is weighted toward competence based trust, the mediating effect of institutionalized narrative will be dominated by considerations of competence (whether positive or negative) in shaping public trust.*

(b) *For individuals whose aggregation of particularized trust is weighted toward goodwill based trust, the mediating effect of institutionalized narrative will be dominated by considerations of goodwill (whether positive or negative) in shaping public trust.*

DISCUSSION AND CONCLUSIONS

This chapter has made the stakeholder perspective a central consideration in understanding trust and predicting how stakeholders approach trust in organizations, and how it connects to public trust. We argue that all stakeholders will value both goodwill and competence-based trust, but that the emphasis on each will vary across stakeholder roles. Further, those differences will play a significant role in the levels of trust stakeholders have in particular firms.

Another contribution of the theoretical model is its consideration of sense-making, scripts, and mental models, that all suggest the power of language, culture, and framing to shape how we look at a given phenomenon.[31] One of our contentions is that societal narratives about business tend to be overwhelmingly negative. Individuals must make sense of these institutionalized narratives, but we have suggested that people are generally quite skeptical of business and tend to have very little trust, particularly when it comes to integrity and goodwill. One need only read the daily newspaper (or internet blog), go to a children's movie, or have a conversation with a friend to run into discussions of business that reinforce the notion that corporations (and those who act on their behalf) are amoral entities that will do almost anything to increase profits – including lie, cheat, and steal if need be. Yet these narratives can certainly vary in their intensity, based on geographic location or other institutional factors.

Given that stakeholders operate in context, and that culture and language shape their perceptions, we believe that sense-making will play a significant role in determining trust levels in business as a whole, and this dimension of the model bears further exploration, especially given the hypothesized disconnect between stakeholder trust and public trust. Indeed, this is one of the insights from our examination of stakeholder roles, organizational trust, and public trust: that societal and institutional narratives can serve as a wedge

---

[31] See, e.g., Gioia, 1992.

between stakeholder trust in specific organizations and perceptions of business generally.

These theoretical considerations highlight a number of practical implications arising from the chapter. The most direct and obvious concern relates to the direct effects of low public trust. Businesses have reason to be concerned about low public trust; low public sentiment can result in increased regulation and more centralized or governmental control over markets. While this suggests some connections between research on trust and existing work on regulation, future work could explore this connection in more detail. Other direct effects could be measured in terms of other extra costs (for both businesses and consumers) of doing business – for example, a need for additional guarantees, insurance, and the use of third parties, as well as lost sales.

Our focus also pushes us to think about more indirect effects of these results for businesses. Rather than thinking about trust in the aggregate, this study highlights the need to more carefully examine the role that trust plays in the operations of a given firm, and more specifically, the kind of relationships it seeks to create with stakeholders in the value chain. As Wicks *et al.* have demonstrated, trust is costly and more trust is not always better – either for the firm as a whole or in its relationships with specific stakeholders.[32] Firms should think about optimal levels of trust for their operations, specifically in terms of the kinds of relationships they have with various stakeholders. Thus, as we understand the phenomenon of public trust in more detailed terms and examine its relationship to stakeholder roles and trust in particularized business, researchers can more fully grasp when public trust levels become a problem: both overall and for relationships with particular stakeholders.

Building on the focus of optimal trust and firm-centered implications of this work, the present study also makes salient the importance of trust (and its absence) in the day-to-day operations of the company. Resolving contracting problems in an efficient and

[32] Wicks *et al.*, 1999.

highly fluid manner that reduces costs and makes the parties involved better off is a central focus of the literature on transaction cost economics. The relative absence of trust in business has implications for thinking through how successful and resource intensive the efforts of management will be in resolving contracting issues with particular stakeholders. This also raises the importance of a focus on the role that stakeholders play in this process. The relative absence, or abundance, of stakeholder responsibility will go a long way in helping determine the firm-level implications of trust levels.[33] In cases where stakeholders act with high levels of integrity and have a strong ethic of responsibility, firms may be able to readily adapt to declining levels of trust. In instances where stakeholder responsibility is low, the erosion of trust may provide circumstances that significantly impact the costs of contracting with stakeholders.

Going forward, researchers need to focus less on absolute levels of trust in business, though these may still be important indicators, and more on levels of trust in business that are reasonable or workable given their relative need for trust. Gaining traction on this issue may involve not only thinking about recent trends, but what levels are attainable, what kinds of costs and trade-offs may be involved in changing those levels, and what role public trust plays in the operation of global financial markets as well as the success or failure of specific firms. Low public trust is troubling, and we can see some of the costs of its absence, but until we know more about these parameters it is difficult to know how to best address the problem of public trust.

Finally, our research builds on the work of others by highlighting the importance of a stakeholder perspective for thinking about public trust.[34] Such global and generalized constructs have value, but without connections back to the more concrete roles of stakeholders, the kinds of trust that are important for firms, and the specific role that trust plays in their operations, these constructs have limited value and relevance for managers. Future work needs to explore these

---

[33] Goodstein and Wicks, 2007.   [34] See, e.g., Pirson and Malhotra, 2007; 2008.

connections in further detail, both to explore their micro-level implications, but also to connect them back to these meso- and macro-level questions. It is precisely in seeing these interconnections, and the relationships that govern them, that researchers can shed valuable light on the subject of the public trust and its significance for management.

REFERENCES

Aaker, J. L. (1997), 'Dimensions of brand personality.' *Journal of Marketing Research*, 34(3), 347–356.

Aguilera, R. V., Rupp, D. E., Williams, C. A., and Ganapathi, J. (2007), 'Putting the "S" back in corporate social responsibility: A multilevel theory of social change in organizations.' *Academy of Management Review*, 32(3), 836–863.

Ashforth, B. E., Kreiner, G. E., Clark, M. A., and Fugate, M. (2007), 'Normalizing dirty work: managerial tactics for countering occupational taint.' *Academy of Management Journal*, 50(1), 149–174.

Auger, P. and Devinney, T. (2007), 'Do what consumers say matter? The misalignment of preferences with unconstrained ethical intentions.' *Journal of Business Ethics*, 76(4), 361–383.

Baier, A. (1986), 'Trust and antitrust.' *Ethics*, 96(2), 231–260.

Baron, D. P. (2007), 'Corporate social responsibility and social entrepreneurship.' *Journal of Economics and Management Strategy*, 16(3), 683–717.

Berger, P. L. and Luckmann, T. 1967. *The Social Construction of Reality*. New York: Doubleday.

Berman, S. L., Wicks, A. C., Kotha, S., and Jones, T. M. 1999. 'Does stakeholder orientation matter? The relationship between stakeholder management models and firm financial performance.' *Academy of Management Journal*, 42(5), 488–506.

BRICE (2004), *Mapping the Terrain: Issues That Connect Business and Ethics*. Charlottesville, VI: Business Roundtable Institute for Corporate Ethics (available at www.darden.virginia.edu/corporate-ethics/pdf/mapping_terrain_business_ethics_2004.pdf).

Bromiley, P. and Cummings, L. L. (1995), 'Transactions costs in organizations with trust.' In Bies, Sheppard, and Lewicki (eds.), *Research on Negotiation in Organizations*. Greenwich, CT: JAI Press, vol. V, 219–247.

Bromiley, P. and Harris, J. D. (2006), 'Trust, transaction cost economics, and mechanisms.' In R. Bachmann and A. Zaheer (eds.), *Handbook of Trust Research*. Cheltenham, UK: Edward Elgar, 124–143.

Casciaro, T. and Lobo, M. S. (2008), 'When competence is irrelevant: the role of interpersonal affect in task-related ties.' *Administrative Science Quarterly*, 53(4), 655–684.

Dirks, K. T. (1999), 'The effects of interpersonal trust on work group performance.' *Journal of Applied Psychology*, 84(3), 445–455.

Dyer, J. H., and Chu, W. (2000), 'The determinants of trust in supplier–automaker relationships in the US, Japan, and Korea.' *Journal of International Business Studies*, 31(2), 259–285.

Dyer, J. H. and Chu, W. (2003), 'The role of trustworthiness in reducing transaction costs and improving performance: empirical evidence from the United States, Japan, and Korea.' *Organization Science*, 14(1), 57–68.

Fournier, S. (1998), 'Consumers and their brands: developing relationship theory in consumer research.' *Journal of Consumer Research*, 24(4), 343–373.

Freeman, R. E. (1984), *Strategic Management: A Stakeholder Approach*. Boston, MA: Pitman.

Freeman, R. E. 1994. 'The politics of stakeholder theory: some future directions.' *Business Ethics Quarterly*, 4(4), 409–421.

Garcia, T. (2009), 'Trust in business at 10-yr. low.' February 2, 2009, 3, *PR week*.

Gioia, D. A. (1992), 'Pinto fires and personal ethics: a script analysis of missed opportunities.' *Journal of Business Ethics*, 11, 379–389.

Glac, K. (2009), 'Understanding socially responsible investing: the effect of decision frames and trade-off options.' *Journal of Business Ethics*, 87, 41–55.

Goodstein, J. and Wicks, A. C. (2007), 'Corporate and stakeholder responsibility: making business ethics a two-way conversation.' *Business Ethics Quarterly*, 17(3), 375–398.

Grant, A. M. (2007), 'Relational job design and the motivation to make a prosocial difference.' *Academy of Management Review*, 32(2), 393–417.

Haney, C., Banks, W. C., and Zimbardo, P. G. (1973), 'Interpersonal dynamics in a simulated prison.' *International Journal of Criminology and Penology*, 1: 69–97.

Heide, J. B. and John, G. (1990), 'Alliances in industrial purchasing: the determinants of joint action in buyer-supplier relationships.' *Journal of Marketing Research*, 27(February 1990), 24–36.

Jap, S. D. and Anderson, E. (2003), 'Safeguarding interorganizational performance and continuity under ex post opportunism.' *Management Science*, 49(12), 1684–1701.

Kahn, W. A. (1990), 'Psychological conditions of personal engagement and disengagement at work.' *Academy of Management Journal*, 33, 692–724.

Liberman, V., Samuels, S. M., and Ross, L. (2004), 'The name of the game: predictive power of reputations versus situational labels in determining prisoner's dilemma game moves.' *Personality and Social Psychology Bulletin*, 30(9), 1175–1185.

Lui, S. S. and Ngo, H. Y. (2004), 'The role of trust and contractual safeguards on cooperation in non-equity alliances.' *Journal of Management*, 30(4), 471–486.

McEvily, B., Perrone, V., and Zaheer, A. (2003), 'Trust as an organizing principle.' *Organization Science*, 14(1), 91–103.

Milgram, S. (1963), 'Behavioral study of obedience.' *Journal of Abnormal and Social Psychology*, 67(4), 371–378.

Nord, W., Brief, A., Atieh, J., and Doherty, E. (1990), 'Studying meanings of work: the case of work values.' In A. Brief, and W. Nord (eds.), *Meanings of Occupational Work*. Lexington, MA: Lexington Books.

Parker, S. L. and Parker, G. R. (1993), 'Why do we trust our congressman?' *Journal of Politics*, 55(2), 442–453.

Pirson, M. and Malhotra, D. (2007), 'What matters to whom? Managing trust across multiple stakeholder groups.' Working paper, Hauser Center for Nonprofit Organizations, Harvard University.

Pirson, M. and Malhotra, D. (2008), 'Unconventional insights for managing stakeholder trust.' *MIT Sloan Management Review*, 49(4), 43–50.

Pratt, M. G. and Ashforth, B. E. (2003), 'Fostering meaningfulness in working and work.' In K. S. Cameron, J. E. Dutton, and R. E. Quinn (eds.), *Positive Organizational Scholarship: Foundations of a New Discipline*. San Francisco, CA: Berrett-Koehler.

Saparito, P. A., Chen, C. C., and Sapienza, H. J. (2004), 'The role of relational trust in bank – small firm relationships.' *Academy of Management Journal*, 47(3).

Siegel, D. S. (2009), 'Green management matters only if it yields more green: an economic/strategic perspective.' *Academy of Management Perspectives*, 23(3), 5–16.

Sluss, D. M. and Ashforth, B. E. (2008), 'How relational and organizational identification converge: processes and conditions.' *Organization Science*, 19(6), 807–823.

Sonenshein, S. (2006), 'Crafting social issues at work.' *Academy of Management Journal*, 49(6), 1158–1172.

Spreitzer, G. (1995), 'Psychological empowerment in the workplace: dimensions, measurement, and validation.' *Academy of Management Journal*, 38, 1442–1465.

Wicks, A. C., Berman, S. L., and Jones, T. M. (1999), 'The structure of optimal trust: moral and strategic implications.' *Academy of Management Review*, 24(1): 99–116.

Williamson, O. E. (1993), 'Calculativeness, trust, and economic organization.' *Journal of Law and Economics*, 36(April 1993), 453–486.

Zaheer, A., McEvily, B., and Perrone, V. (1998), 'Does trust matter? Exploring the effects of interorganizational and interpersonal trust on performance.' *Organization Science*, 9(2), 141–159.

8 Creating more trusting and trustworthy organizations: exploring the foundations and benefits of presumptive trust

Roderick Kramer

EXECUTIVE SUMMARY

THE SITUATION

Low trust has become virtually a default assumption, especially when it comes to the public's expectations regarding the fundamental trustworthiness of American business and its leaders.

KEY QUESTIONS

What precisely can be done to remedy this low trust in business? How can it be "fixed"? Who should do it and how might they go about doing it? How does contemporary trust theory and research move us toward any useful answers to these important questions?

NEW KNOWLEDGE

Presumptive trust – trust that is taken for granted – is one of the bedrocks of the high trust organization. It is only when trust has a solid, secure, and virtually taken-for-granted quality that it operates at maximum effectiveness and durability.

Four key types of expectations are critical to presumptive trust in organizational settings: (1) identity-based expectations; (2) role-based expectations; (3) rule-based expectations; and (4) leader-based expectations.

KEY LESSONS

Trust works best when it has acquired an almost tacit or taken-for-granted quality.

The constructive role that leaders play in setting positive expectations regarding the general level of trust and trustworthiness within their organizations is key to the emergence and maintenance of presumptive trust.

In situations where the costs of misplaced trust are high, too much presumptive trust can create potential vulnerabilities and risks.

Presumptive trust, without actual trustworthiness, would be a hollow achievement and potentially sets the stage for costly abuses of the public's trust.

INTRODUCTION

The substantial and myriad benefits associated with high levels of trust in a society's business organizations and public institutions have been amply documented in numerous studies.[1] Such research suggests that high trust constitutes one of the vital lubricants facilitating more efficient and effective transactions at all levels of social organization. If high trust levels do contribute so centrally to the production of more cooperative and productive transactions, then the absence of such trust is obviously costly and, in the end, tragic.[2] Thus, creating and sustaining high levels of trust ought to be a societal imperative and one situated high on our list of national priorities.

Unfortunately, despite the obvious desirability of high trust, the contemporary score card with respect to either its creation or sustainability remains rather dismal.[3] In one particularly thoughtful appraisal of the state of trust in US organizations, Frankel argued that Americans have become so habituated to the routine abuse of their trust, that low trust has become virtually a default assumption,

---

[1] Cook *et al.*, 2009; Fukuyama, 1995; Putnam, 2000.
[2] Hetherington, 2005; Lorsch *et al.*, 2005.
[3] Edelman and Associates, 2012.

especially when it comes to the public's expectations regarding the fundamental trustworthiness of American business and its leaders.[4]

Frankel's claims, while perhaps extreme along some dimensions, are nonetheless amply buttressed by findings from numerous recent surveys assessing Americans' perceptions of the general lack of trustworthiness of organizations and their leaders across a variety of sectors.[5] For example, one thorough survey conducted by the Center for Public Leadership reported that, when asked to indicate the extent to which they trusted what leaders of organizations had to say, more than 50 percent indicated "not much" or "not at all" when it comes to business leaders.[6] Moreover, nearly 70 percent of Americans surveyed indicated "not much" or "not at all" when it comes to media leaders. In fact, in a sample of twenty major nations, respondents in every case reported significantly less trust in business today than even a year ago.[7]

Within the United States, moreover, respondents indicated not only sharply declining trust in general, but also sharply diminishing expectations that business leaders can be counted on to "do what is right" in addressing this dismaying perceived trust deficit.[8] Additionally, trust in American business experienced a staggering 20-point drop from 58 percent to 38 percent. As Frankel went on to argue in her sobering assessment of the state of trust in contemporary society, Americans should be concerned about this sorry state of affairs because "dishonesty and mistrust are not free ... [they] can destroy the foundation of our economy and prosperity."[9] This decline of the public's trust in business organizations and their leaders is starkly evident, it bears emphasizing, well beyond academic circles. Politicians and social critics alike have argued the need to take steps to restore public trust in organizations and their leaders.[10]

Granted, the picture with respect to trust in business and business leadership is abysmal, but what precisely can be done to remedy

---

[4] Frankel, 2006.   [5] Most recently, Edelman and Associates, 2012.
[6] Center for Public Leadership, 2009, 410.   [7] Edelman and Associates, 2009, 2.
[8] Ibid., 3.   [9] Frankel, 2006, 5.
[10] See e.g., Cook et al., 2009; Frankel, 2006; Kramer, 2009.

this situation? Who should do it and how might they go about doing it? Does contemporary trust theory and research move us toward any useful answers to these important questions? In this chapter, I answer in the affirmative and attempt to articulate one perspective on the problem of restoring trust in organizations and their leaders. To set the stage for this analysis, I should point out that my research approaches the problem of low trust in organizations, in one sense, "from the inside out." In other words, rather than tackle this problem from the perspective of how organizations or organizational leaders might repair their tarnished images or improve impression management when it comes to perceptions of their trustworthiness,[11] my research is predicated on the assumption that what's needed first and foremost is to create more genuinely trustworthy organizations – those, in short, that actually merit our trust. To learn how to do so, moreover, we need to study those organizations and leaders who have been shown to do demonstrably superior jobs at cultivating the public's trust in their products, services, and performance. What do such trustworthy organizations and leaders do differently? What can we learn from them?

To explore these questions, I've organized this chapter as follows. First, I briefly introduce and describe a concept that I term *presumptive trust*. Presumptive trust, I propose, is one of the bedrocks of the high trust organization: it is only when trust has a solid, secure, and virtually taken-for-granted quality, I argue, that it operates at maximum effectiveness and durability. Trust must become, in short, a "background expectation" that animates action within an organization without conscious calculation or premeditation on the part of organizational members. Such presumptive trust, I argue, translates in turn into genuinely trustworthy performance. In advancing these arguments, I first situate the construct of presumptive trust within related conceptions of trust. I then elaborate on some of the antecedents and determinants of such presumptive trust. Finally, I conclude by offering a few suggestions as to where future explorations of this

---

[11] See Elsbach, 2004.

topic might take us. I should note that, because of limitations of length, I do not elaborate here on the beneficial consequences of presumptive trust for two reasons. First, I have tackled this task at considerable length elsewhere.[12] Second, in this chapter I wish to emphasize that it is the *creation* of presumptive trust, I would argue, that presents the more urgent challenge in today's world – and it is this goal, of course, that is a central, underlying concern of the present volume.

CONCEPTUALIZING PRESUMPTIVE TRUST

The topic of trust has been a productive focus of organizational theory for several decades now.[13] As a result of this widespread interest, contributions to the conceptualization of trust have come from virtually every social science discipline, including sociology, psychology, economics, anthropology, and political science,[14] as well as the newer subdisciplines of behavioral economics[15] and neuroscience.[16] Despite some differences in how trust is conceptualized across these disciplines, they converge on the recognition that, whatever else it may encompass, trust is fundamentally a psychological state. As a psychological state, trust is characterized by several components, the most important of which is some sort of positive expectation regarding others' probable future behavior.

In an early and influential contribution, for example, Barber characterized trust in terms of "a set of socially learned and socially confirmed expectations that people have of each other, of the organizations and institutions in which they live, and of the natural and moral social orders that set the fundamental understandings of their lives."[17] Subsequently, Lewis and Weigert conceptualized trust as the willingness to undertake "a risky course of action on the confident

[12] Kramer, 2003.
[13] Barber, 1983; Kramer and Tyler, 1996; Lane and Bachmann, 1998; Lewicki and Bunker, 1995; Mayer *et al.*, 1995.
[14] Cook *et al.*, 2009.   [15] Bohnet and Huck, 2004; Frey and Stutzer, 2007.
[16] Kosfeld *et al.*, 2005; Rule and Ambady, 2008; Zak, 2012.
[17] Barber, 1983, 164–165.

expectation that all persons involved in the action will act competently and dutifully."[18] In one of the most influential treatments, Mayer *et al.* conceptualized trust in terms of "the willingness of a party to be vulnerable to the actions of another party based on the expectation that the other will perform a particular action important to the trustor, irrespective of the ability to monitor or control that other party."[19]

Given this consistent and singular emphasis on the role that positive social expectations play in the development and maintenance of trust, researchers have afforded considerable attention to identifying the foundations or underpinnings of such expectations. These efforts have yielded fruitful results, implicating an impressive variety of cognitive, affective, and behavioral factors that contribute to individuals' trust-related expectations.[20] Complementing these individual, psychological factors, researchers have also identified a variety of social[21] and organizational factors,[22] influencing trust-related expectations. In the context of laying a foundation for restoring and enhancing trust in organizations, these variables can be construed as constitutive of what Knez and Camerer have aptly termed "expectational assets"[23] that social perceivers can draw on when trying to assess others' trustworthiness. The efficacy or potency of such expectational assets, moreover, will be especially high in situations conducive to the creation of benign beliefs regarding others' trustworthiness.[24]

As a positive social expectation, one can argue that such trust works best when it has acquired an almost tacit or taken-for-granted quality. In a discussion of how trust is experienced when operating at an optimal level in social relationships, Brothers suggested it is akin to being in a gravitational field: we experience fully gravity's invariant

---

[18] Lewis and Weigert, 1985, 971.   [19] Mayer, Davis, and Schorrman, 1995, 712.

[20] Lount, 2010; Lindskold, 1978; McAllister, 1995.

[21] Brewer, 2008; Fine and Holyfield, 1996.

[22] Bohnet and Huck, 2004; Farrell, 2009; Zucker, 1986; Kramer, 1999; Meyerson *et al.*, 1996.

[23] Knez and Camerer, 1994, 101.   [24] Kramer, 1994.

tug, but remain oblivious to its presence as we go about our routine activities.[25] In a similar fashion, I would suggest, when trust is in place, we seldom note the constructive "pull" it exerts on our relationships and transactions. It acquires, in short, exactly the presumptive, taken-for-granted, tacit quality associated with gravity.[26]

Viewed in aggregate, then, the available evidence supports the basic notion that, when it comes to deciding who they trust and why, individuals can be viewed as vigilant social perceivers or "auditors" who are attentive to a variety of ambient cues within their environment which shape and condition their trust-related expectations. These cues include an impressive variety of personal, social, and situational factors that are construed as diagnostic or predictive of others' likely trustworthiness.[27]

One way of thinking about the impact of these assorted cues on individuals' trust-related expectations is that they represent observable features of what Bacharach and Gambetta (2001) aptly termed the "trust-warranting properties" of social actors or agents and/or the situations in which they find themselves.[28] In developing this notion, Bacharach and Gambetta proposed that these trust-warranting properties are manifested observationally in terms of at least three distinct categories of information. The first category pertains to the observable personal attributes of prospective trustees, including such things as their age, race, gender, and attire. The second pertains to the social or relational ties that exist between them, including such considerations as whether they share membership in a social network or group. The third pertains to the particular situational contexts within which their trust-related transactions occur or are embedded, whether it involves a contentious negotiation or cooperative brainstorming

[25] Brothers, 1995.
[26] See Baier, 1986 for a similar position, albeit one advanced on philosophical and normative grounds.
[27] See, e.g., Bacharach and Gambetta, 2001; Cook et al., 2009; Cook et al., 2004; Kramer, 1996.
[28] Bacharach and Gambetta, 2001, 151.

exercise. In aggregate, it is the cumulative presence or absence of such cues, Gambetta and Bacharach posit, that directly influence individuals' expectations regarding others' likely trustworthiness in any given situation.[29]

According to Bacharach and Gambetta, these cues influence individuals' trust-related expectations in two ways. First, they can influence by shaping their expectations regarding the *benevolence* or benign motivation of prospective trustees. Second, they can influence individuals' trust-related expectations by influencing their perceived ability or *competence*. Both of these attributes – an actor's perceived intentions and capabilities – have been shown to be important when assessing others' trustworthiness in organizational settings.[30] Mayer *et al.*, I should note, propose further that perceptions of integrity are yet another important component of trust-related expectations, and summarize the evidence in favor of this position.[31]

But where, then, do individuals' expectations regarding others' intentions and capabilities come from? Relatedly, what role do they play in the emergence and maintenance of presumptive organizational trust, as I've defined the construct thus far? To pursue these questions, it is helpful first to review what is known about the foundations of trust within the simpler context of dyadic relationships.

To a large extent, social psychological and game theoretic research on dyadic trust has construed the development of individuals' positive expectations regarding another's trustworthiness as interaction-dependent processes.[32] According to such models, trust between interdependent actors increases or decreases as a function of their cumulative history of personal interaction. Social interaction histories are relevant to trust building because they give decision makers useful diagnostic information when attempting to assess others' potential trustworthiness. Specifically, such information provides a basis for drawing inferences regarding another's likely

---

[29] Bacharach and Gambetta, 2001.   [30] Cook *et al.*, 2004.   [31] Mayer *et al.*, 1995.
[32] Lewicki and Bunker, 1996; Lindskold, 1978; Weber *et al.*, 2005.

trustworthiness with respect to anticipated or expected future inter-actions (Lindskold, 1978).

Boyle and Bonacich's analysis of trust development in dyadic contexts is representative of such arguments. Individuals' expectations about a specific other's trustworthiness, they argued, tend to change "in the direction of experience and to a degree proportional to the difference between this experience and the initial expectations applied to it."[33] In this regard, history-based trust can be construed as an important form of individuated or personalized knowledge-based trust.[34]

As trust theorists attempt to move from the comparatively simple dyadic case to more complex collective contexts – precisely the sort routinely encountered within large, highly differentiated organizations – they encounter the difficulty that the requisite history of individualized interpersonal interaction is not available. Recogniz-ing this potential chasm between the grounds for personalized and more generalized forms of social expectation, Putnam cogently observed that trust in such situations necessarily entails making predictions regarding the behavior of others. "In small, close-knit communities ... this prediction is based securely on ... a belief that rests on intimate familiarity with this individual."[35] However, in larger and more complex organizational settings, he goes on to argue, "a more impersonal or indirect form of trust is required."[36] It is precisely this less personal and less direct form of presumptive trust that is of interest to me in this chapter.

It's helpful at this point to indicate more clearly how the grounds for presumptive trust in other organizational members might differ from the grounds on which their interpersonal trust is usually predicated. Interpersonal trust encounters clearly involve a specific truster and designated trustee. In the case of a cancer patient's trust in

---

[33] Boyle and Bonacich, 1970, 130.
[34] Lewicki and Bunker 1995; Shapiro et al., 1992; Sheppard and Tuckinsky, 1996.
[35] Putnam, 1993, 171.   [36] Ibid.

her physician, for example, the foundations of that trust might be predicated on such things as: (1) the training and institutional affiliation of the physician; (2) the history of interpersonal interaction between them; (3) the reputation of the medical institution employing the physician and within which the patient's care is provided; (4) the nature of the medical complaint or malady; and (5) any other information construed as diagnostic of trustworthiness. Thus, a patient with cervical cancer might trust a physician trained at Harvard Medical School, affiliated with the Mayo Comprehensive Cancer Center, and who has specific expertise in gynecologic oncology because all of these cues are construed by the patient as trust warranting.

In organizational settings, as already noted, the grounds for trust-related expectations about others become more complicated. Obviously, multiple trusters find themselves transacting with multiple individual trustees, and there are multiple domains onto which their trust-related concerns may be mapped. Moreover, there may be important differences among the interdependent actors – such as differences in their power, status, or autonomy – which further complicate the formation of trust-related expectations. As a consequence, the particular evidentiary grounds on which expectations are predicated in collective contexts are less obvious and clear-cut compared to the simpler dyadic context discussed above.

Nonetheless, I argue, organizational actors still typically possess some general grounds for assessing the trustworthiness of the average or prototypic member within the organization. In aggregate, these grounds form the basis for what I am characterizing as presumptive trust. With respect to the example provided above, for instance, the pertinent unit of analysis for presumptive trust becomes what the *prototypical* Mayo Clinic physician is perceived to be like rather than any individual physician. In a sense, it is the truster's *stereotype* of the prototypic organizational member that provides the content for presumptive trust in the other.

I should note, parenthetically, that use of the word stereotype is often construed somewhat negatively in ordinary language usage, and taken to imply unflattering or unduly simplistic examples of the members of a social category. Importantly, and in contrast, my use of the term here does *not* presume such negative overtones or connotations. Instead, I would emphasize the point that in many social settings the content of social stereotypes can be positive and facilitating, especially if they augment or enhance expectations that are conducive to more trusting expectations and resultant cooperative interactions. For example, stereotypes that create high expectations of perceived or anticipated warmth or competence would greatly enhance the prospects for trustworthy interactions.[37]

In the present view, accordingly, presumptive trust in other organizational members constitutes a generalized social expectation perceivers confer on the collective or organization as a whole. Stated in somewhat different terms, presumptive trust constitutes a *diffuse* expectation insofar as its object or target is a perceived social aggregate encompassing the generic features of all the members of that collective. In this sense, it is also a *bounded* social expectation, insofar as it applies only to those individuals who are considered "in-group" members (i.e., individuals included within the social category of organizational membership). Accordingly, presumptive trust is conceptualized as a positive expectation that is founded upon, and coextensive with, knowledge of shared membership in an organization and what that shared membership connotes or signals.

With these conceptual elaborations and clarifications in mind, I can turn now to explicating in more detail the psychological and organizational bases of presumptive trust.

FOUNDATIONS OF PRESUMPTIVE TRUST IN ORGANIZATIONS

In this section, I identify and describe some of the distinct forms of expectational assets that have been identified in recent empirical research on presumptive trust in organizational settings. I characterize

---

[37] Fiske *et al.*, 2002; Fiske *et al.*, 2007.

these as: (1) identity-based expectations; (2) role-based expectations; (3) rule-based expectations; and (4) leader-based expectations.

Identity-based expectations. Several organizational theorists have argued that a positive relationship exists between psychological identification with others and trust in them.[38] Consistent with these arguments, numerous empirical studies support a causal association between identification with others and trust. Brewer was the first to systematically theorize that membership in a shared social category or group might constitute the foundations for trust in other group members. She noted a number of reasons why shared social or common group identities might provide a basis for generalized trust in other members. First, shared membership in a given social identity group can serve as a default rule for defining the boundaries of what she construed as a "low-risk interpersonal trust that bypasses the need for personal knowledge and the costs of negotiating reciprocity" when interacting with other members of that social group.[39] Because of the positive cognitive consequences of in-group categorization, she reasoned, individuals tend to attribute favorable characteristics such as honesty, cooperativeness, and trustworthiness to other in-group members.[40] As a result, individuals may experience what she characterized as a "depersonalized" trust in other in-group members. Depersonalized trust, conceptualized in these terms, is predicated simply on: (1) awareness or psychological salience of shared or common category membership; and (2) what that awareness or salience of shared membership connotes to the social perceiver. Such attributions provide a "cognitive bedrock," as it were, for presumptive trust.

In one of the first experimental explorations of such depersonalized trust, Brewer and her colleagues demonstrated that trust in other group members predicted individuals' own self-restraint, at least in the context of a laboratory simulation of a depleting, shared resource pool.[41] Subsequent experiments explored more directly the relationship

---

[38] See, e.g., Lewicki and Bunker, 1995; Shapiro *et al.*, 1992.
[39] Brewer, 1981, 356.   [40] Brewer, 1996.   [41] Messick *et al.*, 1983.

between psychological salience of collective-level social identities and willingness to trust other in-group members.[42] In fact, numerous experimental studies now support Brewer's initial hypothesis.[43]

In a recent effort to explicate more precisely the psychological underpinnings of such trust, Foddy et al. distinguished between two possible causal mechanisms.[44] The first, which they termed the *stereotype-based trust hypothesis*, is based on the general finding, noted above, that stereotypes of in-group members are generally more positive than stereotypes of out-group members. Along these lines, Platow et al. showed that in-group members perceive each other as more trustworthy compared to out-group members.[45] The second possibility, which Foddy et al. termed the *expectation of generalized reciprocity hypothesis*, is based on the idea that group members entertain a generally positive expectation of diffuse or indirect reciprocity within the boundaries of a shared identity or group.[46]

Experiments by Tanis and Postmes provide additional evidence of such a relationship. Using an investment dilemma frequently used to study trust, they found that the rate of trusting behavior (operationalized as sending money via ostensibly linked computer terminals to an allocator) was significantly higher when the allocator was an in-group versus out-group member.[47] In addition, perceived or expected reciprocity was higher for others believed to be in-group members. Importantly, these researchers found that in-group versus out-group members did not differ with respect to ratings of the allocator's trustworthiness. Hence, their findings did not support the positive stereotype hypothesis. Instead, the findings reflected the fact that there was a stronger expectation among in-group members that others would adhere to a principle or norm of generalized reciprocity.

---

[42] Kramer and Brewer, 1984.

[43] See reviews by Brewer, 2008; Foddy et al., 2009; Kramer and Brewer, 1986; McEvily et al., 2006.

[44] Foddy et al., 2009.   [45] Platow et al., 1990.

[46] Foddy et al., 2009. See also Yamagishi et al., 1999; Yamagishi and Kiyonari, 2000; Yamagishi and Yamagishi, 1994; Yuki et al., 2005.

[47] Tanis and Postmes, 2005.

Viewed in concert, the results of these studies support the expectation of generalized reciprocity hypothesis over the stereotype-based
hypothesis.

To conclude, there is considerable evidence that simply increasing the psychological salience of a shared organizational identity provides one important basis for presumptive trust in others. In a separate
investigation, Lewicki and Bunker theorized that identification-based
trust would be greater when there was high perceived congruence of
individual personal values with group values.[48] We should note that
this assumes the content of the organizational identity consists of
positive expectations and associations.

As important as shared social or organizational identities might
be for providing a basis for positive expectations, are there other
grounds on which presumptive trust in others might be predicated?
In the next section, I turn to evidence that organizational roles also
can influence members' trust-related expectations.

Role-based expectations. From the arguments and evidence
presented in the previous section, one can readily see how presumptive trust in others might be facilitated by the existence of a single,
positive "superordinate" organizational identity. Individuals' shared
presumption that they are pretty much all alike becomes a potent
basis, as I've argued and as empirical evidence attests, for coordinating
trust-related expectations among organizational members.

Unfortunately, most organizations tend to be highly differentiated social systems, comprising multiple subgroups, each with their
own corresponding subordinate identities.[49] In other words, they are
typically differentiated along formal and functional, as well as informal
and social lines. As a consequence of this functional and social differentiation, organizational members possess a variety of subordinate
identities aligned with the various organizational roles they occupy.
In aggregate, the functional roles that individuals occupy within an
organization (e.g., marketing, human resources, finance, etc.) create

[48] Lewicki and Bunker, 1996.   [49] See Kramer, 1991.

an intricate nexus of social relations that underpin or undergird the organization of work, but also – potentially at least – introduce psychological cleavages or fault lines.

Consequently, information about organizational roles – and their content – constitutes another form of impersonal knowledge providing a basis for assessing role occupants' trust-related motives and capabilities. Role-based knowledge becomes a basis for positive expectations about others insofar as those expectations are predicated on knowledge that individuals occupy particular roles in the organization, rather than on specific, individuated knowledge regarding their capabilities or intentions.

I should emphasize at this juncture that early theorizing regarding the relationship between subordinate and superordinate group identities almost universally posited an inherent discontinuity and tension between these different levels of competing identification and role occupancy. For example, Kramer reviewed empirical evidence that the salience of subgroup identities would enhance intergroup bias and competitive orientations, thereby undermining trust and cooperation.[50] Along these lines, Putnam argued there exists a fundamental tension between what he characterized as the *bonding* social capital that arises within subgroups versus the *bridging* social capital that might help subgroups cooperate.[51] It is worth adding, however, that these arguments were predicated on the presupposition that there exists an inherent conflict between social identities at different levels. In theory, however, it is possible that various identities may enjoy complementary relations with each other. If so, they might conceivably produce compatible – and even synergistic – effects. In particular, if subgroup identities are defined in terms of positive interdependent role relations, and complementary role inputs, that enhance the collective organizational welfare, and are, in turn, supported by and integrated with the collective identity, then no such inherent tension or dysfunction need exist among them.

[50] *Ibid.*   [51] Putnam, 2000.

In fact, knowledge about subgroup identities and role occupancy may provide a basis for presumptive trust among interdependent and coordinated role occupants.

Unpacking this argument, I posit that roles can serve as constructive proxies for personalized knowledge about other organizational members in several ways. First, as Barber noted, strong expectations regarding trustworthy performance are often aligned with roles in organizations in ways that do work reasonably well to produce integrative or coordinative behavior.[52] First, role occupants are expected to fulfill the fiduciary responsibilities and obligations associated with the roles they occupy – and our experience with other people in organizations suggests that they frequently do. Thus, to the extent that people within an organization have confidence in the fact that role occupancy signals both the requisite motivation to fulfill such obligations and the requisite competence required for carrying them out, individuals can trust those role occupants presumptively, i.e., simply on the basis of their knowledge of role occupancy and the system of role relations, even in the absence of personalized knowledge regarding the individual in the role.

Consistent with these ideas, numerous scholars have noted that it is not the person in the role that is trusted so much as the *system* of expertise that produces, organizes, and ensures the role-appropriate behavior of role occupants.[53] As Dawes aptly observed in this regard, "We trust engineers because we trust engineering and believe that engineers are trained to apply valid principles of engineering."[54] Moreover, Dawes notes, "We have evidence every day that these principles are valid when we observe airplanes flying."[55] The strength of such trust arises from, and is sustained by, people's common knowledge or beliefs regarding what role occupancy implies or means. These include such things as the severity of barriers to entry into the organizational role (i.e., the *selectivity* of the organization in placing

---

[52] Barber, 1983.   [53] *Ibid.*; Dawes, 1994; Meyerson *et al.*, 1996.
[54] Dawes, 1994, 24.   [55] *Ibid.*

individuals in roles). They include also their beliefs regarding the adequacy and effectiveness of the training and processes that role occupants undergo (the efficacy of their *socialization* into the role). Finally, they encompass their perceptions of various social mechanisms intended to ensure/maintain good, faithful compliance with role behavior (e.g., vigilant monitoring, sanctioning for role violations or lapses, etc.).

As with the other foundations for presumptive trust described thus far, role-based trust functions to reduce uncertainty regarding role occupant's trust-related intentions and capabilities. They thus lessen the perceived need to verify trustworthiness when interacting with role occupants: if you're in the role, you're presumed to be up to the task.

Rule-based expectations. If knowledge about organizational roles provides one valuable source of diagnostic information regarding others' potential trustworthiness, then *organizational rules* constitutes another. Organizational rules constitute codified norms for conduct. As such, they provide a formal enunciation of collective expectations about how organizational members ought to and will behave.[56]

In this respect, organizational norms can shape expectations in two distinct and often complementary, ways.[57] First, *injunctive norms*, which are formulated and expressed in terms of "ought's," prescribe what good organizational members should do. They constitute, in other words, moralistic codes of expected conduct. *Descriptive norms*, in contrast, capture what is simply characteristic of the "normal" or prototypic group member. Despite their differences, each of these distinct kinds of norms provides a basis for coordinating expectations about others' trust-related behaviors. In particular, when the content of injunctive and descriptive norms are positive and overlapping, they provide a powerful basis for converging expectations regarding what the other members of one's group are likely to do in a given situation.

---

[56] Messick and Tenbrunsel, 1996. [57] Cialdini *et al.*, 1990.

Rule-based trust is not predicated, I should note, on members' ability to predict specific others' trust-related behaviors, but rather on their shared understandings regarding the normatively binding structure of rules guiding – and constraining – both their own and others' conduct. March and Olson noted along these lines that rule-based trust is sustained within an organization "not [by] an explicit contract ... [but rather] by [members'] socialization into the structure of rules."[58] When those socialization processes are perceived as efficacious, trust results. When they are perceived as weak, ineffectual, and lacking normative power, it does not.

A study by Fine and Holyfield provides an additional illustration of how a set of explicit rules, and the tacit understandings those rules produce, can function to create and sustain high levels of presumptive trust within an organization.[59] Their study examined the bases of trust among members of the Minnesota Mycological Society, an organization that consists of amateur mushroom collectors. This organization provided a rich setting in which to study the basis of trust for several reasons. First, the costs of misplaced trust in members' motivation and competence can be quite severe: eating mushrooms that someone else in the organization has mistakenly declared safe for consumption can lead to serious illness and even, in rare instances, death. Given such risks, Fine and Holyfield noted, credibility is lost immediately unless a mistake is reasonable. Consequently, members are likely to be highly vigilant when it comes to assessing the level of prudent or sensible trust. Second, because membership in the organization is voluntary, exit is comparatively costless. If doubts about others' trustworthiness become too great, therefore, members will take their trust elsewhere and the organization will cease to exist. Thus, the organization's very survival depends upon its ability to successfully create strong and stable perceptions of mutual trustworthiness among its members.

Fine and Holyfield identified three important foundations of presumptive trust within this organization, which they termed

---

[58] March and Olson, 1989, 27.   [59] Fine and Holyfield, 1996.

awarding trust, managing risk, and *transforming trust.* One way trust is created, they observed, is to award trust to others even when confidence in them may be lacking. For example, considerable social pressure is exerted on novices to consume dishes at banquets prepared by other members. As Fine and Holyfield put it, there is an *insistence* on trust. Thus, even if new members remain privately anxious, their public behaviors – even if somewhat coerced – connote high levels of trust. Collectively, these behavioral displays of trust in other members constitute a potent form of social proof to members that their individual acts of trust are sensible.

Fine and Holyfield further argue that, as members acquire knowledge about the organization, the nature of trust itself is transformed over time. Early on, the organization is simply (in their terminology) a *validator* of trust for new members. It eventually becomes, however, an "arena in which trusting relations are enacted and organizational interaction serves as its own reward."[60]

This insistence on presumptive trust is adaptive, of course, only if collective trustworthiness is fully warranted. Accordingly, a second crucial element in the management of presumptive trust within this organization (or any organization for that matter) occurs through practices and arrangements that ensure requisite competence and due diligence. This result is achieved partially through the meticulous socialization processes to which newcomers to the organization are subjected. Novices participate in these socialization processes with appropriate levels of commitment because it helps them personally manage the risks of mushroom eating. It also helps them secure acceptance in the social order of the group. In turn, more seasoned organizational members teach incoming novices out of a sense of obligation, having benefited from the instruction from those who came before them.

The presumptive trust created here, I should note, is not simply trust in the expertise and motivation of specific individuals, but rather

---

[60] *Ibid.,* 29.

trust in a *system* of rules that create and sustain collective expertise and motivation. Rules contribute to presumptive trust not only through their influence on individuals' expectations regarding other members' behaviors, but also by shaping their expectations regarding their own behavior. In other words, rules also influence their self-perceptions and expectations. Miller offered an excellent example of this kind of self-reinforcing dynamic. In discussing the underpinnings of mutual trust and cooperation at Hewlett-Packard (HP), he noted that, "The reality of cooperation is suggested by the open lab stock policy, which not only allows engineers access to all equipment, but encourages them to take it home for personal use."[61] From a strictly economic perspective, of course, HP's policy simply reduces monitoring and transaction costs. However, its consequences are more subtle and pervasive. As Miller observed, "The open door symbolizes and demonstrates management's trust in the cooperativeness of the employees."[62] Because such acts are so manifestly predicated on trust in others, moreover, they tend to breed trust in turn. As with many forms of social behavior, trust is governed by generalized expectations of reciprocity: all else being equal, if *I* think *you* ought to trust *me*, then *I* ought to trust *you* in return.[63]

Rule-based practices of this sort can exert subtle but powerfully self-reinforcing influences on organizational members' reciprocal expectations. As Miller noted in this regard, by eliminating time clocks and locks on equipment room doors at Hewlett-Packard, the organization built "a shared expectation among all the players that cooperation will most likely be reciprocated." The result, he went on to argue, is "a shared common knowledge in the ability of the players to reach cooperative outcomes."[64]

In sum, I have identified a number of structural and procedural factors that can contribute to the emergence and maintenance of

---

[61] Miller, 1992, 197.   [62] *Ibid.*

[63] And, indeed, this is just what Foddy *et al.*, 2009 and Tanis and Potsme, 2005 found in their empirical investigations.

[64] Miller, 1992, 197.

presumptive trust in organizations. Obviously, one of the most salient, and potentially impactful, variables on organizational functioning is the leadership of the organization. Trust, in some sense, starts at the top and trickles down. In the next section, accordingly, I consider some of the ways in which leaders can facilitate presumptive trust in their organizations.

How organizational leaders contribute to presumptive trust. If presumptive trust is predicated, as I have argued, on a confluence of ambient cues indicating the reasonableness of trusting other organizational members, then the signals that organizational leaders send constitute a particularly potent source of such trust. Leaders tend to be highly salient focal points for organizational sense-making. Not surprisingly, therefore, subordinates often pay a great deal of attention to what those in positions of power or authority do and say, as well as what they don't do and don't say.

Recognizing the central role leaders play in the trust-building process, organizational scholars have attempted to elaborate more fully the nature and impact of this relationship.[65] In one recent assessment of the literature, Dirks and Ferrin performed a useful meta-analysis of nearly four decades of research on the positive effects of trust on organizational performance.[66] They found that trust in leaders had a significant relationship with respect to a variety of important organizational outcomes, including constituents' commitment to a leader's decisions, their commitment to the organization itself, reductions in reported intentions to turnover jobs, enhanced job performance and satisfaction, and increased levels of organizational citizenship behaviors. In a similar vein, Davis *et al.* found that trust in leadership was associated with improved sales and profits, along with reduced turnover.[67] In another study, Dirks reported a relationship between players' trust in their head coach and winning in the National Basketball Association.[68] Finally, and more recently, Grant

---

[65] Dirks, 2006; Dirks and Skarlicki, 2004. [66] Dirks and Ferrin, 2002
[67] Davis *et al.*, 2000. [68] Dirks, 2000.

and Sumanth found that trust in leaders was associated with enhanced pro-social motivations and behaviors among employees, at least within the context of service organizations.[69]

Although these studies employ different outcome measures, in aggregate they suggest the constructive role that leaders play in setting positive expectations regarding the general level of trust and trustworthiness within their organizations – in short, the kind of expectations we've associated in this chapter with the emergence and maintenance of presumptive trust.

There are several specific mechanisms, I should note, by means of which leaders might contribute to the creation of presumptive trust. From an attributional perspective, leaders garner a large share of the causal credit for things that happen – and don't happen – inside their organizations. This association is so powerful that Hackman characterized the tendency as the *leader attribution error*.[70] As the label suggests, the leadership attribution error can be a source of trouble (e.g., when individuals misattribute the reasons for organizational successes or failures to leaders rather than exogenous factors). With respect to trust-building initiatives, however, it's a bias that might be beneficially exploited. Specifically, a leader can use this proclivity to heighten the sense that trust is reasonable because he or she will make sure the requisite grounds for trustworthiness are created and maintained. Evidence for this constructive role of the organizational leader as an architect or conduit of presumptive trust at the collective level emerges also, I should point out, in studies of "swift trust" in temporary organizations.[71]

From a leadership perspective, one might argue that presumptive trust must start at the top of an organization and trickle down. The leader sets the tone when it comes to trust-related expectations. Pixar Animation Studios, and its distinctive brand of leadership, provides one nice illustration of the downward flow of presumptive trust. Pixar is world renowned for its creative excellence, producing such

[69] Grant and Sumanth, 2009.   [70] Hackman, 2002.   [71] Meyerson et al., 1996.

cinematic breakthroughs as *Toy Story* and *The Incredibles*. But behind the company's technological creativity with respect to producing such innovative and successful feature-length animated films is another form of creativity – and that is its creativity with respect to creating a culture of mutual trust and assured trustworthiness. As Pixar's leader, Ed Catmull notes, "It's sometimes difficult to get creative people to work together. That takes trust and respect, which we as managers can't mandate; they must be earned over time."[72] To foster such trust, Catmull notes, "What we can do is construct an environment that nurtures trusting and respectful relationships and unleashes everyone's creativity. If we get that right, the result is a vibrant community where talented people are loyal to one another and their collective work." He concludes, "I know what I'm describing is the antithesis of the free-agency practices that prevail in the movie industry, but that's the point: I believe that community matters."[73]

Pride in work and reputation for competence and concern are among the valued attributes within Pixar's organizational culture that contribute to such trust. In fact, Pixar's reputation on these dimensions turns out to be a source of competitive advantage for securing talent. Catmull noted along these lines that the feeling of Pixar's employees that they are part of an extraordinary enterprise – and its well-earned reputation for being the best place for ambitious, idealistic animators to work makes Pixar "a magnet for talented people coming out of schools or working at other places."[74] However, concerns about trust and trustworthiness don't stop at the boundary of the organization. Pixar's leaders care not only about the cultivation of presumptive trust among its talented employees within the organization, but also care about fulfilling deeply felt obligations to the public it serves. In particular, its leaders are committed to fulfilling the public's expectations that all of Pixar's products will honor the intelligence and social values of the parents and children who go to see their

---

[72] Ed Catmull, 2008, 67.   [73] *Ibid.*, 69.   [74] *Ibid.*, 71.

films. As Pixar's then-Chief Creative Officer John Lasseter once proclaimed, "At Pixar, we always like to over deliver. We want the audience to be entertained from the very beginning to the very end."[75] One final point that merits making here is that presumptive trust does not arise in its most mature and efficacious form when only one or two of these ingredients are in place. Ideally, deep and enduring trust (and the resultant trustworthiness such trust engenders) emerges only when multiple, converging, and mutually reinforcing influences come together in just the right way. To be truly resilient and max-imally impactful, presumptive trust must be "overdetermined" trust.

SOME CONCLUSIONS AND SUGGESTED DIRECTIONS FOR FURTHER INQUIRY

The two primary aims of this brief chapter have been to, first, introduce the construct of *presumptive trust*, and, second, to explicate some of its psychological, social, and organizational antecedents. I have argued that presumptive trust provides an important relational foundation for organizations – one that nurtures the emergence of mutual trust and trustworthiness among organizational members. High levels of such reciprocal trust and trustworthiness can be thought of as a form of "social capital" which benefits not only individual organizational members but also the entire organization in terms of more productive exchanges and reduced transaction costs. When presumptive trust is present, I have argued, the perceived necessity for negotiating its conditions or protecting against breaches of trust are greatly mitigated.

A secondary, but not less important, aim of this chapter has been to suggest a practical, prescriptive framework for thinking about some of the necessary conditions and concrete antecedents for leaders to focus attention on when hoping to create groups and organizations high in such presumptive trust. The framework presented in this chapter, in effect, constitutes a sort of organizational "blueprint" for

---

[75] Quoted in Catmull, 2008, 70.

motivated leaders to use when trying to think about how they might go about creating more trusting and trustworthy organizations from the inside-out and ground up.

The present framework, obviously, does not fully exhaust the range of psychological, social, and organizational variables that a more comprehensive or integrative framework might address. The nature of presumptive trust might vary across organizational and institutional domains. Nonetheless, I hope, the present framework provides a useful starting point upon which future efforts might build.

In that spirit, it might be helpful to briefly entertain some ideas regarding further extensions of this framework and its implications. One important extension would be to connect the ideas presented in this chapter regarding the antecedents of presumptive trust (as a psychological state) with other recent approaches for dealing with low trust, including exciting new work on trust repair.[76] This research addresses the vital question of whether trust in an organization or its leadership can be reestablished or restored after it has been damaged or undermined. Several promising new models and research streams suggest solid grounds for optimism on this front. Gillespie *et al.*, for instance, have articulated a powerful and practical multivariate framework for restoring institutional trust.[77] An attractive feature of their model is that it includes concerns about corporate governance, external regulation, reputation, and other factors which can be leveraged in order to begin to rebuild trust in tainted organizations or their leaders. Of course, one must expect such a rebuilding process to be slow and effortful, but their research suggests there is at least a starting point for undertaking such an initiative.

Approaching this general problem from a different theoretical vantage point – a procedural justice framework – Brockner and Bianchi have elaborated on the importance of a variety of process

---

[76] See: Kramer and Lewicki, 2010; Kramer and Pittinsky, 2012, for recent literature reviews.
[77] Gillespie at al., 2012.

and outcome variables that influence trust in decision-making authorities.[78] An important implication of their framework is that presumptive trust will likely be high only when such authorities manage adroitly perceptions and attributions of *both* organizational procedures and their outcomes. Finally, Lewicki and Polin have documented in considerable detail the importance of effective apologies for trust repair.[79] Given the low trust that currently exists in business and its leaders around the globe, their research suggests, a few appropriate and even long overdue "mea culpas" might help jump-start the slow process of restoring the public's lost trust.

Although useful, such approaches should not be construed as offering sure-fire quick fixes or panaceas. Indeed, in some cases, rushing to restore trust is the last thing we ought to do. Accordingly, another important topic for further exploration is how presumptive trust might sometimes get organizations or their leaders in trouble. In situations where the costs of misplaced trust are high, too much presumptive trust can obviously create potential vulnerabilities and risks. As one illustration, President Ronald Reagan's presumptive trust in his aides and advisers was ill-served during the Iran–Contra controversy that nearly toppled his presidency. Similarly, President Kennedy's initial high levels of trust in his CIA and military advisers during the planning for the ill-fated Bay of Pigs invasion presented him with one of the worst fiascoes of his administration.[80] Finally, and more recently, too much trust in other organizational members' diligence and competence may get interdependent decision-making groups in trouble, as evidenced during the disastrous failure of the US intelligence agencies to coordinate and cooperate effectively with each prior to the 9/11 terrorist attacks on American soil.[81] As I have argued elsewhere on the basis of such examples, too much presumptive trust in a group or organization – manifested as inappropriately high levels of delegation, deference, and complacency – is a recipe for disaster.[82]

---

[78] Brockner and Bianchi, 2012.   [79] Lewicki and Polin, 2012.
[80] Kramer, 1998, 2008.   [81] Kramer, 2005.   [82] Kramer, 2009.

And that observation leads to one final important point for me to make before closing this chapter. I hope by now it is obvious that the central conceit behind the notion that there are virtues to presumptive trust is that such trust is predicated on actual, underlying trustworthiness. Presumptive trust without actual trustworthiness, obviously, would be a hollow achievement and potentially sets the stage for further and costly abuses of the public's trust – as the examples in the previous paragraph illustrate. This raises the thorny question: how much presumptive trust is optimal in any group or organization? Stated another way, when is some form of presumptive distrust – or its weaker cousins, wariness and suspicion – actually warranted and welcomed? I have addressed this important question at length elsewhere,[83] using a judgment and decision-making framework. For the present purposes, I would simply highlight the important point that presumptive trust, when operating effectively, should be thought of as a "tempered" or disciplined form of trust.[84] Presumptive trust, as such, functions to keep one's level of trust firmly anchored or grounded in the extant evidence of just how much trust is appropriate or warranted. To be truly adaptive and generative, our trust-related expectations must always be calibrated so as to match or "fit" the ecologies in which they are embedded.

REFERENCES

Bacharach, M., and Gambetta, D. (2001), 'Trust in signs.' In K. S. Cook (ed.), *Trust in Society*. New York: Russell Sage Foundation, 148–184.

Baier, A. (1986), 'Trust and anti-trust.' *Ethics*, 96, 231–260.

Barber, B. (1983), *The Logic and Limits of Trust*. New Brunswick, NJ: Rutgers University Press.

Bohnet, I., and Huck, S. (2004), 'Repetition and reputation: implications for trust and trustworthiness when institutions change.' *American Economic Association Proceedings*, 94, 362–366.

Boyle, R. and Bonacich, P. (1970), 'The development of trust and mistrust in mixed-motives games.' *Sociometry*, 33, 123–139.

---

[83] Kramer, 1998; Kramer, 2002.   [84] Kramer, 2009.

Brewer, M. B. (1981), 'Ethnocentrism and its role in interpersonal trust.' In M. B. Brewer and B. E. Collins (eds.), *Scientific Inquiry and the Social Sciences*. San Francisco, CA: Jossey-Bass.

Brewer, M. B. (1996), 'In-group favoritism: The subtle side of intergroup discrimination.' In D. M. Messick and A Tenbrunsel (eds.), *Behavioral Research and Business Ethics*. New York: Russell Sage.

Brewer, M. B. (2008), 'Depersonalized trust and in-group cooperation.' In J. I. Krueger (ed.), *Rationality and Social Responsibility: Essays in Honor of Robyn Mason Dawes*. New York: Psychology Press, 215–232.

Brockner, J. and Bianchi, E. C. (2012), 'Breaking the vicious cycle of low trust in decision-making authorities: it's what they do and how they do it.' In R. M. Kramer and T. L. Pittinsky (eds.), *Restoring Trust in Organizations and Leaders: Enduring Challenges and Emerging Answers*. New York: Oxford University Press, 257–274.

Brothers, D. (1995), *Falling Backwards: An Exploration of Trust and Self-experience*. New York: Norton.

Catmull, E. (2008), 'How Pixar fosters collective creativity.' *Harvard Business Review*, 86, 65–72.

Center for Public Leadership (2009), *National Leadership Index 2009: A National Study of Confidence in Leadership*. Cambridge, MA: Harvard Kennedy School.

Cialdini, R. B., Reno, R. R., and Kallgren, C. A. (1990), 'A focus theory of normative conduct.' *Journal of Personality and Social Psychology*, 58, 1015–1026.

Cook, K. S., Kramer, R. M., Thom, D. H., Stepanikova, Mollborn, S. B., and Cooper, R. M. (2004), 'Trust and distrust in physician-patient relationships: Antecedents and consequences.' In R. M. Kramer and K. S. Cook (eds.), *Trust in Organizations: Dilemmas and Approaches*. New York: Russell Sage, 65–98.

Cook, K. S., Levi, M., and Hardin, R. (2009), *Whom Can We Trust: How Groups, Networks, and Institutions Make Trust Possible*. New York: Russell Sage Foundation.

Davis, J., Schoorman, F. D., Mayer, R. C., and Tan, H. (2000), 'The trusted general manager and business unit performance: empirical evidence of a competitive advantage.' *Strategic Management Journal*, 21, 543–576.

Dawes, R. M. (1994), *House of Cards: Psychology and Psychotherapy Built on Myth*. New York: Free Press.

Dirks, K. T. (2000), 'Trust in leadership and team performance: evidence from NCAA basketball.' *Journal of Applied Psychology*, 85, 1004–1012.

Dirks, K. T., and Ferrin, D. L. (2002), 'Trust in leadership: meta-analytic findings and implications for research and practice.' *Journal of Applied Psychology*, 87, 611–628.

Dirks, K. T. (2006), 'Three fundamental questions regarding trust in leaders.' In R. Bachmann and A. Zaheer (eds.), *Handbook of Trust Research*. Northampton, MA: Edward Elgar, 15–28.

Dirks, K. T. and Skarlicki, D. P. (2004), 'Trust in leaders: existing research and emerging issues.' In R. M. Kramer and K. S. Cook (eds.), *Trust and Distrust in Organizations: Dilemmas and Approaches*. New York: Russell Sage Foundation, 21–40.

Edelman and Associates (2009), *Trust Barometer: The Tenth Global Opinion Leader Survey*. New York: Edelman and Associates.

Edelman and Associates (2012), *Trust Barometer: The 2012 Global Opinion Leaders Study*. New York: Edelman and Associates.

Elsbach, K. (2004), 'Managing images of trustworthiness.' In R. M. Kramer and K. S. Cook (eds.), *Trust and Distrust In Organizations: Dilemmas And Approaches*. New York: Russell Sage Foundation, vol. VII, 275–291.

Farrell, H. (2009), 'Institutions and midlevel explanations of trust.' In K. S. Cook, M. Levi, and R. Hardin (eds.), *Whom Can We Trust? How Groups, Networks, and Institutions Make Trust Possible*. New York: Russell Sage Foundation, 127–148.

Fine, G. and Holyfield, L. (1996), 'Secrecy, trust and dangerous leisure: generating group cohesion in voluntary organizations.' *Social Psychology Quarterly*, 59, 22–38.

Fiske, S. F., Cuddy, A. J., and Glick, P. (2007), 'Universal dimensions of social cognition: warmth and competence.' *Trends in Cognitive Sciences*, 11, 77–83.

Fiske, S. F., Cuddy, Glick, P., and Xu, J. (2002), 'A model of (often mixed) stereotype content: competence and warmth follow from perceived status and competition.' *Journal of Personality and Social Psychology*, 82, 878–902.

Foddy, M., Yamagishi, T., and Platow, M. (2009), 'Group-based trust in strangers: the role of stereotypes and expectations.' *Psychological Science*, 20, 419–422.

Frankel, T. (2006). *Trust and Honesty: America's Business Culture at a Crossroad*. New York: Oxford University Press.

Frey, B. S., and Stutzer, A. (2007), *Economics and Psychology: A Promising New Cross-Disciplinary Field*. Cambridge, MA: MIT Press.

Fukuyama, F. (1995), *Trust: The Social Virtues and the Creation of Prosperity*. New York: Free Press.

Gambetta, D. (1988), 'Can we trust trust?' In (ed.) D. Gambetta, *Trust: Making and Breaking Cooperative Relationships*. Cambridge: Blackwell, 213–237.

Gillespie, N., Hurley, R., Dietz, G., and Bachmann, R. (2012), 'Restoring institutional trust after the global financial crisis: a systemic approach.' In R. M. Kramer and T. L. Pittinsky (eds.), *Restoring Trust in Organizations and Leaders: Enduring Challenges and Emerging Answers*. New York: Oxford University Press, 185–211.

Grant, A. M. and Sumanth, J. J. (2009), 'Mission possible? The performance of prosocially motivated employees depends on manager trustworthiness.' *Journal of Applied Psychology*, 94, 927–944.

Hackman, J. R. (2002), *Leading Teams: Setting the Stage for Great Performances*. Boston, MA: Harvard Business School Press.

Hetherington, M. J. (2005), *Why Trust Matters: Declining Political Trust and the Demise of American Liberalism*. Princeton, NJ: Princeton University Press.

Knez, M. and Camerer, C. (1994), 'Creating expectational assets in the laboratory: coordination in "weakest link" games.' *Strategic Management Journal*, 15, 101–19.

Kosfeld, M., Heinrichs, M., Zak, P. J., Fischbacher, U., Fehr, E. (2005), 'Oxytocin increases trust in humans.' *Nature*, 435, 673–676.

Kramer, R. M. (1991), 'Intergroup relations and organizational dilemmas: the role of categorization processes.' In L. L. Cummings and B. M. Staw (eds.), *Research in Organizational Behavior*. Greenwich, CT: JAI Press, vol. XIII, 191–228.

Kramer, R. M. (1994), 'The sinister attribution error: paranoid cognition and collective distrust in groups and organizations.' *Motivation and Emotion*, 18, 199–231.

Kramer, R. M. (1996), 'Divergent realities and convergent disappointments in the hierarchic relation: trust and the intuitive auditor at work.' In R. M. Kramer and T. M. Tyler (eds.), *Trust In Organizations: Frontiers of Theory and Research*. Thousand Oaks, CA: Sage, 216–245.

Kramer, R. M. (1998), 'Paranoid cognition in social systems.' *Personality and social psychology review*, 2, 251–275.

Kramer, R. M. (1999), 'Trust and distrust in organizations.' *Annual Review of Psychology*, 50, 569–598.

Kramer, R. M. (2002), 'When paranoia makes sense.' *Harvard Business Review*, 80, 62–71.

Kramer, R. M. (2003), 'The virtues of prudent trust.' In R. Westwood and S. Clegg (eds.), *Debating Organization: Point-Counterpoint in Organizational Studies*. New York: Blackwell, 339–356.

Kramer, R. M. (2005), 'A failure to communicate: 9/11 and the tragedy of the informational commons.' Special issue titled 'Organizational perspectives on the 9/11 Commission Report,' *International Journal of Public Management*, 8, 1–20.

Kramer, R. M. (2008), 'Presidential leadership and group folly: re-appraising the role of groupthink in the Bay of Pigs decisions.' In C. L. Hoyt, G. R. Goethals, and D. R. Forsythe (eds.), *Leadership at the Cross-Roads*. Westport, CT: Praeger, vol. I, 230–249.

Kramer, R. M. (2009), 'Rethinking trust.' *Harvard Business Review*, 87, 68–78.

Kramer, R. M. and Brewer, M. B. (1984), 'Effects of group identity on resource use in a simulated commons dilemma.' *Journal of Personality and Social Psychology*, 46, 1044–1057.

Kramer, R. M. and Brewer, M. B. (1986), 'Social group identity and the emergence of cooperation in resource conservation dilemmas.' In H. Wilke, C. Rutte, and D. Messick (eds.), *Experimental Studies of Social Dilemmas*. Frankfurt: Peter Lang, 46–61.

Kramer, R. M. and Lewicki, R. J. (2010), Repairing and enhancing trust: approaches to reducing organizational trust deficits. In J. P. Walsh and A. P. Brief (eds.), *Academy of Management Annals*. New York: Routledge, vol. IV, 245–278.

Kramer, R. M. and Pittinsky, T. L. (2012), *Restoring Trust in Organizations and Leaders*. New York: Oxford University Press.

Kramer, R. M. and Tyler, T. (1996), *Trust in Organizations*. Newbury Park, CA: Sage Publications.

Lane, C. and Bachmann, R. (1998), *Trust within and between Organizations: Conceptual Issues and Empirical Applications*. New York: Oxford University Press.

Lewicki, R. J. and Bunker, B. B. (1996), 'Trust in relationships: a model of trust development and decline.' In R. Kramer and T. Tyler (eds.), *Trust in Organizations*. Newbury Park, CA: Sage, 114–139.

Lewicki, R. J. and Bunker, B. B. (1995), 'Trust in relationships: a model of trust development and decline.' In B. B. Bunker and J. Z. Rubin (eds.), *Conflict, Cooperation, and Justice*. San Francisco, CA: Jossey-Bass.

Lewicki, R. J., and Polin, B. (2012), 'The art of the apology: the structure and effectiveness of apologies in trust repair.' In R. M. Kramer and T. L. Pittinsky (eds.), *Restoring Trust in Organizations and Leaders: Enduring Challenges and Emerging Answers*. New York: Oxford University Press, 95–128.

Lewis, J. D. and Weigert, A. (1985), 'Trust as a social reality.' *Social Forces*, 63, 967–985.

Lindskold, S. (1978), 'Trust development, the GRIT proposal, and the effects of conciliatory acts on conflict and cooperation.' *Psychology Bulletin*, 85, 772–793.

Lorsch, J. W., Berlowitz, L., and Zelleke, A. (2005), *Restoring Trust in American Business*. Cambridge, MA: MIT Press.

Lount, R. B., Jr. (2010), 'The impact of positive mood on trust in interpersonal and intergroup interactions.' *Journal of Personality and Social Psychology*, 98, 420–433.

McAllister, D. J. (1995), 'Affect- and cognition- based trust as foundations for interpersonal cooperation in organizations.' *Academy of Management Journal*, 38, 24–59.

McEvily, B., Weber, R. A., Bicchieri, C., and Ho, V. T. (2006), 'Can groups be trusted? An experimental study of trust in collective entities.' In R. Bachmann and A. Zaheer (eds.), *Handbook of Trust Research* Northampton, MA: Elgar, 52–67.

March, J. G. and Olsen, J. P. (1989), *Rediscovering Institutions: The Organizational Basis of Politics*. New York: Free Press.

Mayer, R. C., Davis, J. H., and Schorrman, F. D. (1995), 'An integrative model of organizational trust.' *Academy of Management Review*, 20, 709–734.

Messick, D. M. and Tenbrunsel, A. E. (1996), *Codes of conduct: Behavioral Research into Business Ethics*. New York: Russell Sage Foundation.

Messick, D. M., Wilke, H., Brewer, M. B., Kramer, R. M., Zemke, P. E and Lui, L. (1983), 'Individual adaptations and structural change as solutions to social dilemmas.' *Journal of Personality and Social Psychology*, 44, 294–309.

Meyerson, D., Weick, K. and Kramer, R. M. (1996), 'Swift trust and temporary groups.' In R. M. Kramer and T. R. Tyler (eds.), *Trust in Organizations: Frontiers of Theory and Research*. Thousand Oaks, CA: Sage.

Miller, G. J. (1992), *Managerial Dilemmas: The Political Economy of Hierarchies*. New York: Cambridge University Press.

Platow, M., McClintock, C. G., and Liebrand, W. (1990), 'Predicting intergroup fairness and in-group bias in the minimal group paradigm.' *European Journal of Social Psychology*, 20, 221–239.

Putnam, R. D. (1993), *Making Democracy Work: Civic Traditions in Modern Italy*. Princeton, NJ: Princeton University Press.

Putnam, R. D. (2000), *Bowling Alone*. New York: Simon & Schuster.

Rule, N. O. and Ambady, N. (2008), 'First impressions: peeking at the neural underpinnings.' In N. Ambady and J. J. Skowronski (eds.), *First Impressions*. New York: Guilford, 35–56.

Shapiro, D. L., Sheppard, B. H., and Cherakin, L. (1992), 'Business on a handshake.' *Negotiations Journal*, 8, 365–377.

Sheppard, B. H. and Tuchinsky, M. (1996), 'Micro-OB and the network organization.' In R. M. Kramer and T. R. Tyler (eds.), *Trust in Organizations*. Thousand Oaks, CA: Sage.

Tanis, M. and Postmes, T. (2005), 'A social identity approach to trust: interpersonal perception, group membership, and trusting behavior.' *European Journal of Social Psychology*, 35, 413–424.

Weber, J. M., Malhotra, D., and Murnighan, J. K. (2005), 'Normal acts of irrational trust: motivated attributions and the trust development process.' In B. M. Staw and R. M. Kramer (eds.), *Research in Organizational Behavior*. New York: Elsevier Press, vol. XXVI, 75–102.

Yamagishi, T and Yamagishi, M. (1994), 'Trust and commitment in the United States and Japan.' *Motivation and Emotions*, 18, 129–166.

Yamagishi, T., Jin, N., and Y Kiyonari, T. (1999), 'Bounded generalized reciprocity: in-group boasting and in-group favoritism.' *Advances in Group Processes*, 16, 161–197.

Yamagishi, T. and Kiyonari, T. (2000), 'The group as the container of generalized reciprocity.' *Social Psychology Quarterly*, 63, 116–132.

Yuki, M., Maddux, M., Brewer, M. B., and Takemura, K. (2005), 'Cross-cultural differences in relationship- and group- based trust.' *Personality and Social Psychology Bulletin*, 31, 48–62.

Zak, P. (2012), *The Moral Molecule: The Sources of Love and Prosperity*. New York: Dutton.

Zucker, L. G. (1986). 'Production of trust: institutional sources of economic structure, 1840–1920.' In B. M Staw and L. L. Cummings (eds.), *Research in Organizational Behavior*, 8, 53–111.

9 Building trust through reputation management

Paul Argenti

EXECUTIVE SUMMARY

THE SITUATION

Business scandals, coupled with the adoption of digital communications platforms such as social networks, have created a perfect storm of distrust. Never has there been such public awareness of corporate malfeasance, and never have there been so many channels through which constituents can voice their concerns.

KEY QUESTIONS

What is the relationship between trust and reputation? How can social media affect the erosion of trust? What is the importance of authenticity in times of crisis? How can poor leadership escalate a reputational crisis?

NEW KNOWLEDGE

Identity is the only part of reputation management that an organization can actually create and control. It is critical that identity be strategically shaped.

Stakeholders' access to social media tools lends them a profound ability to impact a business's success or failure.

Reputation is a source of tangible economic value in terms of analyst valuations and stock performance. The less tangible aspects of a strong reputation can also result in competitive advantage. Companies with strong reputations attract and retain the best talent, as well as loyal customers and business partners, all of which contribute positively to growth and success.

KEY LESSONS

A company's communications strategy must correlate with its desired outcome. If you want your audience to understand a message, explain it to them clearly. But if you're trying to sell them something, you need to get them involved in the process. And today that means using digital and social media to communicate with key constituencies.

Reputation is more than just another public relations strategy or ad campaign; it is the basis for trust. Reputational success, once earned, must be managed, measured, and nurtured through an effective reputation management strategy. Reputation is now an integral driver in a company's success and credibility, but many managers who have not thought about corporate reputation continue to underestimate its value.

In a crisis, embracing social media as a means of enhancing conversations with disgruntled stakeholders can be beneficial. Finding a way to talk positively to restore consumer confidence is more important than ever. Many companies, however, are afraid to talk much at all. In an era where every company should be looking to build trust, too many have gone quiet. Companies willing to address problems head-on are the ones who will win back confidence.

INTRODUCTION

Trust in business, as measured by professional polling agencies, academics, and media surveys, has been on the decline for over thirty-five years in the United States. Due to a variety of corporate scandals at the beginning of the twenty-first century and the financial crisis that has lingered into this decade, that decline has accelerated even more dramatically in the past year. In fact, a 2011 Gallup Poll reveals that less than 20 percent of Americans now have confidence that business acts responsibly.[1]

This stems, in part, from a succession of corporate scandals that started in 2001 with the infamous dissolution of Enron, and that has continued with the fall of storied investment banks Bear Stearns,

[1] Gallup, 2011.

Merrill Lynch, and Lehman Brothers; the SEC investigations into prominent financial institutions including Goldman Sachs and AIG, and the BP Deepwater Horizon disaster of 2010, to name only a few. These events, coupled with the adoption of digital communications platforms such as social networks, have created a perfect storm: never has there been such public awareness of corporate malfeasance, and never have there been so many channels with which constituents can voice their concerns.

The Occupy Wall Street (Occupy) movement is an excellent recent symbol of the skepticism and anger that permeates the current business environment. This movement, which started in September 2011 as a largely peaceful protest over growing income inequity in the United States, captures the current zeitgeist for mistrust. Protesters focused on the growing inequity between executive compensation and unemployment, and made extensive use of social media, publishing an online daily newspaper to communicate news and marching orders to participants. Organizers also executed a branding campaign for the movement based on the slogan "we are the 99 percent," meant to highlight the growing income gap between the top 1 percent of earners and the remaining 99 percent. Although critics derided the movement for its lack of clear focus and actionable objectives, by early 2012, Occupy had spread to cities around the globe, including Paris, London, Berlin, Hong Kong, and Rome.[2]

Occupy's dramatic growth underscores a central irony of today's environment: never has trust in business been lower, yet never has it been more important. The 2012 Edelman Trust Barometer also found that people believe that trust, transparency, and honest business practices influence corporate reputation more than the quality of products and services or financial performance of a company.[3] Clearly, companies that can establish and maintain trustworthiness in this environment have a competitive advantage. Edelman's and other studies suggest that in today's environment, corporate

[2] Argenti, 2012.   [3] Edelman, 2012.

reputation has emerged as a key factor influencing consumer behavior and, ultimately, a company's financial performance.[4] Understanding the relationship between trust and reputation is therefore one of the critical challenges of our time.

THE CURRENT ENVIRONMENT FOR REPUTATION AND TRUST IN BUSINESS

As referenced above, a number of factors have come together over the course of the last decade to catalyze a massive decline in trust: a wake of corporate scandals and a turbulent economy, intense public scrutiny of business, disillusionment over excessive executive pay, and the growth of digital communications platforms. In the past year, all of this seems to have erupted into historically low levels of trust in business, and a focus on corporate reputation.

In this section, we will look at three case studies that help define the current environment for reputation and trust from different perspectives. The first looks at how social media can play into the erosion of trust, the second underscores the importance of authenticity in times of crisis, and the third illustrates how poor leadership can escalate a reputational crisis.

NETFLIX GETS LOST IN THE (E)MAIL

Perhaps no single phenomenon has changed the nature of trust in business more than the emergence and continuing adoption of digital communications platforms. As Courtney Barnes and I wrote about in our 2009 book *Digital Strategies for Powerful Corporate Communications*, this phenomenon grew as a result of globalization, stakeholder empowerment, and the network revolution. The rapid spread of information has led to greater scrutiny of business.

Before the digital explosion at the turn of the twenty-first century, corporations' reputations were shaped by one-dimensional messaging that was pushed down the corporate ladder and disseminated

---

[4] Gillen, 2011.

without discussion. But, with an ever-growing list of new tools, stakeholders – companies' employees, customers, or shareholders – have
become empowered to talk back. Social communities and blogs give
stakeholders the ability to disseminate their own messages about
an organization, and to share and build communities around that
information. The rise in corporate scandals and the credit crisis,
combined with the emergence of these new channels, has radically
altered the business landscape.

This convergence has occurred on a global level: technology has
strengthened communication channels around the world to produce
what Canadian philosopher Marshall McLuhan foresaw decades ago –
the creation of a world so interwoven by shared knowledge that it
becomes a "global village." This trend has had a monumental impact
on trust in business, particularly over the last decade.

Through the internet, people have discovered and invented
new ways to share relevant knowledge with blinding speed. The data
are staggering: by the end of 2011, nearly 80 percent of the world's
population had a mobile cellular phone subscription, and more than
32 percent regularly used the internet.[5] Collectively, we created nearly
1.8 trillion gigabytes of information in 2011.[6] These numbers translate
into communications issues that simply didn't exist in the corporate
world ten years ago. The current global connectivity accentuates the
volume at which negative feelings can be heard, and makes it difficult
for companies to prevent negative – and positive – news from reaching
people. Data suggests that these numbers will only continue to
increase as consumers assume further control of corporate reputations
and communicate with each other in real time, 24/7.

An excellent case of how this instantaneous interaction–
feedback–accountability loop can torch a corporate reputation is
Netflix's 2011 faulty pricing and business strategy. In July 2011,
Netflix announced that it was separating its DVD and streaming
services and creating two separate pricing plans. The decision was

[5] Miniwatts, 2011.   [6] Gantz and Reinsel, 2011.

presented by Netflix as one that would give its customers more choice, when in reality, subscription prices had actually been raised by 60 percent for its DVD service. This triggered a storm of criticism online that translated into a serious decline in subscriptions: between June and September 2011, the company lost 800,000 subscribers and more than $2 billion in market value.[7]

In September, CEO Reed Hastings issued a public apology, at the same time making a further announcement that Netflix was rebranding its DVD service under a new name, "Qwikster." A month later, Qwikster was cancelled.

This chain of announcements, apologies, and reversals damaged both Netflix's reputation and stock price. Prior to the restructuring of its services, Netflix had been celebrated as a company known for its market penetration and ability to deftly cross technological divides.[8] Netflix was the nine-time consecutive winner of the ForeSee Results Top 100 Online Retail Satisfaction Index, an annual metric that is based on "the scientific methodology of the American Customer Satisfaction Index (ACSI), which predicts sales, loyalty, and word of mouth recommendations."[9] Where exactly did Netflix go wrong, and how did its communications strategy hurt its reputation and ultimately erode the trust of its customers?

In many ways, Netflix's mistake was not the proposed price increase: while a 60 percent jump is substantial, Netflix could have rationalized to its customers that because the cost of licensing content was rising, the old subscription fee of $10 was not sustainable.[10] Moreover, the company was understandably taking strides toward evolving with the digital revolution, rather than against it, like many of its competitors (including Blockbuster and Borders).[11]

The real error was the way Netflix communicated to its customers, and its lack of awareness of what mattered to them. Netflix's decision to split its services was a fairly typical consultant-driven

[7] Wingfield, 2011.   [8] Kardashian, 2011.   [9] ForeSee, 2012.
[10] Kardashian, 2011.   [11] Sudhaman and Holmes, 2012.

choice: management acted in secret, without gathering feedback from the marketplace.[12] In the past, this strategy might have worked. The concept may have fallen flat, but, silently, without the thunderous echo that can reverberate online. Twenty years ago, maybe even ten, Netflix would have been in control of its own misstep and had time to fix the problem and implement a solution before putting its reputation on the line.

In its failure to communicate with perhaps its most important constituency – Netflix customers – the company missed something intangible: subscribers liked knowing they could get a DVD, even if they didn't use the service. As French writer Antoine de Saint-Exupéry wrote in *The Little Prince*, "What is essential is invisible to the eye." In this case, Netflix didn't account for the emotional attachment its customers had to the DVD service and the drama that would ensure from its cancellation.[13]

Had Netflix engaged with its customers online, it could have avoided considerable damage to both its reputation and financial bottom line. One of the benefits of the two-way conversation enabled by social media is the opportunity to communicate directly with constituents. On Facebook and Twitter, customers can be included in corporate decisions, and in fact, in today's environment, they must be. Stakeholders' access to social media tools lends them a profound ability to impact a business's success or failure. Messaging no longer belongs to the company alone, but can be disseminated and reinterpreted by special interest groups, lone bloggers, activist investors, and any other individual with a laptop and an opinion. Had Netflix invested resources to establish a more intimate understanding of its customers' identities and preferences, a clear picture of an innovation that would have enhanced their brand identity might have emerged, along with the awareness of the risks and failures that could derail that innovation.

The broader lesson is that a company's communications strategy must correlate with its desired outcome. If you want your

[12] Kardashian, 2011.   [13] *Ibid.*

audience to understand a message, explain it to them clearly. But if you're trying to sell them something, you need to get them involved in the process. And today, that means using digital and social media to communicate with key constituencies.

BP BLOWS A GASKET

While Netflix's branding crisis severely damaged their corporate reputation, it passed the moral smell test: no one died, and no animals or environmental ecosystems were harmed in the process. The BP Deepwater Horizon oil spill, however, traded in more than DVDs. It traded in human lives, and was one of the biggest natural disasters in US history. While some members of the public might have been willing to forgive BP for what might have been a series of accidents or the fault of one of its partners, the context of the spill in the company's overall PR and reputation strategy pushed many from healthy skepticism to rage.

In July of 2000, BP launched what has since become known as one of the greatest greenwashing campaigns in the history of advertising, a $200 million corporate advertising and public relations campaign designed by Ogilvy & Mather with the goal of positioning BP as environmentally friendly. Not only did the company introduce a new corporate slogan, "Beyond Petroleum," but it replaced its green shield logo with the Helios symbol, a green and yellow sunburst. Some found this campaign refreshing for a large oil company, but those who knew the industry found it ludicrous. The campaign focused on BP's smallest energy sector, renewable energy, while ignoring its major one: the business of extracting oil. Although BP spent $45 million to purchase a solar energy company in 1999, that investment dwarfs in comparison to the $26 billion spent on ARCO (a drilling operations company) the year before.[14] Prior to 2010, BP had been accused of environmental regulation breaches, oil and propane gas price manipulation, safety violations, falsifying inspection reports, and hazardous substance

[14] Landman, 2010.

dumping, not to mention its involvement in the highly controversial oil sands project in Alberta, Canada.[15] The oil sands investment, in particular, was criticized by many environmental activists as an environmental disaster and a forewarning of a company that prized profit over responsibility. It's clear in retrospect that BP had already been at the center of great controversy prior to the Gulf leak.

Environmental irresponsibility aside, BP also showed signs of a significant management problem. Leaks in the Alaskan pipeline, exploding tanks in Texas, financial issues in London, and the resignation of its CEO after a sordid affair all pointed to a failure of management that made the campaign aspirational more than representational. In fact, the White House Oil Commission ultimately concluded that the cause of the Deepwater explosion and subsequent leak was "a systematic management failure at BP" that was in place long before 2010.[16]

Despite these realities, the campaign seemed to work. Sales from 2004 to 2005 rose from $192 billion to $240 billion then to $266 billion in 2006. Moreover, a Landor Associates survey of consumers found that 21 percent of them thought BP was the most green oil company. BP claimed that from 2000–2007, its brand awareness went from 4 percent to 67 percent.[17] Perhaps because of this success, incoming CEO Tony Hayward decided to move the company back to its more traditional focus on extraction and finances, rather than marketing. In 2008, Hayward reduced spending on corporate advertising to $53.5 million, down from $75 million in 2007; in 2009, that number was further reduced to $32.8 million.[18] By the time Deepwater exploded, most of the communications infrastructure that had been in place just a few years before was gone. BP had not only reduced its investment in brand equity, but the most recent marketing campaign it could point to was one that was completely at odds with reality. Had Deepwater been the disaster of Exxon Mobil,

---

[15] Wikipedia, 2012.   [16] *Guardian*, 2011.
[17] *Environmental Leader*, 2008.   [18] James, 2010.

the public may have been less surprised. The 1989 Exxon Valdez disaster had been the worst oil spill of its kind in US history. Even Shell, the perpetrator of decades of environmental neglect in Nigeria, was more likely to be associated in the eyes of the public with environmental irresponsibility. But BP in a failure to articulate and authenticate their brand in relation to their culture and business, had positioned themselves as the "good guys" in the energy sector.

As the disaster unfolded in the summer of 2010, any reputational capital that BP still had in place through the campaign began to erode. Protests in front of BP's London headquarters, boycotts at BP gas stations, and 24-hours news coverage of the "BP oil spill" helped to degrade trust and belief in BP's brand image, as well as leading to a 52 percent drop in stock value, net quarter loss of $17 billion, and over $3 billion in clean-up costs. Perhaps worse was BP's ensuing marketing campaign, a series of apologetic ads that promised to make things right, including a widely ridiculed message from CEO Hayward, who only days before had been caught in an insensitive gaffe claiming he "wanted his life back."[19] In the spirit of repentance, BP senior executives gave up their bonuses in 2010 in an effort to restore trust in the company, but by 2011, were awarded a 3,000 percent increase, the highest over the past thirty years.[20]

Two years later, the company continues to dig itself out of endless litigation and public mistrust. BP represents a cautionary tale of the role authenticity must play in modern marketing campaigns. Reputation is more than just another public relations strategy or ad campaign. It is the basis for trust.

LISTENING SKILLS LEAD TO PROBLEMS AT NEWS CORPORATION

Newspapers may be black and white, but corporate reputations rarely are. The phone hacking scandal that forced the UK's *News of the World* to shut down in July 2011 was so shocking that it's hard to

---

[19] *Huffington Post*, 2010.   [20] Namezee, 2011.

imagine, in retrospect, that it could have been avoidable. The events themselves may have unfolded the same – clearly, whatever corporate culture in which such acts could have occurred had been simmering for many years – but the response of the executives running the paper, not the facts themselves, was what ultimately brought things to a boil.

In June 2007, British newspaper the *Guardian* exposed that a murdered school girl's phone messages were hacked and deleted at the height of the investigation into her disappearance by journalists at *News of the World*. At the time the messages were hacked, the victim had not yet been found, and her mother, along with the police investigating the case, believed that Milly had checked her messages and was still alive. Along with this heart-wrenching betrayal, the 168-year-old tabloid had hacked into the phones of other crime victims, members of the royal family, prominent celebrities, and politicians.

The story became one of the most damaging to ever hit the international news media, and, as the days passed, more and more twisted details emerged: revelations ranging from the attempted suicides of staffers to an executive-level conspiracy against the police added a macabre layer to an already shocking story. Public ire was such that News Corp managers hired security guards out of fear for their personal safety.

At the center of the company's fall was the Murdoch family, not only the legendary founder Rupert, but his son James, who was at the time News Corp's Chief Executive. When the scandal broke, the younger Murdoch's first reaction was silence: under the guidance of his legal counsel, James did not initially publicly comment on the story. Worse, as the weeks passed and James was called to testify in Parliament, he denied knowledge of the dubious methods by which his journalists had obtained information.

This "I didn't know" argument was what ultimately undermined News Corp's reputation.[21] Rather than demonstrating remorse and transparency, Murdoch's poor decision making seemed

---

[21] Sudhaman and Holmes 2012.

to escalate the story.[22] The Murdoch name was already tarnished with a destructive reputation and alleged history of manipulating politicians for personal gain, and public trust in the family and their companies continued to wane.[23] As a result, nearly six months later, News Corp is still playing catch-up with both the UK and US governments as well as media outlets, who, one suspects, have been waiting for this moment a long time.

Imagine how things could have been different: had James Murdoch come forward a few months earlier and said that News Corp had conducted an internal investigation with a strong outside group of esteemed citizens; that he had found that some reporters were hacking phones and that this had been condoned by managers like Rebekah Brooks, who was being let go immediately; that he acted contrite, apologetic and said all the right things about behavior such as "this cannot be condoned," and had talked about a new strategy as he took the reins from his father, Rupert.

In this scenario, James would have gotten control of the story early enough to shape its destiny, and his company's. And, perhaps most important of all, he would have seemed prepared to handle a crisis of this magnitude.

SUMMARY

The above example, along with Netflix and BP, illustrate how a poorly managed reputation – whether because of a lack of understanding of social media or a lack of transparency and authenticity – can hurt not just a company's image, but also its bottom line.

However, reputation does not only involve risk. As we will see in the next section of this chapter, companies that successfully build strong reputations benefit from higher share prices, and high customer loyalty and forgiveness. First, we must develop a thorough understanding of why an organization must align its identity, vision, and values to achieve a strong reputation.

---

[22] Curtis, 2011.   [23] Robinson, 2011.

SURVIVING THE CURRENT CRISIS THROUGH
REPUTATION MANAGEMENT

In the changed environment for business, corporate reputation has gained visibility and importance in the eyes of many constituencies. Reputation is now an integral driver in a company's success and credibility, but many managers who have not thought about corporate reputation continue to underestimate its value. This error is partly due to a lack of understanding about what corporate identity, brand, image, and reputation are all about, and what they can do for a business. Skeptics should understand that an inappropriate identity can be as damaging to a firm as poor financial performance. Individuals are seeking trust and transparency, and if perceptions about a company fail to mesh with reality, constituents will take their money elsewhere.

WHAT ARE IDENTITY, BRAND, IMAGE, AND REPUTATION?

A company's identity is the actual manifestation of the company's reality as conveyed through the organization's name, logo, motto, products, services, building, stationery, uniforms, and all other tangible pieces of evidence created by the organization and communicated to a variety of constituencies. Constituencies then form perceptions based on the messages that companies send in these tangible forms. If the images accurately reflect an organization's reality, the identity program is a success. If the perceptions differ dramatically from the reality, then either the strategy is ineffective, or the corporation's understanding of itself needs to be modified.[24]

Because identity is the only part of reputation management that an organization can actually create and control, it is critical that it is strategically shaped. One of the key factors that contribute to a successful corporate identity is a careful brand: a name or logo that differentiates the goods and services of one seller from those of its competitors. Branding is much more complex and nuanced than a

---

[24] Argenti, 2008.

swoosh or a pair of golden arches, however. A brand can provoke an emotional reaction from the consumer; a brand is a promise that sets an expectation of an experience. As marketing expert Kevin Keller explains, "the power of a brand lies in the minds of consumers."[25] A company's value can be considerably influenced by the success of its corporate branding strategy. Coca-Cola, for instance, has a value that far exceeds its total tangible assets because of its strong brand name.[26]

An organization's image is a function of how constituencies perceive the organization, based on all the messages it sends out through names, logo, and self-presentation. It is the organization as seen from the viewpoint of its constituencies. But image is in the eye of the beholder: Depending on the vantage point of a particular constituency, a company can have many different images. For example, employees will perceive their company's image differently than customers. Even customers who have never interacted with a product will have preconceived notions (just because you've never eaten a McDonald's hamburger doesn't mean you don't have certain perceptions about the company and the product). Large, diversified companies may also struggle to define their images. What is the image for a company as large as Tata, or one as diverse as General Electric?

Reputation is the sum of all of an organization's constituencies' perceptions. It differs from image in that it is built gradually, and is therefore not simply a perception in any moment of time. It differs from identity because it is a product of both internal and external constituencies, whereas identity is constructed by the company itself. A strong reputation has important strategic implications for a company, as we shall see.

WHY REPUTATION MATTERS

The importance of reputation is evidenced by several prominent surveys and rankings that seek to identify the best and worst among

---

[25] Keller, 1997.   [26] Interbrand, 2011.

them: the *Fortune* "Most Admired" list, *BusinessWeek* and Interbrand's "Best Global Brands" ranking, and the Reputation Institute's
Global RepTrak Pulse studies. These highly publicized rankings
are evidence of what many business leaders already know: that
companies with strong reputations have financial and competitive
advantages and experience greater stability.[27]

Reputation is a source of tangible economic value. According to
the 2008 Hill and Knowlton *Corporate reputation watch*, more than
90 percent of analysts agree that if a company fails to look after the
reputational aspects of its performance, it will ultimately suffer financially. Reputation does indeed correlate with higher market valuation
and stock price, and with less stock price volatility. A comprehensive
study by the Munich-based Market-Based Management Institute
compared the reputation and stock-market performance of 60 blue-
chip companies over the course of five years. The 25 percent (Top 25)
of companies with the best reputations considerably outperformed
the companies with poorer reputations and, compared to price movements on the DAX 30 in general, the Top 25 returned greater yield
with lower risk.[28]

The less tangible aspects of a strong reputation can also result in
competitive advantage. Companies with strong reputations attract
and retain the best talent, as well as loyal customers and business
partners, all of which contribute positively to growth and success.
Reputation "calls attention to a company's attractive features and
widens the options available to its managers; for instance, whether
to charge higher or lower prices for products and services, or to
implement innovative programs."[29] Companies whose corporate
communications promote sincerity and accuracy have greater operating leverage and the power to buck negative trends in the economy
and in their respective industries. Being able to weather a corporate
crisis is a particularly valuable position in an age of skepticism and
mistrust, where information travels at lightning speed.[30]

[27] Argenti, 2008.   [28] Ketchum, 2012.   [29] Aaker, 1996.   [30] Argenti, 2008.

Jet Blue, for example, learned how important stores of goodwill can be in times of crisis. But on February 14, 2007, the airline faced a reputational crisis that put customer loyalty to the test: during a particularly nasty nor'easter, the airline had an operational meltdown that resulted from a combination of bad luck, flawed decision making, and multiple systematic failures. The airline canceled more than 1,000 flights, incurring millions of dollars in losses and tarnishing its sterling reputation among customers who were stranded at its hub, JFK Airport. Yet, after a publicity nightmare and an enquiry from Congress, CEO and founder David Neeleman was inspired to search for inventive solutions to win back his constituents' loyalty. Some of those solutions, like the industry's first ever customer bill of rights, were groundbreaking, and helped JetBlue to regain, if not exceed, its reputational standing in the eyes of its customers.[31]

Against the backdrop of the current business environment, organizations are increasingly appreciating the financial and competitive advantages of a strong reputation. How does an organization know where it stands? How does it build trust? Since reputation is formed by the perceptions of all of their constituencies, companies must first uncover what those perceptions are and then choose their reputation strategy accordingly.

MEASURING AND MANAGING REPUTATION

You can't manage what you don't measure. This adage rings especially true when looking at corporate reputation. In assessing its reputation, an organization must examine the perceptions of all of its constituencies. Only when perceptions and identity are in alignment will a strong reputation result.

Many consulting firms, like the Reputation Institute (RI), have developed diagnostics for helping companies conduct this research. Nearly all of these tools require constituency research. The RI's RepTrak Alignment Monitor, for example, conducts extensive

---

[31] *Ibid.*

internal analysis of employee alignment. Such tools exist because companies run into trouble when they do not practice the values that they promote internally. Walmart is perhaps one of the best examples of a company that has frequently been entangled in contradictions between the values it espouses and its employees' perceptions. The company, which defines its three basic beliefs and values to be respect for the individual, service to its customers, and striving for excellence,[32] has been embroiled in a constant stream of lawsuits, including what would have been the largest employment discrimination class action in US history.[33] However, Walmart has made significant attempts to close the gap that exists between its identity and image in other areas of its business, as we shall later discuss.

SUMMARY

An organization with a clear corporate identity that represents its underlying reality and is aligned with the images held by all of its constituencies will be well on the path toward achieving a strong reputation, an irreplaceable asset in an intensely skeptical global business environment. Reputational success, once earned, must be managed, measured, and nurtured through an effective reputation management strategy.

REPUTATION MANAGEMENT STRATEGIES THAT BUILD TRUST

Once a strong corporate reputation is established, what strategies can a company employ to safeguard that reputation and beyond that, to maximize trust?

FOCUS ON VALUES AND PRINCIPLES-BASED LEADERSHIP

As mentioned earlier, the level of concern about corporate responsibility and trust has increased dramatically in recent years, and has been amplified by the ability of digital platforms to

---

[32] Walmart Corporate, 2012.   [33] Liptak, 2011.

democratize access to information. Stakeholders are increasingly demanding value for their money when purchasing goods and services, and are also expecting to see a strong set of values in the companies with which they do business. As we've seen before, companies that embrace digital tools to engage individual stakeholder groups in the context of their corporate responsibility efforts will prosper over those who forgo opportunities to communicate.

Ever the innovator, CEO Howard Schultz of Starbucks incorporated a revolutionary crowdsourcing strategy into his plan to transform the coffee retailer, following years of overexpansion and sliding stock prices. Schultz's challenge was to "rekindle an emotional attachment with customers," and in 2009, the brand created www.mystarbucksidea.com, a forum where customers could literally submit ideas on how to make the brand better.[34] The ideas were categorized, and users could then vote on which ones they thought should be implemented. Schultz also invested heavily in Starbucks' "shared planet" campaign, which marketed the company's dedication to being "bigger than coffee."[35] Whether these crowdsourcing and corporate social responsibility (CSR) initiatives can be directly related to a bump in stock price is difficult to prove, but Starbucks' popularity, at least, has grown in the three years since these programs were implemented: in 2010, Starbucks reported record fiscal revenue of $10.7 billion.[36] Schultz was able to intuit that Starbucks customers wanted more than just coffee.

Another company whose brand has transcended the products it sells is PepsiCo, whose "refresh" campaign positively illustrates the current shift toward value and values. PepsiCo understands what academic Dennis Whittle argues is a "value-oriented" paradigm, in which progressive corporate leaders know that engaging their companies and employees in social enterprise efforts pays off – internally by attracting and retaining high-quality workers, and externally with positive impacts on their brand.[37]

[34] Miller, 2011. [35] Starbucks, 2012.
[36] Starbucks Investor Relations, 2012. [37] Bryan, 2012.

Starting in January 2010, Pepsi decided to take a massive gamble in their marketing strategy: they pulled their multi-decade, multimillion dollar Super Bowl opening ad and traded it in for a $20 million social campaign. At its core, the Pepsi Refresh Project is about getting the global community to nominate projects that need funding in local communities. Participants enter online by uploading a video or project profile and lobbying the community for votes. In the past two years, the company has contributed over $40 million to small-scale, community-based social enterprise efforts. More importantly, in return for their initial $20 million investment, Pepsi has donated to community service around the country, built strong relationships with customers, built their brand, encouraged a two-way flow of communication between their company and their customers, increased consumer awareness, and generated exposure for their products. A year after the campaign was implemented, it had assisted Pepsi in attaining over 56,000 followers on Twitter, 700,000 views on YouTube, and over 3 million "likes" on Facebook.[38]

Although the financial return on the Refresh campaign is hard to measure, PepsiCo is building its reputational capital for years to come, which may be a critical factor to survival in an environment where its core products are being increasingly called into question in the nation's ongoing debate over nutrition and healthcare. Even if Americans start to question PepsiCo products from a health care perspective, they may be persuaded to remain loyal because of the company's focus on social enterprise.

FOCUS ON STRATEGIC CSR

The Pepsi Refresh project underscores the argument that in today's environment, CSR plays a significant role in forming customers' perceptions of a brand. Reputational risk now transcends simply staying out of trouble; rather, stakeholders are far more proactive in seeking out information about companies and wanting to know more

[38] PepsiCo, 2012.

about what they stand for. Study after study demonstrates that "good corporate citizenship" directly correlates with the strength of a company's reputation, and its bottom line. For examples, see the 2010 Cone Cause Evolution Study, the annual Edelman Trust Surveys, and Reputation Institute's Global RepTrak Pulse reports.

Consumers are increasingly preoccupied with the values and reputations of the companies with which they interact: The 2010 Cone Cause Evolution Study, for example, reveals that 83 percent of Americans want more of the products, services, and retailers they use to support causes. It has been found that 85 percent of consumers have a more positive image of a product or company when it supports a cause they care about, and 90 percent of consumers want companies to communicate to them the ways in which they are supporting causes. Strategically directed CSR programs can be key vehicles for the creation of competitive advantage.[39]

When a company understands what each of its constituencies is concerned about, what matters to them, and what they already think about the company, it is well positioned to structure the right kinds of CSR programs. Walmart is an example of a company that has made significant progress in enhancing its corporate reputation by focusing its CSR efforts on one of the key issues which its constituents have been most publicly concerned about – environmental sustainability. In 2005, Walmart hired a sustainability and energy think-tank to conduct an efficiency overhaul and audit, and then outlined three clear environmental goals: to be supplied entirely by renewable energy, to create zero waste, and to sell products that sustain resources and the environment. The implementation of the plan cost Walmart more than $500 million, but by talking the talk in its logistics, operations, and sales practices, the retailer has hugely enhanced its perceived environmental impact.[40] In the 2010 Newsweek Green Rankings, a ranking of the top 100 global companies based on their environmental impact, green policies and

[39] Cone Communications, 2010.   [40] MSNBC, 2005.

performance, and reputation, Walmart ranked 39th, up from 59th the year before.[41]

To summarize, CSR programs can greatly contribute to a company's reputational capital and provide a distinct competitive advantage in an environment where constituencies increasingly expect responsible and accountable behavior, along with profit. To respond to this demand, executives must manage and measure stakeholders' perceptions, and implement new and creative ways to position themselves.

BACK ALL RHETORIC WITH CLEAR-CUT ACTION – CONSTITUENCY TRUST CANNOT BE REGAINED

In the area of reputation management, one of the most unforgiveable mistakes is an insincere apology. The Susan G. Komen for the Cure Foundation recently learned this lesson the hard way when their founder and CEO decided to pull funding from Planned Parenthood, without enacting a solid reputation management strategy.

Since 2007, Susan G. Komen has provided hundreds of thousands of dollars to Planned Parenthood in funding toward breast cancer care, screenings, and referrals, but in March 2011, decided to abruptly end their commitment to the family provider. Initially, Komen claimed that it was halting funding because Planned Parenthood is under investigation by Congress. Komen later defended its decision as being part of an ongoing effort to exact "stronger performance criteria for our grantees," but many Planned Parenthood supporters have accused Komen of caving to pressure from powerful conservative groups and letting politics play a role in women's reproductive rights and health care.[42]

Instead of getting ahead of the announcement, Komen tried to quietly end the relationship, severely underestimating the backlash from its power base. As the news spread online, politicians, celebrities, breast cancer survivors, and women's activist groups from all over the

[41] Newsweek, 2010.   [42] Konigsberg, 2012.

country became involved in the discussion. Komen CEO and Founder Nancy Brinker appeared on MSNBC 48 hours later to defend her organization's decision, but she appeared nervous and uncomfortable, and was not able to confidently express why the congressional investigation necessitated the cut. The next day, prominent *Washington Post* columnist Sally Quinn called Brinker out for compromising the organization's mission. Brinker responded in a letter of her own, but she changed her story, claiming this time that Planned Parenthood's screening program was inefficient, which would have been a valid reason were it not obvious that Brinker was covering up for the previous, more thinly veiled explanation. In her letter, Brinker apologized, but she didn't say for what, or explore the mistakes she made. Nor did she offer a concession: critics wanted to see Planned Parenthood's funding restored, but Brinker merely hinted that it was eligible to reapply, making the overall letter appear insincere.[43]

Komen bungled the communications of the entire Planned Parenthood scandal from the start. Leaders who make public apologies cannot stop halfway – they must describe what they are sorry for, what mistakes they realize they've made, and what they plan to do to keep them from ever happening again in the future. That level of sincerity allows for a clear-cut, actionable plan to repair the crisis and to begin reestablishing trust with constituents.

HARNESS SOCIAL MEDIA TO BUILD TRUST

The Susan G. Komen example above illustrates a change that has emerged out of an increasingly digital world: whereas corporate communications professionals formerly fed their messaging to stakeholders in a one-way conversation, they now find themselves at the mercy of the people they once controlled, and their organizations' reputations hang in the balance. The Komen–Planned Parenthood scandal erupted from an old-fashioned press release, and less than 24 hours after the announcement, Komen faced a massive social

---

[43] McGregor, 2012.

media backlash from angry people flocking to its message boards, Twitter, and Facebook wall to announce that they would no longer donate to the breast cancer charity. In this instance, Komen under-estimated the degree to which digital communications have evolved. Their stakeholders have gained enormous influence in shaping cor-porate messaging and virtually stole Komen's news out from under them. Komen would have been in a stronger position had it announced the news differently and actually had a conversation with its many passionate followers.[44]

Many companies have learned exactly this lesson: in a crisis, embracing social media as a means of enhancing conversations with inflamed stakeholders can be hugely beneficial. Dell is an example of a company that decided early on to embrace social media rather than ignore it. Back in 2005, the computer manufacturer's reputation was thrown for a loop when an irate blogger named Jeff Jarvis lambasted the company for poor customer service ("Dell Hell," he called it). Within hours, hordes of customers who were in agreement with Jarvis's claims posted comments on his blog and their own, creating a maelstrom of negative publicity.[45] The company struggled for months as a result of failing to address the criticism, but in July 2006 it launched its own blog, where executives could at last join the conversation. The blog allowed customers to comment freely on this and later crises, and in February 2007 Michael Dell launched IdeaStorm.com, a permanent forum in which customers could give the company advice (Dell, 2012). Metrics showed that the company's customer-service rating rose significantly immediately afterwards. In fact, Dell's communica-tions team estimates that since Dell began using social media, nega-tive comments about the company have gone down by 30 percent.[46]

FOCUS ON STRUCTURE

Dell executives recognized that, in order to remain competitive, they needed to rethink the way they positioned themselves internally to

[44] Bassett, 2012.　[45] *Bloomberg Business Week*, 2005.　[46] Lacorte, 2009.

have a positive impact externally. By 2009, IdeaStorm employed a chief blogger and a team of forty-two people who worked hand in hand with the broader corporate communications function. Dell evolved its organizational structure to meet changing stakeholder demands, integrating an entirely new division within its communications function and giving it visibility within the company.[47]

This is a critical lesson: at world-class companies, digital communications has morphed from a backroom tactical department to a strategic liaison between an organization and its many stakeholder groups. HP, as well, employed a digital communications team to facilitate conversations between its constituents during a period of incredible change – its 2002 merger with Compaq. Recognizing the challenges behind aligning different cultures and information management systems, HP executives developed @HP, a business-to-employee portal that acted as a gateway to the merging HP and Compaq intranets. The platform served as the infrastructure to communicate messages to all 88,000 plus employees around the globe, and ensured that the right messages were delivered to the right internal audiences. The intranet embodied the new corporate culture.[48]

FOCUS ON AUTHENTICITY AND TRANSPARENCY

The kind of transparency practiced at HP during its $87 billion merger with Compaq might strike some as scary in an age when a lone employee blogger can derail even the most thought-out strategy, but in fact the reverse is true. Radical transparency is exactly what is needed to survive in the current business environment, assuming a brand is built on authenticity.

Given that less than half of all members of the public now have trust in business, finding a way to talk positively to restore consumer confidence is more important than ever. Many companies, however, are afraid to talk much at all. In an era where every company should be looking to build trust, too many, like News Corp in the previous

---

[47] Menchaca, 2011.   [48] Eschbach and Morgan, 2012.

example, have gone quiet. Worse, many are living up to the public's negative impressions of cost-cutting measures during a recession, scaling back on community efforts and reducing employee benefits to cut costs and please shareholders.

Companies willing to address problems head-on are the ones who will win back confidence. After the credit crisis first erupted in 2007, the banks whose reputations remained intact were those that communicated most transparently. As an example, JPMorgan decided in one of the worst financial markets in history to take the opportunity to encourage discussion about its customers' concerns. JPMorgan set up a new website called the Way Forward that acknow-ledged consumer fears while also reassuring them with an appeal to values of responsible investing. In addition, CEO Jamie Dimon stepped out as one of the most visible leaders in the sector, actively collaborating with Washington in setting the terms of the bail-out plan.[49] Compare that with Goldman Sachs, whose hallowed reputa-tion sustained a considerable blow at the height of the crisis after CEO Lloyd Blankfein referred to himself and the company as doing "God's work."[50]

Why JPMorgan stood out from all of the other banks that issued apologies and reassuring messaging in the wake of the credit crisis is that its message rang true. The bank didn't lay off employees in 2009, or reduce bonuses. The way JPMorgan ran its business in the wake of the crisis – especially the way it treated its employees – resonated with customers. Radical transparency worked for JPMorgan because the messaging was on point:

> Our commitment to corporate responsibility extends to every facet of our business – in both good economic times and bad. We are proactively assisting customers and clients as well as supporting efforts to achieve financial market stability throughout these unprecedented economic times.[51]

[49] Argenti, 2011.   [50] Weil, 2009.   [51] JP Morgan Chase, 2012.

The message is clear: we're acknowledging that the current environment is challenging, but we won't forsake our values in bad times.

This kind of authenticity is even more important in the era of social media, when it is so easy for consumers to find their own information to test the veracity of a company's claims. Volkswagen, for instance, tried to get out of having to fix a design flaw in their seatbelts by saying customers were using them incorrectly – a stance that blew up in their face online.[52] By contrast, Dell's IdeaStorm actually encourages consumers not only to talk to one another but also to offer advice to management. With social media tools, it's now a given that customers will talk among themselves. The smartest companies are those that preempt the conversation in a meaningful way.

SUMMARY

Companies must take a long, hard look at their reputation strategies and determine if they are still viable in the current era of customer mistrust. In the past, many companies may have pushed messages in one-way conversations that no longer make sense in the era of two-way, interactive conversations enabled by digital communications platforms. Being a reputation-driven company that drives and maintains customer trust is a painstaking endeavor that now requires principles and values-based leadership, a clear-cut action plan in times of crisis, and an understanding of and willingness to embrace social media. As if that weren't a long enough list, they must also communicate all of the above with attention to transparency and authenticity. Those that rise to the challenge, however, will gain competitive advantage in a world that is looking for institutions it can trust in the long term.

CONCLUSION: WHAT SUCCESS WILL LOOK LIKE

From an executive's vantage point, the current landscape is a daunting place. The ongoing economic recession and growth of digital platforms

---

[52] Argenti, 2009.

has produced an environment in which business fortunes change overnight. Perhaps even more unsettling is that we are living in a time when one of the most commonly accepted tenants of our society – that businesses operate in our best interests – has collapsed. In the face of this instability, how do we move forward? Two years ago the answer might have been increased government regulation. That argument no longer stands. One of the most remarkable results from the 2012 Edelman Trust Barometer is that government has experienced an even more dramatic drop in trust than business; in fact, 17 out of 25 countries reported that they now mistrust government.[53]

The way forward looks strikingly like a retreat from the espoused corporate values of twenty years ago, when executives made top-down strategic decisions and could dismiss or even punish signs of discontent. Now, employees and customers have more channels with which to communicate their dissatisfaction with corporate decisions, and they don't seem to have much faith in the people making them anyways. The voices that constituents do seem to listen to are their own, and those of their peers. One need only look at the recent history of peer-to-peer trust to realize that it mirrors the public's trust in business.

Since the term was first tracked and measured in 2003, trust in peers jumped consistently until 2009, when it began to feel the effects of the financial crisis. The subsequent drop in peer trust from 2009 to 2010 reflects a shift to trust in sources of specialized expertise and authority during the crisis. But events in Europe, Japan, and elsewhere over the last twelve months have undermined trust in authority, and driven a return to trust in peers.

Peer-to-peer trust is now higher than ever: regular people and employees are twice as trusted spokespersons, government officials, or CEOS.[54] Additionally, there's been a huge rise in "trust in persons like yourself," which explains the incredible growth of social media: people want to exchange information with their peers, not be fed

[53] Edelman, 2012.   [54] Ibid.

messaging that they don't feel they can trust. The message behind all of this seems to be that executives should act less like CEOs, and more like one of their employees.

The rankings of the world's most reputable companies support this trend. The RepTrak 100, a leading measurement tool, reveals that having strong and visible leaders, such as Bill Gates, Larry Page, and Sergey Brin, helps position companies as visionaries, but the results also show that a high-profile leader doesn't have to be present for a company to make the top 10. BMW, SONY, Volkswagen, Intel, and Daimler are all in the top 10 without a strong public profile of their leaders.[55]

Smart businesses will take advantage of this dispersion of authority. They will engage in authentic and transparent conversations with their employees and customers, empowering them to continue driving the conversation among their peers not only about the company's performance, but also its broader role in society.[56] They will act less like autocrats and instead take a more democratic approach to decision making. Through these strategies, they will harness that most rare commodity in today's environment: the trust of their constituents that is the lifeblood of any business looking to sustain itself in the long term.

REFERENCES

Aaker, D. (1996), *Corporate Communications: Building Strong Brands*. New York: Free Press.

Argenti, P. A. (2008), *Corporate Communication*, 5th edn. New York: McGraw-Hill

Argenti, P. A. (2009), 'Authenticity above all.' *Tuck Today*. Fall.

Argenti, P. A. (2011), 'Digital strategies for powerful corporate communications.' *European Financial Review*. February 17.

Argenti, P. A. (2012), *Corporate Communication*. New York: McGraw-Hill/Irwin

Argenti, P. A. and Barnes, C. M. (2009), *Digital Strategies for Powerful Corporate Communications*. New York: McGraw Hill.

Arthur W. Page Society (2012), 'Building belief: a new model for activating corporate character and authentic advocacy.' March, 2012.

[55] Reputational Institute, 2011.   [56] Arthur W. Page Society, 2012.

Bassett, L. (2012), 'Karen Handel, Susan G. Komen's Anti-Abortion VP, drove decision to defund Planned Parenthood.' *Huffington Post*. February 6.

Bloomberg Business Week (2005), 'Hanging up on Dell?' October 10.

Bryan, B. (2012), 'An interview with Dennis Whittle.' Icosa. www.theicosamagazine.com/charitable-giving-redesigned (accessed March 20, 2012).

Cone Communications (2010), 'Cone cause evolution study.'

Curtis, A. (2011), 'Rupert Murdoch: a portrait of satan,' BBC. January 30, 2011 www.bbc.co.uk/blogs/adamcurtis/2011/01/rupert_murdoch_-_a_portrait_of.html (accessed February 15, 2011).

Dell (2012), Ideastorm.com (accessed March 20, 2012).

de Saint-Exupéry, A. (1943), *The Little Prince*. New York: Harcourt Brace & World.

Edelman and Associates (2012), *2012 Edelman trust barometer: Global decks*. January.

Environmental Leader (2008), 'Beyond Petroleum pays off for BP.' January 15.

Eschbach, P. and Morgan, J. (2012), 'Unlocking the value of HP's employee portal.' *PR news* (accessed October 4, 2012).

ForeSee (2012), www.foreseeresults.com (accessed June 22, 2012).

Gallup Poll (2011), Confidence in institutions. June 9, www.gallup.com/poll/1597/confidence-institutions.aspx (accessed February 25, 2012).

Gantz, J. and Reinsel, D. (2011), 'IDC IView: extracting value from chaos.' Sponsored by EMC Corporation.

Gillen, S. (2011), 'IRM enterprise risk management SIG: quantifying the value of reputation.' Institute of Risk Management presentation, February 2011.

Gregory, J. (2010), 'BP's oil and brand equity spill in the Gulf.' *Branding Strategy Insider*. May 6.

Guardian (2011), 'BP cost-cutting blamed for "avoidable" Deepwater Horizon oil spill.' January 6.

Huffington Post (2010), 'BP CEO Tony Hayward new oil disaster ad: sincere or damage control?' June 3, 2010.

Interbrand, *Best Global Brands 2011*, www.interbrand.com/Libraries/Branding_Studies/Best_Global_Brands_2011.sflb.ashx (accessed February 25, 2012).

JP Morgan Chase (2012), 'Corporate responsibility.' JPMorganChase.com (accessed March 19, 2012.)

Kardashian, K. (2011), 'In bad company,' *Tuck today*, November.

Keller, K. (1997), *Strategic brand management: Building, measuring, and managing brand equity*. 1st edn. New York: Prentice Hall.

Ketchum (2012), 'Reputation capital: building and maintaining trust in the 21st century.' White paper.

Konigsberg, R. D. (2012), 'Susan G. Komen apologizes: hoisted on its own pink ribbon?' *Time Magazine*. February 3.

Lacorte, V. L. (2009), 'Digital communication at Dell.' Tuck School of Business at Dartmouth, McNamee Centre For Digital Strategies. 2009.

Landman, A. (2010), 'BP's "Beyond Petroleum" campaign losing its sheen.' *PR watch*. May 3.

Liptak, A. (2011), 'Justice rule for Walmart in class-action bias case.' *New York Times*. June 20.

McGregor, J. (2012), 'Komen leader's latest apology about Planned Parenthood fiasco only goes halfway.' *Washington Post*. February 9.

Menchaca, L. (2011), 'FIR interview: Dell chief blogger.' *Social Media Today*. September 1.

Miller, C. C. (2011), 'A changed Starbucks. A changed CEO.' *New York Times*. March 13.

Miniwatts Marketing Group (2011), *Internet World Stats, Usage, and Population Statistics: World*, www.InternetWorldStats.com (accessed March 20, 2012).

MSNBC (2005), 'Is Wal-Mart going green?' October 25.

Namezee, M. (2011), 'Hargreaves says rising executive pay undermines trust.' *Washington Post with Bloomberg Business*. April 19.

Newsweek (2010), 'Green rankings: US companies.' *Daily Beast*. October 18.

PepsiCo (2012), 'Refresh everything.' www.refresheverything.com (accessed March 20, 2012).

Reputational Institute (2011), 'The Global Reptrak 100.'

Robinson, J. (2011), 'Phone hacking: 58 percent of UK public say they have lost trust in papers.' *Guardian*. November 14

Starbucks (2012), 'Being a responsible company,' www.starbucks.com/responsibility (accessed March 20, 2012).

Starbucks Investor Relations (2010), 'Starbucks reports record fourth quarter and fiscal 2010 results.' November 4, http://investor.starbucks.com/phoenix.zhtml?c=99518&p=irol-newsArticle&ID=1492291&highlight= (accessed March 20, 2012).

Sudhaman, A. and Holmes, P. (2012), 'The top 10 crises of 2011.' *Holmes Report*, January 25.

Walmart Corporate (2012) 'What we do.' http://walmartstores.com/AboutUs/8123.aspx (accessed March 20, 2012).

Weil, J. (2009), 'Blankfein invokes god and man at Goldman Sachs,' bloomberg.com. November 11 (accessed October 4, 2012).

Wikipedia (2012), http://en.wikipedia.org/wiki/BP#Environmental_record

Wingfield, N. (2011), 'Netflix market value shrivels.' *New York Times*, October 25.

10 Can trust flourish where institutionalized distrust reigns?

Reinhard Bachmann and Edeltraud
Hanappi-Egger

EXECUTIVE SUMMARY

THE SITUATION

The global financial crisis has made one thing abundantly clear: trusting too much, particularly without having any reliable control mechanisms in place, is a very risky strategy. If we trust too much and ignore the possibility of opportunistic behavior, greed, and fraud, we are likely to be disappointed and bitterly regret it.

KEY QUESTIONS

What can provide protection from the forces of untamed capitalism? Clearly, trust and distrust have their legitimate places in business relationships. The crucial question, however, is how these two mechanisms may fruitfully coexist.

NEW KNOWLEDGE

With reference to the two-tiered governance systems of incorporated companies in Austria and Germany, it is shown how interpersonal trust can coexist with institutionalized distrust mechanisms within organizations.

Reliance on a dominant form of interpersonal trust between organizational members, meant to create checks and balances within the network, could result in negative effects such as complicity and corruption. The latter, however, can be avoided by strong institutionalized forms of distrust that exist alongside trust within the organization.

Such structures may be conducive to (re)establishing and maintaining the perceived trustworthiness of business organizations.

Rather than indicating the absence of a relationship, distrust is in fact a useful component of a relationship. Trust is not always an option when the risk of misplaced trust is too high. In this type of situation, a substitute for trust – i.e., another mechanism which can fulfill the same function of coordinating expectations and interaction between two actors – is needed. Paradoxically, this can be addressed through *distrust*. If distrust – as opposed to the sheer absence of trust – emerges between two potential actors, then it can be a starting point for the governance of a social relationship.

KEY LESSONS

Although a high level of distrust can cause a number of serious problems in the corporate world as well as the societal level, we can also *create* grave risks when we ignore distrust and simply employ trust as the exclusive mechanism for governing a relationship.

Institutionalized distrust can contribute to effectively coordinating social interactions between a supervisory board and an executive board.

There are different forms of trust and distrust. We need to integrate these in such a way that we can benefit from specific combinations when it comes to designing organizations and finding solutions for governance problems. In particular, we should recognize that institutionalized forms of distrust can help improve our interpersonal relationships and allow more trust to emerge.

Only when distrust is adequately institutionalized can public trust flourish.

INTRODUCTION

If the global financial crisis has made one thing abundantly clear, then it is the fact that trusting too much without having any reliable control mechanisms in place can be a very risky strategy. Since the 1980s, governments and investors had trusted the financial services industry to a historically unprecedented degree. In the wake of neo-liberal ideology, regulations were massively weakened and the financial sector was believed to control itself along the lines of what market forces toward a perfect equilibrium would suggest anyway.[1] The complete absence of distrust resulted in outright fraudulent practices as, for example, revealed in the Bernie Madoff case and – more dramatically – in a global disaster which involved the breakdown of building societies and (investment) banks in autumn 2008.[2] The consequences of these events are ongoing: low or negative growth rates, high levels of unemployment, fractures of social cohesion, and even an increase of radical political parties.[3] Chances are that we will have to live with severe austerity measures for at least a decade or so to make up for the losses of private and public equity. The basic lesson to learn from these events is clear and simple: if we trust too much and ignore the possibility of opportunistic behavior, greed, and fraud we may easily be disappointed and bitterly regret it.

Distrust has meanwhile become much more prominent in the business world compared to only a few years ago. In many cases, shareholders, employees, and other stakeholders keenly seek shelter from exuberant risks which they do not find acceptable any longer, not even in the name of creativity and innovation. But what can really provide protection from the forces of untamed capitalism? The common view suggests moral appeals and to take business ethics more seriously. In our perspective, this is not a very promising approach as it puts the entire burden on the shoulders of individuals who in theory may be free to make their own choices but whose decisions and actions are in reality deeply embedded in an environment which forcefully imposes its logic and incentive structure onto individuals' behavior. We believe, rather, that a solution lies in fact in political action aimed at the (re)establishment of rules and control structures which can reliably encourage or discourage relevant actors' behavior.

---

[1] Ferber and Nelson, 2003; Foley, 2002.   [2] Gillespie et al., 2012.
[3] Hochschildt, 2010; Roemer, 2010; Hanappi-Egger and Hanappi, 2011.

To safeguard against too high levels of risk and the misuse of power we have, for example in the political arena, checks and balances designed into the relationships between legislative, executive, and legal constitutional bodies, and hardly anyone would see this as superfluous and suggest to simply insist on moral norms of conduct instead. Similarly, the governance of large commercial organizations is in some countries, such as Austria and Germany, based on a system of rules and control. The two-tier structure, which is obligatory for virtually every large firm in these countries, consists of an executive board, on the one hand, and a powerful supervisory board, on the other. This structure can be taken as a case of institutionalized control, maintaining an effective level of distrust and keeping relevant actors wary of potential opportunistic behavior or fraud and can thus be deemed a way to avoid unhealthy forms of trust in the governance of (large) business organizations.

Of course, even in the face of corporate scandals and the global financial crisis we should not diminish the advantages that trust has in the world of business. After all, it is not by accident that managers and scholars alike have placed so much emphasis on firms' capabilities to build trust-based relationships to suppliers, customers, horizontally linked collaborators, and other stakeholders,[4] and now indeed try to explore viable ways of how to effectively repair it.[5] Trust can, for example, tremendously save transaction costs.[6] If a firm has a trust-based relationship to a supplier it will not need to continuously monitor the quality of inputs received from this supplier or search for a new, potentially better, supplier each time a new purchase of inputs is considered. Equally, trust is vital to facilitate some forms of innovation. Especially where two organizations have complementary resources, these brought together can spark off the development of new products, services and production processes which would otherwise not be possible.[7] These observations are all valid, not least in

---

[4] Bachmann and Zaheer, 2006.   [5] Gillespie and Dietz, 2009.
[6] Bromely and Harris, 2006.   [7] Nooteboom, 2000.

times of economic crisis. The important insight which we need to take seriously is simply that it would be naïve to assume that very strong forms of trust are always and everywhere beneficial to anyone involved in whatever kind of relationship. It is certainly true that an exceedingly high level of distrust can cause a number of serious problems in the corporate world as well as the societal level. But there are also dark sides of trust which we need to take into account, specifically when trust is employed as the exclusive mechanism to govern a relationship.[8]

Clearly, trust and distrust have their legitimate places in business relationships. The crucial question, however, is how these two mechanisms may fruitfully coexist. In answering this question, it is, in our view, important to discern different forms of trust and distrust because it seems that some trust–distrust combinations are workable whereas others are not. In this chapter we will examine an empirical case where institutionalized distrust can prevent dysfunctional forms of trust in the governance structure of an organization and thus be conducive to the creation and maintenance of intra-organizational trust as well as public trust in an organization. In so doing we will refer to the two-tier corporate governance system in Austria and Germany and explore a perspective which focuses on the dialectics of trust and distrust between the involved actors.

In the following we will *first* develop a conceptual framework to analyze the mechanisms and processes of trust and distrust in general as well as in relation to their function in the corporate governance system in Austria and Germany. In this context, we will analyze the roles of institutionalized and personal forms of trust and distrust at different phases of the establishment and operation of relationships between supervisory board members and the members of the executive board. *Second,* we will present empirical data which we have collected in thirteen semi-structured interviews with supervisory board members in Austria. These will cover both the selection of

---

[8] Gargulio and Ertug, 2006.

supervisory board members by the shareholders as well as the supervisory board members' task of nominating and appointing the members of the executive board. *Third*, we will re-evaluate the roles and effectiveness of trust and distrust in the examined corporate governance system, and provide an assessment of the contribution that this system can make with regard to the (re)development of internal and public trust in business organizations. The chapter will finally conclude with some thoughts about future directions in trust research.

TRUST AND DISTRUST AS MECHANISMS TO COORDINATE INTERACTION

In the literature on organizational trust we can mainly find two competing lines of argument, each based on a specific definition of trust. First, trust is seen as an attitude or "state of mind."[9] This is a view very much embraced by organizational psychologists. It locates trust inside individuals while showing only limited interest in the institutional environment which influences the actual behavior of social actors. By contrast, institutionalist management researchers tend to pin the phenomenon down as an "organizing principle"[10] or as a "coordination mechanism."[11] The latter approach, in our view, has a number of advantages as it opens up a much broader and richer perspective, both in terms of theory development and with regard to conducting relevant empirical research. Hence, we prefer this definition of trust and focus on the observable forms of social behavior, rather than just attitudes, when exploring the roles of trust and distrust in the Austrian and German corporate governance system.

In order to gain a deeper understanding of what it implies when trust is conceptualized as a coordination mechanism, we suggest the following perspective: trust is a basic social mechanism which can effectively facilitate interaction between two individuals who might

[9] Rousseau *et al.*, 1998. [10] McEvily *et al.*, 2003. [11] Bachmann, 2001.

otherwise find no possibility to engage in any meaningful exchange at all. Before entering into a relationship, an actor who has little information about the other party will – if he or she is considering trust as a basis for interaction – make specific assumptions about the latter's future behavior.[12] While in principle any actor (potential trustee) is free to any form of behavior, it is essential that one party (the potential truster) decides to select some very specific possibilities as to how the other party (the potential trustee) is likely to behave in the relevant future and ignore all other possibilities. Especially where actors are unknown to each other, the potential truster has no rational basis for such expectations, let alone guarantees that the potential trustee will behave as expected.[13] Thus, a potential truster has to make a "leap of faith"[14] in that he or she decides to accept the unavoidable risk of being betrayed, which will then also put the trustee into a situation where he or she will be able to make specific assumptions about the future behavior of the truster. Subsequently, a whole system of social interaction can emerge on the basis of coordinated mutual expectations. It is in this sense that trust can be described as a prime coordination mechanism wherever knowledge about the other party is limited, i.e., fuzzy and/or incomplete.

Undoubtedly, there are also many instances where trust is not really an option for someone who tries to engage in a social relationship because, for example, the risk of misplaced trust may be too high.[15] What is needed then is a substitute for trust, i.e., another mechanism which can fulfill the same function of coordinating expectations and interaction between two actors. This, in our view, can be distrust. It may sound a bit counterintuitive but if distrust – as opposed to the sheer absence of trust – emerges between two potential actors then it seems equally possible to find a starting point for a social relationship. Expectations can be formed and coordinated in a way very similar to situations where trust is the dominant coordination principle. A potential distruster would do nothing else but also

---

[12] *Ibid.*   [13] Luhmann, 1979.   [14] Möllering, 2006.   [15] Bachmann, 2001.

make specific assumptions about the future behavior of the other party, i.e., the distrustee.

It is no less of a "leap," even though we may describe it as a "leap of negative faith" rather than a "leap of positive faith" if a distruster starts to make assumptions about the distrustee's future behavior in the face of limited information being available about the potential distrustee. Thus, the expectation that another actor will behave untrustworthily can also provide an effective basis for coordinated interaction between two actors, just as trust would do.

When the distrustee realizes that the distruster makes these assumptions about his or her future behavior, this would also allow him or her to make specific expectations about the distruster's future behavior. In this way, a whole system of coordinated interaction can emerge on the basis of distrust, very similar to the case where trust is the basic coordination mechanism. The difference is only that a truster makes positive assumptions about the other party's future behavior whereas a distruster selects negative ones. Both, on the basis of trust as well as on the basis of distrust, we may conclude, actors can quickly and effectively align their mutual expectations and coordinate their expectations and interaction.

If applied to a specific empirical context such as the Austrian and German corporate governance system, this perspective seems to provide a useful conceptual approach to the question of whether trust and distrust might be combined in the same empirical setting. If trust and distrust are seen as not only fulfilling the same function but also as functioning in very similar ways, then we indeed have good reasons to assume that trust and distrust may coexist or even complement each other in one and the same social interaction system.

DIFFERENT FORMS OF TRUST AND DISTRUST

Trust comes in different shapes and sizes, and a number of useful classifications can be found in the literature. One of the earliest classifications of trust in business contexts[16] suggests discerning contract trust, i.e., trust that the other party will at least feel obliged to fulfill a contract which it has signed; competence trust, i.e., trust that the other party is competent enough to live up to its promises; and goodwill trust, i.e., trust that is based on the willingness to take the other party's interests into account, almost as if they were one's own. In a similar vein, Lewicki and Bunker suggest the following three forms: calculation-based trust, knowledge-based trust, and identity-based trust. In this classification the order goes from the weakest to the strongest form of trust and can also be read as a stage model of trust development.[17] One of the most cited classifications has been suggested by Mayer et al.[18] It makes a very fundamental insight explicit which also shines through in many other categorizations. In their view, the object of trust can be either the integrity or the ability of a trustee. These are seen as two very different but equally generic forms of trust. If both come together and the relationship includes some extra mutual flexibility then they would call this benevolence-based trust and count it as a third form of trust. In our view, the classification suggested by Mayer et al. seems very useful for researching many empirical contexts, including the two-tier corporate governance system which we are looking at in this chapter.[19]

Another very fundamental differentiation which is relevant in the context of our empirical case refers to the question of whether trust is produced largely on the basis of two actors' interpersonal chemistry or whether it is constitutively embedded in an institutional framework which shapes their preferences and interests. The latter is often called "institutional-based trust."[20] It can in many cases substitute for interpersonal trust and is described as a vital form of trust in any advanced socio-economic system. This form of trust prevails where the institutional order provides reliable patterns of behavior which are of restrictive as well as an enabling nature. The risk that

---

[16] Sako, 1992.   [17] Lewicki and Bunker, 1996.
[18] Mayer et al., 1995.   [19] Ibid.   [20] Zucker, 1986.

any truster has inevitably to accommodate, namely the risk that the trustee defects, will in these situations be considerably lower than where such institutions are not in place. The latter may be taken as a good reason by the (potential) truster to deem the risk of trust relatively low, even if no prior interpersonal contact has occurred between the two actors and helped reduce the risk of trust. Thus we can say that the mere existence of institutionalized patterns of behavior can encourage a potential truster to actually invest trust in a relationship with another party. Institutional trust can do its job swiftly and is thus often preferable to trust developed solely at the interpersonal level, the latter usually requiring considerable on-the-spot effort on part of the individuals involved in a specific relationship.[21]

From our analysis of trust we can derive some important insights also into the forms of distrust that may play a role in systems of social interaction, such as the Austrian and German two-tier corporate governance. What we suggest is that it is not only interpersonal distrust but also institutional distrust which can be an important mechanism to coordinate expectations and interaction between two actors. If there are institutionalized rules in place which shape relevant actors' behavior in such a way that distrust emerges on a routine basis or incentives to distrust the other party are systematically encouraged, then we may well view the actors' behavior as being based on institutional distrust. In a similar vein, we can – in parallel to Mayer *et al.*'s classification of trust – differentiate between ability-based distrust, integrity-based distrust, and benevolence-based distrust.[22] If, for example, an actor distrusts that the other party is able to do something, then this does not necessarily mean that he or she has doubts with regard to that party's integrity. If a distruster feels that the distrustee is unwilling to fulfill his or her commitments, there is no reason to assume that this inevitably implies that the distruster is also unable to do so. And if another actor's benevolence is distrusted, this does not always include distrust in the integrity and

---

[21] Bachmann and Inkpen, 2011.   [22] Mayer *et al.*, 1995.

Trust   Distrust

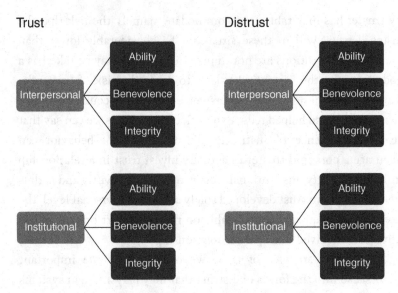

FIGURE 10.1 Forms of trust and distrust

ability of the distrustee, at the same time. Hence we propose a classification system for distrust which simply replicates the main distinc-
tions which we usually make with regard to trust. Figure 10.1
includes the resulting forms of trust and distrust which might all in
principle be relevant when a social system such as the two-tier governance structure is under review.

THE TWO-TIER CORPORATE GOVERNANCE SYSTEM:
A FORM OF INSTITUTIONALIZED DISTRUST

If the above analysis holds true, trust as well as distrust can be seen as
being highly effective social coordination mechanisms. It depends,
however, largely on the empirical context how these two mechanisms
can be combined and what particular forms of trust and distrust come
into play then. Figure 10.2 depicts the forms of trust and distrust that
we found to be dominant in the Austrian and German corporate governance system. This figure also identifies the location where these
forms occur and interact in this system. While the relationship between
the supervisory board members and the CEOs is at the heart of our

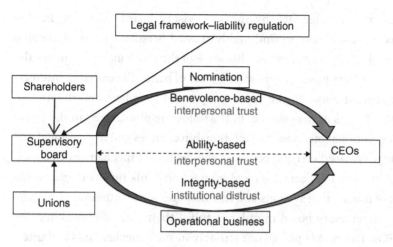

FIGURE 10.2 Trust, distrust, and control in two-tier governance structures

interest we also included the unions and specifically the shareholders in the figure as these are the actors who ultimately rule the firm.

In the Austrian and German corporate governance system, the members of the supervisory board are appointed by capital owners and thus act in accordance with the shareholders' interests while employees' representatives deputize for employees' interests and also have a strong influence on key decisions of this board.[23] The role that supervisory boards play is relatively complex and multilayered as they need to balance the demands of different shareholders, on the one hand, and other stakeholders' interests, on the other hand. Supervisory boards are primarily controlling committees vis-à-vis the CEOs but they act as consulting bodies for the top management at the same time. Their tasks include hiring and firing the members of the executive board as well as nominating external accountants.

According to government regulation, supervisory board members are held personally liable if corruption, other forms of mismanagement, or bankruptcy occurs. Against the background of this arrangement, it is not surprising that the nomination of the CEOs is

[23] See Hanappi-Egger and Mensi-Klarbach, 2010.

seen as a crucial task by the supervisory board members. In this process, they have to find highly trusted personalities who are able to lead the organization. At this stage of the relationship – namely the nomination phase – a very strong form of benevolence-based interpersonal trust between the supervisory board members and the (potential) CEOs is of the essence. In the following phases, i.e., in the phase of operational business, the relationship changes and institutionalized integrity-based distrust becomes the dominant mechanism to coordinate mutual expectations and interaction. This means that a whole set of monitoring systems and risk-management systems are set up by the supervisory board in order to fulfill their task of controlling the CEOs. Distrust is played out strongly in such mechanisms and interpersonal trust has to stand back once the CEOs are appointed.

Despite the fact that it is chiefly institutionalized distrust that we find incorporated in the structures of the two-tier corporate governance system, we do not ignore the possibility of the continuation of interpersonal trust in the operational mode of this system. But where this is the case, above all, trust appears as ability-based which means that the supervisory board members have trust in the competence of the CEOs. In the operational phase of the relationship other forms of interpersonal trust, i.e., whether integrity or benevolence based, are not supposed to develop and in fact will hardly occur – since the risk of being made liable for overlooked managerial misbehavior on part of the executive board is high. Below, the multifaceted aspects of the trust–distrust relationship in the tow-tier system will be illustrated by the results of empirical research which we recently conducted in Austria.

EMPIRICAL EVIDENCE

In a one-year research project (2009–2010)[24] on the need for diversified skills in Austrian supervisory boards, semi-structured interviews were

---

[24] The project was a joint project of staff members and students of the Gender and Diversity Management Group and the Institute of Change Management and Management Education of WU Vienna.

conducted with members of such bodies, all highly respected personalities in the Austrian business world and frequently mentioned in the
Austrian press as "The Who is Who of corporate Austria". They all
represented shareholders (rather than the unions) on supervisory
boards.

The sample of interview subjects was identified by utilizing our
personal networks. This seemed most promising as it is relatively
difficult to find people of our target group who agree to participate in
academic studies. A list of forty potential candidates was drawn up
(due to the low quota of female board members only four of them were
women) and out of these fourteen board members were willing to give
an interview, one female and thirteen male. The interviews were done
in 1 to 1.5 hour face-to-face sessions and were recorded. These interviews were then transcribed and interpreted by applying content analysis techniques such as described by Mayering.[25] Since the female board
member was an exceptional case (in terms of background, nomination
procedure, and role), for the purpose of this chapter, only the thirteen
male board members' interviews are included in our analysis below.

The sample of interviewees consisted of the people as set out in
Table 10.1.

Although the research project originally focused on the qualifi-
cation and skills necessary to fulfill the tasks of non-executive board
members[26] the interview protocols also included very interesting data
on the subjects' self-understanding as counterpart of the executive
boards. Thus, we decided to revisit our interview transcripts for the
purpose of this chapter and elucidated aspects of control, trust, and
distrust in the supervisory boards' relationships to shareholders and
the CEOs. The relevant empirical results are presented below: first,
the nomination process of supervisory board members by shareholders, and CEOs by supervisory board members, will be highlighted with
respect to interpersonal benevolence trust. Second, the views of

---

[25] Mayering, 2007.
[26] See also Hanappi-Egger and Mensi-Klarbach 2010; Hanappi-Egger, 2011.

Table 10.1 *Sample of interviewees*

	Professional background	Age	Qualification
I1	Manager	70	University degree: business
I2	Manager	37	University degree: law
I3	Manager	58	University degree: business
I4	Manager	n.a.	n.a.
I5	Entrepreneur	64	University degree: business
I6	Entrepreneur	52	University degree: informatics
I7	Manager	74	University degree: governance
I8	Manager	n.a.	Polytechnic education & US management college
I9	Entrepreneur	55	University degree: law & economics
I10	Manager	61	Polytechnic education
I11	Entrepreneur	64	University degree: law
I12	Manager	59	University degree: business
I13	Manager	59	University degree: mathematics

supervisory board members related to the CEOs' integrity in the phase of operational business, i.e., after the executive board members have been appointed, will be discussed. Here, it will be shown that institutionalized integrity-based distrust plays the dominant role.

The nomination processes. All our thirteen interviewees confirmed that they were nominated on the basis of their private networks and because of the trust shareholders had in their integrity. This is nicely illustrated by the following quotes.

> Shareholders of course nominate somebody with whom they have a positive relationship, they will not nominate somebody agitating against their interest … Trust is the main topic in this game.
>
> *(I1)*

> Well, I think that in Austria in boards trust is the most important thing – trust is even more important than qualification.
>
> *(I4)*

The nomination of supervisory board members is a highly selective process where trust is undoubtedly of the essence. When shareholders decide who they trust to run the firm they often prefer candidates with a similar understanding of doing business.[27] According to our data, shareholders choose supervisory board members who best fit their own values and norms, trusting that in this way their interests are best represented in the non-executive board.

While trust is seen as most important in the process of selecting supervisory board members by the shareholders, it seems to play a very similar role where the members of the supervisory board nominate the members of the executive board. When executive board members are hired this is done equally on the basis of strong forms of interpersonal benevolence-based trust. As the supervisory board members are legally liable vis-à-vis the shareholders (and the wider circles of stakeholders) they take the task of selecting CEOs very seriously and would not appoint anybody who they cannot fully trust.

> The most important task is the selection of the CEO...
> The non-executive board member is searching for the right
> CEO, finding him, installing him and then he is working with
> him, ok?
>
> *(I10)*

Our interviewees almost never directly referred to the CEOs' competences. But, evidently, competence has to be proved in daily business and is observed by the supervisory board members. In cases where the respondents did refer to the competence of the CEOs, we found them generally not worrying too much about this issue. The competence to lead a large organization was something that our interviewees more or less assumed to be a given when they were considering the crucial issues in their relationships with the executive board members.

---

[27] Hanappi-Egger, 2011.

This is exactly the strength of our current CEO – being remarkably visionary. I think that this is so important in the globalized world of today, because business models and established structures are not functioning anymore. The flexibility and being visionary are skills a manager needs today.

(I3)

Of course I look for a clean track ... if you hire somebody you are looking for the marks one left, which skills the person has, which personality – and if everything fits, then you approach the person.

(I11)

While it is not so much the CEOs' competences, that the supervisory board members were interested in, the question of whether they could trust the executive board members in terms of their agency role and integrity.

The short-term performance is referred to for everything ... Hence, there should be adequate characters in the top management.

(I3)

You must have the trust of the shareholders or access to shareholders so that you really know what they want or what they don't want ... Then the supervisory board member has to ensure that the CEOs are implementing the will of the shareholders.

(I7)

These examples confirm that non-executive board members are interested in finding adequately qualified and, particularly, loyal CEOs who they can trust. Nevertheless there were also doubts expressed by our interviewees concerning the latter. Many statements include hints to a considerable degree of distrust concerning the integrity of CEOs.

Operational business. In interpreting our data it came to light that it is very important to differentiate between the nomination phase and the phase of operational business which starts once the CEOs are appointed. In the operational phase, institutionalized distrust – i.e., distrust encouraged by the structure and logic of the two-tier governance system – becomes an important part of the relationship between the supervisory board members and the executive board. The supervisory board members we interviewed clearly defined their responsibility in the company as appointing the CEOs but also to controlling them tightly thereafter.

> It has to be assured that a first-class management is nominated ... and then controlling is needed, leading to a profound risk calculation.
>
> *(I6)*

> The non-executive board is mainly a control committee.
>
> *(I8)*

> The main task is to specify objectives for the CEOs.
>
> *(I10)*

> It is important that the management and non-executive board has a clear distribution of roles ... The non-executive board has primarily a control task.
>
> *(I11)*

> The non-executive board is responsible for control mechanisms ... In our system there is a strict division.
>
> *(I13)*

Our interviews clearly show that supervisory board members were conscientiously considering their tasks in the governance structure of their firm. Despite the fact that the supervisory board members place great emphasis on the trustworthiness of the CEOs when they hire them, a high level of distrust in their integrity and the necessity to control them was expressed when our interviewees referred to their relationships to the executive board members once they had appointed them.

> Top managers don't want to be controlled.
>
> *(I6)*

> You can never exclude the possibility that a manager will turn away
> from a firm moral base.
>
> *(18)*

Another interviewee confirmed this very clearly, while yet another added an interesting interpretation of it.

> If you hire managers, they usually haven't been entrepreneurs
> themselves ... and so they don't have an entrepreneurial spirit.
>
> *(19)*

DISCUSSION

Our empirical data suggest that trust generally plays a crucial role in the two-tier corporate governance system. Without trust it would hardly be possible to identify and allocate key tasks to key actors, both with regard to the supervisory board and the executive board. More than many other social systems, corporate governance systems build constitutively on trust. The complexity of tasks and the unpredictability of the tasks and responsibilities which are delegated from shareholders to supervisory board members as well as from supervisory board members to CEOs make it unavoidable to utilize trust as a key coordination principle in these relationships.

Within the two-tier governance structure, distrust is also very important and may coexist with trust in such a way that both mechanisms appear in different forms and at phases of the relationship between the supervisory board members and the executive board members. While the members of the supervisory board have to rely on the shareholders' benevolence-based trust in a typical principal–agent situation,[28] the supervisory board members themselves usually have strongly personalized relationships based on benevolence-based interpersonal trust with individuals who they deem suitable for a post in the executive board. But it is essential to see that benevolence-

---

[28] Eisenhardt, 1989.

based interpersonal trust is only so important in the nomination process while integrity-based institutionalized distrust becomes dominant when the relationship changes into the operational mode. In other words, trust can only coexist with distrust in one and the same relationship if we differentiate between different forms of trust and distrust and, particularly, two different phases: the nomination phase and the operational phase of the relationship.

If strong forms of interpersonal trust and distrust emerged simultaneously in time we would probably find many ambiguous situations or counterproductive frictions between both mechanisms in the relationship between the members of both boards. What might also occur in such circumstances is that the conflict between the principles of trust and distrust may sooner or later result in either trust or distrust becoming so dominant that little room is left for the other mechanism. This would equally lead to an unproductive situation. On the one hand, namely in situations where trust rules supreme, we would expect problems of the kind which we know from corporate corruption and accounting scandals as well as from the unhealthy relationship that financial institutions had (and sometimes still have) with investors and borrowers before the (near) collapse of the global financial system. On the other hand, where the level of distrust leaves no room for trust, we would also expect massive problems. The latter are well known and described for regions of the world where massive social and political upheaval exists. A healthy and balanced mixture of both principles can be achieved through trust dominating in the nomination phase and distrust in the phase of operational business.

What can hardly be overrated in this context is the fact that trust and distrust occurred in specific forms. Distrust was not created at the interpersonal level but appeared in depersonalized form, ingrained in rules which everyone has to follow and which do not provide any opportunity to misuse them for egoistical purposes. This type of distrust can indeed coexist with interpersonal trust. Had it been the opposite combination, namely a combination of institutionalized trust and interpersonal distrust, the consequences might well have been very different. In such cases we will not have a situation where the goodwill of individuals flourishes within a given system of generally accepted rules, but a situation where the involved individuals develop idiosyncratic strategies to control their exchange partners in the absence of generally accepted rules. The latter scenario is likely to produce a high level of conflict and at the same legitimizes conspiracy and other forms of cooperation which are not beneficial for the functioning of the social system as whole. By contrast, the combinations of trust and distrust which we have studied in the Austrian corporate governance systems do not result in unproductive arrangements of this kind but in fact lead to a healthy balance of trust and distrust in the relationships between shareholders, supervisory board members, and the CEOs. This is certainly one of the noteworthy, and in fact not necessarily self-understood, results of our research. In our view, the two-tier corporate governance system has great advantages over governance structures and could, if applied more widely, play a crucial role, not least with regard to re-establishing of public trust in business organizations in and beyond the German-speaking part of the world.

CONCLUSION

In our view, the two-tier corporate governance structure is a good example of a balanced system of trust and distrust which can function to the benefit of the internal actors of the firm as well as its external stakeholders. More empirical studies which adopt such a perspective are necessary. Trust research needs to move away from the naïve belief that pure trust is always good and beneficial and that we can never have enough of it. The global financial crisis as well the many corporate scandals which we have witnessed in recent years should open our eyes. Trust repair is certainly in many cases something positive and necessary but we should not repair it in a way which conjures up exactly the same problems as those which we have just gone through and are indeed still going through. What we need is to safeguard against opportunism and establish the basis of a more mature understanding of the role of trust business relationships. The latter should lead us to study and create systems of more balanced combinations of trust and distrust in future practice and practice.

In this context it will be of the essence to understand that there are different forms of trust and distrust, and we need to integrate these in such a way that we can benefit from specific combinations when it comes to designing organizations and finding solutions for governance problems. In particular, we should recognize that institutionalized forms of distrust can help improve our interpersonal relationships and allow more trust to emerge than would be the case if we were only to rely on moral claims which have no fit with the socio-economic world in which we live today.

Our research implies that only if distrust is adequately institutionalized, can public trust flourish. We have studied this with reference to the two-tier corporate governance structure in Austria and found that this system has important advantages compared with governance structures which place less emphasis on the clear separation of the supervisory and executive boards. In the face of irresponsible practices of money lending and selling extremely risky financial products, as well as the widespread corporate scandals in other industries, we believe that the Austrian and German two-tier governance system could be seen as a suitable mechanism to (re)establish trust in business organizations. However, for public trust to flourish it also requires that in cases of corruption and bribery the responsible actors are duly held to account. This cannot always be taken for granted, not even in Austria. In fact, it is a hot topic in the current Austrian political debates since in several recent cases the liability mechanisms have in reality proven to be not always effective enough. Or as an interviewee described it: "A weakness of the Austrian system is that the liability is not yet a real threat for non-executive board members" (I6). This shows that the best governance system cannot prevent opportunism and complacency if it is not applied decisively. Thus we can conclude that the balance of trust and distrust in the two-tier corporate governance system deserves further scholarly analyses and legal protection to ensure that key actors can indeed be held to account for their decisions.

REFERENCES

Bachmann, R. (2001), 'Trust, power and control in trans-organizational relations.' *Organization Studies*, 22, 337–365.

Bachmann, R. and Inkpen, A. (2011), 'Understanding institutional-based trust building processes in inter-organizational relationships.' *Organization Studies*, 32, 281–301.

Bachmann, R. and Zaheer, A. (eds.) (1996), *Handbook of Trust Research*. Cheltenham, UK: Edward Elgar.

Bourdieu, P. (1977), *Outline of a Theory of Practice*. New York: Cambridge University Press.

Bromiley, P. and Harris, J. (2006), 'Trust, transaction cost economics, and mechanisms.' In R. Bachmann and A. Zaheer (eds.), *Handbook of Trust Research*. Cheltenham, UK: Edward Elgar.

Byrne, D. E. (1971), *The Attraction Paradigm*. New York: Academic Press.

Eisenhardt, K. M. (1989), 'Agency theory: an assessment and review.' *Academy of Management Review*, 14, 1, 57–74.

Ferber, M. A. and Nelson, J. A. (eds.) (2003), *Feminist Economics Today: Beyond Economic Man*. Chicago, IL and London: University of Chicago Press.

Foley, D. (2002), 'The strange history of the economic agent.' Retrieved 12.10.2010, from http://homepage.newschool.edu/~foleyd/ecagent.pdf.

Gargiulo, M. and Ertug, G. (2006), 'The dark side of trust.' R. Bachmann and A. Zaheer, *Handbook of Trust Research*. Cheltenham, UK: Edward Elgar.

Gillespie, N. and Dietz, G. (2009), 'Trust repair after an organization-level failure.' *Academy of Management Review*, 34, 127–145.

Gillespie, N., Hurley, B., Dietz, G. and Bachmann, R. (2012), 'Restoring institutional trust after the global financial crisis: a systemic approach.' In: R. Kramer and T. Pittinsky (eds.), *Trust Restoring in Organizations and Leaders: Enduring Challenges and Emerging Answers*. Oxford: Oxford University Press, 185–215.

Hanappi-Egger, E. (2011), *The Triple M of Organizations: Man, Management and Myth*. New York and Vienna: Springer.

Hanappi-Egger, E. and Hanappi, H. (2011), Exploitation Re-visited: New Forms, Same Ideologies? AHE Conference, Nottingham, UK, 06.07.–09.07.2011.

Hanappi-Egger, E. and Mensi-Klarbach, H. (2010), Dealing with complexity: dealing with diversity: on the meaning of diversity in Austrian incorporated companies.

Workshop on Top Management Teams and Business Strategy Research, Valencia, Spain, 22.03.–23.03.2010.

Heidrick and Struggles (2009), *Boards in Turbulent Times*. Corporate governance report 2009. Heidrick and Struggles International, Inc.

Hochschild, J. (2010), 'How did the 2008 economic crisis affect social and political solidarity in Europe?' (at: www.iwm.at/read-listen-watch/transit-online/how-did-the-2008-economic-crisis-affect-social-and-political-solidarity-in-europe).

Kim, B., Burns, M. L. and Prescott, J. E. (2009), 'The strategic role of the board: the impact of board structure on top management team strategic action capability.' *Corporate Governance: An International Review*, 17, 728–743.

Lewicki, R. J. and Bunker, B. B. (1995), 'Developing and maintaining trust in work relationships.' In R. Kramer and T. R. Tyler (eds.), *Trust in Organizations: Frontiers of Theory and Research*. Thousand Oaks, CA: Sage, 114–139.

Luhmann, N. (1979), *Trust and Power*. Chichester, UK: Wiley.

McEvily, B., Perrone, V., and Zaheer, A. (2003), 'Trust as an organizing principle.' *Organization Science*, 14, 91–103.

Mayer, R. C., Davis, J. H., and Schoorman, F. D. (1995), 'An integrative model of organizational trust.' *Academy of Management Review*, 20(3), 709–734.

Mayring, P. (2007), *Qualitative Inhaltsanalyse: Grundlagen und Techniken*. Weinheim u.a.: Beltz Verlag.

Möllering, G. (2006), *Trust: Reason, Routine, Reflexivity*. Amsterdam: Elsevier.

Nooteboom, B. (2000), 'Institutions and forms of co-ordination in innovation systems.' *Organization Studies*, 21, 915–939.

Roemer, J. (2010). *Ideology, Social Ethos, and the Financial Crisis*. New Haven, CT: Yale University Press.

Rousseau, D. M, Sitkin, R. S., Burt, R. S., and Camerer, C. (1998), 'Not so different after all: a cross-disciplinary view of trust.' *Academy of Management Review*, 23, 393–404.

Sako, Mari (1992), *Prices, Quality and Trust: Inter-Firm Relations in Britain and Japan*. Cambridge University Press.

Saunders, M. N. K. (2007), 'Conceptualizing trust and distrust and the role of boundaries: an organizationally based exploration.' Paper prepared for the 4th EIASM Workshop on Trust within and between Organizations, Amsterdam.

Zaheer, Aks and Harris, J. (2006), 'Interorganizational trust.' In O. Shenkar and J. Reuer (eds.), *Handbook of Strategic Alliances*. Thousand Oaks, CA: Sage, 169–197.

Zucker, L. G. (1986), 'Production of trust: institutional sources of economic structure 1840–1920.' *Research in Organizational Behavior*, 6, 53–111.

11 Roles of third parties in trust repair: lessons from high-tech alliances for public trust

Rosalinde Klein Woolthuis, Bart Nooteboom, Gjalt de Jong

EXECUTIVE SUMMARY

THE SITUATION

The relationship between organizations and their stakeholders has become increasingly problematic due to breaches of trust. This trust problem is at the heart of the recent financial crisis in which individuals and whole societies were shown to be highly dependent on large corporations. For example, banks have control over savings, mortgages, and pensions, while – individually and often even collectively – affected stakeholders have no means of control over these parties.

KEY QUESTIONS

What is the role of third parties in trust repair? Given power imbalances, can trust be repaired, and if so, how?

NEW KNOWLEDGE

This chapter presents one of the first empirical tests of the role of third parties in trust repair.

Third parties are tasked with repairing damage to trust that results from three disruptive events among partner organization: legal haggling, misuse of power, and cultural distance.

With regard to legal haggling, the process of drawing up a contract and its actual use tend to evoke distrust unless a third party steers it clear from suspicion. Third parties can help eliminate misunderstandings, clarify causes of disappointed expectations, and help negotiate altered conditions. Under the guidance of a third party, legal haggling need not harm trust.

Likewise, power plays may not be viewed as threatening if third parties can help to clarify intentions or help negotiate conditions. Specific demands may be prejudged as a power play until an objective outsider can show that they are reasonable or necessary. The third party can also prevent demands that are indeed unreasonable. The authors expect that this occurs especially in innovation. There, the third parties may be needed to clarify why something seemingly irregular does make sense.

Cultural distance could not be mitigated by the use of a third party. Seemingly, cultural mind frames can be persistent, and the gaps between them difficult to bridge for a third party. A possible explanation for this is that legal and power struggles relate to the business side, rather than the personal side of the relationship and hence have no direct relation with the cultural and internalized values, beliefs, and understandings of the parties involved.

KEY LESSONS

The need for flexibility and a continuous rebalancing of interests will form a potential source for conflict and breakdown of trust. It is here, in particular, that third parties can be of value.

Third parties should be impartial and independent as trust suffers from causal ambiguity. Third-party roles facilitating the relationship between business and society do exist, but generally fail to meet the requirement of impartiality and independence. This raises the question as to which third parties are actually actively playing a role in supporting public trust, and which additional functions are needed to restore the current trust crisis.

Cultural distance – especially on the level of fundamental differences in norms, values, and beliefs – might hamper public trust. The negative effect of cultural distance among partner firms could not be eliminated by third-party involvement and the same may hold true for public trust.

Distrust can stem from situations that conflict with common norms and values and are perceived as morally wrong. No logical or independent explanation can counter such deeply anchored emotional judgment. If business wants to repair public trust, business leaders will need to continually align their business models to the prevailing norms and values in society at large.

INTRODUCTION

Trust is of pivotal importance to the functioning of our modern networked economies, which has become clear in recent crises and a growing literature on legitimacy of organizations[1] and public trust.[2] The relationship between organizations and their stakeholders has become increasingly problematic due to a breach of trust. Trust is defined as the expectation that a partner will not engage in opportunistic behavior, even in the face of opportunities and incentives for opportunism, irrespective of the ability to monitor or control that party.[3] Key to this definition is a truster's vulnerability and inability to control the other that he/she has entrusted something to (trustee). This trust problem is at the heart of the current crisis in which individuals and whole societies are highly dependent on large corporations and banks for example for their savings, mortgages and pensions, while – individually and often even collectively – having no means of control over these parties. Yet, a breach of trust is disadvantageous for both sides as distrust breaks down relationships and paralyzes consumption, investment, and economic growth. This raises the important question: can trust be repaired, and, if so, how? For instance, can pension funds restore public trust in their institution after losing the money that people had entrusted them? Can companies repair trust after scandals of administrative fraud, excessive bonuses, and malignant products? Can the trustees regain trusters'

---

[1] Lamin and Zaheer, 2012; Pfarrer et al., 2008; Sullivan et al., 2007.

[2] Moriarty, 2009.

[3] Klein Woolthuis et al., 2005; McAllister, 1995; Bradach and Eccles, 1989; Nooteboom, 1996.

trust? Trust repair will have to involve some form of independent judgment to enable a reinterpretation of events, and to take away the suspicion of opportunism by the trustee, for instance by attributing the breach of trust to other factors than self-interest seeking with guile. This is where third parties come in.

In this study we built upon knowledge from an interorganizational context to shed light on the role of third parties in trust repair. We investigate how third parties can help partners to rebuild and repair interorganizational trust in high-tech alliances. Highly effective collaborative relationships are typically associated with high trust between alliance partners.[4] High-tech alliances are crucially important for innovation, and thereby for the competitiveness of firms[5], as well as regions and nation states.[6] As these relationships are complex, characterized by uncertainty, and risks of spillover and opportunism, their governance has attracted much attention.[7] Although aspects of trust such as uncertainty, (relational) risks, and control are addressed in most studies, thereby implicitly emphasizing the vulnerability of trust in alliances, research on how to repair trust – or how to deal with distrust – has only recently emerged.[8]

The role of third parties is another area that has received relatively little attention in the alliance literature. For instance, a review of more than 150 papers on alliances and alliance governance[9] does not mention the role of third parties in supporting such relationships, and only recently has the role of third parties in mediating and arbitrating in inter-firm relationships received more attention.[10] We consider the question of what to do once trust is under pressure a highly relevant one, as in business relationships trust will always be vulnerable to trust-reducing forces such as competition for knowledge, resources, and market position.[11] The contribution of this chapter is to address the role of third parties in trust repair.

---

[4] Bachmann, 1998; Becerra et al., 2008; Krishnan et al., 2006.
[5] Klein Woolthuis et al., 2005; De Man and Duysters, 2005.   [6] Edquist, 2005.
[7] Nooteboom, 1999.   [8] Dirks et al., 2009; Tomlinson and Mayer, 2009.
[9] Ireland et al., 2002.   [10] Howells, 2006; Mesquita, 2007.   [11] Mesquita, 2007.

The importance of third parties or intermediaries has been noted[12] and some proposals for specific roles of third parties have been made.[13] However, the literature is still eclectic, as most studies see the role of the intermediary as tangential to their main field of enquiry.[14] The literature is still in the phase of theory building,[15] or provides at best case study results or secondary data.[16] Empirical tests of the roles of third parties are few and far between, and also the attention to the function of third parties is limited. Whereas many studies acknowledge the role of third parties in gathering, translating, and encoding information, there are only few studies that relate third parties to alliance governance. An important strand in the alliance literature[17] emphasizes how third parties can obtain advantage by playing off two parties against each other, according to the principle of the "laughing third" (tertius gaudens). This principle is found in the earlier work of Simmel,[18] who did, however, also recognize the positive roles third parties can play to help two parties to collaborate. This role was later elaborated on by Obstveld in his description of the tertius iungens, the helping third.[19]

The contribution of this chapter is as follows. It considers the possible roles of third parties that are recognized in the literature, elaborates and operationalizes some of their effects on trust repair. In particular, we look at potential trust-destroying effects of power play, legal haggling, and cultural misunderstandings. While this does not cover all possible roles that third parties can play, it does address some of the key roles as identified in the recent literature. We test our hypotheses in a sample of 391 high-tech alliances, thereby presenting one of the first empirical tests of the role of third parties in trust repair.

---

[12] Fukuyama, 1995; Shapiro, 1987; Williamson, 1985; Zucker, 1986.
[13] Gould and Fernandez, 1989; Nooteboom, 1999.   [14] Howells, 2006.
[15] Bijlsma-Frankema et al., 2008; Mesquita, 2007.
[16] Bidault and Fischer, 1994; Bryant and Reenstra-Bryant, 1998; Morgan and Crawford, 1996.
[17] In particular, Burt, 1992.   [18] Simmel, 1950.   [19] Obstveld, 2005.

The outline of this chapter is as follows. In the next section, we explain the theoretical foundations of our study. A discussion of the research methodology and our empirical results follows. We conclude with an appraisal of the results, derive lessons for public trust, and suggest avenues for future research.

THEORY AND HYPOTHESES

The role of trust in high-tech alliances

Firms in an alliance can use different mechanisms to manage the relationship, such as control by contracts or hierarchy. In recent years, alliance research identified trust as a key governance mechanism for alliance success.[20] Trust has value because, for example, it reduces the need for hierarchical control and improves openness and problem solving.[21] However, it has disadvantages as well: it takes a long time to develop, is vulnerable to pressures of survival, can easily be broken down and then is difficult to restore.[22] In all stages of an inter-firm alliance – from initiating contacts to developing collaboration, contract negotiations, monitoring behavior, and renegotiations – critical events may occur that can break down trust. For instance, the active use of power by a stronger partner may induce feelings of anger and revenge and therefore dismantle trust. Even without the stronger partner using its power, perceived vulnerability or lacking self-confidence may generate enough suspicion to dismantle trust.[23] Trust can also deteriorate as a result of a lack of communication, misunderstandings, differences in perception, or as a result of cultural distance.[24] This may all result in a premature ending of the relationship, whereas innovation requires durable relationships between interdependent actors that can work through changing circumstances and adjust expectations. Along the way, parties will have to rethink their projects, and

---

[20] Das and Teng, 2001; Fryxell et al., 2002; Poppo and Zenger, 2002.
[21] Gulati, 1995; Zaheer et al., 1998; Zand, 1972.
[22] Nooteboom, 2002.   [23] Klein Woolthuis et al., 2005.
[24] Bijlsma-Frankema et al., 2008; Nooteboom, 1999.

renegotiate their relationship. The need for flexibility and a continuous rebalancing of interests will form a potential source for conflict and breakdown of trust. It is here, in particular, that third parties can be of value.

Roles of third parties

The analysis of the role of third parties goes back a long way, but has surprisingly not led to a rich and coherent body of literature.[25] A classic source of the "tertius" is Simmel.[26] Some of his work was picked up and diffused by Burt (1992) in his seminal work on third parties as boundary spanners of structural holes, but this was more focused on how to profit as a third party ("tertius gaudens") than on solving problems of collaboration.[27] More recently, studies have reported on an increasing trend in relying on external support if a firm lacks sufficient internal competencies.[28] The third party has acquired many labels, depending on the aim of the research – which usually focuses on one function of a third party under particular circumstances – labels such as intermediaries in innovation,[29] gatekeepers in technological knowledge transfer,[30] boundary spanners in networks,[31] or "impannatore" (specialist coordinators) and "superstructure organisations" in clusters are used.[32]

Recently, several studies have attempted to structure the different roles of third parties. Howells,[33] for example, looked at the role of intermediaries in innovation. Mesquita theorized on the role of third parties as trust facilitators for clustered firms.[34] However, it is especially in situations where trust is under pressure that the role of third parties becomes important, as truster and trustees are themselves too much "part of the problem" to be able to for instance arbitrate, mediate, and interpret. Hence, it makes sense to involve independent

---

[25] Howells, 2006. [26] Simmel, 1950. [27] Burt, 1992.
[28] Chiesa, Manzini, and Pizzurno, 2004; Grant and Baden-Fuller, 2004; Hislop, 2002; Morgan and Crawford, 1996.
[29] Stankiewicz, 1995. [30] Friedman and Silberman, 2003; Siegel et al., 2003.
[31] Burt, 1992. [32] Lynn et al., 1996. [33] Howells, 2006. [34] Mesquita, 2007.

and knowledgeable third parties to fulfill such functions. This role of third parties to prevent the breakdown of trust, or turn a situation around once conflicts or distrust has arisen, has recently been acknowledged in literature on trust building and trust repair.[35]

For this chapter we build upon the categorization of Nooteboom, who specifically addresses the role of go-betweens in innovation alliances and distinguishes eight roles.[36] The first role, presented also in transaction cost economics, is "trilateral governance."[37] When transactions are small or infrequent, it is not worth the cost and effort to set up an extensive governance structure. In this case it is more efficient to set up an incomplete contract and involve a third party to serve as an arbitrator or mediator to solve problems of legal haggling in setting up the contract and settling disputes. A second role is in the value assessment of information or knowledge before it is divulged or sold. Knowledge specialists that can assess and transfer the knowledge necessary for the innovation process should fulfill this role. This role has often been described as intermediary.[38] A third role lies in helping to bridge cultural distance. In collaboration processes, third parties can "translate" behavior. Such translations can also be necessary between technology fields, for example, to optimize "absorptive capacity."[39] This role has also been termed "knowledge or technology brokers"[40] and comes close to the role of the "tertius iungens," defined as a person who brings parties together and aims to improve collaboration.[41] Fourth, third parties can reduce the negative effects of power play, by preventing it or eliminating suspicion and mistaken interpretations of actions. A fifth role is to guard spillover through the monitoring of information flows, which role is also referred to as that of the gatekeeper.[42] A sixth role is that as a keeper of hostages to secure conformity to agreements.[43] The seventh role that Nooteboom distinguishes is in assisting a timely and minimally destructive

---

[35] Bijlsma-Frankema et al., 2008; Mesquita, 2007.   [36] Nooteboom, 2004.
[37] Williamson, 1985.   [38] See, e.g., Callon, 1994.
[39] Cohen and Levinthal, 1990.   [40] Hargadon, 1998; Wolpert, 2002.
[41] Simmel, 1950.   [42] Cohen and Levinthal, 1990.   [43] Williamson, 1985.

ending of relationships, so that a future potential remains for parties to collaborate.[44] A final role refers to the support of reputation mechanisms by intentional "gossip" as a means to deter opportunistic behavior.

Because our study focuses on the role of the third parties in high-tech alliances in which uncertainty and risk – and hence trust – plays a crucial role, we choose to focus on those roles that directly relate to rebuilding trust or preventing its breakdown once it is under pressure, that is: (1) the role of a mediator in legal disputes in the absence of hierarchical control or complete contracts; (2) the role of moderating power play whereby the disruptive nature of such events can be lessened and trust maintained; for instance by making use of reputation mechanisms; and (3) the role of bridging cultural distance to enhance understanding and hence facilitate the process of trust where this is problematic.

Interorganizational trust

Before we continue, we need to find a working definition of interorganizational trust. A key challenge is the applicability of the concept of "trust" to different contexts and levels of analysis, which easily creates confusion.[45] Hence, the first issue is the level of analysis, given that the referent of trust may vary.[46] For this chapter, the distinction between interpersonal and interorganizational trust is relevant.[47] In the first approach trust is a micro-level phenomenon and has its basis in individuals. A distinction has been made between trusting behavior and trust as a psychological disposition. Since there is no psychology on the organizational level, the common wisdom is to say that organizations as such cannot trust. However, if we see disposition in a more general sense, we can very well see an organizational disposition to trust, on the basis of its culture, style of governance (more legal or more informal), and level of risk acceptance,

[44] Nooteboom, 2004.   [45] Inkpen and Currall, 2003.   [46] Dirks and Ferrin, 2002.
[47] De Jong and Klein Woolthuis, 2008; Zaheer et al., 1998.

which are embodied and maintained in personnel selection, training, decision structures and procedures, reporting procedures, etc. Organizations can also be the object of trust (trustee), on the basis of their reputation, experience, structure, and process. Clearly, to have trust in an organization one must also trust the individuals that enact the policies of the organization, which again depends, in part, on organizational culture, structure, and processes. Conversely, it is not enough to trust the employees of the organization one is dealing with, their commitments should be supported by their role and position within their organization. In other words, personal and organizational trust should be in line.[48]

In the present study we focus on trust in the organization of a partner (trustee), as judged by respondents that can reliably express the experience of the focal firm (truster). In small firms the owner-manager is the most reliable source. Hence we derive our working definition of interorganizational trust as a positive perception of the partner's behavior, that is, the perception by the respondent of the focal firm that a partner organization will not engage in opportunistic behavior, even in the face of opportunities and incentives to do so.[49] We can expect trust to be present in situations where: (1) the trustee in the business relationship shows forbearance from opportunism; and (2) is known to behave carefully and with concern (integrity, goodwill, and benevolence); and where (3) the truster shows limited control behavior. Hence, our definition characterizes interorganizational trust as a multi-component construct based on three related components: forbearance from opportunism, care and concern, and limited control. This conceptualization operationalizes interorganizational trust as a relational rather than a dispositional feature as it can be more reliably observed than underlying dispositions. This is important in this study to reduce single-source bias that occurs in surveys in which one asks the same respondent about both antecedents and outcomes. In what follows, we consider three disruptive events for

[48] Nooteboom, 2002.   [49] Hosmer, 1995.

interorganizational trust that we hypothesize can be tempered by third parties, namely legal haggling in the absence of formal hierarchy, active misuse of power, and cultural distance.

Legal haggling

The relation between trust and contracts is somewhat ambivalent. On the one hand, having been able to reach an agreement, and writing this down in a formal written contract, forms a "safe haven" to fall back upon in case of trouble and can hence make it easier for trust to develop. On the other hand, it has been argued that parties that trust each other more have less incentive to write contracts as they rely on their mutual willingness to solve problems as they arise. This is interesting because it is exactly their trusting relationship that would make it easier to arrive at detailed written agreements as there will be less hesitance to accept (inter)dependence and commit to an agreement in writing.[50] Cynically one could conclude that contracts are easiest to draw up when they are not needed, that is, when parties (still) trust each other and have good working relationships, and most needed in situations where they are difficult to draw up, that is, in situations where parties are haggling over the agreement or its execution. Legal haggling relates to all disputes that may arise in the design, execution, use, and renegotiation of the contract between alliance partners. Such disputes may include squabbles of interpretation, demands for compliance, threats and execution of sanctions or litigation, and requests for adjustments.[51] This is likely to affect trust in several ways and a third party can help to moderate its negative effects.

First of all third parties can play an important role by guiding contract negotiations as an impartial, independent "moderator." This can reduce distrust arising from the emphasis placed on contracts that may be interpreted as a sign of distrust. Furthermore, a third party can help in the design and monitoring of the contract, in

---

[50] Klein Woolthuis *et al.*, 2005. [51] Williamson, 1985.

resolving misunderstandings, reinterpretation of events, pointing out risks of escalating conflicts, and helping to renegotiate the contract. This is all part of "trilateral governance" as identified in transaction cost theory. Nooteboom adds to this that the third parties may play a role in determining whether deviance from the contract rests on a misunderstanding, lack of competence, or bad intentions, that is, not only the actions counts, but also the intentions behind actions as they yield the most resilience in trust development.[52] The impossibility of obtaining this information from an objective source may lead parties to unfoundedly distrust each other, start shirking, or retaliating. Trust suffers from "causal ambiguity:" when something goes wrong, there is the dilemma of interpretation since the cause of the trouble may not be opportunism but an accident or lack of competence. However, it is precisely the opportunist who will claim that an error occurred.[53] In this way accidents can escalate to mutual distrust. The third party can fulfill an objective mediating role and thereby take away doubts, reduce the risk of false accusations, and help to maintain or restore an atmosphere in which disputes can be constructively resolved. This may prevent parties from calling upon means of ultimate appeal or "revenge," and thus the third party can reduce the detrimental effects of contract enforcement. This is the first role of the third parties in restoring trust. We therefore hypothesize:

> *Hypothesis H1a. Legal haggling will dismantle interorganizational trust.*
> *Hypothesis H1b. Third parties can help to solve legal haggling and thus restore interorganizational trust.*

Power play

In an inter-firm alliance, parties can resort to social (e.g., trust), legal (e.g., contract), or private ordering mechanism to "encourage" desired

---

[52] Nooteboom, 2002.   [53] *Ibid.*

behavior of their counterpart. Private ordering includes the deliberate use of one's relative position of power, that is, by imposing one's will, demands, views, approaches, and actions. A strong power position by one of the alliance partners may already have an unintended negative effect because it may create a fear of power abuse or opportunistic behavior.[54] Power play, however, relates to the active and intentional use of power to enforce for instance the (beneficial) terms of an agreement, (unfair) execution of, or (disproportional) gains from an agreement. Of course, such power play will have strong effects on the relationship. It may provoke defensive behavior or breakdown of trust and thus carries the risk of harming the alliance.[55] It may also lock the relationship into a straitjacket that leaves little room for learning and innovation. However, use of power or having clear power dependence between partners does not always have to be bad. Having "one captain on the ship" can make it possible to push a project forwards and achieve results within planned time frames and budgetary constraints.[56] It is when power play crosses the borders of perceived fairness that it will have a particularly detrimental effect on the level of trust between parties and hence on the quality of the relationship. It is especially in a situation of power play that a third party has a role to play.

In the event of actual use of power, a third party can assist the abused party to address and discuss this behavior with the alliance partner. He or she may show the adverse effects of power play on motivation and trust, and on reducing both the space and the motivation for the abused party to take initiative and contribute to the best of his/her ability. The third party may also show the negative impact of the misuse of power on the reputation of the company. "Spreading the news" on benevolent or opportunistic parties will have more credibility when done by the third parties than by parties holding a direct interest, whose words may be seen as malicious, strategic gossip. Because the third parties cannot afford to take part in a gossip

---

[54] Hart and Saunders, 1997.   [55] Bachmann, 2001.   [56] Klein Woolthuis, 1999.

campaign, (s)he can be trusted to function as a sieve and amplifier by checking accusations of opportunistic or incompetent behavior and transmitting them only if correct.[57] Hence, third parties can moderate power play directly or indirectly by supporting the reputation mechanism. This brings us to the following hypotheses:

> *Hypothesis H2a. Power play will dismantle interorganizational trust.*
>
> *Hypothesis H2b. Third parties can help to restrict the misuse of power and thus restore interorganizational trust.*

Cultural distance

In inter-firm relationships dissimilarities between parties can create problems of understanding and judging the other's competences and intentions.[58] In highly dynamic technological fields, this process may take too long for timely reactions to new developments. Third parties can help to bridge the gap between mental frameworks and guide the processes that are needed to increase mutual understanding of capabilities and mind frames, thereby inducing trust into the relationship. It is especially when doubts emerge during the alliance or disputes that occur due to a lack of understanding of the other that the third parties can play a crucial role. He or she may offer second opinions on the progress of the project, verify information, form an objective judgment on the success of the partnership, and "translate" knowledge, information, and judgments. This is the "bridging" role of third parties as identified earlier. We therefore hypothesize that:

> *Hypothesis H3a. Cultural distance will dismantle interorganizational trust.*
>
> *Hypothesis H3b. Third parties can help to bridge distance and thus restore interorganizational trust.*

---

[57] Nooteboom, 2002.   [58] Nieto and Santamaria, 2007.

METHODS

Data collection, sample, and measures

This study focuses on business relationships between two or more firms and/or research institutes that operate in high-tech industries (biotechnology, new material development, information technology, maritime technologies, and environmental technology). The lifecycle of R&D in these industries is usually short. Much of the new technological knowledge quickly becomes outdated, often even before it has been incorporated in new products and/or services. Hence, in the high-tech industries in particular, we find many collaborative efforts between firms, including rival firms. Furthermore, environmental uncertainty and project complexity make partnerships in high-tech innovation a challenge as flexibility, learning, and adaptability are core qualities a relationship in this context should have. Because of all these relationship characteristics, we expect trust to play a vital role in these relationships.

Our data collection proceeded in two phases. In the preparatory phase of the fieldwork, we conducted twenty-five semi-structured interviews with consultants of the Dutch Ministry of Economic Affairs who were involved in policy programs to stimulate inter-firm collaboration on innovation. Additionally, the consultants selected twenty cases (ten successful and ten less successful ones) that we studied in great detail to obtain in-depth knowledge of the high-tech collaboration. Case research is suitable for exploratory research where understanding is the primary objective.[59] The twenty cases dealt with collaborative innovation and hence involved complex transactions for which close collaboration between partners was necessary over a considerable period of time. The cases involved legally independent partners that shared costs and benefits more or less evenly. All cases entailed uncertainty and/or complexity, and specific assets, and hence risks of dependence, opportunism, and "hold-up." Under strict confidentiality, we received full access to all

[59] Yin, 2003.

documents of the cases – including the inter-firm contracts but also project plans, annual reports of the companies involved, personal notes and letters, and half-yearly progress reports – that were available at the Ministry. Among other things, this allowed us to examine the content of the contracts with respect to the clauses that were laid down in the contract and the exact content of each clause. Also, clippings from newspapers and trade magazines concerning the collaborations were collected. To enable comparison between the cases and to ensure the quality of the case analysis, a case protocol was written to describe the alliance's history, development, and outcome.[60] The interviews with the consultants were transcribed into interview reports and sent back for verification and agreement. Hence, all this allowed us to reconstruct the development of high-tech alliances and to check the data from the interviews with the secondary sources. We used this information to design our survey. The survey was field-tested using a sample of ten companies involved in R&D alliances. This resulted in a number of modifications to the questionnaire.

In the second stage, a research team conducted telephone interviews with 572 business managers of inter-firm R&D collaboration. Prior to these interviews, all managers received an explanatory letter inviting them to participate. We briefed the team on the features of R&D, high-tech industries, and inter-firm relationships. The team made three attempts to identify and interview the selected respondents. The case firms were identified from a database of Dutch inter-firm high-technology alliances published by the Ministry of Economic Affairs. This enabled us to identify the business managers who were responsible for interfacing with the partner firms. They were considered to be the most knowledgeable informants about the inter-firm relationships. During the interview, main topics such as the history and purpose of the alliance as well as contracts, investments, and industry dynamics were discussed. One of the first questions required the respondents to identify the business partner in the alliance in question.

[60] *Ibid.*

We used this information to cross-validate the information from the database. Because high-tech alliances are typically concerned with specific projects and goals, we also asked the respondents to identify one project that was the most important to the inter-firm alliance. By focusing on inter-firm collaboration within one sector (high-tech industries), we reduced the range of extraneous variations such as the level of uncertainty or competition that might influence the constructs of interest. Some open questions were added to enable the respondents to tell their own story to some extent. In total fifty main questions (often divided in several sub-questions) were asked. An outcome of this was that the interviews that were designed to take half an hour would sometimes take up to one hour depending on the respondent.

We obtained 391 usable responses, giving an effective response rate of 68.5 percent. This rate is considerably higher than those observed in prior studies on inter-firm relationships that usually are in the 10 to 33 percent range.[61] It was also satisfactory considering this studies' requirement for direct senior management involvement and the confidentiality of some of the requested information.

The non-response is low (31.5 percent), especially considering that only 10.5 percent actually refused to be interviewed; 20.1 percent could not be contacted within the three attempts that the interviewers used to try to get in touch with the respondent. To investigate whether the non-response incurs a bias, the non-cooperating respondents (10.5 percent) were asked for their reasons for not participating. The reasons for refusal were on the one hand a lack of time and interest, and on the other hand, irritation because they had recently cooperated in another survey. Although these reasons can hide their true motive for not participating in the survey (such as an unsuccessful cooperation), the low non-response and the reasons for not participating do not raise serious doubts on the implications of non-response.

Studies of this type, where one asks the same respondent about both dependent and explanatory variables, are in principle vulnerable

---

[61] Parkhe, 1993; Poppo and Zenger, 2002; Subramani and Venkatraman, 2003.

to common-method bias, in particular common-source bias.[62] For the aim of this study, reliance on key informants such as our respondents seems to be the only realistic and feasible way to obtain the required information.[63] We used the following actions to address possible concerns of validity. First and foremost, we used a complex model specification with interaction terms that is recognized as one of the most important solutions to prevent common-source bias.[64] Second, available data can be tested for convergence by triangulation with secondary data.[65] We compared the outcomes of the self-reported data in the questionnaire with the archival data on the twenty cooperative projects that we studied in the first phase of data collection. The congruence of the data from the questionnaires and case studies supports the accuracy of the reported data. Third, we asked questions concerning objective events rather than subjective expectations or opinions. Fourth, via the sequence of our questions we aimed to minimize the effects of consistency artifacts. Whereas Salancik and Pfeffer suggest letting the independent variable follow, rather than precede, the independent variables, Podsakoff and Organ argue that correlations will be similar using either method.[66] In our opinion, a life-cycle approach would best serve an accurate reflection of the inter-firm collaboration. Hence, for the purpose of this study, we structured the questions in the survey from past interactions through partner selection, contract negotiations, contract execution, and outcomes of the inter-firm collaboration. Fifth, we conducted Harman's single-factor test and this gave no indication of common-method bias. In sum, in our case it is unlikely that the findings can be attributed to common-source bias.

Control variables

We included three control variables in our model. First, we included focal firm size as a variable to control for extraneous factors such as

---

[62] Podsakoff and Organ, 1986.   [63] Huber and Power, 1985.
[64] Aiken and West, 1991; Brockner et al., 1997.   [65] Keats and Hitt, 1988.
[66] Podsakoff and Organ, 1986; Salancik and Pfeffer, 1977.

bargaining power and resource base.[67] These factors may influence the governance because large firms have more legal resources, experience, and staff as a result of which they are likely to be less dependent on governance mechanisms such as interorganizational trust to protect their business interests. Second, we include the perceived importance of institutions in the form of the role of norms and values over formal alliance management. Those also may affect trust, particularly in the Dutch (or broader continental European) culture in which "voice" is the prevalent option for solving problems.[68] Third, we included the strategic importance of the alliance partner.[69] More specifically, we included the value that the focal firm places on the knowledge that the partner firm has to offer. In high-tech alliances, knowledge is important, and alliance partners that have relevant knowledge will be able to obtain a strategically better position. An alliance with a strategically important partner will receive more attention that will foster interorganizational trust. Also, professionals exchanging technical information may have more affinity and initial respect for each other that may serve as a basis for trust.[70]

Measures

Table 11.1 provides an overview of the items that we used to measure the constructs of our theoretical model.

We used five items to measure interorganizational trust. Our definition characterizes interorganizational trust as a multi-component construct based on three related components: forbearance from opportunism (measured by two items), care and concern (measured by two items), and lack of monitoring (measured by one item). The choice

---

[67] Ariño and Reuer, 2004.   [68] Bachmann, 1998.   [69] Reuer *et al.*, 2006.

[70] The question arises whether alliances with and those without the use of third parties differ not only in the effects of the explanatory variables on trust, but also, perhaps, in other respects that might affect the results of the explanatory variables. For example, do they differ also in the effects of the control variables on trust? We tested for this by also appending the condition of using an intermediary or not to the control variables, and we found no significant difference.

Table 11.1 *Concepts and measures*

Constructs, items, and scales	Factor loading
Interorganizational trust, alpha = 0.78	
1. We did not feel that we constantly had to keep an eye on [name partner].	0.76
2. During the relationship, [name partner] treated our problems constructively and with care.	0.76
3. I never had the feeling of being misled by [name partner].	0.77
4. [Name partner] tried to reap disproportional gains from the cooperation relative to its input.	0.71
5. [Name partner] withhold important information from us.	0.74
(1 = strongly disagree, 5 = strongly agree)	
Go-between	
1. Did you during the start of the relationship with [name partner] and the execution of the project ever ask the help of a third party (with a third party we mean a non-contract party)?	n.a.
(1 = yes, 0 = no)	
Contracting process	
1. It was easy to design the contract with [name partner]	n.a.
(1 = strongly disagree, 5 = strongly agree)	
Active contract use	
1. The contract is, also after it has been drawn up, actively used to manage the relationship with [name partner].	n.a.
(1 = strongly disagree, 5 = strongly agree)	
Use of power	
1. The partner forced us to do the things they wanted them to.	n.a.
(1 = strongly disagree, 5 = strongly agree)	
Cultural distance, alpha = 0.72	
1. Cultural differences between us and [name partner] have resulted in problems.	0.89
2. Due to different ways of communicating, problems in discussions and meetings with [name partner] often occurred.	0.89
(1 = strongly disagree, 5 = strongly agree)	

Table 11.1 (cont.)

Constructs, items, and scales	Factor loading
Strategic importance of the alliance partner	
1. [Name partner] supplied us with important information on new technologies.	n.a.
(1 = strongly disagree, 5 = strongly agree)	
Relative importance of institutions	
1. Informal norms and values were in our relationship with [name partner] more important than the formal contract.	n.a.
(1 = strongly disagree, 5 = strongly agree)	
Size of focal firm, alpha = 0.82	
1. What is the number of employees in your firm?	0.92
(1 = 0 − 10; 3 = 100 − 250; 5 > 1000)	
2. What is the annual sales revenue of your firm?	0.92
(1 < 500.000; 3 = 1 − 10M; 5 > 50m)	

Notes: The original questions are presented in the table. Prior to the empirical analysis, the scales for items 4 and 5 for interorganizational trust and for contracting process have been reversed to maintain consistency.

and specification of these items is based on earlier studies.[71] The use of third parties, ease of the contracting process, the active use of a contract to manage the alliance, power play by the alliance partner, the strategic importance of the alliance partner, and the relative importance of institutions were measured by one item that directly relates to the particular construct. The size of the focal organization was measured by two items: the number of employees and the annual sales. Cultural distance was also measured by two items: the perceived cultural differences between the partners and the degree to which communication problems had occurred due to cultural differences.

[71] McAllister, 1995; Nooteboom *et al.*, 1997

EMPIRICAL RESULTS

With our model, we seek to explain how interorganizational trust breaks down as a result of legal haggling, power play, and cultural distance, and how third parties can mitigate these detrimental effects. We split up the effects on trust in two classes: for collaboration without an intermediary (66 percent of the cases) and for collaboration in which an intermediary was used (34 percent). This is specified in the form of interaction variables for the presence or absence of third parties and each of the three trust-breaking conditions. Here we expect a negative effect for cases without intermediary, and a significantly lesser or zero negative effect for cases with an intermediary. The means, standard deviations, and correlations among composite indicators are shown in Table 11.2. The hierarchical OLS regression results are provided in Table 11.3. We standardized the explanatory variables before entering them into the regression model. The baseline specification (Model 1) presents the control variables. Model 2 reports the interactions of the disruptive events without and with the use of a third party. In preparation for the regression analysis, we performed the regular tests to obtain reliable estimates. The latter tests gave satisfactory results: neither heteroscedasticity nor non-normality is an issue. We tested for possible biases caused by co-linearity among variables by calculating the variance inflation factor (VIF) for each of the regression coefficients. The VIF values were well below the cutoff value of 10 recommended by Neter et al.[72]

The various fit parameters show that our models increasingly fit the data better. Conclusions from the empirical results are twofold. First, as expected, the disruptive events of legal haggling, power play, and cultural distance do have a detrimental effect on interorganizational trust, if no use of an intermediary is made. The effects in Model 2 report a negative and strongly significant effect of legal haggling

[72] Neter et al., 1985.

Table 11.2 Correlations, means, and standard deviations

	Mean	S.D.	(1)	(2)	(3)	(4)	(5)	(6)	(7)	(8)	(9)
1. Interorganizational trust	22.366	3.673	1.000								
2. Go-between	0.512	0.501	0.023	1.000							
3. Contracting process	4.199	1.241	0.263**	0.008	1.000						
4. Active contract use	2.209	1.583	−0.192**	−0.031	−0.223**	1.000					
5. Use of power	1.315	0.836	−0.320**	0.049	−0.217**	0.093*	1.000				
6. Cultural distance	3.118	1.909	−0.426**	0.029	−0.199**	0.217**	0.385**	1.000			
7. Importance partner	3.798	1.388	0.120**	0.001	0.023	0.059	−0.055	−0.014	1.000		
8. Importance institutions	4.151	1.201	0.259**	0.082	0.208**	−0.180**	−0.100*	−0.260**	0.072	1.000	
9. Size of focal firm	6.711	2.293	−0.001	−0.080	−0.053	−0.025	−0.015	−0.020	0.071	0.032	1.000

Note: * $p < .05$; ** $p < .01$

Table 11.3 *Third parties and interorganizational trust in high-tech alliances*

	Model 1	Model 2
Constant	22.38 ***	22.38 ***
	(0.98)	(0.98)
Control variables		
Firm size focal organization	−.01	.00
	(.08)	(.06)
Value of the alliance partner	.13 **	.14 ***
	(.13)	(.10)
Relative importance of institutions	.20 ***	.12 ***
	(.15)	(.12)
Independent variables		
Contracting process × (1 − go-between)		−.26 ***
		(.13)
Active contract use × (1 − go-between)		−.14 **
		(.13)
Use of power × (1 − go-between)		−.22 ***
		(.25)
Cultural distance × (1 − go-between)		−.54 ***
		(.12)
Contracting process × go-between		−.07
		(.14)
Active contract use × go-between		−.01
		(.13)
Use of power × go-between		−.05
		(.27)
Cultural distance × go-between		−.54 ***
		(.12)
Model fit indices		
R^2	.06	.46
Adj. R^2	.05	.44
F	7.74 ***	28.81 ***

Notes: * $p < 0.10$; ** $p < 0.05$; *** $p < 0.01$; the entries in the table are standardized coefficients (βs). The numbers in brackets are standard errors.

within the contracting process ($\beta = -0.26$, p $<$.01) and by the active use of contracts to enforce behavior ($\beta = -0.14$, p $<$.05), for instance, power play by the alliance partner ($\beta = -0.22$, p $<$.01), and cultural distance between the alliance partners ($\beta = -0.54$, p $<$.01). Second, the empirical results confirm three of the four mitigating roles of third parties. That is, Model 2 shows that in those cases where a third party is involved, the two dimensions of legal haggling have a negative but non-significant effect on interorganizational trust ($\beta = -0.07$, n.s.; and $\beta = -0.01$, n.s.). A similar conclusion can be obtained for the impact of power play: with a third party involved, the significant effect is transformed into a non-significant relationship ($\beta = -0.05$, n.s.). For cultural distance, however, we cannot find a difference in the effects without and with the use of third parties. This may indicate that third parties did not manage to solve such problems. However, there is another possibility. The question concerning cultural distance was whether differences in culture affect trust. Perhaps third parties manage to reduce cultural difference and what we see here is the effect of any remaining difference that they did not manage to eliminate. Then using a third party should have a negative effect on cultural distance. We tested for this, again using the control variables, and indeed a negative effect on cultural distance of using a third party was found but it was not statistically significant. These third parties did not seem to be able to either reduce cultural distance or mitigate its negative effect on trust.

CONCLUSIONS

In this chapter we examined the role that third parties can play in repairing trust in high-tech alliances. Collaboration is rife with triggers of suspicion under causal ambiguity and misunderstanding that third parties may help to unravel – with expertise and a sobering attitude – taking the emotions and the sting out of mishaps that inevitably occur. Our contribution is to provide an empirical test of some of the potential roles of third parties, and drawing lessons from this for public trust.

The literature so far has categorized third parties' roles,[73] and has theorized their trust-mitigating role between collaborating firms.[74] Other literature has implicitly addressed the role of third parties by focusing on trust-restoring processes, while implicitly acknowledging the role of third parties in this process by taking this role upon themselves as independent researchers.[75] Our empirical test forms a step toward substantiating the proposed roles of third parties identified in these earlier studies.

On the basis of our empirical study we conclude the following. First, as expected, legal haggling, power play, and cultural distance have a negative effect on trust between alliance partners. Second, with the involvement of third parties, these negative effects can in two out of three cases be eliminated. With regard to legal haggling, we conclude that both the process of drawing up a contract and its actual use tend to evoke distrust, unless a third party steers it clear from suspicion, presumably by eliminating misunderstandings, clarifying causes of disappointed expectations, and for instance helping to negotiate altered conditions. This, we believe, is an important result. It is partly in line with earlier views of contract use as an action of last resort, but corrects it with the finding that under the guidance of a third parties it need not harm trust.

We find a similar result for power play. Apparently, pressure by one party, seeking to impose its views on the other, may not be seen as threatening if third parties can help to clarify intentions or help negotiate conditions. Demands may be prejudged as power play until an objective outsider can show that they are reasonable or necessary, or will be compensated. The third party can also prevent demands that are indeed unreasonable. We can imagine that this occurs especially in innovation. There, the third parties may be needed to clarify why something seemingly irregular does make sense, or why one should work toward deadlines and budgets where there might still be so much to explore.

[73] Howells, 2006.   [74] Nooteboom, 2002; Mesquita, 2007.
[75] Bijlsma-Frankema *et al.*, 2008.

Last, we found that cultural distance also yields a problem. This, however, could not be mitigated by the use of a third party. Seemingly, cultural mind frames can be persistent, and the gaps between them difficult to bridge for a third party. A possible explanation for this is that legal and power struggles relate to the business side, rather than the personal side of the relationship and hence have no direct relation with the cultural and internalized values, beliefs, and understandings of the parties involved. Legal and power issues can be discussed and (re)negotiated, whereas cultural differences lie closer to the heart and rest on personal and stable beliefs and interpretations. Even with the help of third parties, it will be difficult to reinterpret situations which conflict with parties' beliefs and values.

LESSONS FOR PUBLIC TRUST — AVENUES FOR FURTHER RESEARCH

Whereas a study of trust in high-tech alliances cannot be linearly extrapolated into the domain of public trust, it can inspire some basic conditions and principles of roles that third parties may have in supporting or restoring public trust. The lessons from the inter-firm context as such help to formulate a research agenda for public trust.

As argued in this chapter, it is especially in situations where trust is under pressure that the role of third parties becomes important, as parties themselves are too much "part of the problem" to be able to for instance arbitrate, mediate, and interpret; hence such functions are better fulfilled by independent and knowledgeable third parties.[76] The role of independent third parties does not only exist in the inter-firm context, it also exists in the public domain to ensure trust in our institutions: rating agencies, watchdogs, financial auditors, certification offices, commissions, and courts are some of the many organizations that fulfill the role of "independent third" that can help to make, break, or repair trust. An important difference

[76] Mesquita, 2007.

between the inter-firm context and the public trust domain is that, whereas the inter-firm context is generally characterized by personal relationships between managers with decision power and a considerable level of mutual dependence as the rationale for collaboration, public trust is characterized by impersonal relationships and large power asymmetry. Public trust is therefore a more abstract phenomenon as it cannot relate to real trust as defined by Nooteboom.[77] Real or thick trust relates to trust that is personal and specific to the exchange relationship.[78] This raises the complex question of how public trust can be supported or repaired, and how third parties can assist in this process.

In a similar vein, third parties in inter-firm relationships are often trusted persons or experts, whereas in public trust the third party appears more like a function: general ratings and comparisons for customer products, certifications, and audits for business performance, and for instance watchdogs and financial authorities for market and price fixing. In the terms of Nooteboom,[79] public trust therefore has its base in macro sources of trust which are general and impersonal, and not specific to an exchange relation.[80] Macro sources arise from the institutional environment of laws, norms, values, standards, and agencies for their enforcement. This yields "institution-based" or "thin" trust. Thin trust is "borrowed" from the trust we have in those institutions that verify, support or enforce the trustworthiness of people and organizations. This coins the question on how the function of an independent and impartial third party can prosper in absence of personal relationships. Can the role of third parties to build, maintain or repair trust be fulfilled by impersonal institutions?

Whereas any extrapolation from inter-firm to public trust should bear in mind the above questions, we do believe that there are lessons that can be learned from the inter-firm context. First, and most important, are the conditions for a third party to be effective in

---

[77] Nooteboom, 2002.   [78] Deutsch, 1973; Shapiro, 1987.
[79] Nooteboom, 2002.   [80] Williams, 1998; Bachmann, 1998.

building, maintaining, or restoring trust. Third parties should be impartial and independent as trust suffers from causal ambiguity.[81] Third-party roles facilitating the relationship between business and society do exist, but generally fail to meet the requirement of impartiality and independence. Consumer organizations defend the interests of customers, rating agencies are paid by the companies they rate, and brokers and advisers of, for example, pensions and financial products are incentivized by sales commissions on the most profitable products. This raises the question as to which third parties are actually actively playing a role in supporting public trust, and which additional functions are needed to restore the current trust crisis.

Our empirical research into trust breakdown in high-tech alliances as a result of legal haggling, power play, and cultural quarrels leads to more specific suggestions and considerations for the study of public trust. Whereas the lessons above mainly related to the *conditions* that a third party should adhere to (independent and personal), the lessons from the specific relational problems relate more to some basic *principles* that play a role in trust breakdown and repair, such as power asymmetry and fairness. We draw on these lessons to formulate further research questions on how these principles pan out in the public trust domain.

First, legal haggling in an inter-firm context supposes that contracts can be (re)negotiated with an eye on mutual interests and fairness. In public trust, the (re)negotiation of agreements will be hard, if not impossible, as the relationship is highly asymmetrical: a single consumer or citizen cannot renegotiate conditions with its larger counterpart, nor defend their own interests. This is why institutions and safeguards have been put in place, such as compensation schemes for failing banks and antitrust regulations to prevent price fixing. However, individuals generally do not have a real "voice," nor personal contacts with people in large organizations that are able to weigh individual interests and make decisions accordingly with

---

[81] Nooteboom 2002.

mutual consent. This makes the public–business relationship a unilateral contract in which the truster is a "contract-taker." The imbalance inherent to the relationship will make it difficult to build or repair trust. This makes the individual vulnerable, and trust very fragile. One way to deal with this vulnerability is to try to establish beforehand the trustworthiness of the trustee. The fast rise of providers of independent and impartial information on e.g. the internet (rating and review websites) can be seen as an illustration of this quest for information. An interesting avenue for further research is to see which parties fulfill the role of the independent third in the public domain. How, and with what effect? Further questions relate to the nature of the relationship between business and society: how can trust function when unilateral contracts and impersonal contacts characterize the relationship? And what is the role of "thin" trust and institutions in this context?

Second, power play was found detrimental to the relationships, but the negative effects could be eliminated by the involvement of a third party. In the inter-firm context, issues arising from power play could be steered clear from conflict by moderating dependence, for instance through the reputation mechanism. The business–society relationship is characterized by a large power gap, whereby asymmetry is the logical consequence of modern business. Asymmetry, however, is known to greatly hinder trust buildup and lead to defensive behavior, lack of openness, and destructive conflict.[82] Like in the inter-firm domain, power symmetry also appears a problem in the business–society interface. There is a growing trend of large citizen and consumer movements conquering the hegemony of large business, by for instance organizing customer boycotts and cyber-attacks. However, like with legal haggling, a "real" third-party function, which should focus on moderating power distance through alignment of interests, is lacking. Instead, the mediating "third" is often organized according to an "us vs. them" logic, whereas the real challenge

---

[82] Klein Woolthuis et al., 2005.

lies in the creation of value for all stakeholders involved. Promising in this respect are the new business models evolving around the concept of shared value[83] in which the creation of value for all is the central aim. This aligns interests and supports (public) trust as direct relationships are restored between business and its stakeholders.[84] Whereas front-runner organizations are quick to adapt these new business models, the question remains how the general breakdown of public trust can be countered, and what the role of third parties could be in aligning interests to facilitate this process. Like in the inter-firm context, reputation mechanisms can be used to affect the legitimacy of organizations, and this function has spontaneously evolved into, for instance online forums where experiences are shared and reputations can be made or broken. Are such functions sufficiently effective to moderate the power asymmetry between business and society? Which other mechanisms exist to mediate power asymmetry? Which role could third parties play in this process and how could they weigh and align interests? And, how can institutions, but also sanctions and safeguards, be employed to prevent power play?

Lastly, cultural distance might hamper public trust. This is a deeper problem than a superficial alignment of consumer products to local preferences or speaking the other's language. It refers to fundamental differences in norms, values, and beliefs that can lead to a breakdown of trust. In our study we found that the negative effect of cultural distance could not be eliminated by third-party involvement. We believe that the same will hold true for public trust. A breach of trust resulting from issues such as excessive executive bonuses while "normal people" are losing their pensions cannot be repaired by outsiders. These situations conflict with common norms and values and are hence perceived as morally wrong. No logical, nor any independent explanation can counter such deeply anchored emotional judgment. It is therefore up to businesses to realign their business models to the prevailing norms and values in society at large to repair

---

[83] Porter and Kramer, 2011.   [84] Senge et al., 2010.

public trust. This chapter contributes to this aim by identifying some of the key problems in the trust relationship between business and society, giving leads to redesign the business–society relationship, and defining roles and conditions for third-party involvement in public trust.

REFERENCES

Aiken, L., and West, S. (1991), *Multiple Regression: Testing and Interpreting Interactions*. Thousand Oaks CA: Sage.

Ariño, A. and Reuer, J. J. (2004), 'Designing and renegotiating strategic alliance contracts.' *Academy of Management Executive*, 18(3), 37–48.

Bachmann, R. (1998), 'Trust – conceptual aspects of a complex phenomenon.' In C. Lane, and R. Bachmann (eds.), *Trust within and between Organizations*. Oxford: Oxford University Press, 298–322.

Bachmann, R. (2001), 'Trust, power, and control in trans-organizational relations.' *Organization Studies*, 22(2), 337–365.

Becerra, M., Lunnan, R., and Huemer, L. (2008), 'Trustworthiness, risk, and the transfer of tacit and explicit knowledge between alliance partners.' *Journal of Management Studies*, 45(5), 691.

Bidault, F. and Fischer, W. A. (1994), 'Technology transactions – networks over markets.' *R and D Management*, 24(4), 373–386.

Bijlsma-Frankema, K., Sitkin, S., and Weibel, A. (2008), *Breaking out of Distrust: Judges and Administrators in a Court of Law*. EGOS. Bergen.

Bradach, J. L. and Eccles, R. G. (1989), 'Price, authority and trust: from ideal types to plural forms.' *Annual Review of Society*, 15, 97–118.

Brockner, J., Siegel, P. A., Daly, J. P., Tyler, T., and Martin, C. (1997), 'When trust matters: the moderating effect of outcome favorability.' *Administrative Science Quarterly*, 42(3), 558–583.

Bryant, T. A., and Reenstra-Bryant, R. A. (1998), 'Technology brokers in the North American software industry: getting the most out of mismatched dyads.' *International Journal of Technology Management*, 16(1–3), 281–290.

Burt, R. S. (1992), *Structural Holes: The Social Structure of Competition*. Cambridge, MA: Harvard University Press.

Callon, M. (1994), 'Is science a public good?' *Science, Technology and Human Values*, 19, 395–424.

Chiesa, V., Manzini, R., and Pizzurno, E. (2004), 'The externalisation of R and D activities and the growing market of product development services.' *R and D Management*, 34(1), 65–75.

Cohen, W. M. and Levinthal, D. (1990), 'Absorptive capacity: a new perspective on learning and innovation.' *Administrative Science Quarterly*, 35(1), 128–152.

Das, T. K. and Teng, B. S. 2001. 'Trust, control, and risk in strategic alliances: an integrated framework.' *Organization Studies*, 22(2), 251–283.

De Jong, G., and Klein Woolthuis, R. J. A. (2008), 'The institutional arrangements of innovation: antecedents and performance effects of trust in high-tech alliances.' *Industry and Innovation*, 15(1), 45–67.

Dirks, K. T. and Ferrin, D. L. (2002), 'Trust in leadership: meta-analytic findings and implications for research and practice.' *Journal of Applied Psychology*, 87(4), 611–628.

Dirks, K. T., Lewicki, R. J., and Zaheer, A. (2009), 'Repairing relationships within and between organizations: building a conceptual foundation.' *Academy of Management Review*, 34(1), 68–84.

Edquist, C. (2005), *Systems of National Innovation*. Oxford: Oxford University Press.

Friedman, J., and Silberman, J. (2003), 'University technology transfer: do incentives, management, and location matter?' *Journal of Technology Transfer*, 28, 17–30.

Fryxell, G. E., Dooley, R. S., and Vryza, M. (2002), 'After the ink dries: the interaction of trust and control in US-based international joint ventures.' *Journal of Management Studies*, 39(6): 865–886.

Fukuyama, F. (1995), *Trust: The Social Virtues and the Creation of Prosperity*. London: Hamish Hamilton.

Gould, R. V. and Fernandez, R. M. (1989), 'Structures of mediation: a formal approach to brokerage in transaction networks.' *Sociological Methodology*, 19, 89–126

Grant, R. M. and Baden-Fuller, C. (2004), 'A knowledge accessing theory of strategic alliances.' *Journal of Management Studies*, 41(1), 61–84.

Gulati, R. (1995), 'Does familiarity breed trust – the implications of repeated ties for contractual choice in alliances.' *Academy of Management Journal*, 38(1), 85–112.

Hargadon, A. B. (1998), 'Firms as knowledge brokers: lessons in pursuing continuous innovation.' *California Management Review*, 40(3): 209–+.

Hart, P., and Saunders, C. (1997), 'Power and trust: critical factors in the adoption and use of electronic data interchange.' *Organization Science*, 8(1), 23–42.

Hislop, D. (2002), 'The client role in consultancy relations during the appropriation of technological innovations.' *Research Policy*, 31(5), 657–671.

Hosmer, L. T. (1995), 'Trust – the connecting link between organizational theory and philosophical ethics.' *Academy of Management Review*, 20(2), 379–403.

Howells, J. (2006), 'Intermediation and the role of intermediaries in innovation.' *Research Policy*, 35(5), 715–728.

Huber, G. P. and Power, D. J. (1985), 'Retrospective reports of strategic-level managers – guidelines for increasing their accuracy.' *Strategic Management Journal*, 6(2), 171–180.

Inkpen, A. C. and Currall, S. C. (2003), 'Strategic alliances and the evolution of trust across levels.' In M. A. West, D. Tjosvold, and K. G. Smith (eds.), *International Handbook of Organizational Teamwork and Cooperative Working*. New York: Wiley-Blackwell.

Ireland, R. D., Hitt, M. A., and Vaidyanath, D. (2002), 'Alliance management as a source of competitive advantage.' *Journal of Management*, 28(3), 413–446.

Keats, B. W. and Hitt, M. A. (1988), 'A causal model of linkages among environmental dimensions, macro organizational characteristics, and performance.' *Academy of Management Journal*, 31(3), 570–598.

Klein Woolthuis, R. J. A., Hillebrand, B., and Nooteboom, B. (2005), 'Trust, contract, and relationship development.' *Organization Studies*, 26(6), 813–840.

Krishnan, R., Martin, X., and Noorderhaven, N. G. (2006), 'When does trust matter to alliance performance?' *Academy of Management Journal*, 49(5), 894–917.

Lamin, A. and Zaheer, S. (2012), 'Wall Street vs. main street: firm strategies for defending legitimacy and their impact on different stakeholders.' *Organization Science*, 23(1), 47–66.

Lynn, L. H., Reddy, N. M., and Aram, J. D. (1996), 'Linking technology and institutions: the innovation community framework.' *Research Policy*, 25(1): 91–106.

McAllister, D. J. (1995), 'Affect-based and cognition-based trust as foundations for interpersonal cooperation in organizations.' *Academy of Management Journal*, 38(1), 24–59.

Man de, A. P. and Duysters, G. (2005), 'Collaboration and innovation: a review of the effects of mergers, acquisitions and alliances on innovation.' *Technovation*, 25(12), 1377–1387.

Mesquita, L. F. (2007), 'Starting over when the bickering never ends: rebuilding aggregate trust among clustered firms through trust facilitators.' *Academy of Management Review*, 32(1), 72–91.

Morgan, E. J. and Crawford, N. (1996), Technology broking activities in Europe – a survey. *International Journal of Technology Management*, 12(3), 360–367.

Moriarty, B. (2009), 'The dynamics of public trust in business – emerging opportunities for leaders: a call to action to overcome the present crisis of trust in business.' In A. M. Mulcahy (ed.), *Society and Business Roundtable Institute for Corporate Ethics* (at: www.corporate-ethics.org/pdf/innovation_ethics.pdf).

Nieto, M. J. and Santamaria, L. (2007), 'The importance of diverse collaborative networks for the novelty of product innovation.' *Technovation*, 27(6–7), 367–377.

Nooteboom, B.. (1996), 'Trust, opportunism, and governance: a process control model.' *Organization Studies*, 17(6), 395–424.

Nooteboom, B. (1999), *Interfirm Alliances: Analysis and Design*. London: Routledge.

Nooteboom, B. (2002), *Trust: Forms, Foundations, Functions, Failures, and Figures*. Cheltenham, UK: Edward Elgar.

Nooteboom, B. (2004), *Interfirm Collaboration, Learning, and Networks: An Integrated Approach*. London: Routledge.

Nooteboom, B., Berger, H., and Noorderhaven, N. G. (1997), 'Effects of trust and governance on relational risk.' *Academy of Management Journal*, 40(2), 308–338.

Obstveld, D. (2005), 'Social networks, the Tertius Iungens orientation, and involvement in innovation.' *Administrative Science Quarterly*, 50(1), 100–130.

Parkhe, A. 1993. 'Strategic alliance structuring – a game-theoretic and transaction cost examination of interfirm cooperation.' *Academy of Management Journal*, 36(4), 794–829.

Pfarrer, M. D., Smith, K. G., Bartol, K. M., Khanin, D. M., and Zhang, X. M. (2008), 'Coming forward: the effects of social and regulatory forces on the voluntary restatement of earnings subsequent to wrongdoing.' *Organization Science*, 19(3), 386–403.

Podsakoff, P. M. and Organ, D. W. 1986. 'Self-reports in organizational research – Problems and prospects.' *Journal of management*, 12(4): 531–544.

Poppo, L. and Zenger, T. (2002), 'Do formal contracts and relational governance function as substitutes or complements?' *Strategic Management Journal*, 23(8), 707–725.

Porter, M. E. and Kramer, M. R. (2011), 'Creating shared value.' *Harvard Business Review*, 89(1–2), 62–77.

Reuer, J. J., Arino, A., and Mellewigt, T. (2006), 'Entrepreneurial alliances as contractual forms.' *Journal of Business Venturing*, 21(3), 306–325.

Salancik, G. R. and Pfeffer, J. (1977), 'Examination of need–satisfaction models of job attitudes.' *Administrative Science Quarterly*, 22(3), 427–456.

Senge, P. M., Kruschwitz, N., Smith, B., Laur, J., and Schley, S. (2010), *The Necessary Revolution: How Individuals and Organisations Are Working Together to Create a Sustainable World*. London and Boston, MA: Nicholas Brealey Publishing.

Shapiro, S. P. (1987), 'The social-control of impersonal trust.' *American Journal of Sociology*, 93(3), 623–658.

Siegel, D. S., Waldman, D., and Link, A. (2003), 'Assessing the impact of organizational practices on the relative productivity of university technology transfer offices: an exploratory study.' *Research Policy*, 32(1), 27–48.

Simmel, G. (1950), 'Individual and society.' In K. H. Wolff (ed.), *The Sociology of George Simmel*. New York: Free Press.

Stankiewicz, R. (1995), 'The role of the science and technology infrastructure in the development and diffusion of industrial automation in Sweden.' In B. Carlsson (ed.), *Technological Systems and Economic Performance: The Case of Factory Automation*. Dordrecht: Kluwer, 165–210.

Subramani, M. R. and Venkatraman, N. (2003), 'Safeguarding investments in asymmetric interorganizational relationships: theory and evidence.' *Academy of Management Journal*, 46(1), 46–62.

Sullivan, B. N., Haunschild, P., and Page, K. (2007), 'Organizations non gratae? The impact of unethical corporate acts on interorganizational networks.' *Organization Science*, 18(1), 55–70.

Tomlinson, E. C. and Mayer, R. C. (2009), 'The role of causal attribution dimensions in trust repair.' *Academy of Management Review*, 34(1), 85–104.

Williamson, O. E. (1985), *The Economic Institutions of Capitalism*. New York: Free Press.

Wolpert, J. D. (2002), 'Breaking out of the innovation box.' *Harvard Business Review*, 80(8), 77.

Yin, R. K. (2003), *Case Study Research: Design and Methods* (3rd edn). Thousand Oaks, CA: Sage.

Zaheer, A., McEvily, B., and Perrone, V. (1998), 'Does trust matter? Exploring the effects of interorganizational and interpersonal trust on performance.' *Organization Science*, 9(2), 141–159.

Zand, D. E. (1972), 'Trust and managerial problem solving.' *Administrative Science Quarterly*, 17(2), 229–239.

Zucker, L. G. (1986), 'Production of trust: institutional sources of economic structure.' In B. M. Staw and L. L. Cummings (eds.), *Research in Organizational Behavior*. Greenwich, CT: JAI Press, 53–112.

12 The repair of public trust following controllable or uncontrollable organizational failures: a conceptual framework

Laura Poppo and Donald J. (DJ) Schepker

EXECUTIVE SUMMARY

THE SITUATION

Prior research suggests that organizations tend to misunderstand how to repair trust. Many organizations fail to supply explanations for key events, or provide explanations that are so vague that they lack real information. As a result, trust can be easily damaged or destroyed through organizational failures and from the inability to repair it.

KEY QUESTIONS AND APPROACH

How should organizations repair trust among external stakeholders? In what situations are communications to the public and institutional reforms likely to rebuild public trust following a competence violation or an integrity violation? How can companies rebuild trust when direct observation and interaction with the public cannot readily occur?

NEW KNOWLEDGE

Institutional reforms can be used to prevent distrust and to signal an organization's commitment to integrity or competence, and, as such, can effectively rebuild trust.

Controllability conditions the choice of trust repair strategies. Controllability assigns "blame" or "fault" to the organization, such as how much to hold another accountable for the failure, even if the organizational actions or inactions are deemed to be the root cause of the failure.

Public communication (such as apologies, accounts, and plans) are best conceptualized as a weak signal, but when bundled with more credible signals (such as institutional reforms), communication results in higher levels of public trust than communication or costly actions alone.

KEY LESSONS

Greater measures will be necessary to restore public trust following competence violations than integrity violations.

Response strategies for rebuilding public trust differ. In repairing trust, firms should bundle both communicative strategies with strategic and structural reforms to signal an organization's commitment to restoring its competence or integrity following an organizational failure.

Not all failures are easily or readily classified into violations of integrity or competence.

Because communication does not provide assurance that the other party can be trusted it does not constitute much as a signal of trustworthiness.

INTRODUCTION

Public trust, the degree to which external stakeholders, such as consumers, potential consumers, and the more distant remaining others hold a collective trust orientation toward an organization, is an important area of study.[1] Given the public's role as a key stakeholder group, the firm's ability to survive and prosper may be dependent on the public's ability to trust the firm's actions and the goods or services it produces.[2] Consistent with this logic, others assert that reputation provides legitimacy and can be utilized as a resource to help firms

---

[1] Poppo and Schepker, 2010.
[2] Freeman, 1984; Coombs and Holladay, 2002; Fitzpatrick and Rubin, 1995.

achieve competitive advantage.[3] Yet, when an organization violates its legitimacy, it breaches and thus fails to fulfill its promised obligations and commitments to the public. Prior works show that within organizations, breaches of psychological contracts are associated with a loss of trust,[4] withdrawal, and lower commitment to the organization.[5] For organizations, failure to appropriately respond to such violations may not only harm the organization's legitimacy or reputation in the marketplace,[6] thereby damaging a firm's future revenue stream, but also pave the way for government regulation.

An obvious managerial gap and research opportunity is to study how organizations should repair trust among external stakeholders. Prior research suggests that organizations tend to be poor at knowing how to repair trust,[7] as many organizations fail to supply explanations for key events or provide explanations that are so vague that they lack real information.[8] As a result, trust can be easily damaged or destroyed through organizational failures[9] and from the inability to repair it.[10]

Despite its importance, public trust is an understudied concept in strategic management. Most prior work focuses on the collective trust in interorganizational exchanges, its effects on organizational outcomes, and its relational origins.[11] Absent in this literature are its more dynamics properties, such as how to repair unmet expectations. Another stream of literature examines trust repair among individuals – for example between an employee and his/her manager,[12] or how a CEO should rebuild trust with his or her organization's employees.[13] This literature suggests organizations will seek to repair their image in the eyes of others by using various impression management and interactional justice techniques[14] and implementing institutional reforms to regulate distrust.[15] In addition, scholars generally agree

---

[3] Fombrun and Shanley, 1990; Barney 1991.
[4] Robinson, 1996; Coyle-Shapiro, 2002.   [5] Coyle-Shapiro and Kessler, 2000.
[6] Bradford and Garrett 1995; Fombrun, 1996.   [7] Schwartz and Gibb, 1999.
[8] Folger and Skarlicki, 2001; Shaw et al., 2003.
[9] Slovic, 1993; Nakayachi and Watabe 2005.   [10] Lewicki and Bunker 1996.
[11] See Zaheer and Harris, 2005.   [12] Kim et al., 2004; Kim et al., 2006.
[13] Gillespie and Dietz, 2009.   [14] Bies, 1987; Carter and Dukerich, 1998.
[15] See, e.g., Gillespie and Dietz, 2009.

that organizational responses to integrity violations are decidedly different than competence violations: the nature of the transgression is pivotal in determining the success of the firm's repair efforts.[16]

Yet, we know of few published works that extend how to repair *public* trust following integrity or competence violations. Rather, existing works focus on restoring legitimacy following an integrity violation[17] and restoring employee trust following an integrity or competence violation.[18] Our analysis demonstrates that optimal strategies for repairing public trust following integrity and competence violations differ from those proposed in the above works. For example, while Gillespie and Dietz advocate the use of interpersonal strategies to rebuild employees' trust following a competence violation, this strategy cannot be applied to public trust simply because the public lacks an intimate, direct relationship with managers.[19] That is, the public does not directly interact with and observe managerial actions and communications – at most, their access is indirect and filtered through the media. Alternatively, Pfarrer and colleagues propose that legitimacy can be reestablished following an integrity violation, while our analysis suggests that trust can be restored following integrity and competence violations, but greater measures will be necessary to restore public trust following competence violations.[20]

Based on these differences, we infer that the public, as a stakeholder group, is a critical context variable and boundary constraint, making a generalized theory or generic perspective of organizational responses strategies to trust violation unlikely. This guides our research query: when do communications to the public and institutional reforms likely rebuild *public* trust following a competence violation and an integrity violation? We propose that while the choice of institutional reforms depends on the type of violation, such reforms can be used to both prevent distrust as well as signal an organization's

[16] Gillespie and Dietz, 2009; Dirks *et al.*, 2009; Kim *et al.*, 2004; 2006.
[17] Pfarrer *et al.*, 2008.   [18] Gillespie and Dietz, 2009.
[19] *Ibid.*   [20] Pfarrer *et al.*, 2008.

commitment to integrity or competence, and as such can effectively rebuild trust. We further propose that controllability conditions the choice of trust repair strategies. Controllability assigns "blame" or "fault" to the organization, such as how much to hold another accountable for the failure, even if the organizational actions or inactions are deemed to be the root cause of the failure.[21] Third, we propose that public communication (such as apologies, accounts, and plans) are best conceptualized as a weak signal, but when bundled with more credible signals (institutional reforms) result in higher levels of public trust than communication or costly actions alone.

PUBLIC TRUST: INTEGRITY AND COMPETENCE DIMENSIONS

Public trust is defined as the "degree to which the general public as a stakeholder group holds a collective trust orientation toward an organization."[22] Admittedly, the public is a very broad population of individuals, including consumers, potential consumers, and more distant "others." Considerable heterogeneity is likely to exist, such as individual differences in the propensity to trust others or to trust business.[23] Yet, as a collective group they can have considerable influence. If companies (or industries) fail to produce an acceptable level of trust, governments, especially those in more developed, western economies, generally fill the void through regulation. Most companies do not desire greater regulation. Alternatively, if public trust diminishes significantly for a particular firm or industry (such as fears of tainted milk production in China), then it is unlikely that organizational repair efforts will sway public opinion. Companies risk failure as consumers buy the product from more reputable companies or go without the product.

A second interesting facet is that the trust building process is fundamentally different for the public and organizations, for each

---

[21] Weiner, 1986; Tomlinson and Mayer, 2009.   [22] Poppo and Schepker, 2010, 126.
[23] See, e.g., Yamagisha, 1988.

group cannot personally interact with and directly observe the other. By definition, trustworthiness requires parties to be willing to be vulnerable to the actions of others;[24] so how do companies rebuild trust when direct observation and interaction with the public cannot readily occur? We suspect that given the arm's-length stance between the public and companies, the media and background "stories" will influence trusting perceptions a great deal. We return to this issue later in this chapter.

A final interesting facet of public trust is that the public's trust in business varies over time. Some argue that trust between organizations and the public is a given, such that individuals trust organizations until such trust is violated. These arguments suggest that as intervals pass where organizations fail to violate the public's trust, the public regains comfort with organizations, and the public begins to lose lingering distrust that may exist from prior violations. However, when organizations repeatedly violate the public's trust over a relatively short time period, public trust is likely to wane considerably. For instance, when economic periods provide for wealth creation and benefit all members of the public, public trust is likely to be high. However, when violations occur which negatively impact the public's trust and suggest that organizations act opportunistically at the public's expense, the public is likely to lose trust in business as a whole; such was the case during the recent subprime mortgage crisis. These arguments suggest that the public's general attitude toward business (e.g., the existing level of trust) will affect how violations of public trust are framed. For instance, when public trust is high, an isolated violation may have less impact on the public's trust in business as a whole than when multiple violations by several firms, whether in one industry or multiple industries, occur in a short time period.

In order to ground our definition and framing of public trust in the relevant literature, we examine the definition of

---

[24] Rousseau *et al.*, 1998.

interorganizational trust: the extent to which members of one organization hold a collective trust orientation toward another organization.[25] Based on our review of this literature, we focus on two components of trust – competence and integrity – as critical dimensions underlying the public's willingness to trust an organization.[26] Integrity-based trust is based upon the truster's perception that the trustee adheres to a set of principles the truster finds at least acceptable.[27] An integrity-based violation is an indication that a party to the relationship is violating a principle agreed upon within the relationship,[28] which may be linked to self-interest or opportunism.[29] Integrity is also linked to upholding promises, such as good-faith efforts to behave in accordance with implicit or explicit commitments or perceptions of acting honestly or fairly.[30] Without integrity, individuals acting on the organization's behalf are likely to act dishonestly; that is, they may deceive, lie, or cheat for their own gain. Competence-based trust refers to the perception that the trustee possesses the requisite skills and knowledge necessary for the task.[31] Thus, a trust violation may occur when organizational actors are not trained or lack adequate knowledge to competently perform their function.[32] The public, in particular, is concerned with an organization's competence (and, relatedly, with its competence-based trust), as competence directly impacts the outputs the firm produces or serves to the public.

ORGANIZATION-LEVEL FAILURES

In developing our conceptual framework, we focus on violations of the public's trust as the result of organization-level failures that take the form of a single major incident or a cumulative series of incidents

[25] Zaheer et al., 1998; Zaheer and Harris, 2005.
[26] Mayer et al., 1995; Schepker and Poppo, 2010; Zaheer and Harris, 2005.
[27] Mayer et al., 1995; Kim et al., 2004; Sitkin and Roth, 1993.
[28] Kim et al., 2006.   [29] Williamson, 1996.
[30] See, e.g., Cummings and Bromiley, 1996; Zaheer et al., 2002; Husted and Folger, 2004; Poppo et al., 2008.
[31] Butler and Cantrell, 1984.   [32] Kim et al., 2004, 2006.

that arise as consequences to actions or inactions of organizational agents. Thus, the locus of control of the failure is perceived to be internal: it is due to actions or inactions of organizational agents. Such events are defined as a failure when they pose a significant threat to the organization's legitimacy and inflict harm on one or more stakeholders.[33] Legitimacy "is a generalized perception or assumption that the actions of an entity are desirable, proper, or appropriate within some socially constructed system of norms, values, beliefs, and definitions."[34] Legitimacy, thus, is a collective concept which implies that an organization can deviate from a social norm at the individual level without consequences as long as the public does not disapprove of the divergence or as long as the public is not aware of its deviance.

As illustrated in Figure 12.1, and based on our discussion of the importance of competence and integrity with respect to trust, we focus on two primary types of organizational level failures, those related to organizational integrity and competence. Integrity violations indicate that some of the organization's agents are acting in an intentionally dishonest, deceitful manner which may involve lying, cheating, or stealing. Such violations may include deceit, scandal, or accounting fraud and may be large or small in scale, such as a few deceitful individuals, or a large-scale systemic failure orchestrated by many deceitful individuals. Competence violations indicate the organization is not skilled enough to carry on operations without causing harm to others, such as product safety scandals, plant explosions, and environmental accidents. While prior works examining the repair of stakeholder trust advance that organizations should apologize, assume responsibility, and disclose reasons for the failure,[35] we extend these works by showing how response strategies for rebuilding public trust differ. We also extend prior works by arguing that in repairing trust, firms should bundle both communicative strategies with strategic and structural reforms to signal an

---

[33] Anheier, 1999; Gillespie and Dietz, 2009.   [34] Suchman, 1995, 574.
[35] Pfarrer et al., 2008; Gillespie and Dietz, 2009.

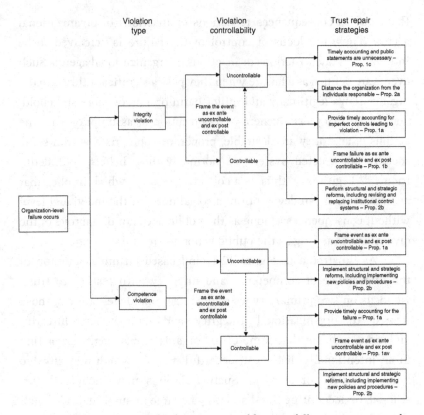

FIGURE 12.1 Strategies for restoring public trust following integrity and competence violations

organization's commitment to restoring its competence or integrity following an organizational failure.

In order to create a tractable framework and approach, we assume that organizational failures can be readily classified as violating trust with regards to integrity or competence, which is similar to prior works that examine trust repair at the individual level of analysis[36] as well as at the organizational level of analysis.[37] We recognize, however, that not all failures are easily or readily classified into

---

[36] Dirks et al., 2009; Kim et al., 2004, 2006.
[37] Gillespie and Dietz, 2009; Pfarrer et al., 2008.

violations of integrity or competence (such as recent failures at Toyota and bank failures on Wall Street) and discuss in the last section of our chapter possible extensions of our research to consider these more complex types of failures.

Following the classification of an organizational failure as integrity or competence violations, we next propose that controllability conditions the choice of trust repair strategies. Controllability assigns "blame" or "fault" to the organization, such as how much to hold another accountable for the failure, even if the organizational actions or inactions are deemed to be the root cause of the failure.[38] For our purposes, this is a defining feature of the controllability attribution; in hindsight, does the public view the organization responsible for not exerting more control over the outcome when the organizational actions or inactions are deemed the root cause of the failure. For example, if the public does not believe the organization at "fault" then the trustee will be seen as less culpable or blameworthy;[39] while trust repair strategies are important, they will not be as extensive, since the organization has little control over the violation's occurrence. Such is likely to be the case for integrity violations stemming from a few individuals within a company (e.g., embezzlement, fraud). While organizations devise institutional control systems to minimize organizational failures, and create a legitimate understanding of the organization, they cannot regulate and control the values of each employee – some individuals are inherently dishonest and will cheat or steal if given the opportunity.

Yet, there are other types of organizational failures which invariably occur due to imperfect controls. Well acknowledged across a broad set of literatures is that controls, including incentive systems, monitoring, and standard procedures, are imperfect governance mechanisms; that is, they cannot provide complete assurance that integrity and competence violations will not occur.[40] Relatedly, they cannot

---

[38] Weiner, 1986; Tomlinson and Mayer, 2009.   [39] Lewicki and Bunker, 1996.
[40] Williamson, 1993; Pratt and Zeckhauser, 1995; Shapiro, 2005.

completely mitigate public distrust: "confident negative expectations regarding another's conduct."[41]

Controls are necessary in organizations because monitoring of agent actions and information by the principal (e.g., the CEO, the intermediary, or the public) is both imperfect and costly.[42] The failure to perfectly monitor agent behavior creates agency costs. Solutions, that is controls, to the agency problem are second best (e.g., imperfect). For example, when monitoring is expensive and substitutes are cheaply implemented (such as incentives), managers monitor the actual behavior less and what monitoring occurs is of poorer quality since information may be ascertained by looking at the results of activities, rather than the activity itself. Performance and outcome measurement is imperfect as such activities do not measure the actual behavior.[43] Relatedly, monitoring may only focus on a subset of activities, while multiple tasks involve many activities, which allows agents to exert effort only on the tasks they know are monitored.[44]

Examples of violations that may arise from the gap between what the principal knows and what the agents do are numerous.[45] An employer sets compensation, but lacks direct information on the opportunities and risk associated with employee decisions: that is, the employer can only obtain such information from the employees. Thus, directors may have a final say on the degree of investment decisions, but they rely on divisional employees to provide information regarding the profitability and risk of the new venture. For these situations, information advantages exist because the agent has exclusive access to specialized information. Armed with an informational advantage, agency costs can increase as agents attempt to influence decisions to their advantage. Agents can do so through the manipulation of information that they provide to the principal – which may

---

[41] Lewicki *et al.*, 1998, 439; Sitkin and Roth, 1993.
[42] Pratt and Zeckhauser, 1995; Shapiro, 2005.
[43] Jacobides and Croson, 2001.   [44] Holmstrom and Milgrom, 1991.
[45] Milgrom and Roberts, 1988; Pratt and Zeckhauser, 1995; Shapiro, 2005.

mean lying about the facts, omitting unfavorable and useful information, or a relentless framing of the decision to highlight the favorable information.[46] Such incentive problems can lead to integrity
violations, either a few individuals gaming the system or a large-
scale assault (such as incentivizing mechanics to make unnecessary
repairs or incentivizing bankers to disregard the risk associated
with loans).

A related factor contributing to organizational failures is that
formal bureaucratic controls, such as the use of explicit operating
procedures or goal specification, are inherently incomplete because
of bounded rationality and transaction costs.[47] Thus, while the goal
of explicit, complete specifications is to increase the predictability
and reliability of employees' actions,[48] crafting a complete set of
formal controls is either cost prohibitive or simply not possible
because the task environment in which the firm operates is both
complex and uncertain. This logic suggests the trade-offs involved in
selecting which activities to regulate and monitor through formalized routines, responsibilities, and procedures. Because of the complexity of the situation and bounded rationality of the decision
makers, controls may inadvertently redirect efforts toward efficiency or time-to-market at the expense of product safety. As a
result, integrity and competence violations may occur because
bureaucratic controls were not fully or well specified, yet the public
may not view the organization at fault, ex post, because the
public views that the firm could not have plausibly foreseen
the outcome (violation) occurring. That is, ex post the organization
is not at fault for the violation, even though its controls (or lack of
controls) caused it.

Thus, our framework views controllability as a critical factor
affecting the initial framing scope of the trust repair strategies.
We detail these relationships in the remaining sections.

---

[46] Milgrom and Roberts, 1988.   [47] Macneil, 1978; Williamson, 1996.
[48] Sitkin and Roth, 1993.

COMMUNICATION AND THE REPAIR OF PUBLIC TRUST

When an organization violates public trust, it breaches and thus fails to fulfill its promised obligations to the public. Organizational efforts to resolve the conflict and repair trust can be readily categorized into those that focus predominantly on communication to the affected party, the public, and those that require more costly investments, such as paying damages, product recalls, and institutional reforms. In this section we first review justice and impression management approaches to trust repair, which are based on the specific context of violations that affect individual(s) within an organization, and then in subsequent sections extend this logic to consider the repair of public trust.

Prior work suggests that interactional justice and impression management are critical to reestablishing trust following a violation. Through direct communication, managers can reestablish an image, restore perceptions of fairness, and thus reestablish a psychological contract such that both parties share similar or perhaps identical perceptions of the situation.[49] Interactional justice research further suggests that the communication needs to be conveyed in a particular manner in order to positively manage the impression: (1) the party that inflicted damage to others treats individuals with respect and dignity; and (2) the verbal message provides justifications or explanations of the event.[50] Central to this logic is that the communication alters perception of the violation and the organization such that it reestablishes a basis of trust compared to violations in which communication does not occur.[51]

An alternative perspective, however, is that communication does not reestablish trust because it is a form of "cheap talk." According to signaling literature, the effectiveness of any action a

---

[49] Rousseau and McLean Parks, 1993; Bottom *et al.*, 2002.

[50] Bies, 1987; Bies and Moag, 1986; Bies and Shapiro, 1988; Bottom *et al.*, 2002; Kim *et al.*, 2004; 2006; Pfarrer *et al.*, 2008; Gillespie and Dietz, 2009.

[51] Seeger, 2006; Coombs, 1999.

firm takes to build a perception of trust depends on whether the act credibly signals the party's intent. Signals are observable features "which are intentionally displayed for the purpose of raising the probability the receiver assigns to a certain state of affairs."[52] The key feature of a signal is that it is too costly for those with an untrustworthy quality to display. In a classic article, Spence argues that a diploma reveals the underlying quality of the individual; low-ability individuals will find it too costly to obtain a college education compared to high-ability individuals.[53] Thus, the key issue is that the repair mechanisms must be costly, such that it would be too costly for untrustworthy organizations or poor-quality organizations to undertake such a repair. Thus, according to this logic, communication tactics which embody interactional justice and impression management aspects do not credibly separate trustworthy companies from untrustworthy types because management can simply create a feasible account and a sincere apology in a timely fashion. For a self-interested party, such forms of communication are unverifiable and relatively costless; managers can easily communicate as if it were a trustworthy type.[54] Thus, because communication does not provide assurance that the other party can be trusted it does not constitute much as a signal of trustworthiness.

Contrary to the above perspective, however, empirical works show the value of communication following failures, such as voluntary disclosures that provide a rationale for the failure or specify what party, if any, is responsible it.[55] Consistent with this, management scholars argue that communication is an important initial response to an organization-level failure which can begin to rebuild trust.[56] When managers are willing to communicate with stakeholders, such transparency allows the public greater information with which to form an impression, limit distrust, and begin to trust the organization.

---

[52] Gambetta, 2009, 170.   [53] Spence, 1973.   [54] Bottom et al., 2002, 500.
[55] Bottom et al., 2002; Ferrin et al., 2007; Lee et al., 2004.
[56] Gillespie and Dietz, 2009; Pfarrer et al., 2008.

Without being transparent, the organization risks alienating stakeholders as well as appearing to conceal information.

The contingent value of timely, "uncontrollable" explanations in competence vs. integrity violations

For impression management scholars, explanations that account for
how the violation occurred positively impact others' impressions and
perceptions.[57] Related works in interactional justice also advise that
providing an explanation for the violation is a central feature for how
individuals rebuild cooperative behavior[58] and trust.[59] The primary
objective of the explanation is to limit negative expectations
and create positive expectations about future trustworthiness.[60]
These works suggest that the account for why the violation occurred
need to be truthful and transparent, as well as treat the offended party
with respect and dignity.[61] Thus, when responding to an organizational failure, the firm that provides an explanation of how the organizational failure occurred based on an internal investigation is more
likely to reestablish trust.[62]

Second, this literature proposes that the explanation must
occur in a timely fashion, since the ultimate objective is to reframe
the account of the failure.[63] An immediate response to the failure
with a promise for a timely internal investigation (if the explanation
is not known immediately) helps shape public reaction and provides
details to prevent false information from being reported, such as
information that may develop through negative reporting and/or
blogs.[64] Thus, many argue that in order for an explanation to be
successful at reframing the organizational failure, it must be timely,
transparent, and adequate.[65] If the explanation provides sufficient

---

[57] Hooghiemstra, 2000.   [58] Bottom et al., 2002.
[59] Bies and Shapiro, 1988; Kim et al., 2004.   [60] Gillespie and Dietz, 2009.
[61] Folger and Bies, 1989; Pfarrer et al., 2008; Gillespie and Dietz, 2009.
[62] Gillespie and Dietz, 2009; Pfarrer et al., 2008.
[63] Bies, 1987; Cody and McLaughlin, 1990.
[64] Seeger, 2006; Reynolds, 2006; Coombs, 1999.   [65] Seeger, 2006; Coombs, 1999.

substance and matches the severity of the offense, then parties are more likely to believe it.[66]

Left unexplored in this literature, however, is an additional factor that shapes the positive reframing of the organizational failure: whether the feedback frames the organizational failure as ex ante controllable (foreseeable) by the organization or not. Decision theorists' logic highlights the criticality of hindsight bias and whether the type of feedback contained in the explanation will affect the public's reframing of the unexpected event. Hindsight bias is the tendency of people to "consistently exaggerate what could have been anticipated in foresight."[67] This work suggests that the most damaging judgment following an organizational failure is the attribution that "management should have known this all along." That is, management could have easily and simply avoided the failure; it was a "controllable" organizational failure. Recall that, if the public attributes the failure as "controllable," then they attribute the organization as at fault for the failure; that is, the competence or integrity failure could have been avoided through a simple set of tasks. Under such situations, trust repair is more difficult, for the public holds the organization responsible for not acting on what they should have known.

Alternatively, if the public is provided with an explanation that convinces them of the complexity of the tasks that led to the failure, then the public is more likely to infer management could *not* have known this would occur and thus avoided it. That is, the failure was only controllable in hindsight. Critical to an explanation is whether the organization could have anticipated the organizational failure, and thus ex ante avoided its occurrence.[68] Therefore, an explanation that is timely and transparent – but also details the complexity of the tasks that led to the failure which management could not have foreseen ex ante – is more likely to produce a positive, uncontrollable reframing of the organizational failure, and in doing so minimize hindsight bias.

---

[66] Bottom *et al.*, 2002.   [67] Fischhoff, 1975; Hoch and Loewenstein, 1989, 605.
[68] Hoch and Loewenstein, 1989.

We extend this logic by arguing that the effectiveness of an explanation is likely to depend on the type of violation. Following an integrity-based trust violation, an explanation can disclose the ongoing investigation and root causes behind the integrity violation. Yet, some integrity-based violations are rooted in the values of the individual, rather than those of the organization itself. For such "uncontrollable" integrity violations, explanations are less effectual in trust repair: these violations are due to individual greed and thus blame needs to be assigned to the identifiable individuals rather than to the organization itself. There is little other information that could be used to reframe the account, as the organization's control systems could not be designed to prevent all potential integrity violations. Even the most well-designed control systems fail when co-opted by multiple individuals. As long as the organization provides evidence it has attempted to limit and prevent such behavior within reason, the public will be more likely to view the violation as uncontrollable. Since the root cause is outside the control of the organization, communication that addresses plans to rectify the situation is not effective; in fact, communication of such a plan may be damaging as it suggests that the problem is not rooted in a few individuals, but is in fact characteristic of the behavior of many in the company.

Following competence-based or large-scale (systemic) integrity violations (e.g., indicative of improperly designed or absent institutional control systems), however, communication will be more critical since the failure is inextricably intertwined with the firm's operations and structure. Without a timely explanation that focuses on the complexity of the factors that led to the failure, the firm may not be able to convince the public to continue supporting and trusting the organization going forward. The merit of this approach, however, may be necessarily limited, for the public may or may not accept the account of the event and whether or not it was unforeseeable. Yet, if the organization can provide a credible explanation of the complexity of factors that led to the failure, trust repair is facilitated. Alternatively, if management does not provide a full account of the reasons for the failure, it suggests that the failure may have been ex ante controllable. Second, management should also communicate a plan that suggests how a company will prevent the failure from occurring again. This communication is critical, for without such action the public will not view the firm as a credible and legitimate provider of services or products. The early communication of such a plan represents an initial public commitment that the firm will put in places changes that will prevent an organizational failure from occurring in the future. Communicating a plan of action suggests that the firm is taking steps to resolve the issue and to prevent future trust violations.

Consistent with this logic, competence violations reflect a problem typically rooted in the core of a firm's operation; a failure that occurs because of poor product safety or quality reflects the firm's failure to properly oversee its operations. Even in situations where the firm does not directly contribute to the violation itself, such as Mattel's outsourcing of manufacturing, the firm has responsibility for the product or service it provides to the marketplace. In this example, after the initial announcement of lead based products in their toys, Mattel responded quickly to assure stakeholders that an investigation was being undertaken, and quickly produced the results following an internal probe. Furthermore, Mattel identified solutions that were to be put in place in order to prevent future quality control issues from occurring with its toys. The swift response, coupled with a plan regarding actions taken as well as explanations for the failure, were communications that the firm made in order to assure public of the safety and quality of Mattel's toys.

A similar type of communicative response is necessary to begin trust repair following a large-scale integrity violation. Because a number of employees contributed to the organizational failure, it may be harder for management to offer a credible communication that only in hindsight could they have known that faulty controls fostered widespread gaming and strategic self-interest. Yet, as organizations grow in size and complexity, sub-units may be geographically dispersed, making monitoring more difficult. Related, specialized sub-units (those that focus on product safety and those that focus on time-to-market) may compete against one another, and in doing so commit unethical activities in order to promote their performance and possibly their survival.[69] Thus, even if managers cannot reframe the event as ex ante controllable, they need to account for how the faulty controls enabled the failure, and how this created an unethical environment that either implicitly or explicitly facilitated integrity violations, and they need a plan that will stop the failure from reoccurring.

> *Proposition 1a: For competence violations, the more timely the accounting of the complexity and credible framing that the failure was "ex ante uncontrollability," followed by an ex post plan for "controllability," the greater the impact on public trust compared to less timely and simple accounts of the failure in which no ex post plan for controllability exists.*
>
> *Proposition 1b: For large-scale integrity violations, the more timely the accounting of the imperfect institutional controls that lead to the violation and credible framing of the failure as "ex ante uncontrollable," followed by an ex post plan for "controllability," the greater the impact on public trust compared to the alternatives (e.g., less timely, weak accounts of the failure in which no ex post plan for controllability exists; or timely account but inability to frame as "ex ante uncontrollable," followed by an ex post plan for "controllability").*
>
> *Proposition 1c: For small-scale integrity violations, public statements are less necessary, timely, and effective to rebuild public trust (as integrity violations are likely due to a few culpable parties that do not represent the values of others and do not require changes to existing systems and structures).*

---

[69] Vaughan, 1983.

While timely accounting of an organizational failure is a somewhat costly way to indicate reasons for the failure, it is still a form of cheap talk. Because both competent and incompetent firms can craft an explanation for the failure, the impact of this communication strategy on the repair of public trust is necessarily limited. A firm may stand to regain trust and credibility further by instituting costly actions and reforms designed to signal its true intentions to prevent future violations. While prior works suggest this route to repair trust, they do not specify and thus propose which types of reforms are most effective in rebuilding trust given the type of violation: competence or integrity.[70]

CREDIBLE SIGNALS AND THE REBUILDING OF PUBLIC TRUST: STRUCTURAL AND STRATEGIC

An alternative focus of trust repair is the actions, not the communications, that a firm undertakes to restore trust. Because the public is not intimately involved in a company's operations, coordinating information, and activities, trust repair is unlikely to follow traditional vehicles such as personal or relational bases of trust. This lack of interdependence prevents relational and process-based trust from developing between the organization and the public,[71] as advocated in other frameworks, such as those focusing on repairing employee trust following violations.[72] Instead, trusting perceptions are influenced through communication channels that inform the public of more credible and legitimate reforms.

The distance of the public as a stakeholder group from an organization, including its operations, requires trust to be built through legitimate institutions.[73] Such formal institutions substitute administratively and symbolically for other vehicles of trust.[74] Public trust is likely to be built through institutional reforms that are both structural and strategic. Institutional sources that are structural

---

[70] Pfarrer *et al.*, 2008; Gillespie and Dietz, 2009.
[71] Kramer, 1999; Zaheer and Harris, 2005; Zucker, 1986.
[72] See Gillespie and Dietz, 2009.   [73] Zucker: 1986, 55.
[74] Sitkin and Roth, 1993.

include internal actors (e.g., the board), external firm representatives (e.g., independent auditors), and the organization's specific roles and procedures. To produce public trust, trust must be generated at the local level and transferred in a meaningful level to the aggregate stakeholder – the public – through an objective, standardized interaction or format. The public then uses such structures to determine the organization's legitimacy or redetermine the level of integrity with which the organization will conduct its business.

Relatedly, organizations may build public trust by enlisting prominent intermediaries with specific reputations, or by employing individuals in salient, high-level positions who may possess specific characteristics or belong to certain categories, such as gender, ethnicity, national origin, or age to influence others. Some refer to this as a strategic form of legitimacy since managers can willingly extract and manipulate legitimacy, like a resource, given the cultural environment.[75] Critical to its effectiveness is the public's sense of the legitimacy of the specific reputation, position, or category; that is, whether it will affect the behavior or actions of the firm.[76] In general, these mechanisms are more idiosyncratic and transitional, and thus are associated with lower levels of legitimacy.[77] However, they may play a significant role when building new institutions or transforming disturbing ones. A critical facet in communicating these changes to the public is to work with media to ensure that the story being told is that the new leadership is not simply a cosmetic change, but will transform the practices, behaviors, and values of its employees.

In general, few works examine how a firm can rebuild trust with stakeholders.[78] Furthermore, trust may be bestowed upon organizations as long as no evidence to the contrary exists.[79] However, mistrusted organizations must exhibit trustworthiness in order to reestablish trust following violations of such trust expectations.[80]

[75] Suchman, 1995; Pfeffer, 1981.   [76] Zucker, 1986.
[77] Suchman, 1995.   [78] Thomas, 1998.   [79] McKnight et al., 1998.
[80] Kim et al., 2004; Schweitzer et al., 2006.

Institutional repair mechanisms

A dominant perspective in the management literature is that institutional vehicles of trust production (e.g., bureaucratic or legalistic controls and procedures) cannot be equated to the trust produced through close, personal relationships and interactions.[81] Unresolved, however, are the specific effects or types of institutional reforms on trust production following competence and integrity violations. Sitkin and Roth argue formal controls and procedures can only effectively regulate task-specific reliability, such as those that provide assurance in organizational competencies that underlie manufacturing and service.[82] Thus, an inherent limit of institutional controls is that they cannot regulate value congruence, such as in the instances underlying integrity violations. Gillespie and Dietz argue to the contrary, that because formal controls are designed to prevent future malevolent acts they will be viewed as "more convincing and effective" as a trust repair strategy for integrity violations than for competence violations.[83]

We present an alternative perspective: the effectiveness of the institutional reform depends on the type of violation, and institutional reforms can function to symbolize value congruence. When an integrity violation occurs, affected parties lack trust as they believe violators are likely to act opportunistically again.[84] Integrity violations may occur as a select group of individuals take advantage of imperfectly developed institutional control systems at the expense of those for whom such a system works well with more representative values of society. We submit that in such cases of essentially uncontrollable integrity violations structural institutional reforms are not necessary, as they will not deter integrity violations that represent unusual, aberrant cases. The organization's lack of control over such events does not enable it to craft controls to prevent its occurrence.

---

[81] Granovetter, 1985; Ghoshal and Moran, 1996.
[82] Sitkin and Roth, 1993.   [83] Gillespie and Dietz, 2009, 140.
[84] Sitkin and Roth, 1993; Gillespie and Dietz, 2009.

In fact if managers craft such a system and publically announce it, they are suggesting that this practice may be more widespread than initially communicated. For such small-scale, or non-systemic, violations, public trust may be more easily resolved by limited structural reforms which distance the organization from the individuals involved in the violation.

However, for systemic, controllable integrity violations, the firm must do more than merely remove the individuals responsible for the violation. Controllable integrity violations represent situations where the firm has fostered or created an unethical environment that either implicitly or explicitly allows for integrity violations. Organizations in such situations cannot argue that control systems have been devised to the best of their ability, as such systems led to the violation itself. Instead, organizations must also revise and replace existing institutional control systems in order to prevent future integrity violations from occurring. Without changing the systems that promoted or allowed for integrity violations to occur, future violations can be expected to continue. Revisions of such systems following a systemic integrity violation may be seen as an admission of guilt by the firm that existing systems were not designed to promote integrity; yet because designing optimal control devices is at times complex or at best imperfect, revisions are not damaging. Rather, they are credible vehicles for minimizing future organizational failures, and as such can effectively rebuild trust. Again, the media can influence this process by reporting the changes in the incentive systems to the general public; their review can further validate the shortcomings of the former control systems as well as the benefits of the new ones.

For competence violations, different, strategic efforts are necessary in order to rebuild competence-based trust in the organization. By definition, competence violations result from a lack of due diligence, whether knowingly or not, in managing and coordinating the firm's operations. Because the violation is not person specific, it symbolizes an organization's inability to ensure the existence of a proper structure for ensuring competence. Given the root problems associated with competence violations, organizations are more likely to restructure the organization in order to better direct and align employee activities.

> Proposition 2a: Distancing of the organization from employees responsible for a violation has a greater positive impact on public trust following an uncontrollable integrity violation than a competence violation or controllable integrity violation.
>
> Proposition 2b: Structural and strategic reforms, such as the revision and replacement of institutional control systems and employment of individuals with a reputation for integrity, have a greater positive impact on public trust following a controllable integrity violation than an uncontrollable integrity violation or competence violation.
>
> Proposition 2c: Structural and strategic reforms, such as the institution of new policies and procedures and creation of oversight positions, have a greater positive impact on public trust following a competence violation rather than an integrity violation.

The value of a bundle of signs, weak signals, and signals

Cheap talk and costly action

As previously discussed, a fundamental limitation of communication strategies is that dishonest, incompetent firms can act like honest, competent firms at a relatively low cost. Accordingly, we suggest that the communication strategies advanced in Proposition 1 have a relatively lower impact on public trust relative to institutional reforms because institutional reforms represent costly actions that are likely to be too costly for a firm to fake. For instance, one such structural reform is to hire a person with a prestigious reputation for integrity. Such an individual is unlikely to join a company which has numerous and system-wide problems in competence and integrity or is not fully committed to restoring integrity throughout the firm. Reputable hires would be unable to effectively change systemic problems in competence and integrity, and therefore would decline top offers in order to not risk damaging their reputation. Relatedly, a truly incompetent organization would find the costs of structural reform too high, as the entire operations would need to be reworked, not simply the part associated with the competence failure. Thus, the critical distinction is that the institutional reform represents a significant cost to an organization, which would be too costly for a firm that lacks the competence or system-wide integrity to make.

This logic is consistent with prior works. For instance, Bottom *et al.* examine trust repair following opportunistic behavior and note that cooperation can be rebuilt through apologies and simple explanations, but most importantly, trust repair requires substantive amends made by the deceiving party.[85] Furthermore, the extant literature has also noted that hostage posting, or placing a firm under voluntary regulation, following a trust violation can illustrate a commitment to preventing future trust violations and results in greater trust.[86]

Proposition 3a: Institutional reforms for competence or integrity violations have a greater impact on public trust than communication strategies.

While institutional reforms are necessarily more credible signals, we do not advise that firms should neglect undertaking the less costly and noisier signals (e.g., communication strategies). In general, signals are rarely perfect; they are semi-shorting, and while they do convey information, they do not do so perfectly. As Gambetta concludes, "We rarely encounter a fully mimic-proof signal."[87] More critically, a noisy signal, such as a verbal account of the failure, is not necessarily cheap talk, as advanced by others.[88] We submit that it is not without cost: it is costly to display in a permanent fashion (e.g., formal public statement) an account of the failure, because the communication

---

[85] Bottom *et al.*, 2002.   [86] Nakayachi and Watabe, 2005.
[87] Gambetta, 2009, 173.   [88] Bottom *et al.*, 2002.

cannot be forgotten or unknowingly changed to accommodate new information. In effect, it is a permanent record that informs as well as constrains future actions and communications of the firm. This may account for the observations that most managers do not effectively communicate in response to failure.[89]

When a signal is partial, such as for communication strategies, it causes the receivers to "probe and seek more credible signals."[90] If communication functions as an initial signal of commitment to publicly resolving the violation, the organization will take further action to demonstrate persistence to this cause. This kind of process approach – events unfolding over time – is endorsed by the descriptive propositions of Gillespie and Dietz and Pfarrer et al. Both papers advise that following organizational failures, organizations should employ both communication strategies as well as costly actions in order to reestablish legitimacy and trust.[91]

Our logic suggests that organizations build trust following an organizational failure in an incremental fashion by making numerous investments in actions to strengthen the initial signal: an organization's commitment to restoring its competence or integrity following an organizational failure. Thus, the initial signal of commitment will be to communicate to the public. These communications provide an initial accounting for the failure, demonstrate compassion and concern, and begin to lay the foundation for institutional reforms to occur. As the organization gains additional information on the causes of the trust violation, further reforms can be instituted to attempt to solve the issues that led to the initial violation. Thus, the bundling of communication and institutional reforms sends a stronger signal of commitment to restoring trust than either one.

Proposition 3b: Organizations that employ communicative strategies followed by institutional reforms have a greater

---

[89] Folger and Skarlicki, 2001; Shaw et al., 2003.
[90] Gambetta, 2009, 174.   [91] Pfarrer, et al., 2008; Gillespie and Dietz, 2009.

*impact on public trust than organizations that perform only
institutional reforms or communicative strategies.*

DISCUSSION

Public trust in organizations is an understudied area that is particularly relevant in today's business climate. Routinely, organizations
encounter crisis situations due to organizational failures; however,
little is known about what strategies are most effective for organizations to repair trust and credibility with the public following such
failures. We propose that the type of violation – integrity or competence – as well as the controllability of the violation, represents
a critical boundary constraint and conditions the actions firms need
to take in order to rebuild public trust. Our primary contribution is to
develop a conceptual framework toward understanding public trust –
its relationship to other forms of trust; how it is primarily built
through institutional mechanisms; why institutional mechanisms
are prone to be imperfect governance devices; and which trust repair
strategies are more effective. This approach informs the nascent literature on trust repair, and the nonexistent literature on the repair of
public trust. It also demonstrates, consistent with prior works, the
importance of distinguishing the type of trust violation, as response
strategies appear to be contingent on the kind of violation.[92]

A second contribution of this research is establishing that
the stakeholder group, whether it is an individual, employees, or
the public, appears to be an important boundary constraint in considering the effects of violations on trust and trust-repair responses.
The stakeholder group is likely to evaluate different actions undertaken by the organization from a different perspective from that of
other stakeholder groups. The public, due to its limited interaction
with the firm, is likely to seek out explanations for why a failure
occurred and what the organization is planning on doing to prevent
such a failure in the future. Our analysis argues that for small-scale

---

[92] See, e.g., Kim *et al.*, 2004, 2006; Gillespie and Dietz, 2009.

violations, merely disassociating the firm from the violators is enough to begin to restore trust. For large-scale or systemic violations, the organization must implement structural reforms related to organizational control systems to ensure that such behavior is identified in the future.

Organizations have limited direct channels when communicating to the public. Thus, an organization's ability to disseminate information to the media is critical.[93] Media attention focused on an organizational failure can have a negative impact on the firm's overall reputation,[94] by making the event more salient, exposing the severity of the failure, as well as by raising issues regarding the company's integrity and competence.[95] Organizations can use the media in order to help manage the public's trust in the firm.[96] By providing information to the media, having senior management appear on news networks to communicate firm responses, and by communicating detailed response strategies to visible external stakeholders, the firm can help promote a positive image to the public. Finally, the amount of accessible information in the media can add additional legitimacy to the firm and helps to construct a positive image, as well as allows the firm to control the framing of the account.[97] Overall, providing additional information to the media promotes a positive image of the firm and displays compassion and concern for affected stakeholders, which facilitates trust repair.

One limitation of our approach lies in that these views are particularly Western centric and may not apply in other cultures or societies. The theories developed in this chapter are meant to apply primarily to responding to violations of public trust in the United States. We recognize that integrity is based on a social, moral conviction that people in business should not intentionally cheat, lie, manipulate information, and deceive others. This is a salient ideal

---

[93] Seeger, 2006; Ulmer, 2001.
[94] Fombrun and Shanley, 1990; Weinberger and Romeo, 1989.
[95] Zyglidopoulos, 2001.   [96] Seeger, 2006; Ulmer 2001.
[97] Seeger, 2006; Coombs, 1999.

that pervades many literatures such as those on organizations, economics, and ethics. Yet, we also realize that, over time, other moral convictions may become collectively agreed upon, and as a result our proposed framework would be necessarily incomplete.

Future research

Our research suggests that the stakeholder group conditions organizational responses to competence or integrity violations. Another obvious avenue for future research is examining situations that have elements of both integrity and competence violations. We suspect that these violations often become significantly larger in scope, and according to our framework could be limited by timely accounting for the initial failure and by the use of institutional reform mechanisms as outlined in Figure 12.1. In addition, firms who suffer from violations of both integrity and competence could use a mixture of strategies in order to repair the public's trust. For instance, Mattel's quest to constantly lower margins for greater profitability led to contracts with Chinese manufacturers, which were forced to lower standards or lose business. Mattel failed to properly oversee its suppliers to know what its products were being composed of (a competence violation), while also creating a climate in which cutting corners was beneficial and necessary for the supplier (an integrity violation). We also suspect that violations that involve dimensions of both competence and integrity may well begin as either competence failures that are improperly handled (e.g., such as Toyota's lack of follow-up on initial concerns about product safety) or integrity violations (e.g., managers deceiving their bosses as to the risk and return of their investment portfolios), and then may extend to include reporting that presents top management as either conspiring in a "cover-up" or failing to properly oversee the firm's operations.

Additionally, the propositions presented above represent ways in which individual firms may help restore the public's trust following violations; however, future research can begin to examine in greater detail how business as a whole can regain the public's trust. Future research may examine how specific industries develop solutions to both build the public's trust when at a low point and repair it following violations. For instance, following the subprime mortgage crisis, public trust in the banking and finance industry reached a new low. The loss of the public's trust led to significant distrust of financial institutions. Furthermore, this distrust negatively affected all financial institutions, including those who were not directly involved in the crisis. Such situations require greater institutional and structural reforms for an entire industry, rather than merely within one firm. Finally, the lingering distrust of all financial institutions suggests that such violations of public trust may have a contagious effect within an industry. Future research could examine under what conditions violations may be contagious within industries and the effects of such distrust of firms who are related to firms who violate the public's trust. For instance, following the Deepwater Horizon oil spill off the Gulf of Mexico, the public lost trust not only in British Petroleum, but was concerned about the operations of all firms who were involved in drilling for oil. Future research would be well served to continue to expand and understand the public's trust in business beyond the individual firm level.

In sum, we believe trust repair is an important area of research and hope that our framework contributes to better understanding and empirical testing of optimal strategies.

REFERENCES

Anheier, H. K. (ed.) (1999), *When Things Go Wrong: Organizational Failures and Breakdowns.* Thousand Oaks, CA: Sage.

Barney, J. (1991), 'Firm resources and sustained competitive advantage.' *Journal of Management*, 17, 99–120.

Bies, R. J. (1987), 'The predicament of injustice: the management of moral outrage.' *Research in Organizational Behavior*, 9, 289–319.

Bies, R. J. and Moag, J. (1986), 'Interactional justice: communication criteria of fairness.' *Research on Negotiation in Organizations*, 1, 43–55.

Bies, R. J. and Shapiro, D. L. (1988), 'Voice and justification: their influence of procedural fairness judgments.' *Academy of Management Journal*, 31, 676–685.

Bottom, W. P., Gibson, K., Daniels, S. E., and Murnighan, J. K. (2002), 'When talk is not cheap: substantive penance and expressions of intent in rebuilding cooperation.' *Organization Science*, 13, 497–513.

Bradford, J. L. and Garrett, D. E. (1995), 'The effectiveness of corporate communicative responses to accusations of unethical behavior.' *Journal of Business Ethics*, 14, 875–892.

Butler, J. and Cantrell, R. (1984), 'A behavioral decision theory approach to modeling dyadic trust in superiors and subordinates.' *Psychological Reports*, 55, 19–28.

Carter, S. and Dukerich, J. (1998), 'Corporate responses to changes in reputation.' *Corporate Reputation Review*, 1, 250–270.

Cody, M. and McLaughlin, M. (eds.) (1990), *The Psychology of Tactical Communication*. Bristol, PA: Multilingual Matters.

Coombs, W. T. (1999), *Ongoing Crisis Communication*. Thousand Oaks, CA: Sage.

Coombs, W. T. and Holladay, S. J. (2002), 'Helping crisis managers protect reputational assets.' *Management Communication Quarterly*, 16, 165–186.

Coyle-Shapiro, J. A. (2002), 'A psychological contract perspective on organizational citizenship behavior.' *Journal of Organizational Behavior*, 23, 927–946.

Coyle-Shapiro, J. and Kessler, I. (2000), 'Consequences of the psychological contract for the employment relationship: a large scale survey.' *Journal of Management Studies*, 37, 903–930.

Cummings, L. L. and Bromiley, P. (1996), 'The organizational trust inventory (OTI): development and validation.' In R. Kramer and T. Tyler (eds.), *Trust in Organizations: Frontiers of Theory and Research*. Thousand Oaks, CA: Sage, 302–330.

Dirks, K., Lewicki, R., and Zaheer, A. (2009), 'Special topic forum on repairing relationships within and between organizations.' *Academy of Management Review*, 34, 68–84.

Ferrin, D. L., Kim, P. H., Cooper, C. D., and Dirks, K. T. (2007), 'Silence speaks volumes: the effectiveness of reticence in comparison to apology and denial for responding to integrity- and competence-based trust violations.' *Journal of Applied Psychology*, 92: 893–908.

Fischhoff, B. (1975), 'Hindsight ≠ foresight: the effect of outcome knowledge on judgment under uncertainty.' *Journal of Experimental Psychology: Human Perception and Performance*, 1, 288–299.

Fitzpatrick, K. R. and Rubin, S. M. (1995), 'Public relations vs. legal strategies in organizational crisis decisions.' *Public Relations Review*, 21, 21–33.

Folger, R. and Bies, R. J. (1989), 'Managerial responsibilities and procedural justice.' *Employee Responsibilities and Rights Journal*, 2, 79–90.

Folger, R. and Skarlicki, D. P. (2001), 'Fairness as a dependent variable: why tough times can lead to bad management.' In R. Cropanzano (ed.), *Justice in the Workplace: Volume II – From Theory to Practice*. Mahwah, NJ: Erlbaum, 97–118.

Fombrun, C. J. (1996), *Reputation: Realizing Value from the Corporate Image*. Boston, MA: Harvard Business School Press.

Fombrun, C. and Shanley, M. (1990), 'What's in a name? Reputation building and corporate strategy.' *Academy of Management Journal*, 33, 233–258.

Freeman, R. E. (1984), *Strategic Management: A Stakeholder Approach*. Boston, MA: Pitman.

Gambetta, D. (2009), 'Signaling.' In P. Bearman and P. Hedstrom (eds.), *Oxford Handbook on Analytical Sociology*. New York: Oxford University Press, 168–194.

Ghoshal, S. and Moran, P. (1996), 'Bad for practice: a critique of transaction cost theory.' *Academy of Management Review*, 21, 13–47.

Gillespie, N. and Dietz, G. (2009), 'Trust repair after an organization-level failure.' *Academy of Management Review*, 34, 127–145.

Granovetter, M. 1985. 'Economic action and social structure: the problem of embeddedness.' *American Journal of Sociology*, 91: 481–510.

Hoch, S. J. and Loewenstein, G. (1989), 'Outcome feedback: hindsight and information.' *Journal of Experimental Psychology*, 15, 605–619.

Holmstrom, B. and Milgrom, P. (1991), 'Multitask principal–agent analyses: incentive contracts, asset ownership, and job design.' *Journal of Law, Economics, and Organization*, 7, 24–52.

Hooghiemstra, R. (2000), 'Corporate communication and impression management – new perspectives why companies engage in corporate social reporting.' *Journal of Business Ethics*, 27, 55–68.

Husted, B. and Folger, R. (2004), 'Fairness and transaction costs: the contribution of organizational justice theory to an integrative model of economic organization.' *Organization Science*, 15, 719–729.

Jacobides, M. and Croson, D. (2001), 'Information policy: shaping the value of agency relationships.' *Academy of Management Review*, 26, 202–223.

Kim, P., Ferrin, D., Cooper, C., and Dirks, K. (2004), 'Removing the shadow of suspicion: the effects of apology versus denial for repairing competence-versus integrity-based trust violations.' *Journal of Applied Psychology*, 89, 104–118.

Kim P., Dirks, K., Cooper, C., and Ferrin, D. (2006), 'When more blame is better than less: the implications of internal vs. external attributions for the repair of trust after a competence- vs. integrity-based trust violation.' *Organizational Behavior and Human Decision Processes*, 99, 49–65.

Kramer, R. (1999), 'Trust and distrust in organizations: emerging perspectives, enduring questions.' *Annual Review of Psychology*, 50, 569–598.

Lee, F., Peterson, C., and Tiedens, L. (2004), 'Mea culpa: predicting stock prices from organizational attributions.' *Personality and Social Psychology Bulletin*, 30, 1636–1649.

Lewicki, R. and Bunker, B. B. (1996), 'Developing and maintaining trust in work relationships.' In R. M. Kramer and T. R. Tyler (eds.), *Trust in Organizations: Frontiers of Theory and Research*. Thousand Oaks, CA: Sage, 114–139.

Lewicki, R. J., McAllister, D. J., and Bies, R. J. (1998), 'Trust and distrust: new relationships and realities.' *Academy of Management Review*, 23, 438–458.

McKnight, D. H., Cummings, L. L., and Chervany, N. L. (1998), 'Initial trust formation in new organizational relationships.' *Academy of Management Review*, 23(3), 473–490.

Macneil, I. R. (1978), 'Contracts: adjustment of long-term economic relations under classical, neoclassical, and relational contract law.' *Northwestern University Law Review*, 72, 854–905.

Mayer, R., Davis, J., and Schoorman, D. (1995), 'An integrative model of organizational trust.' *Academy of Management Review*, 20, 709–734.

Milgrom, P. and Roberts, J. (1988), 'An economic approach to influence activities in organizations.' *American Journal of Sociology*, 94, 154–179.

Nakayachi, K. and Watabe, M. (2005), 'Restoring trustworthiness after adverse events: the signaling effects of voluntary "hostage posting" on trust.' *Organizational Behavior and Human Decision Processes*, 97, 1–17.

Pfarrer, M., Decelles, K., Smith, K, and Taylor, M. S. (2008), 'After the fall: reintegrating the corrupt organization.' *Academy of Management Review*, 33, 730–749.

Pfeffer, J. (1981), *Power in Organizations*. Marshfield, MA: Pitman.

Poppo, L. and Schepker, D. J. (2010), 'Repairing public trust in organizations.' *Corporate Reputation Review*, 13, 124–141.

Poppo, L., Zhou, K., and Ryu, S. (2008), 'Alternative origins to interorganizational trust: an interdependence perspective on the shadow of the past and the shadow of the future.' *Organization Science*, 19, 39–55.

Pratt, J. and Zeckhauser, R. 1995. 'Principals and agents: an overview.' In J. Pratt and R. Zeckhauser (eds.), *Principals and Agents: The Structure of Business*. Boston, MA: Harvard Business School Press, 1–35.

Reynolds, B. (2006), 'Response to best practices.' *Journal of Applied Communications Research*, 34, 249–252.

Ring, P. S. (1996), 'Fragile and resilient trust and their roles in economic exchange.' *Business and Society*, 35, 148–175.

Robinson, S. L. (1996), 'Trust and breach of the psychological contract.' *Administrative Science Quarterly*, 41, 574–599.

Rousseau, D. M. and McLean Parks, J. (1993), 'The contracts of individuals and organizations.' In L. L. Cummings and B. M. Staw (eds.), *Research in Organizational Behavior*. Greenwich, CT: JAI Press, 1–43.

Rousseau, D., Sitkin, S., Burt, R., and Camerer, C. (1998), 'Not so different after all: a cross-discipline view of trust.' *Academy of Management Review*, 23, 393–405.

Schwartz, P. and Gibb, B. (1999), *When Good Companies Do Bad Things: Responsibilities and Risk in an Age of Globalization*. New York: Wiley.

Schweitzer, M. E., Hershey, J. C., and Bradlow, E. T. (2006), 'Promises and lies: restoring violated trust.' *Organizational Behavior and Human Decision Processes*, 101, 1–19.

Seeger, M. W. (2006), 'Best practices in crisis communication: an expert panel process.' *Journal of Applied Communication Research*, 34, 232–244.

Shapiro, S. (2005), 'Agency theory.' *Annual Review of Sociology*, 31, 263–284.

Shaw, J. C., Wild, E., and Colquitt, J. A. (2003), 'To justify or excuse? A meta-analytic review of the effects of explanations.' *Journal of Applied Psychology*, 88, 444–458.

Sitkin, S. and Roth, N. (1993), 'Explaining the limited effectiveness of legalistic "remedies" for trust/ distrust.' *Organizational Science*, 4, 367–392.

Slovic, P. (1993), 'Perceived risk, trust, and democracy.' *Risk Analysis*, 13, 675–682.

Spence, M. (1973), 'Job market signaling.' *Quarterly Journal of Economics*, 87, 355–374.

Suchman, M. (1995), 'Managing legitimacy: strategic and institutional approaches.' *Academy of Management Review*, 20, 571–610.

Thomas, C. W. (1998), 'Maintaining and restoring public trust in government agencies and their employees.' *Administration and Society*, 30, 166–193.

Tomlinson, E. and Mayer, R. (2009), 'The role of causal attribution dimensions in trust repair.' *Academy of Management Review*, 34, 85–104.

Ulmer, R. R. (2001), 'Effective crisis management through established stakeholder relationships.' *Management Communication Quarterly*, 14(4), 590–615.

Vaughan, D. (1983), *Controlling Unlawful Organizational Behavior: Social Structure and Corporate Misconduct*. Chicago, IL: University of Chicago Press.

Weiner, B. (1986), *An Attributional Theory of Motivation and Emotion*. New York: Springer-Verlag.

Weingerger, M. G. and Romeo, J. B. (1989), 'The impact of negative product news.' *Business Horizons*, 32(1), 44–50.

Williamson, O. E. (1993), 'Calculativeness, trust, and economic organization.' *Journal of Law and Economics*, 36, 453–502.

Williamson, O. E. (1996), *The Mechanisms of Governance*. Oxford: Oxford University Press.

Yamagishi, T. (1988), 'The provision of a sanctioning system in the United States and Japan.' *Social Psychology Quarterly*, 51, 32–42.

Zaheer, A. and Harris, J. (2005), 'Interorganizational trust.' In O. Shenkar and J. J. Reurer (eds.). *Handbook of Strategic Alliances*. Thousand Oaks, CA: Sage, 169–197.

Zaheer, A., Lofstrom, S., and George, V. (2002), 'Interpersonal and organizational trust in alliances.' In F. Contractor and P. Lorange (eds.), *Cooperative Strategies and Alliances: What We Know 15 Years Later*. London: Elsevier, 347–377.

Zaheer, A., McEvily, B., and Perrone, V. (1998), 'Does trust matter? Exploring the effects of interorganizational and interpersonal trust on performance.' *Organization Science*, 9, 141–159.

Zucker, L. G. 1986. 'Production of trust: institutional sources of economics structure, 1840–1920.' In B. Staw and L. L. Cummings (eds.), *Research in Organizational Behavior*. Greenwich, CT: JAI Press, vol. VIII, 53–111.

13 Toward a better understanding of public trust in business

Jared D. Harris, Andrew C. Wicks,
Brian T. Moriarty

The research compiled in this volume, the consistently dismal poll results, and continued public interest in the role of business in society give rise to a number of opportunities to further improve our understanding of public trust in the institution of business. One of our primary objectives in commissioning these chapters was to stimulate further scholarly thinking and research on the subject of trust in the institution of business; as such, a number of questions offer potential avenues for additional analysis and inquiry.

DEFINITION AND ANTECEDENTS

We need a better conceptual understanding of what constitutes "public trust" and how we might define it in terms that build on the existing literature and extend our theoretical understanding. Given the potential importance of trust in business as an institution, there is an opportunity for scholars to bring more precise understanding to what exactly respondents are talking about when they talk about public trust in business writ large. How much of one's trust in business as an institution arises from one's direct experiences with various specific businesses? How much is attributable to a particular stakeholder role or mindset? How is one's generalized trust in business influenced by observations about *others'* experiences, or the observed behavior of firms with which one has no direct experience? We need to better understand the drivers of trust in business as an institution. Several chapters in this volume begin to offer theory about how public trust is formed, but many questions remain.

OPTIMAL PUBLIC TRUST

As many of the chapters in this volume point out, public trust in business right now is low, and this potentially poses a major problem for both individual firms and for the economy. Yet the historical data reveal that public trust has been low for quite a long time – even in the boom eras before Occupy, during time periods with few business scandals making the front pages, and coupled with the election of politicians promising to unleash the power of the private sector. What, then, should we infer from this relatively "stable" state of low public trust in business? Given the ideas presented by Bachmann and Hanappi-Egger in Chapter 10, does the low level of trust in the institution of business represent an absence of trust, or an outright distrust? And if such a distinction can be made at the institutional level, is a certain amount of distrust actually useful as a governance mechanism? What constitutes a healthy or appropriate level of public trust in business? If organizational trust can be "optimal,"[1] what does this mean for ideal levels of trust in business as an institution?

One confounding factor is the ephemeral nature of public trust in business as an institution, which requires better understanding. Trust in business as an institution, for example, may ultimately involve trusting an idea, rather than trusting something tangible. The institution of business may simply be our collective sense of a prototypical business that may or may not bear a close relationship to the individual businesses we interact with and participate in on a daily basis. Thus, it is possible that we may have fairly robust levels of trust in the grocery store we patronize (or even the whole chain of affiliated grocery stores) yet not trust "business" much at all. Part of this can be explained by psychological biases revealed in research from other fields, including work done on politics and politicians; Americans tend to have low levels of trust in Congress (even lower than in business as an institution!), but relatively high levels of trust

---

[1] Wicks *et al.*, 1999.

in their local representative.[2] Yet the existence of this bias may help us understand why we might trust "business" less than a specific company, but it doesn't tell us about what levels of trust or distrust (in either case) are healthy, desirable, or why they gravitate toward a certain point.

Both executives and researchers also need to better understand how to "move the dial" – to actually take steps to affect the overall level of public trust (whether positively or negatively) – and how such movement can be influenced. For instance, if it turns out that regulatory efforts such as the Sarbanes–Oxley and Dodd–Frank bills in the United States cost billions of dollars to create and implement but do little to alter levels of public trust in business, this may have implications regarding the usefulness of such legislation. One might suggest that higher levels of public trust might lead to lower levels of government regulation (and vice versa), yet even if there were compelling evidence for such a claim, are there particular tipping points that suggest significant shifts in levels and degree of regulation? To what extent can institutional distrust substitute for such regulation?

IMPACT

Why should business leaders (or anyone else) care? It was evident that the executives we spoke to back in 2007 viewed the crisis in public trust as a topic of immediate concern and impact on their specific businesses. But what, exactly, are these implications? Research needs to better understand the implications of public trust – its outcomes and effects – not only at the current low level of trust in business, but also when public trust increases or decreases. For instance, are the supposed negative effects of low public trust on specific firms observable, and measurable? How, precisely, does low public trust negatively impact individual businesses? How do different levels of public trust alter specific-firm corporate governance practices? What

---

[2] Parker and Parker, 1993.

about forms of insurance and their cost – if generalized trust in business declines, might that not impact the cost of insurance?

Perhaps some might argue that except in extreme cases, most businesses may have little reason to worry about levels of public trust. They might say: as long as the trust levels we have with our own specific stakeholders are robust and in line with what we need to make our business function well, low public trust may not impact our direct operations. But whether or not this is true is ultimately an empirical question. After all, it seems more likely that low public trust would have a negative impact on specific firms. For instance, if people trust the institution of business less, might they be predisposed to distrust specific executives since they are part of "business"? And, if so, won't that impact the ability of my business to solve "commitment problems" with key stakeholders in efficient, inexpensive, and value-generative ways?

SOCIETAL NARRATIVES ABOUT PUBLIC TRUST

Another area of fruitful exploration involves public trust in business and the societal "story" told about business – our background narrative. Embodied within everyday media accounts is a story about what a business is, how it operates, and what we can expect of it. Thus, not only is the decline of public trust interesting as a phenomenon and potentially influential on both regulatory efforts and day-to-day operations of a business, it may also reflect an underlying societal narrative about the trustworthiness of business and its role within society. This gets to the heart of "enacted capitalism" and the way in which the media both reflects and responds to actual business practice.

And if such societal narratives matter, research ought to further examine how it is formed and how it can be influenced. And what is the role of fragmented or selected narratives? We live in an era where we are bombarded with information, much of it about business, and not all with the same point of view. Are there certain messages that tend to dominate those narratives? Why? And under what circumstances? Does hearing different stories about business – whether more favorable or less so – over a period of time alter our own assumptions about business as an institution? Will that in turn affect our trust in individual businesses? How does the increased fragmentation and niche nature of specialized media accounts impact public attitudes toward business as an institution?

Furthermore, what are the implications of this for normative debates about what business "should be"? Societal narratives about the role of business are intertwined with scholarly and public discussions about our normative conceptions of global capitalism. A better understanding of media narratives may enable us to focus and shape the discourse around normative business ethics – much as some scholars have argued that moral psychology needs to help mold the kind of normative theories philosophers develop to describe the "should" aspects of life.[3] If our biology or psychology prevent us from doing something, does it make sense to say we have a moral duty to do it? Many scholars have argued that "is" and "ought to" need to be brought in closer proximity and inform each other.[4] Similarly, one can make the case for normative business ethics needing to better understand societal narratives and our collective sense of what businesses are.

THE WAY FORWARD

The recent global financial crisis has once again raised the specter of widespread economic calamity – and, more disconcertingly, has illustrated that, in matters involving public goods, markets may not reliably self-correct and exemplify the "invisible hand" of Adam Smith. If we all have a collective sense that there is something broken in modern global capitalism, what can be done to address it? What kinds of changes need to be made that will enable us to rest well and boost confidence in markets, companies, managers, and other stakeholders – encouraging them to naturally behave in ways that lead the collective greater good?

---

[3] Appiah, 2008.   [4] See, e.g., Harris and Freeman, 2008; Searle, 1964.

Society's heightened collective sense of economic anxiety invites us to examine what various changes need to be made to restore confidence. The work in this volume suggests that improving public trust in the institution of business is not likely to be accomplished by simple means, or by any one specific approach. Regulation, corporate governance practices, individual assessments, stakeholder relations, cultural context, supporting institutions, and societal media-driven narratives would all appear to be candidates for further scrutiny. If public trust in business is a topic of central concern to modern capitalism, then all these facets of public trust beg further scrutiny – not just for individual investigation, but also for the way in which their interrelationships and the dynamic interplay between them impact the complex global economy.

CONCLUSION

Although rich research opportunities remain, the chapters in this volume are intended to offer a jump-start to further scholarly inquiry on this timely topic. *Public trust in business* is a book whose time has come. Trust has proven to be a critical lens through which to understand the health of relationships and institutions, and is an integral feature of our social fabric. We tend to pay attention to it when it becomes frayed or torn, yet it remains important even when it is intact. Our current moment – the aftermath of a global economic crisis whose effects are still being felt – provides a rich opportunity to draw interest to this topic, precisely because our current circumstances underscore just how vital public trust in business is to our society, and to our society's future. This collection of research chapters makes a convincing case for why such further investigation is important and what kinds of questions we should be asking, as well as providing the beginnings of theories and insights for better understanding this phenomenon.

REFERENCES

Andersen, K. (2011), 'The protester.' *Time*, December 26, 53–89.
Appiah, K. (2008), *Experiments in Ethics*. Cambridge, MA: Harvard University Press.

Apps, P. (2011), 'Wall Street action part of global Arab Spring?' Reuters, October 11, 2011, retrieved November 24, 2011.

Ashforth, B. E. and Kreiner, G. E. (1999), 'How can you do it: dirty work and the challenge of constructing a positive identity.' *Academy of Management Review*, 24, 413–434.

Becker, B. (2011), 'The Hill Poll: fears about income inequality grow.' *The Hill*, October 31.

Bolton, R., Freeman, R. E., Harris, J. D., Moriarty, B., and Nash, L. (2009), *The Dynamics of Public Trust in Business – Emerging Opportunities for Leaders*, Charlottesville, VA: Business Roundtable Institute for Corporate Ethics, white paper.

Business Roundtable Institute for Corporate Ethic (2004), *Mapping the Terrain: Issues that Connect Business and Ethics*, white paper.

Brossard, M. A. (1996), 'Americans losing trust in each other and in institutions', *Washington Post*, 28 and 29 January, A1.

Cavazos D. E. and Rutherford M. (2011), 'Examining how media coverage impacts the regulatory notice and comment process.' *American Review of Public Administration*, 41(6), 625–638.

Deloitte (2011), *A Risk Intelligent View of Reputation* (white paper: Risk Intelligence Series, no. 22).

Economist (2012), 'The never-ending crisis,' (July 24).

Economist Intelligence Unit (2005), *Reputation: Risk of Risks* (white paper).

Fombrun, C. J. and Rindova, V. (1996) 'Who's tops and who decides? The social construction of corporate reputations,' New York University, Stern School of Business, working paper.

Fukuyama, F. (1995), *Trust: The Social Virtues and the Creation of Prosperity*, New York: Free Press.

Gallup (2011), 'Honesty/ethics in the professions.' (Nov. 28–Dec. 1).

Gerzema, J. and Lebar, E. (2008), *The Brand Bubble: The Looming Crisis in Brand Value and How to Avoid It*. San Francisco, CA: Jossey-Bass.

Hargrave, T. (2009), 'Moral imagination, collective action, and the achievement of moral outcomes.' *Business Ethics Quarterly*, 19(1), 87–104.

Harris, J. D. and Freeman, R. E. (2008), 'The impossibility of the separation thesis.' *Business Ethics Quarterly*, 18(4), 541–548.

Hughes, E. C. (1958), *Men and Their Work*. Glencoe, IL: Free Press.

Mufson, S. and Vargas, T. (2010), 'BP loses 15 percent of market value as US launches criminal probe of spill.' *Washington Post*, June 2.

Ovide, S. (2011), 'Billionaire tells Occupy Wall Street to get off his lawn.' *Wall Street Journal*, October 11, retrieved October 23, 2011.

Parker, S. L. and Parker, G. R. (1993), 'Why do we trust our congressman?' *Journal of Politics*, 55(2), 442–453.

Porter, E. (2012), 'The spreading scourge of corporate corruption.' *New York Times*, July 10.

Searle, J. R. 1964. 'How to derive "ought" from "is."' *Philosophical Review*, 73(1), 43–58.

Toobin, J. (2012), 'Money unlimited.' *New Yorker*, May 21.

Towers Perrin (2007–2008) *Closing the Engagement Gap: A Road Map for Driving Superior Business Performance* white paper.

Van de Ven, A. H. and Ring, P. S. (2006), 'Relying on trust in cooperative inter-organizational relationships.' In R. Bachmann and A. Zaheer (eds.), *Handbook of Trust Research*, Cheltenham, UK: Edward Elgar, p. 144.

Wicks, A. C., Berman, S., and Jones, T. (1999), 'The structure of optimal trust: moral and strategic implications.' *Academy of Management Review*, 24(1), 99–116.

Index

Printed in the United States
By Bookmasters